*Volume 3 of Russia and the South Pacific, 1696-1840*
MELANESIA AND THE WESTERN POLYNESIAN FRINGE

This is the third of four volumes on the naval, scientific, and social activities of the Imperial Russian Navy in the South Pacific. In this book, Glynn Barratt focuses on the voyages that touched on Vanuatu (formerly the New Hebrides), Fiji, Tuvalu (formerly the Ellice Islands), and Anuta.

As in the other books in the series, Barratt has made full use of both modern and archival sources in describing the sites and people that the visitors encountered. Emphasizing the Russians' scientific work in botany, linguistics, ethnography, and hydrography rather than the voyages as such, he describes the visits by Captain Vasilii Mikhailovich Golovnin in 1809 to Tana, at the southern end of modern Tuvalu, by Captain Faddei F. Bellingshausen to Ono-i-Lau, Fiji, in 1820, and the Vasil'ev-Shismarev encounters in 1820 with the Polynesians settled on the atoll of Nukufetau, Ellice Islands, and in 1822 with another isolated group of Polynesian speakers on Anuta.

The visit by Golovnin's ship *Diana* to Tana followed a particularly dramatic voyage, and Tana was deliberately chosen as a secret resting spot. Here the Russians, after making contact with an elder by the name of Gunama, bartered for some forty feet of sugarcane, some four hundred coconuts, and yams. Tannese weaponry and artefacts were also brought on board, and full notes were taken on the evidence of tribal warfare, social structure, navigation, husbandry and diet, clothing, ornament, and language.

In underscoring the splendid naval tradition of the Russian empire, Barratt dispels the myth that the Russians were landlubbers. He points out that they made contact with native populations in many areas of the South Pacific and that, in some places, the Russian influence was not inconsiderable.

Of particular interest is Barratt's analysis of the drawings executed by staff artists of the various expeditions, especially those by Pavel Nikolaevich Mikhailov.

GLYNN BARRATT is a professor of Russian at Carleton University and the author of many books on Russia's naval and diplomatic history.

University of British Columbia Press
PACIFIC MARITIME STUDIES SERIES

*Volume 3 of*
*Russia and the South Pacific,*
*1696–1840*

# MELANESIA
## AND THE
# WESTERN POLYNESIAN FRINGE

*Glynn Barratt*

UNIVERSITY OF BRITISH COLUMBIA
PRESS
Vancouver 1990

Printed in Canada

ISBN 0-7748-0338-X
ISSN 0847-0529

∞

Printed on acid-free paper


**Canadian Cataloguing in Publication Data**

Barratt, Glynn.
  Melanesia and the western Polynesian fringe

  (University of British Columbia Press Pacific maritime series; 8)
  (Volume 3 of Russia and the South Pacific, 1696–1840)
  Includes bibliographical references.
  ISBN 0-7748-0338-X
  1. Melanesia – Relations – Soviet Union.
2. Soviet Union – Relations – Melanesia. 3.
Melanesia – Discovery and exploration. 4.
Scientific expeditions – Melanesia – History –
19th century. 5. Soviet Union – History, Naval.
I. Title. II. Series. III. Series: Barratt,
Glynn. Russia and the South Pacific, 1696-1840; v. 3.
DU490.B37 1990    993    C89-091510-5

University of British Columbia Press
6344 Memorial Road
Vancouver, B.C. V6T 1W5

This book has been published with the help of a grant from the Social Science
Federation of Canada, using funds provided by the Social Sciences and
Humanities Research Council of Canada.

# Contents

# ILLUSTRATIONS AND MAPS

MAPS

# INTRODUCTION

This is the third volume in a series entitled *Russia and the South Pacific, 1696–1840*. Like the first two volumes, which deal respectively with Russian interest and dealings in Australia and in Southern and Eastern Polynesia (Easter Island, the Austral Islands, and New Zealand), this surveys the Russians' social, maritime, and scientific enterprise within a geographically delimited (but culturally varied) part of Oceania. That part is Melanesia, more specifically Vanuatu and Fiji and the Western Polynesian fringe (Tuvalu, known until lately as the Ellice Islands, and Anuta in the group of Santa Cruz). A fourth volume is planned, to cover Russian social, maritime, and scientific dealings with the Central Polynesian archipelagoes (Tahiti and the Tuamotus, the Marquesas Islands, and Tonga). Like the two preceding volumes in this series, this survey has been written for non-Russian readers but provides sufficient data in extensive notes and bibliography to meet the needs of those with special skills and interests—in Soviet archival sources, for example, for the history and language of the Lau Group in Fiji or of Tana and Aneityum, Vanuatu. It does not pretend to comprehensive treatment of the subject, long neglected in the West, of the development of Russian knowledge and activity in South Pacific waters. Nor, because it *is* a survey, does it stray—beyond a certain point, at least—into the thickets of linguistics or ethnology.

I have again chosen to stress those sciences pursued by Russians in the course of visits to particular localities in Oceania, and not to dwell upon the strictly naval aspects of the "cruising" (*kreiserstvo*) that gave rise to visits. In the cases both of Tana at the southern end of Cook's New Hebrides (today, Vanuatu) and of the Lau cluster (southern sector of the Fiji archipelago), those sciences included botany, linguistics, and hydrography. The visits here in question were, specifically, those made by *Diana* (Captain Vasilii Mikhailovich Golovnin) to Cook's "Port Resolution" (now Uea Bay), Tana, in 1809; and by the sloops *Vostok* (Captain Faddei F. Bellingshausen) and her escort *Mirnyi* (Captain Mikhail Petrovich Lazarev) to Ono-i-Lau, Fiji, in mid-August 1820. Notice is taken, in a brief separate section of Part Two (pp. 96-101), of later passages by Russian ships into Fijian waters: by *Otkrytie* (Captain Mikhail Nikolaevich Vasil'ev) and *Blagonamerennyi* (Captain Gleb Semenovich Shishmarev); by *Krotkii* (Captain Leontii A. Hagemeister), and *Amerika* (Captain Ivan von Schants). Notice is taken, finally, of the 1820 Vasil'ev-Shishmarev encounter with the Polynesians settled on a low atoll, called then as now, Nukufetau, in Tuvalu (Ellice Islands), and of *Apollon*'s encounter two years later with another isolated group of Polynesian speakers on Anuta (Cherry Island), NNE of the New Hebrides (Vanuatu) and at the easternmost extension of the Solomons (Map 4).

As in preceding volumes in this series, information on specific circumstances and conditions that resulted in a visit is preceded by material on what, if anything, the Russians knew about that place. Again, each part offers a general discussion of the Russian narrative and other evidence. Part One, dealing with Golovnin's activities on Tana, thus begins with a discussion of the Anglo-Russian maritime entente of pre-Napoleonic years, on the mounting of the Kruzenshtern-Lisianskii expedition round the globe (1803-6), and on the part played, in the planning of *Diana*'s later mission, by young Russian naval officers' awareness of Captain James Cook's *Voyages*. (Of Golovnin's and his subordinates' awareness that they were anchoring, in 1809, almost exactly where Cook's *Resolution* had stood in 1774, suffice to comment that they landed with a copy of George Forster's *Voyage Round the World* and of his father Johann Reinhold Forster's *Observations Made During a Voyage* [1778], not just at hand, but in their hands.)

Part Two begins, similarly, with a survey of Ivan F. Kruzenshtern's essential role as human link between his navy and the western European expeditionary experience in Oceania. Even by 1805, Kruzenshtern (alone of his compatriots) was quite familiar with Abel Tasman's 1643 route up to the Fiji Islands. He was for good measure well acquainted with George Tobin (1768-1838), who had sailed with the luckless Captain Bligh in *Providence* (1791) while the latter was composing his account of an extraordinary passage in 1788 in *Bounty*'s open launch, across the Fijis to Batavia via Timor. As Professor Antony G. Cross has shown so clearly in his 1980 book, *By the Banks of the Thames: Russians in Eighteenth-Century Britain*, many Russian Volunteers in the wartime Royal Navy of the mid-1790s had as good an opportunity as Kruzenshtern to pump such officers as Tobin or James Trevenen (1760-90), who had served on Cook's last voyage. None, however, took such full and keen advantage of the chance as he did. The results are plain in several of Kruzenshtern's earlier articles (see Bibliography, "Otkrytiia Tasmana . . .").

In May and June 1804, as I have shown in *Russia in Pacific Waters, 1715-1825* (1981) and *The Russian Discovery of Hawaii, 1804* (1988), the officers and seamen of *Nadezhda* (Captain Kruzenshtern) and of *Neva* (Captain Iurii Fedorovich Lisianskii) had politically and scientifically important contact with the people of the Taio-hae area of Nukuhiva Island in the Washington-Marquesas Group and with Kamehameha's subjects on Hawaii's Kona coast. As shown in Volume 2 (*Southern and Eastern Polynesia*) of this series, *Neva* also had dealings with the Easter Islanders in 1804. Despite the natives' unexpected opposition to attempts to land at Hanga-roa Bay, knives, scissors, mirrors, coins, and cloth were gladly taken in exchange for local artefacts and foodstuffs; and, like Jacob Roggeveen (1722) and Captain Cook, Lisianskii made a broadly accurate albeit hurried study of the Easter Islanders' tattooing, clothing, general physique, huts, craft, carving, and giant coastal statues. Twenty, even thirty years after Cook's death at the Hawaiians' hands, the forms and very emphases of his Pacific explorations were not only borne in mind by the ambitious younger officer from Kronstadt, but were seen as proper to such ventures. Among those emphases were certain scientific ones. It would, in Lisianskii's opinion, have been wholly reprehensible had any effort been neglected to extract the greatest possible advantage to the sciences at large from his arrival on a coast where La Pérouse and Cook and Roggeveen had laboured. For Melanesian studies, it is certainly unfortunate that Melanesia was not visited in 1804-5 by *Nadezhda* or *Neva*. It was not until *Seniavin* (Captain Fedor Petrovich Lütke) entered South Pacific waters in the early weeks of 1827 that an academic *company* arrived in Oceania, under the Russian flag at least, of equal brilliance to that of 1803-6. We may be grateful, on the other hand, that such an able officer and writer as Vasilii M. Golovnin was given command of *Diana*, with instructions to escort *Neva*, on her second voyage, from the Baltic to the North Pacific settlements. Despite its brevity, the Russian visit to Uea Bay ("Port Resolution"), Tana, was fruitful in both practical and scientific terms.

*Diana* had no orders from the Russian naval ministry to call at Tana. Her arrival there was, indeed, a consequence of a dramatic and unlikely series of events, including capture by the British, an escape from Simon's Bay, South Africa, at dusk and in a storm, and an exhausting, uninterrupted passage round Australia and through the Tasman Sea with the intention of avoiding all encounters with the British fleet or British merchantmen. Tana was chosen, as a resting and revictualling spot, as one removed from normal shipping routes and likely to be free of Europeans, yet supplied with ample fruit, some drinking water, and a neatly charted harbour. All, in fact, passed off as well as Golovnin could have desired, after tense initial meetings with a Kwamera-speaking Tannese group led by an elder called Gunama. Drawing maximal advantage from the works of the two Forsters who, as seen, had been at Tana with *Resolution* in 1774, Golovnin proceeded cautiously but amicably. A single day produced, through barter at the water's edge, some forty feet of sugarcane, 400 coconuts or more, and yams. Uea Bay, meanwhile, was surveyed by cutter. Tannese weaponry and other artefacts were stowed aboard. Some are in Leningrad today. Full notes were taken on the evidence of tribal warfare, social structure, navigation, husbandry and diet, clothing, ornament, and language. One could hardly expect more of a company of seamen who, departing from the Baltic, had anticipated no such visit; who needed to pay attention, on arrival, to provisionment and watering above all else; and who were conscious of the need to reach Kamchatka by September, while its seas were safe for shipping.

In itself, and in conjunction with the British evidence of 1774, the Russian record of a call at Tana plays its part in South Pacific and especially in Melanesian studies. *Diana*'s youthful officers, however, soon enough assessed the place as a potential port of call for other vessels on the longer eastward route from South America, around Australia, to Petropavlovsk. Notwithstanding all its natural resources, they concluded, Tana Island was inferior in all respects to Sydney, New South Wales, as a resting and revictualling place for Russian shipping. Tana Islanders had shown no willingness to barter hogs or fowls, gave some evidence of being dangerous, and could suggest no useful source of drinking water other than the swampy pond that Cook had found. In the event, no other Russians called at Tana in the early nineteenth century.

*Diana* headed north from Tana, passing east of all the northerly New Hebrides (see Map 2). The 169th meridian brought Golovnin in sight of Tikopia, a particularly isolated, lofty island. Its height and solitude made it a signpost for a vessel like *Diana*, northward-bound within the zone of southeast trade winds. She was followed through these waters at the far edge of the Solomons and Santa Cruz, where landspecks like Fataka and Anuta (Captain Edward Edwards' "Mitre Isle" and "Cherry Isle," seen from HMS *Pandora* in 1791) served as comparably elevated signposts, by at least two other Russian ships during the early 1800s: *Apollon* (Captain Stepan Khrushchev) in 1822, and *Amerika* (Captain Ivan von Schants) in 1835. Both ships were making for Kamchatka from the friendly port of Sydney. Other vessels, like *Elena* (Captain Vasilii S. Khromchenko) and *Krotkii* (Captain Hagemeister), passed no more than 6° east of Anuta, on their own long northward run. For them, Rotuma was the marker in an empty waste of ocean. One may say, indeed, that "Cherry Isle" and Rotuma lay astride the

Russian Navy's northern highway from Australia. Given prevailing winds and currents in those latitudes in the southern summer, Russian contact with the Polynesian people of Tuvalu was predictable. For Russian sailing patterns of the era, which *Diana* and *Neva* had set together, called for summer navigation *west* of Fiji, in longitudes approximately 175°–180°E.

Russian ships in fact passed through the Fiji Islands seven times in fifteen years (1820–35) en route from Sydney to the North. All had arrived via Brazil on complex, multi-purpose missions; all were following a schedule, so arrived within a twelve-week period (April–June), with the intention of exploiting southeast trade winds to the limit. Other factors, too, produced homogeneity in Russian naval visits to the area: no ship arriving off the Fijis, for example, needed drinking water or supplies. Again, no captain had instructions to investigate those islands. Nonetheless, each of the seven Russian passes through the archipelago produced at least a running survey of the land observed, as well as journal notes. All these materials remain in Leningrad, unpublished. Each visit was made by highly trained observers who, moreover, were required to take daily notes on what they saw. Several officers who passed the Fiji Islands in early April 1820, in the sloops-of-war *Otkrytie* and *Blagonamerennyi*, afterwards tried to publish narratives describing their experiences on the basis of their journals. None succeeded. The involvement of assorted naval officers in the ill-fated coup on 14 December 1825 that heralded the reign of Nicholas I, had predisposed him against publishing any such accounts by their associates. The fate of journals kept by *Otkrytie*'s and *Blagonamerennyi*'s young officers well illustrates how, in a larger way, the fate of source materials relating to, say, Fiji, was dependent on the overall success of a whole voyage in the course of which a visit had occurred, as then perceived by the imperial authorities.

Like the contemporaneous northern and Arctic naval voyages made by the British, by the Rosses, Scoresby, Parry, and by Franklin (1819–21), Captain Bellingshausen's voyage to the fringes of Antarctica and Oceania—during the course of which Ono-i-Lau and its outlyers were found and first described for Europeans—was a product of the international rivalry that stamped the post-Napoleonic age. Now, in another era of tranquillity and competition for resources and strategic gain, the aims of science and of empire were no less fused than they had been a half a century before. As in the days of Captain Cook, knowledge was (real or potential) strength; a reality recognized by both the British and Russian governments. The time had come, it was agreed, to win fresh laurels and political advantage from a scientific voyage of discovery in Cook's and Bougainville's tradition. Better yet, the Russian naval ministry would underwrite a double polar venture. Two vessels would probe the farthest South where, since Cook's return in

1775, no European expedition had attempted any work, while another two pressed north to seek a navigable link between Atlantic and Pacific waters. Like its Arctic counterpart, led with indifferent success by Captain Mikhail Vasil'ev, the southern venture, or the Bellingshausen-Lazarev Antarctic Expedition (1819–21), was in essence an imperial response to mounting pressures, to which Englishmen and Russians alike had contributed. And as the mounting of the double expedition bore the mark of Cook's activities in other days, so did its very form and shape.

Cook had received no orders to concern himself at length with "curiosities," as ethnographica continued to be termed, on his Pacific expeditions. Nonetheless, he and his officers showed a keen, objective interest in native peoples that they met. Officially, the emphasis had fallen on the naval sciences (hydrography, marine astronomy), then on the twin natural sciences (zoology and botany), in which the Forsters and Cook's other men of learning were particularly qualified. In fact, Cook and his people made a comprehensive study of Pacific Islanders within the time limits available at any spot. Such an example was not lost on Kruzenshtern in 1802, nor on Bellingshausen, whose orders were in any case precise in few respects.

Those orders were inevitably cloudy: by its very type, his enterprise was such that its development could not well be determined in advance by a committee. As "Divisional Commander," Bellingshausen was merely told to overlook no area of scientific interest. Whenever feasible, his officers were to assist his (German) naturalists in their work. (In the event, those foreign naturalists missed the boat in the most literal and awkward sense.) Thus, in effect, he was at liberty to read the scientific sections of his orders as he chose; and as had Cook and Kruzenshtern, he chose to read them in a way that favoured study of the South Pacific Islanders. Large quantities of broken iron, buttons, gimlets, beads, scissors, and knives, as well as cloth and other things cheaply and readily obtainable, were stowed for use in large-scale barter. Here the Russians were more fortunately placed than Cook had been. *Vostok* and *Mirnyi* were larger and more roomy vessels than the Englishman's had been, *Vostok* being of 907 tons and *Mirnyi* of 530. Bellingshausen left for South Pacific waters and his meetings with the Maori and Rapa Islanders with larger stores of manufactured articles for barter than his foreign predecessors had enjoyed. Matters thus already augured well for would-be students of Pacific ethnographica.

The Russians were received with hospitality and warmth in New South Wales when, in April 1820, they concluded the initial phase of their Antarctic work and came for rest and fresh supplies. Refreshed and well provisioned by the Governor, Lachlan Macquarie, they proceeded, as they thought, for Rapa Island, which Vancouver had discovered almost thirty years before (1791), but where no landing had been made. Stormy winds compelled the

Russians to amend their plans once in the Tasman Sea, and to proceed to Cook's Queen Charlotte Sound (Totaranui), on the northeast of New Zealand's main ("South") island. That well-sheltered spot was reached and, using Cook's own charts, the Russians stood by Motuara Island and Ship Cove, so often visited by *Resolution* and *Discovery*. As *Neva*'s men had retraced Cook's very footsteps on the shore of Ka'awaloa on Hawaii Island (1804), noting the rock where he had fallen (and assorted British bullets, damaged trees, and other traces of revenge along the coast), so now *Vostok*'s and *Mirnyi*'s officers and versatile young astronomer, Ivan Mikhailovich Simonov (1794–1855), prepared to sight Cannibal Cove and Hippah Island. Of the Russian eyewitness accounts of Maori life and culture, as they were in 1820 at a natural historic intersection between North and South Island communications systems, trade, and war, suffice to say that they remain of major value to this day. This contribution to New Zealand and, more generally, to Polynesian studies, has been recognized in recent years. In *Queen Charlotte Sound, New Zealand* (1987), I myself attempt to summarize the evidence. Deplorably, the value of the 1820 Russian contribution to Tahitian studies has not yet been recognized. Yet it has long been known that Bellingshausen's stay in Matavai Bay, Tahiti, from 22 to 27 July 1820 was essentially a session of comparative ethnography, and that the Russians departed their kindly host, Pomare I, with a heavy store of drawings, artefacts, botanical and other specimens, live animals, and journals in their holds—and that the data are unpublished. Perhaps the Soviet authorities will rectify this situation in good time. An overview of the material will be presented to a Western readership, in any case, in the fourth part of this series.

Heading again for New South Wales, at the end of an especially successful winter cruise among the atolls of the Tuamotu archipelago and to Tahiti, Bellingshausen came upon Vostók Island (3 August). The island, like the Antarctic research station of that name, still keeps the memory of Bellingshausen's sloop alive. From here, the Russians coasted down past Tonga's Vava'u Group and Late Island; the chosen route now lay deliberately between those of La Pérouse and Cook, and the desired prize—discovery— was won. Tuvana-i-Tholo ("Mikhailov Island"), in latitude 21°01'S, longitude 181°19'E as the Russians themselves oddly record it, was sighted on 19 August. Shortly after, both Tuvana-i-Ra ("Simonov Island") and the main island of the group, Ono-i-Lau, were observed. The Russians anchored off the northwest tip of Ono, by the low Yanuya islets, on the 20th. They were at once approached by many little craft and by a large double canoe (Fijian: *ndrua*). Contact once established, friendly ceremonial exchanges were begun with the aid of an expatriate and influential Tongan known as Paul. The island chief himself, Fio or Dio, was both intelligent and welcoming. Barter ensued while, as in other plaes, Bellingshausen's officers collected artefacts, made notes, drew up a word list of the local language, sketched, measured and, every day, recorded full impressions in their journals.

Not the least of many Russian contributions to Fijian studies made during this visit were the drawings of the expeditionary artist, Pavel Nikolaevich Mikhailov (1780–1840). I have twice examined the original portfolio of sketches, now preserved at the Russian State Museum, Leningrad. Under a magnifying glass and spotlights, it is possible to see, beneath the portraits of assorted Ono Islanders who visited *Vostok* and whom Mikhailov immediately drew, remains of lightly pencilled proper names in jumbled Latin and Cyrillic characters. Among these names are Tutenberi, Fio, and Dovili/ Dovli. An enquiry among the Lauans based (and now thriving) in Suva, Fiji, makes apparent that those names have not died out. As for the word list speedily drawn up by Bellingshausen's officers, it too throws light on daily life among a people unsuspected by the Eurocentric world in 1820, for a number of the words were, if not Tongan, Tongan-based. Migrants like Paul had been sailing to the Lau Group for many years and, once settled there, had gained some influence and even power. I am most grateful to Paul Geraghty, of the Fiji Dictionary Project, Suva, for his painstaking analysis of the linguistic evidence of Bellingshausen's 1820 visit. An abbreviated version of his study is included here (see pp. 139–46). Russian eyewitness accounts of *Vostok*'s and *Mirnyi*'s call at Ono are, like Golovnin's account of *Diana*'s Tana visit, complemented by discussion of the evidence itself, for health and diet, clothing, ornament, transport, and warfare (Part Two, Chapter 6). That section of the book is self-explanatory. It is worth observing here that the Russian written evidence for Ono Island (journals, letters, logs, and published narratives) is, like the illustrative evidence provided by Mikhailov, well complemented by the artefacts taken to Russia by *Vostok* and *Mirnyi*. Those Lauan artefacts, notably clubs, spears, and ornaments, are on display today in Leningrad and at Kazan' State University, Kazan'. These matters, too, are dealt with briefly in this book (Part Two, Chapter 7).

The third part of this volume gives an overview of early Russian dealings with descendants of the Polynesian migrants who, some time before the eighteenth century, had voyaged north and west from Tonga (or perhaps Samoa) to the Ellice Islands, now known as Tuvalu, and to "Cherry Isle" (Anuta) in the Santa Cruz Group (see Map 4). Of *Apollon*'s encounter with Anuta Islanders in 1822, Russian evidence supports linguistic, artefactual, and other data indicating that those natives had Tongan antecedents. Though of course Samoan settlers might have arrived and intermarried with an earlier, non-Polynesian populace in prehistoric times, it is significant that the Anutans should immediately have responded to the Russians' use of Admiral Bruni d'Entrecasteaux's short Tongan word list. Similarly, Russian evidence of 1821 shows that the occupants of Nukufetau atoll in Tuvalu shared material and social culture with the Tongans. Four Nukufetauan craft approached the sloop *Blagonamerennyi* off Fale, on the atoll's southwest side, but they had not come out to trade, declined to board the foreign ship, and gave the Russians little chance to make a word list. All the same, several articles were deftly stowed aboard the sloop and several officers made full descriptions of their visitors. Triangular mat sails and essentially identical canoe prows and low sterns were features of the "Western" Polynesian area, as shown by the American ethnologist E. Burrows in the 1930s and re-emphasized by Nikolai Butinov in his little book of 1982 (see Bibliography). The circumstances of this Russian visit are considered on the basis of the visitors' own texts. Subsequent Russian sightings and positioning of northern atolls in Tuvalu, Nanumanga, Nanumea, and the so-called "Gran Cocal" are treated separately and, I hope, at proper length (see pp. 169–89).

Both volcanic, steaming Tana and, especially, Ono-i-Lau were removed from the habitual—if not yet beaten—track of Russian ships plying the South Pacific Ocean in the early 1800s. Whether Sitka- or Kamchatka-bound, most Russian vessels that had called at Sydney, New South Wales, on the longer, eastward passage round the globe steered a good way from the Loyalties and so, given prevailing winds and currents in that latitude, drew closer to the Fijis than to any of the Melanesian clusters scattered liberally to the west, such as Vanuatu. Hardly surprisingly, those ships that did look in at Tana and at Ono were, as seen, on scientific or in other ways unusual (and non-commercial) missions. *Diana*'s voyage, broken by a thirteen-month hiatus in South Africa, had neither precedent nor parallel in Russian naval history. *Vostok* was actually seeking unmapped islands, until the seasons changed and made Antarctic survey work a possibility once more. Brief though the Russian stays at Tana and at Ono might have been, though, they produced a wealth of information for the Russian government and, in time, for Europeans generally. Such officers as had been chosen to participate in voyages like Golovnin's or Bellingshausen's were, by temperament and training, sound observers of the Islands scene. Remote and isolated though "Port Resolution," Tana, and the Lau Group might be, from the perspective of St. Petersburg, the Russian Navy's competent "Pacific branch" drew maximum advantage from the unexpected landfalls made in 1809 and 1820–21. And Melanesian studies are the richer for that fact.

*Part One*

# THE RUSSIANS AND VANUATU
# (NEW HEBRIDES)

# 1

# ANGLO-RUSSIAN MARITIME ENTENTE AND RUSSIAN PLANS FOR OCEANIA

The Russian Navy did its best throughout the eighteenth century to gather data on those South Pacific Islands known to science and geography through Western European publications. It remained, perforce, a second-hand and academic knowledge. Immediate realities were echoed in the fact that, since the mid-1730s, the St. Petersburg Academy of Science and not the Admiralty College held responsibility for study of such distant regions.[1] Still, the notion of a state-supported naval expedition round the world into the North Pacific basin had at least been *entertained* by Russian officers for generations. Nor were even southern routes dismissed as hopeless in the period of general decline for the entire Russian Navy that commenced following the death of Peter Alekseevich (1672–1725), its founder.[2] In that era of despondency and deep frustration for the Baltic fleet, there were a few far-sighted officers who took as genuine an interest in Captain Vitus Bering's half-success and further plans for Arctic Exploration as the late tsar would have done, had he survived to see the first of Bering's expeditions end in 1730. The basic soundness of their arguments in favour of a seaborne expedition round the globe was to be demonstrated fully by the vast effort expended on the Second Bering (Arctic and Pacific) Northern Expedition (1733–42).

Two such officers were Captain Nikolai F. Golovin and Vice-Admiral Thomas Saunders. Both were able men who well recalled the naval glory of the days of Hangö (Gangut), when the Russian fleet had overcome the strength of Sweden (1714). Both deplored Russia's continuing decline as a sea power and had their private reasons for an interest in Bering and in Russia's naval prospects in the East.[3] Count Golovin's father, F.A. Golovin, had in 1686 dispatched the earliest of Russian expeditions to seek out a navigable passage to the Indies from the River Léna's mouth; and in 1689 he had signed the Treaty of Nerchinsk with China on the Russians' part.[4] Bering and Thomas Saunders were related through their wives, the Godwig sisters. Their professional connection would at all events have been inevitable.[5]

Saunders and Golovin had both inspected Bering's written statement of July 1730 on his first Arctic-Pacific expedition and subsequently had met him often in St. Petersburg. They had been struck by his remarks about the painful difficulty of his people's journey overland across Siberia to the Pacific coast. They were aware that another venture was afoot in the remote northeast and east under the cossack Shestakóv and that Ivan Kirillov, Secretary to the Senate and an indefatigable statistician and geographer, was working on a third.[6] Determined that the Navy play its proper part in Bering's coming exercise at least, both drafted memoranda on the matter.[7] Bering's overall experience, they argued, showed the folly and expense of sending seamen and equipment from the capital, or even from Tobol'sk, to the Pacific littoral. The Navy could convey heavy equipment to Kamchatka or Okhotsk by sea, around Cape Horn. The passage had been known for generations; nor, despite the common Russian misconception on that score, were "tropic zones" inevitably dangerous to northern mariners. En route, a Russian cargo might be profitably sold, perhaps in China.

On 12 September 1732, the Admiralty College's representation on these questions, that is, Golovin's and Saunders' complementary proposals, were considered by the Senate. "Members of the Admiralty College," reads the Senate Record for that day, "declared that it *is* possible to send ships to Kamchatka from St. Petersburg. The ships could be repaired there, and it is now proposed that they should be; and naval officers would thereby gain in practical experience."[8] In turn, the Senate sent a paper to the College with instructions that the sending of vessels to Kamchatka from the Baltic Sea be further studied.[9] Golovin and Saunders now refined their own proposals, stressing time that could be saved by sending seamen and equipment by the Southern (Oceanic) route. Bering's experience, they noted, demonstrated that it took two years to convey all the supplies for any Arctic-cum-Pacific expedition to its starting point on Kamchatka or the Siberian coast; and two more years were needed to construct an ocean-going craft or two, and yet two more to make a voyage from Kamchatka, to return, and to report back to St. Petersburg. A vessel, on the other hand, could reach Kamchatka from the Baltic Sea within ten months. An expedition need not last more than three seasons if it sailed around Cape Horn to the peninsula that was the easternmost extension of the empire. There were other either probable or certain benefits from the approach. Denmark and Sweden were methodically developing their commerce overseas, as had the British, French, and Dutch.

Russia also could have a mercantile marine, for which such voyages around the globe would form the necessary officers and men. Too many naval vessels were inactive, even rotting at their moorings in the Baltic. Ships were wanted in the North Pacific region to defend the national interest from the inevitable jealousy of other powers and from native depredations and attacks. Their presence, moreover, would give unruly native peoples an impression of Russia's might. Those same natives conceivably could be trained in naval arts.[10]

Saunders's and Golovin's proposals were submitted to the Senate that October. Golovin was actually working on "Instructions for the Sending of Two Frigates to Kamchatka,"[11] confident that they would sail, when on 28 December 1732 he learned of his political defeat by the proponents of a different approach towards an imminent Great Northern Expedition.[12] Nonetheless, his views and Saunders' marked the dawn of a new age in Russian Admiralty circles, where *Vostochnyi Okean*—the Eastern Ocean— was concerned. Despite those officers' and others' views, the Russian Navy was required to expend enormous energy and manpower on Arctic exploration, in the eighteenth-century attempt to settle whether a ship could reach Kamchatka and the Orient from northern Russian ports or river mouths. But, though frustrated at the time, such men as Golovin and Saunders had already sown a seed that was to sprout, under the influence of Captain James Cook's North Pacific triumphs, as the century drew to its end. It was indeed, and not surprisingly in view of Russia's national interests on North Pacific littorals, essentially within the *North* Pacific context that awareness of Oceania and South Pacific crossings could survive a quarter-century of maritime decline.[13]

Of fruitless efforts to discover and exploit an Arctic navigable passage round the far northeast of Asia to the Orient, suffice to mention that of Navy Captain V. Ia. Chichagóv (1726–1809) in 1765. His three-ship expedition was beset with problems from the time it sailed vainly north from Bellsund for the trackless wastes of ice that lay northwest. The squadron met with solid ice in latitude 80°26′N. On a fresh attempt the following summer it did no better, being stopped by ice four minutes higher, five days earlier (18 July 1766).[14] It was a major disappointment to the Admiralty College, to the venture's leading sponsors in the Senate and at Court, to the distinguished poet-scientist Mikhail Vasil'evich Lomonósov (who had entertained great hopes of its success and helped to plan it), and, above all, to Siberian officialdom.[15] Not even such expensive setbacks, though, could kill the question of a navigable passage to the Orient, which English, Dutch, and Russian mariners had sought in vain and for so long. The vast potential of the China trade had always been acknowledged, and its market was sufficiently extensive to accommodate new Arctic or, indeed, Pacific products. That fact alone sustained at least subliminal awareness, at Kronstadt and in Russian merchant circles with an interest in peltry, of the need to keep a Southern route in view.

Catherine II's accession to the throne in 1762 had, as the launching of the Chichagov Pacific thrust well showed, marked the beginning of another naval age after a night of deep neglect of naval matters by the Crown.[16] Coming to Russia from a land-locked German duchy, she herself had little knowledge of the sea. Not only was she willing to be seen to further Peter I's naval work, however; she also became genuinely interested in the problems of a naval renaissance. She was a pragmatist and therefore flexible as to the means to be employed to re-establish Russia's fleet. Among the measures that were very soon effecting the development of Russian policy and naval strength in the remote Northeast and East were fleet inspections, ship construction programs, acquisition of the latest foreign charts and works on naval and related sciences—the latter with the aid of Russian diplomats abroad,[17] and the acceptance of assorted foreign officers of proven competence into the Baltic fleet itself. Since the conclusion of the Seven Years' War, the British Navy List had been dramatically reduced. As a result, numerous officers were now (1763–65) on half-pay or were simply unemployed. At least a dozen of them joined the Russian naval service in that period. Among these hopefuls was the future admiral and commandant of Kronstadt, Samuel K. Greig of Inverkeithing.[18] Efforts were intensified, meanwhile, to acquire charts and surveys, harbour notes, and published voyages abroad.

Market conditions proved discouraging to Russians where the North Pacific Ocean was concerned. No government was able to oblige the would-be buyers, least of all the Spanish government, which was annoyed even by casual approaches on the topic by the Russian minister then in Madrid.[19] Even the *most* remote northerly reaches of the Great South Sea, the Russian agents were reminded, were the patrimony of the kings of Spain and had been recognized as such by Rome since 1493.[20] Less complacent in its grandiose imperial pretensions now, under the ablest of the Spanish Bourbon kings, Carlos III, Madrid reacted promptly to suggestions that the Russians had pretensions on the fringes of that *mare clausum*. Diplomatic steps were quickly taken in response to urgent rumours, in the sixties, of expanding cossack enterprise around its rim.[21]

It is a commonplace of North Pacific history that, for some thirty years (1760–90), Spain and Russia fenced and feinted on the fur-rich northwest coast of North America and on the equally prolific and commercially desirable Aleutian Island chain. Such Russian scholars as A.V. Efimov, A.P. Sokolov, and V.A. Divin, and in North America such Coast historians as H.R. Wagner, C.E. Chapman, W.L. Cook, and S.R. Tompkins, have discussed the subject fully on the basis of the primary, archival documents.[22]

What has been overlooked, however, is that spectral Spanish action in the North Pacific basin served—at least as adequately as awareness in Moscow of the wonderful potential of the China trade—to keep the thought of Russian seaborne expeditions around the world alive and well. The mere knowledge, by extension, that exploratory and surveillance voyages had actually *been* conducted off the "Russian" Northwest Coast of North America, by Captains Juan Perez (1774–75) and Bodega y Quadra (1775), in response to Cossack ventures around the North Pacific rim, strengthened that thought appreciably. So much is clear from despatches sent to Spain in 1772–75 by Francisco Antonio, Conde de Lacy (1731–92), Spain's ambassador in Russia and, as such, the diplomatic representative entrusted with surveillance of a growing threat of "Muscovite encroachment" north and west of Alta California.[23]

Shortly after a report on its results had reached Madrid, the Russian government had learned, in outline, of the Spanish expedition into North Pacific waters led by Captain G. de Portola (1769–70). From resultant apprehension of attacks on Petropavlovsk-in-Kamchatka by the Spaniards, there had sprung (in Lacy's phrase) a "royal order" dated 5 September 1770 that reflected Russian readiness to take large measures to resist such hypothetical aggression by a foreign naval power. Guns and powder should at once be stockpiled at Petropavlovsk; garrisons should be increased on the peninsula, with Spanish raids in mind; and, more significantly, naval steps should also be envisaged by the Admiralty College and the Senate. In the College, added Lacy (who, contemptuous of Court intrigue and gossip and intolerant of Russia and the Russians, was decidedly ill-suited to the diplomatic life), there had been serious discussion of the prospects for a North Pacific naval pact with Britain. Such a pact, it seemed, had struck senior members of the College as a cost-effective method of preventing Spain from legally administering territories that were hers in the Pacific.[24]

Lacy's despatches were designed to stress the gravity of the Pacific situation, to impress upon Prime Minister Grimaldi the importance of a military initiative in New Spain (Mexico) and of a rapid northward thrust across the Californias. They were alarmist. Even so, they were reflections of political realities; and there is evidence that, notwithstanding Catherine's preoccupation with her Turkish wars and Polish "problems" in the early seventies, there was a feeling in the Admiralty College that an Anglo-Russian naval understanding in the East would be expedient. The notion was abandoned when the news arrived that Captain Portola had reached a northern latitude of only 48°. (He had in fact sailed to 38°. So much for diplomatic reportage.)[25] Russia had, reasonably in the naval and political conditions of the period, looked to Great Britain for assistance in holding Spain at bay from Russian outposts on the North Pacific rim.[26] That nothing came of the idea was itself an indication that sounder judgment finally prevailed in the College, as at Court, in 1771. (Might not the British prove an even greater menace to the Russian economic and strategic interest in the Pacific, once in an alliance?) But the mere fact that Anglo-Russian naval understanding had been hoped for, in the North Pacific context, was prophetic.[27]

So too was de Lacy's long despatch dated 11 May 1773. "The Russian Empress," read Grimaldi in Madrid, "having told the famous Haller [Leonhard Euler], professor at the Academy here, of the discoveries made in America [by cossack hunter-traders—GB], the latter has presented a detailed memorial."[28] When peace had been concluded with the Porte, Euler argued, "part of the Russian squadron from the Greek archipelago should be sent around the Cape of Good Hope to Kamchatka, in the ports of which it could refit after its long voyage. Later, it might continue conquests advantageous to the Empire. According to Haller, that Empire has more right than any other power to America, because America was formerly colonized by inhabitants of Siberia. . . ."

Conde de Lacy's despatch, with its confusing reference to prehistorical events or, possibly, to legends of a mediaeval Russian settlement in North America, is of great interest in the Pacific naval context.[29] There had certainly been earlier suggestions that a Russian squadron sail to Okhotsk or Petropávlovsk-in-Kamchatka by a South Pacific route. There quite possibly had been similar suggestions made in Catherine's own reign. None of these, however, had sent ripples through St. Petersburg or chanceries abroad. Now, for the first time, such proposals caused disturbance outside Russia. It was well for Spain that Euler (1707–83), a physicist and mathematician, was unversed in naval matters, though indeed he had at one time been proposed as a lieutenant in the Russian Baltic fleet.[30]

He had worked at the Academy of Sciences with men who, more than thirty years before, had had professional connections with the Second Bering Northern Expedition—Gerhard Friedrich Müller (1705–83), the historian; Joseph-Nicolas Delisle (1688–1768), cartographer; and Georg-Wilhelm Steller and Johann-Georg Gmelin (1709–55), German botanists, zoologists, and students of Siberia.[31] His correspondence offers ample evidence of long-term interests in Northern exploration and the North Pacific Ocean. As it happened, he had incorrect and exaggerated notions of the Russian Navy's real capabilities which were perhaps excusable in 1773. A Russian squadron, after all, *had*—as he emphasized—been led by Greig of Inverkeithing to a famous victory over the Turks at Chesme Bay in Asia Minor and, with British aid, had entered the Aegean Sea in 1770.[32] (No less than fifteen Russian officers who had participated in that major expedition, whose commander, Elphinston, had joined the Russian naval service in the same summer as Greig, had trained on British men-of-war during the sixties as selected volunteers.[33] An historic demonstration of the value of the Anglo-Russian naval understanding of that period, the victory at Chesme Bay understandably had been borne in mind by Russian advocates of similar entente in the Pacific twelve months later.)[34] In reality, those frigates that had reached Aegean waters were, in 1771, in wretched shape; nor is it reasonable to believe that one of them could, in the absence of a long refitting period, have sailed around the globe as was belatedly proposed.

But Euler was correct in his perception of the meaning and importance that would necessarily attach to the arrival of a Russian naval force in the Pacific by a Southern route. The moment had arrived to play that hand, before a European power made a serious new move in those localities which Catherine herself viewed as a Russian zone of influence, that is, the waters east of Kodiak and north of the Aleutians where *promýshlenniki* (hunter-traders) formed an ever more aggressive Russian presence.[35] Then in 1775 came news of Captain Juan Perez's voyage of investigation to the "Russian" northwest coast of North America from Mexico. Again alarums rang.[36] Again, officials at the Admiralty College and the Commerce College, merchants with an interest in the Siberian-Pacific fur-trade, and affected diplomats reflected publicly on Russian policy in the remote Northeast and East of Asia.[37] Russian policy had been, for twenty years by the mid-1770s, to lend some state assistance to the main backers and agents of the new Pacific fur trade, but not openly.[38] For ten years, Catherine herself had—when occasionally sparing thought for the Pacific and American extremities of her domains—elected not to trumpet her subjects' eastward progress to the world.[39] To advertise that progress, after all, would be to signal pointless messages to London and Madrid. And since the Navy had no warships in the far Northeast and East, how was, for instance, the Aleutian Island chain to be regarded as a safe, still less an integral, portion of the empire?

There were essential disadvantages, as well as great advantages, to any policy involving private traders as the instruments of Russian penetration down the Kurile and Aleutian Island chains and to the east. The nervousness provoked by Captain Perez's surveillance cruise died down and, too preoccupied with European crises and developments in any case to focus on such distant and exotic regions, Catherine maintained her cautious policy: unostentatiously rewarding certain merchants, moving gingerly where Russian interests were rapidly expanding but, if not quite indefensible, at least went undefended by the Crown.[40] In the event, Spain's indecisiveness and failing strength in the Pacific made that policy a viable and cost-effective one for four more years (1775-78). But the stage was set already for the jolt that Captain James Cook's people gave Siberian officialdom and Catherine herself, by unexpectedly appearing first at Unalaska Island in mid-October 1778, then at Petropavlovsk-in-Kamchatka twice, in April-May and August-

October 1779.[41] The very presence of Cook's vessels *Resolution* and *Discovery* in countries that had tacitly been treated as a province of the empire, brought home to many in St. Petersburg as nothing had before the simultaneous defencelessness and economic value of Kamchatka and its hinterland.[42] The time was past when North Pacific projects and proposals that a Russian naval squadron make the voyage round the world could be dismissed, as in the seventies and earlier, as costly follies.

That reality was underlined decisively in 1780 by Russian recognition of the meaning of that new species of fur-trade, which the British had so fortunately stumbled on while at Canton.[43] With the assistance of a group of English merchants in that coastal city, Aleksandr Vorontsóv and other members of the Commerce College learned a year later, John Gore of the ship *Discovery* had easily disposed of mostly torn sea-otter skins that had been casually gathered on the northwest coast of North America for an enormous sum: £2,000.[44] It was impossible to overlook the prospect that the Russians, who had neither well-trained crews nor even ocean-going ships to be relied upon in North Pacific waters, might be kept out of this coast-to-China fur-trade.[45] Not surprisingly, under these circumstances, those Pacific naval plans that were advanced during the eighties and involved a Russian cruise through Oceania revolved essentially around avoidance of exclusion from the coast-to-China fur-trade by the British.[46]

Ever willing to exploit the Anglo-Russian naval nexus when expedient, the empress looked pragmatically to Englishmen for information on that fur-trade and, indeed, on Cook's discoveries in general. Coincidentally, she looked for data on Pacific Islands, management of seaborne exploration, and the British expeditionary experience. In 1779, *Resolution* and *Discovery*, now commanded by Clerke and Gore, had been hospitably received at Petropavlovsk by the civilized Livonian who was then governor of the peninsula, Magnus von Behm (1727–1806).[47] They had, indeed, been welcomed generously and provisioned free of charge. Behm's own reports of British visits had been sent on to St. Petersburg, however, by the xenophobic Colonel F.N. Klichka of Irkutsk.[48] Nor did the procurator-general to whom it was addressed, Prince A.A. Viazemskii, see any reason not to offer it to Catherine in the blackest light. As a result, orders were sent for more guns to be taken overland to Petropavlovsk.

Such suspicions of the British expedition's academic aims and basic object as the empress may have entertained, however, were suppressed when she discussed them with Sir James Harris, then British minister. "The Empress," wrote the latter in a long despatch dated 7 January 1780, "feels the great Utility which must result from such a voyage, & is anxious to promote its success—she expressd a *very* earnest desire of having Copys of such Charts as may tend to ascertain more precisely the extent & position of those remote and unexplored Parts of her Empire."[49] Catherine had reason to "desire Copys": the imperial authorities had all too few "such Charts" as covered littorals and waters north of the Pribylov Islands. With the same aim of exploiting British sources to the full, she later welcomed former members of Cook's final expedition (1776-80), not a few of whom were planning to engage in foreign service by the mid-1780s with a view to exploitation of their earlier connections or their North Pacific projects. Three such men were the Connecticut marine John Ledyard (1751-89),[50] Joseph Billings, mate aboard *Discovery* (who gave the Russians to suppose that he had served as her "astronomer's assistant"),[51] and Lieutenant James Trevenen (1760-90). All three had been deeply struck by the potential of the coast-to-China fur-trade. All intended to exploit their first-hand knowledge of it, and their status as companions of Cook, by drawing Catherine's attention to the "soft gold" (otter skins) of the Pacific and the urgency of shielding Russia's interests in China—by establishing some serviceable maritime connection with the East.

Of purely speculative British otter-hunting voyages, reports of which served to sustain official consciousness of the importance of asserting Russia's rights in the Pacific (and by obvious extension of the three expatriates' own likely usefulness), those that most annoyed Count Vorontsov were the operations of *Sea Otter* (Captain James Hanna, 1785), *Nootka* (Captain John Meares, 1786), and *Mercury* (Captain John Cox, 1788).[52] Of foreign scientific expeditions that performed the same function, the most significant was Jean François de La Pérouse's which, for good measure, put in at Petropavlovsk.[53] His humble social origins forgotten, Captain Billings was awarded command of a sub-Arctic North Pacific expedition at the age of twenty-eight and served the empress in the far Northeast for seven draining years.[54] It is James Trevenen's service that will chiefly interest us now, however, for—unlike Billings and Ledyard—he arrived in Russia hoping to encourage Catherine to send her ships into North Pacific waters from the South.

Trevenen's "Russian plans" derived, like Ledyard's plan to cross Siberia (and then proceed, by Bering Strait, to North America and home), from personal experiences on the northwest coast and, shortly afterwards, in China.[55] For a single broken buckle, as he later told his first biographer and brother-in-law, Charles Vinicombe Penrose, he had obtained an otter skin that fetched $300 at Canton.[56] In 1784 Trevenen was on half-pay and depressed about his prospects in the British Navy. He was luckless in his dealings with the merchants of the City, men of "charters and monopolies" whom he was hoping to involve in trading ventures. He approached Count Semeon R. Vorontsov (1744-1832), brother of the minister of commerce, now Russian minister in London. His approach proved timely. Vorontsov, an influential anglophile, had connections of his own in British Admiralty circles and was following developments, both in the international search for the elusive northern passage to the Orient and in the North Pacific fur-trade, with considerable interest. He knew of Hanna's trading coup. Within six weeks of his arrival on the northwest coast from India, that English shipmaster had stowed 500 otter pelts in prime condition. He had sold them to the Chinese for some $20,000.[57] Now the hunt for the sea-otter was progressing in a region to which Russia had a claim. An edict had been issued on the subject on 22 December 1786, which he had looked through only days before Trevenen's letter reached him. Peltry, poaching, and the North Pacific fur-trade were thus still on his mind. In recent weeks, more British vessels were reported to have traded with the Aleuts and the Tlingit Indians, whom Russians called Kolosh, exchanging guns, powder, and ironware for skins, (as well as burning or bombarding native settlements).

Who could better guard the Russian North Pacific interest than the ex-servant of the British Board of Admiralty? Given Catherine's new stance towards the British (and Bostonian) fur "poachers," James Trevenen's plan to send three vessels from St. Petersburg to deal with them seemed promising. That plan was, fundamentally, commercial in its objects; yet it lent itself to other, warlike ends. Being adaptable, it answered to the needs of the new policy. The minister approved the plan and so, in due course, did the empress.[58] Seizing opportunities, Trevenen left for Russia via Holland and the Russian Baltic provinces (1787).[59]

Trevenen argued in his "North Pacific Project" that the Russians should equip three ships, one of 500 tons, the others of 300, and send them from the Baltic round Cape Horn to Petropavlovsk. They should carry trade goods, smiths, and shipwrights and should leave during September, revictualling at some South Pacific Island. Many were known to European science and cartography, and one charted by Cook might fit the bill. The Russian squadron should, however, make no effort to annex Pacific Islands since the objects of the venture, though imperial in scope and implication, might be gained the more effectively by means of shipbuilding and economic progress further north. Here, Trevenen, who perforce wrote as an Englishman and felt no need to urge the Russians to develop an imperial design in Oceania, had parted company with other foreign authors of Pacific naval projects for Catherine. The Anglo-Dutch adventurer and propagandist, Willem (William) Bolts (1740–1808), for instance, had specifically proposed such annexations, "with a view to the establishment of sugarcane plantations."[60] Sugar, Bolts had argued on 17 December 1782, could be carried from a mid-Pacific Island, in a proper Russian vessel, to Kamchatka, and exported at a profit on the European market. "I would trust to make more profit from a single voyage round Cape Horn, than Russians might from twenty expeditions from Kamchatka." Not surprisingly, given his chauvinist and tactless presentation, Bolts's services were speedily declined.[61]

Trevenen's emphases survived into the early nineteenth century, to be incorporated in the final sailing orders of Ivan F. Krúzenshtern (1770–1846) and Iurii F. Lisianskii (1773–1839) when, commanding *Nadézhda* and *Nevá*, they brought the Russian flag at last to Oceania. Trevenen's project was in many ways an adumbration of the Russian Navy's North Pacific venture of the early 1800s. As he urged before his death in battle in the Russo-Swedish War (1790), Russian vessels on their way to Petropavlovsk did indeed call at a European port of South America before proceeding around the Horn to fertile "Islands in the South Sea" (the Marquesan and Hawaiian archipelagoes). They did indeed take trade goods calculated to appeal to Pacific Islanders, and their commanders strove to trade with Japanese as well as Chinese merchants. Finally, their voyages did lead to numerous discoveries "in the immense extent" of Oceania, and did indeed "create a nursery of seamen" for the Crown.[62]

Trevenen broke a leg on his way across Livonia and lay immobile in a little roadside inn for fifty days, wracked both by fever and by panic lest his golden opportunities of earning fame be lost. His accident was prophetic, for when at length he reached St. Petersburg in September 1787, a Russo-Turkish war was under way. No useful squadron that could serve against the Porte would be sent to the Pacific. In any case, a four-ship squadron that recently had been fitting out at Kronstadt for a North Pacific cruise, if it had not already sailed, thus conceivably avoiding an imperial embargo that was now to be expected, had another young commander named Grigorii Ivanovich Mulovskii.[63] Mulovskii, bastard son of Count Ivan Chernýshev, minister of the marine, had trained on British men-of-war (1769–71) while his father had been minister in London.[64] He had served as naval adjutant to Admiral Sir Charles Knowles when the latter, then in Russian pay, had been directing reconstruction of a small Black Sea flotilla,[65] and was held in high esteem by Knowles and Greig.

Trevenen stifled disappointment, introduced himself to his superiors, and hoped at least for an appointment with Mulovskii. *Kholmogor* (600 tons), *Solovki* (500 tons), *Turukhtán*, and *Sókol* (both of 450 tons) would require many officers, and it was clear that the Crown was lending adequate support to the entire undertaking. Penny-pinching in the Admiralty yards could not be overcome perhaps, but able seamen, new equipment, and a library of charts had all been found.[66] Much time and energy had been devoted to the expedition's planning. A committee drawn from members of the Admiralty College and the Senate had decided how the squadron should advance. From the Baltic Sea, it was to make for the Brazils, then east and under Africa towards Australia (New Holland). Watering, revictualling, and exploring on the Sandwich or Hawaiian Islands found by Cook, it was to split into two units. Two ships would proceed with an investigation of the Kurile Islands and the Amur River estuary and the island or peninsula, whichever it might be, of Sakhalin (Sagalin-anga-ata). Meanwhile, commanded by Mulovskii, the other two would make for Nootka Sound. Sailing from there to the latitude where, almost fifty years before, Captain Aleksei Chirikov had sighted land, Mulovskii would possess himself of "the entire littoral" in Russia's name, here and there leaving behind small iron crests (earlier) marked with 1789–91.[67] The coastline of America north of 55°N, was to be annexed, with proper ceremonies.[68]

For a few weeks, even months, the empress had been ready to accept the risk inherent in a forward policy for the Pacific. That she kept her sense of balance, in a time of heady progress on the Black Sea and of international tension, is apparent from the sudden cancellation of Mulovskii's expedition, once hostilities had begun against the Porte in the south as well as Sweden in the west. Mulovskii's orders are, in any case, replete with points of interest for any student of the origins of Russia's naval enterprise in Oceania. Significantly, first, they nowhere specify whether or not, or in what circumstances, servants of the Navy would take orders from Siberian authorities. Where ordinary seamen were concerned, no doubt, the problem would be academic: they would recognize authority, civilian or otherwise. But what of the commissioned naval officer ashore and his relations with Siberian officialdom? These questions of authority were begged only to rise again, in far more urgent form, aboard *Nadezhda* in 1802–4. Then, when a lordly representative of fur-trade interests, Nikolai Petrovich Rezánov, clashed in public with indignant naval officers.[69]

Second, that section of Mulovskii's orders which relates to naval practices at sea merits attention. What could usefully be borrowed from the British should be borrowed: an improved "nautical stove," for instance, for distilling sea water,[70] and charts recently published in assorted accounts of voyages in the Pacific ("Eastern") Ocean.[71] Lastly, as both Mulovskii's sailing orders and contemporary memoirs to Catherine from A.R. Vorontsov and A.A. Bezborodko indicate, a crucial problem in the effort to maintain a naval presence in Pacific waters had been grasped: that lacking serviceable dockyards in the far Northeast or bases in the South, the Russian Navy was obliged to send its vessels round the world and keep on sending them at heavy cost.[72] The moral was straightforward. Either adequate facilities for the construction and repair of naval vessels of some size must be acquired, or the Crown must bear the burden and accept the inconvenience of sending vessels around the globe to the Pacific settlements.[73] In either case, it was apparent that the Navy needed friendly ports of call, if not revictualling bases of its own, in Oceania.

Mulovskii, like Trevenen, died in action in the Russo-Swedish War (1788–90) that had made the execution of his North Pacific voyage quite impractical. Both officers, though, found the time and opportunity to pass their dreams on to a youthful generation, represented in Mulovskii's frigate *Mstislav* by Midshipman Ivan F. Kruzenshtern[74] and in Trevenen's ship *Ne Tron' Menia* by Cadet Vasilii M. Golovnin (1776–1831).[75] It was as though, before they died, they had established in the Baltic fleet a veritable North Pacific club. Mulovskii spoke to many in his ship about the aborted expedition. Kruzenshtern, in whom by 1802 the Anglo-Russian maritime entente and Russian mercantile-imperial ambitions were embodied, was with his captain as he died. Also in *Mstislav* at the time were Iakov Bering, Vitus Bering's lineal descendant, and Lieutenant Aleksei S. Greig, son of the admiral. A godchild of the empress, A.S. Greig returned to England in June 1789 and from there travelled to Calcutta and Canton. While in the Orient, he was promoted. On returning to the Baltic, he was again promoted before setting out for England for the third, but not the last, time.[76] There were lessons to be drawn from such examples of success: that there was nothing to be lost by an awareness of Eastern trade and promise, for example, and that Portsmouth was as good a gate as any to professional advancement, for a young, ambitious man like Golovnin. An orphaned adolescent, Golovnin had fallen under James Trevenen's influence almost immediately after he boarded *Ne Tron' Menia*.[77] Like others in that anglophile setting, he had very soon perceived the need to speak some English.

It remains to mention Rear-Admiral Vasilii Ia. Chichagov in connection with the early growth of Kruzenshtern's and Golovnin's awareness of the East and the Pacific. Formerly commander of a naval expedition to the ice northwest of Spitzbergen but not, as he had hoped, to the Pacific, Chichagov now led the squadron to which *Mstislav* and *Ne Tron' Menia* were both attached. Mulovskii and Trevenen, Bering, Greig, and Chichagov: there was a pattern of suggestion and example around the youthful Kruzenshtern and Golovnin that was not easily dismissed.[78] Such understanding of the promise of the East as either youth had gained while serving in the Baltic Sea, however, was dramatically increased during the nineties when, with fortunate results for Russia, both saw service with the active Royal Navy in the North Sea, Caribbean, and Atlantic.[79]

British officers and shipwrights had been serving in the Baltic, and in Russian pay, since 1560.[80] For the British naval officer, historical, financial, and political considerations favoured Anglo-Russian maritime entente.[81] As seen, occasional expatriates in Russia such as Saunders and Trevenen attempted to draw the notice of the Russian government to the Pacific and the promise held by circumnavigation. But, despite the fearful cost of transport overland across Siberia, the dangerous fragility of all communication lines with Russia's outposts in the far Northeast and East and in America, and real or imaginary foreign threats to those remote Pacific settlements (embodied by the likes of Cook and Perez, La Pérouse and Bodega y Quadra), those attempts bore little fruit.[82] It took a major shift of balance in the ongoing exchange of personnel between the Russian and British navies, which occurred during the nineties thanks to A.R. Vorontsov's persistence and the start of the Napoleonic Wars (1793), to force imperial authorities to recognize the need for Russian voyages around the world.

Specifically, it took the presence not of Englishmen and Scots at Kronstadt, but of Kruzenshtern and other volunteers in Great Britain and in far-flung British colonies from South America to India, to end the lengthy incubation of the Saunders-Golovnin-Trevenen plan. "Vorontsov's scheme was 'to select twelve young and disciplined lieutenants from the fleet and send them . . . to serve four years without a break on English ships at sea; then to send a similar number of officers for the same period to replace the first group and to repeat this constantly, so that in the space of twenty years we should have sixty men worthy of commanding ships'."[83]

Kruzenshtern, who left for England at the age of twenty-three, was placed aboard the frigate *Thetis* (38 guns); his friend Iurii Lisianskii was appointed to *L'Oiseau*.[84] Both sailed for North America with Rear-Admiral George Murray on 17 May 1794.[85] The squadron's sailing marked the start of many friendships—with Charles Vinicombe Penrose, brother-in-law of James Trevenen, J.P. Beresford, and other officers with knowledge of the East or Russian interests.[86] The Russians saw a number of the British Caribbean and Atlantic colonies (Barbados, Antigua, Guiana) and took a lively interest in their administrations and economies. They were reminded that the Russians, too, had island colonies. They sought extension of their leave and it was granted. From the West, they turned their thoughts to the East Indies. Back in London, Kruzenshtern won the assistance of Count Semeon R. Vorontsov, now full ambassador, in developing the plan he had nurtured to proceed to the East Indies and, if possible, to China; to examine how the British, with the backing of their navy, were effectively controlling certain sections of the China trade; and to consider steps that might be taken to increase the Russians' economic influence in the Far East.[87] Captain Charles Boyles of *Raisonnable*, then at Spithead, was informed that three young Russians would take passage in his vessel to Cape Colony, South Africa, in March 1797. Kruzenshtern, Lisianskii, and their travelling companion and compatriot, Baskákov, duly sailed.[88]

In South Africa, Lisianskii fell victim to the fever which, he thought, he had contracted in the cane fields of Antigua.[89] Kruzenshtern went on alone to British India (Calcutta) and thence, with many difficulties and delays, to China. In Canton, he spent ten months over a systematic study of the workings of the coast-to-China fur-trade. Not untypical of little merchantmen that he observed arriving from the northwest coast was *Caroline*, ex-*Dragon* (Captain Lay), a sloop-rigged craft of fifty tons. She had been fitted out in China, had been gone five months or even less, and had brought a cargo that was promptly sold for $60,000.[90] It was plain to Kruzenshtern that a Russian naval undertaking in the East, that was, the realizing of Trevenen's project, was a matter of the greatest urgency. He wrote a memoir on the subject as he voyaged back to Europe in the spring of 1800:

> I proposed that two ships be sent from Kronstadt to the Aleutian Islands and America, carrying every kind of necessary material for the building and outfitting of vessels; that they also be provided with competent shipwrights, workmen of all kinds, and a navigation instructor, as well as charts, books, and nautical and astronomical instruments. Money acquired from the sale of peltry in Canton might be used to purchase Chinese wares, which could be forwarded to Russia in ships fitted out in the Pacific. . . .[91]

Lisianskii too, meanwhile, had been focusing more consciously on Eastern and Pacific opportunities. From Cape Town, he had sailed in *Sceptre* (Captain Edwards) to Madras and, thence, Bombay where—against the background of Lord Mornington's campaigns in Mysore and along the Malabar—he spent three busy months (February-April 1799).[92] Being at liberty while *Sceptre* underwent a refit, he, of course, surveyed the commerce and administration of Bombay, indulged in sightseeing (the Temple of the Cave, Elephant Island), made social calls.[93] To read his journals of the period, however, is to sense the pull of underlying interests, a pull towards the East and Oceania, away from poverty, intrigue, and local war.[94] There are, for instance, lengthy extracts from the writings of the Welsh-born Admiral Erasmus Gower (1742-1814). Gower had been master's mate in *Dolphin* (Commodore John Byron) on a cruise through Oceania of 1765, returning as lieutenant of *Swallow* under Carteret in 1767.[95] Again, there are reflections on the British naval forces then commanded in the East by Rainier. It is an April 1799 reference to Matthew Flinders' survey work around Australia, however, that most strikingly suggests the main direction of Lisianskii's thought after a season in the East. ("I was just then making ready to go to New Holland in a small frigate, which had been ordered to sail to make surveys of those parts. . . .")[96] Lisianskii evidently hesitated to pursue that plan, for fear of irritating Rainier, his own captain, or—worse—the Russian government. The whole problem was solved by the arrival in early May of formal orders to return to Kronstadt. Anglo-Russian friendship, Lisianskii was told by Semeon R. Vorontsov, had chilled of late. He took passage straight to London, nonetheless, aboard *Royalist*, a homeward-bound India-man, and then spent more than fourteen weeks in England.[97] Like his com-rade Kruzenshtern and like Vasilii Golovnin, his junior by three years in the service, he was fluent and indeed polished in English.[98]

Kruzenshtern's memoir of 1800 was rejected; but another was accepted in 1802 by a new, liberal naval minister, Count Nikolai S. Mordvinov, whom the North Pacific project greatly pleased.[99] That August, Kruzenshtern was named commander of a full-scale, multi-purpose expedition to the North Pacific Ocean, in which Crown and merchant interests would both invest. An age of caution and neglect, it seemed, had ended; and in fact two ships, *Nadezhda* (ex-*Leander*) and *Neva* (ex-*Thames*), both built in England and acquired by Lisianskii at considerable cost,[100] did leave the Baltic Sea for Oceania in August 1803.[101] The central element in Kruzenshtern's design as of Trevenen's was, as seen, that Russians barter with the northwest coastal Indians for otter skins, proceed to China, sell some skins, and purchase Chinese goods before returning to the Baltic Sea. In short, his plan owed much to earlier designs. What must be stressed within the context of Pacific studies, though, is the essential element in his design as finalized in 1802 of which Trevenen and Mulovskii had *not* given early notice: the deliberately scientific element which, happily for Melanesian studies, influenced succes-sive Russian voyages through Oceania during the early nineteenth cen-tury.[102] For forty years after his death in 1779, it is important to recall, James Cook remained the very model for the Russians of the leader of a voyage of discovery and science.[103] Cook's celebrity indeed had permeated Kruzenshtern's (and Golovnin's) earlier service lives, during the course of which the three Pacific *Voyages* had periodically appeared in a dozen lan-guages, including Russian.[104] Golovnin and Kruzenshtern had made the personal acquaintance of the hero's former subalterns and aides. The very emphases of *his* Pacific explorations were not only borne in mind by the ambitious younger officer at Kronstadt, but also were seen as proper to such ventures; and among those emphases were certain scientific ones.

It was a paradox: Cook's own appearance on the empire's extremities in 1778 had caused political concern and had been viewed by the imperial authorities in a strategic, not a scientific, context.[105] Even so, it had disposed the Russian government to be receptive to accounts of any voyages into the North Pacific Ocean from the South, that is, to solid information. Russian consciousness of Oceania thus grew apace, as the activities of Cook and his companions had made it possible, as well as necessary, that it grow. And Cook himself had reinforced that fundamentally disinterested, academic attitude towards the South Pacific Islanders which, of necessity, the Rus-sians had adopted in another age. Cook's own achievements were reflected for the Russians, after all, in the most factual and cool descriptions of those

Islanders and of their homes. Young naval officers like Kruzenshtern and Golovnin especially, who had developed close professional connections with the British and who recognized Cook's eminence, were deeply influenced by his approach to the business of discovery—in short, by Cook the scientist. Because the emphases and practices of Kruzenshtern's Pacific expedition (1803–6) were to influence and shape the management of Golovnin's (1807–9), during the course of which the Russians first had dealings with a Melanesian people (Tana Island, South Vanuatu, in June-July 1809), we may usefully reflect here on Cook's and Kruzenshtern's joint ethnographic legacy to Russia. If *Diana*'s five-week stay at Tana was of scientific value, after all, it was especially as a control on ethnographical material that Cook and his associates had gathered there in August 1774 with *Resolution* and *Adventure*.

On setting out on his Pacific voyages, Cook had received no orders to concern himself particularly or at length with "curiosities." That paragraph of his instructions which related to such "Natives" as he might encounter in Pacific waters was as terse as it was clear, and the same for all three major voyages. "You are likewise to observe the Genius, Temper, Disposition, and Number of the Natives, if there be any, and endeavour by all proper means to cultivate a Friendship and Alliance with them, making them presents of such Trifles as they may value, inviting them to Traffick . . . taking care however not to suffer yourself to be surprized by them."[106] No word, here, of the scientific value of the articles that native tribes might "traffick": the political was to take precedence over the strictly scientific where first contact was concerned. In *Endeavour* it was, first, to gaze on Venus in Tahiti, second, to discover Southern land if possible and, third, to complete a grand botanical design that Cook had sailed. Nevertheless, both he and Joseph Banks had shown a lively and persistent interest in native artefacts, as in the languages, beliefs, and social customs of the South Pacific peoples they encountered, and the pattern was repeated on the second and the final voyages.

Officially, the emphasis was first upon discovery and the attendant naval sciences of hydrography and marine astronomy, then on the twin natural sciences of zoology and botany. In fact, Cook and his people made as full and close study of the native peoples met as time allowed, gathering artefacts (certain of which may now be seen in Leningrad),[107] collecting data, sketching.[108] These examples were not lost on Kruzenshtern in 1802–3, nor were they lost by 1820 when the ablest of his midshipmen aboard *Nadezhda*, Faddei F. Bellinsgauzen (German: Fabian Gottlieb von Bellingshausen, 1778–1852), returned to Oceania as captain of his own ship, *Vostok*, and crossed the Lau Group (Fiji) in Melanesia. Preserved intact by Russian officers too young, like Bellingshausen, to have known even Cook's junior subordinates during the Russo-Swedish War, Cook's very spirit nonetheless went with *Vostok* to the Pacific in a way that set at nought the intervening forty years—the age of Bonaparte. Such occupations as had marked Cook's Melanesian explorations in the mid-1770s, for instance, were deliberately taken up again by well-trained Russian officers.[109]

Of Kruzenshtern's own South Pacific work with *Nadezhda* and *Neva* in 1804, I will simply note that as an officer of academic disposition he inclined to stress its maritime and scientific elements at the expense of its commercial and its (hopeless) diplomatic ones.[110] To the extent that the first Russian seaborne venture in the East and Oceania *was* a success, it was successful as a naval training voyage and, above all, as a scientific exercise. Nor is there any question but that Kruzenshtern's "Marquesan Orders," as dictated when *Nadezhda* was approaching Taio-hae Bay (Hergest's "Port Anna Maria"), Nuku Hiva (9 May 1804), where a Russian company was for the first time to have contact with a South Pacific group ashore,[111] reflected Cook's similar orders of another generation. Since those orders were recalled in 1820 by an older Bellingshausen, then commander of his own Pacific mission, they will bear quotation here at least in extract:

> The principal object of our calling here is to water and take on fresh supplies. Though we might achieve all this without the natives' consent, possible risk both to them and to us prevent our taking any such approach. . . . It will be only natural if, on our coming, novel objects provoke a desire in many to possess them; and you would very gladly barter European goods, mostly trinkets, for the various curiosities of these people. . . . When, and only when, we have furnished ourselves with the provisions necessary for the continuation of our voyage, I shall give sufficient notice for every man to be able to barter his own things for others. . . . To ensure the orderly purchase of foodstuffs for officers and men alike, Lt. Romberg and Dr. Espenberg are hereby appointed: only through them are exchanges to be made. It is emphatically reaffirmed that no member of the lower deck shall use a firearm, on board or ashore, without particular orders to that effect. . . .[112]

In every line of the "Marquesan Orders," by which Russian dealings with the South Pacific peoples would be influenced for many years to come, Cook's influence is plain. So it is also in the interest evinced in native artefacts by Kruzenshtern, Lisianskii (as commander of *Neva*), and their efficient naturalists, Georg Heinrich Langsdorf and Tilesius von Tilenau.[113] Day by day, through peaceful barter, artefacts were gathered by the visitors at Taio-hae Bay and stowed aboard.[114] So it is also in the presence of an expeditionary artist, Stepan Kurliandtsev. Day by day, Kurliandtsev, like another Sydney Parkinson, drew artefacts, and natives using them. Like Bellingshausen later, Kruzenshtern had had the time and liberty to choose his own subordinates and he had done so carefully. All his officers had shown high ability and, more significantly from the standpoint of ethnography, were men of scientific bent.[115] All promised well for South Pacific studies thanks to Kruzenshtern's own strategy. That strategy was, first and foremost, to ensure that the Crown and the directors of the powerful, monopolistic Russian-American Company, trading in furs around the North Pacific rim, would back his venture. That assured, he could develop other, scientific aspects of his project—those specifically suggested by Cook's voyages.[116] It was most fitting that in April 1803 the young commander should be named a corresponding member of St. Petersburg's Academy of Sciences.[117] The honour was on one level an act of faith and on another—the official recognition of the link between his enterprise itself and the Academy. There had indeed been many instances of full co-operation between Admiralty and Academy where distant expeditions were concerned, for example to Arctic and remote Northeastern waters, since the time of Vitus Bering. Now that Naval-Academic link was to be strengthened and developed in a new, and still more distant, Southern context. The Directors of the Company had little choice but to accept the situation and acknowledge that the voyage was no longer overwhelmingly commercial in its aim but rather had a major academic and political significance.[118] They did so on 29 May 1803. Here are the crucial lines in Kruzenshtern's Company Orders: "All that you learn from your observations or may otherwise acquire during your voyage, which has significance for natural history, geography, navigation, or for any other science, you will without fail submit to the Company, together with any maps or descriptions that you may have made. We deem it superfluous to go into detail in these matters, however, having learned of your zeal in this regard. . . ."[119]

The "zealous" Kruzenshtern was thus accorded liberty not only to insist upon, but also to construe, the broadly scientific aspects of his orders. As had Cook, he read his orders in a way that favoured study of the South Pacific peoples. On his personal insistence, broken iron hoops, beads, mirrors, nails, knives, and cloth, all in considerable quantities, were stowed aboard *Nadezhda* and *Neva* for use in trade with the Pacific Islanders. In short, he planned to draw maximum advantage from his cruise through Oceania by a judicious choice of trade goods and of officers and men. As he expressed it, "I wished to fill the spare room in my ship with such men as might contribute to advancement of the sciences; for it seemed to me that our long-awaited sojourn in the Southern Hemisphere must surely offer useful employment for all."[120] His attitude survived intact among the captains of a dozen Russian vessels that traversed the South Pacific from 1805 to 1820, five of whom (Vasilii M. Golovnin, Bellingshausen, Mikhail P.

Lázarev, Gleb S. Shishmarév, Mikhail N. Vasil'ev) had opportunities to study and trade with Melanesians. Golovnin, as seen, brought *Diana* into Cook's "Port Resolution," Tana Island in the New Hebrides (Vanuatu), in 1809. He remained there from 25 to 30 July, in friendly contact with a group led by a Chief Gunama, trading ironware, coarse cloths, and other articles for fresh supplies and native artefacts.[121]

Both Cook's account of *Resolution*'s and *Adventure*'s stay at Tana, thirty-five years previously, and especially the narratives of George (Johann Georg Adam) and Johann Reinhold Forster, Cook's companions and naturalists on the second voyage, were employed to good effect by Golovnin. Then, in the space of five months (April-August 1820), four Russian ships, *Vostók*, *Mirnyi*, *Otkrýtie*, and *Blagonamérennyi*, had encounters with South Pacific peoples. On their passage north from Sydney, New South Wales, to Kamchatka, *Otkrytie* (Captain-Lieutenant Mikhail Vasil'ev) and *Blagonamerennyi* (Captain-Lieutenant Gleb Shishmarev) sighted land in 8°S, 178°20'E.[122] It was the low island of Nukufetau in the Ellice (now Tuvalu) Group. The Russians could not know that, only nine months earlier, it had been sighted by a Captain de Peyster of the merchantman *Rebecca*, then en route from Valparaiso to India.[123] The sighting, which had ot been followed up by an attempted landing, was reported only months after the Russians had departed from the Baltic.[124] Understandably believing they had made a fresh discovery, the latter called the whole visible cluster the "Blagonamerennyi Islands." Large canoes put out towards the sloops, which hove to, west of Fale islet, from southwest of the atoll. Trade ensued despite the islanders' indifference to iron. Cruising south-by-west towards Australia after a summer spent surveying in the Tuamotu Archipelago, at Matavai Bay, Tahiti, and more recently in Southern Tonga (Vava'u), *Vostok* and *Mirnyi* came unexpectedly on Fiji's southeasterly outlyers—Ono-i-Lau, Tuvana-i-Tholo, and Tuvana-i-Ra.[125] Ono-i-Lau was a fertile, lofty island and its populace, whose chief was named Fio (Dio), welcomed the Russians most hospitably. Again excusably, for want of published information, the Russians supposed that they had found a place unknown to Europeans. Ono had in fact been visited by *Matavy*, tender to HMS *Pandora*, in 1791.[126] Again, however, Russians made the first effective survey and the first report to European science. Bellingshausen's and his crew's narratives were complemented both by detailed drawings of Fijians and their artefacts by Pavel Nikolaevich Mikhailov, expeditionary artist,[127] and by objects taken back to Russia. They are on display in Leningrad.[128]

Russian aims and operations in the North Pacific region in the eighteenth and early nineteenth centuries differed from those in other waters. First, they reflected underlying Arctic emphases and were essentially a function of the effort to exploit a Northern passage over Russia and Siberia to Eastern markets. Second, they reflected the exploitative yet secret nature of the Cossack enterprise in the remote Northeast and East, in the Aleutians, and in North America. Not only was the Navy's very presence in those areas linked to the lure of furs and, by extension, to the need to guard those furs from foreign subjects; it had also, from the outset, international implications.[129] Third, the Russians' aims and seaborne operations reflected local weakness in the far Northeast and East, where peculation, graft, and (from the Kronstadt standpoint) maritime incompetence were institutional. While Russian consciousness of the Pacific and American possessions both as threatened borderlands and as a source of peltry placed the Navy in an odd, supportive role, weakness on the high seas made it difficult even for autocrats to cast the Navy in another, grander part. The Russian government was constantly weighing the possible reactions of the courts of Spain, Britain, or both to bolder moves in the Pacific. Accordingly, when danger grew in Europe, resources were withdrawn from the Pacific: hence, the sudden cancellation of Mulovskii's expedition and the modest naval presence in the far Northeast and East until the close of the Napoleonic Wars. The cautious move onto the northwest coast of North America and southward merely emphasized what was peculiar and difficult about the Navy's Eastern function. That move, which in itself neither enhanced nor strengthened Russia's naval presence in the area, was from a power vacuum into "a field of international rivalry, where Russian, Spanish, British, and American imperialism vied for territory and resources."[130] Naval officers were needed in the North Pacific area; yet for political, strategic, and commercial reasons, they were limited to unheroic roles in the Pacific, around the rim of which meanwhile cossack and foreign influence crept unabated. For the forward-looking servant of the Navy, the entire situation was both paradoxical and, by its nature, galling.

But those very factors that had worked against aggressive naval moves and forward policies on the Pacific littoral, and which continued to discourage them into the nineteenth century, encouraged academically disposed young officers with Southern plans. Nor did the long delay imposed upon the implementing of designs for naval moves into the North Pacific basin from the South—by the imperial authorities themselves—discourage scientific aims. On the contrary, the twenty-year hiatus (1779–99) between Cook's death and Kruzenshtern's arrival in Canton allowed many Russians to absorb the basic messages of Cook's and his companions' *Voyages*. Those messages, for Russia, were that Russia still had time (if it were quick) to find the navigable passage over Asia to the Orient; that, failing the discovery of such a passage, there were other routes to China or the northwest coast that lay through Oceania; and that the Navy might exploit those Southern routes and North American resources, incidentally combining trade and science with diplomacy, by using Cook's own *Voyages* to best advantage.

In an age when English was not generally learned by the nobility in Russia, many Russian naval officers *did* read it—a result both of professional connections with the British Navy and of recognition of that navy's primacy among the navies of the world. In any case, Cook's *Voyages* and not a few associated narratives were readily available in French or Russian by the early 1800s.[131] That accessibility contributed to Cook's own posthumous celebrity in Russian naval circles. Not until 1820 did the ablest of younger Russian officers cease to revere Cook's name, nor even later did such influential admirals as Kruzenshtern and Bellingshausen cease to think of Cook's professional descendants—George Vancouver, Matthew Flinders—with a measure of the same profound respect.[132] Perhaps *Nadezhda* and *Neva*, *Diana*, *Riurik*, and other Russian ships sent round the world to Oceania in 1803–17 could not annex new lands or implement imperial designs like those of Spain, France, and Great Britain in the South Pacific Ocean. On the other hand, there was nothing to stop them from developing the coast-to-China trade, from reinforcing Petropavlovsk-in-Kamchatka, and, while crossing Oceania, from seeking glory (in Trevenen's words) "by putting the finishing stroke to the discoveries" of naval powers and by "rendering the globe's geography" complete.[133]

Since 1775 at least, official thinking on the Navy's proper role in the Pacific and the Orient had presented two main obstacles to those like Kruzenshtern and Golovnin who viewed that role as both strategically and scientifically important. First, as seen, there was the problem of the Navy's long involvement with the search for open water in the Arctic as opposed to warmer waters in the East; then there was that to do with long association with the fur-trade as a minor and, at times, clandestine partner. Golovnin addressed himself to the solution of this latter set of problems, Kruzenshtern to settling the former.[134] Both were partially successful. Both contributed directly to the work of a Pacific "special service," expeditions from the Baltic to the North Pacific outposts being linked, at least until the 1830s, with the Baltic German element at Kronstadt and St. Petersburg, science, and prestige.[135] By that token, both men placed their names and reputations in the brightest single column of the Navy's early effort in the North and South Pacific. For the Navy's double failure in provisioning the hungry North Pacific settlements and as an adequate deterrent force along the Russian northwest coast in post-Napoleonic times (1815–21) was counterbalanced by the sum of the achievements of such officers and those who sailed with them in a half-a-dozen sciences, including botany, hydrography, ethnography, and physics.[136]

Modern Melanesian studies are the beneficiary of those achievements as of Russian shipping patterns of the early nineteenth century. Even by 1825, more than a dozen Russian visits to Australia had occurred pleasantly as a result of Anglo-Russian understanding and alliance in the wars against Napoleonic France.[137] A passing glance at any map suggests that vessels on their way to Petropavlovsk or the Russian northwest coast from New South Wales must cross the Melanesian archipelagoes or make a giant eastward arc. Among the vessels that traversed them were *Neva* under Lieutenant L.A. Hagemeister (on her second voyage from the Baltic to the Northwest Coast, in 1807);[138] *Diana*, having sailed around Australia in 1809; the *Apollón* in 1822; *Eléna* in 1825; *Krotkii* in 1829; and *Amerika* in 1832.[139] The 1820 ships, as seen, had all recently visited Sydney, but *Vostók* and *Mirnyi* were on their way towards, not from, that port when they traversed the Lau Group (Southern Fiji). Given the temperaments and training of those ships' young officers and the reality that, in the North Pacific area at least in post-Napoleonic years, "aims of science and of empire were essentially one and the same,"[140] it would have been surprising only had they *not* made useful studies of the Melanesian Islands as they passed.

## VASILII MIKHAILOVICH GOLOVNIN AND THE "DIANA" CRUISE (1807–9)

Vasilii Mikhailovich Golovnin (1776–1831) had been intended by his parents for the Guards but was orphaned at the age of ten and, three years later, was delivered to the Naval Cadet College (Morskoi Kadetskii Korpus) in St. Petersburg. A training there was to be had at smaller cost than at a Guards Corps, and his relatives were unconcerned about its broken windows, barracks discipline, and daily bullying.[141] A studious and able adolescent, Golovnin took refuge in extensive reading and in classes, where he shone. In 1790 he was with Trevenen on an active frigate and was known as a particularly promising cadet. He was commended for his bravery against the Swedes and youth alone delayed promotion. Having studied French and English in his spare time, he read of Cook's Pacific voyages in the original, and learned the details of Bougainville's in French.[142] He took a lifelong interest in exploration, and developed expertise in the related naval sciences: astronomy and trigonometry, hydrography, geography, and navigation.[143] Twice in the mid-nineties his facility in English and acknowledged competence at signalling resulted in his serving as liaison officer between the Russians under Mikhail Makárov and the English under Vice-Admiral Duncan, then on joint blockading duty off the Friesian Islands of Holland.[144] Like Kruzenshtern, he proved a beneficiary of Anglo-Russian understanding and alliance on the eve of the Napoleonic Wars.[145] Rear-Admiral Makarov's favour followed him: in 1802 he went to England as a Russian Volunteer, serving vigorously under Collingwood and Nelson, seeing action in *Plantagenet*, *Ville de Paris*, *Fisgard*, and *Prince of Wales* against French and allied warships(1803–5).[146]

While at liberty, ashore in England, he examined Admiralty yards, attended lectures, and pursued his private studies. As a Volunteer he performed repeated guard and convoy duties. Like his naval predecessors on secondment, he examined the colonial administration of the Caribbean islands that he saw;[147] did well in battle; and, requesting an extension of his foreign tour, agreed to go unpaid. Within three months of his eventual return to Baltic duty, in the spring of 1806, he was attempting to secure an appointment on the 16-gun, 305-ton sloop *Diana*, then being readied for a voyage around the world. Meanwhile, to improve the shining hour, he presented Chichagov, now naval minister, both with a detailed report on the comparative conditions of the Russian and the British fleets and with a code of naval signals on the British pattern, which the Russian Baltic fleet was to employ for twenty years. He was named commander of *Diana* and prepared for a long Pacific cruise.[148]

*Diana*'s voyage was, officially, one of provisionment, surveying, and discovery in North Pacific waters. In reality, as was made clear to Golovnin, the naval ministry had one more end in mind—to demonstrate effective Russian hegemony over certain tracts of water between Asia and the northwest coast of North America. In build, *Diana* was a storeship; but in keeping with her function as supply ship for Pacific outposts, she was notably capacious for her length (88 feet). Both in Russia and abroad, nevertheless, she was regarded as a warship.[149] Golovnin took his instructions, furthermore, not from the Russian-American Company Board but from the naval ministry. But some things seemed unchanging and, as usual, too little time was given for the preparations vital for a lengthy voyage. Thirty days of frenzied yard activity were ended by an order that postponed the sailing date by nine whole months.[150] As a result, even the theoretical connection that the ministry had seen betwen *Diana*'s voyage and *Neva*'s to Petropavlovsk and the northwest coast (which had begun in 1806), was wholly ended.[151] To contend that *Diana* could in any way protect *Neva* in the Pacific was ridiculous. Golovnin's whole enterprise was thus now independent, as was Gagemeister's own aboard *Neva*. That independence was reflected in his management of the entire voyage, in the course of which he watered and provisioned in that bay of Tana Island called by Cook "Port Resolution"—and by Tana Islanders, Uea—in the dark volcanic lee of Mount Yasur.[152]

As his second-in-command, Golovnin chose Petr I. Rikord (1776–1855).[153] Their relationship echoed a pattern set in 1802–3 by Kruzenshtern and

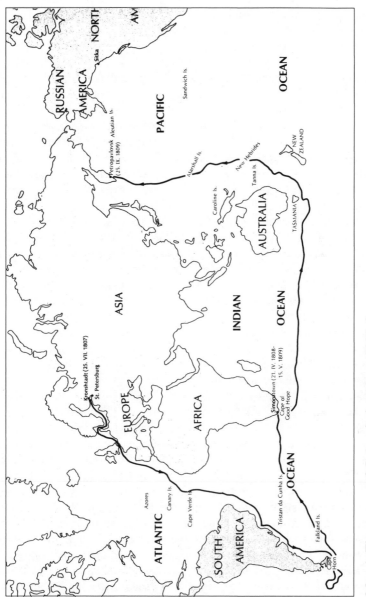

Map 1 The voyage of Golovnin in *Diana*, 1807–9

Lisianskii. They too had met in 1793, at Reval in Estonia; their paths like-wise had crossed during a "North Sea Period." Both men had served under Khanykov for a while. Both had had encounters betwen 1796 and 1801 with Aleksei S. Greig, son of the admiral, who had returned by way of London from the Indies and Canton.[154] Resisting pressure to accept more officers aboard *Diana*, Golovnin instead took on two youthful midshipmen (Il'ia Rudakov and Fedor Mur or Moore) and three cadets (Filatov, Kartavtseve, and Iakushkin).[155] Remembering the value of his practical experience aboard *Ne Tron' Menia* as a cadet, he was to emphasize the need to take cadets on lengthy voyages throughout his service in the fleet.[156] *Diana* sailed on 25 July 1807 with a young and energetic company of fifty-five. Large iron bars and anchors, rigging, cables, tools, and even dry provisions for the North Pacific settlements were used as ballast to increase the cost efficiency. At Petropavlovsk-in-Kamchatka, they were always in demand and short supply.[157]

The political situation on the Continent was tense when Golovnin set out from Kronstadt. It was not supposed, however, that events would move so fast as to affect the exercise. In fact, the Russians saw a British squadron shelling Kronborg Fortress in Copenhagen, and preparing to bombard the Danish capital, if the entire Danish fleet were not surrendered to the British. Cannonballs fell in the water near *Diana* and a drifting, blazing ship threat-ened to set her afire. Watched suspiciously from Nelson's flagship, but unhindered, Golovnin went on his way to Helsingör, which he found aban-doned by its civil population (8-10 August), through the Kattegat, and so to Portsmouth.[158] Copenhagen set the tone for his entire voyage, which was filled with incident and accident.

Britain and Russia were at peace in mid-September 1807. On the other hand, the meaning of the Franco-Russian pact at Tilsit had been obvious for weeks. But *Diana* needed scientific instruments which, following the pattern set by Kruzenshtern in 1803, had been bespoken months before.[159] In the event, the Russian company was well enough received at Portsmouth; nor were difficulties made when Golovnin, having delayed eight weeks while he provisioned for the passage to Brazil and while instruments were tested and delivered to his sloop, suddenly decided to sail on 1 November. He had probably received intelligence that gave him reason to depart; and, shortly afterward, news of a break between the Russian and the British courts was duly published and the British government sent orders to the stations where *Diana* might put in for water and provisions to detain her as an armed belligerent. It also cancelled papers, lately issued to her captain at his embas-sy's request, which guaranteed a safe, unhindered passage through those regions where the British writ then ran.

Golovnin crossed the Equator on 20 December, reaching Santa Catherina

Island in Brazil, where *Nadezhda* and *Neva* had been generously received and cheaply provisioned, on 10 January 1808.[160] The Portuguese authorities again were friendly, and *Diana* and her company, well rested, headed south across the mouth of the La Plata. Cape Horn was rounded on 12 February, but the elements, so helpful hitherto, now turned ferocious and for thirteen days and nights the Russians fought to make a mile of headway westward. Finally the storms prevailed. Recognizing the unlikelihood of better weather at the end of February, Golovnin turned back, setting an eastward course towards South Africa and New South Wales.[161] On the morning of 21 April 1808, *Diana* entered Simon's Bay near Cape Town. She was boarded and detained on the instructions of the British naval officer commanding at the Cape, Admiral Bertie. The detention lasted thirteen months. It would have lasted even longer, had not Golovnin, insulted by demands that his subordinates reduce their rations and repair a British ship in port, and angry that *Diana* was not mentioned in despatches sent from London, made a daring run for freedom on 16 May 1809.[162] The wind was high. Only the frigate *Proserpina*'s sails were unfurled; all other warships in the bay were unprepared to put to sea. "At half past six, in a rainy squall and in overcast weather, I ordered the cables cut. . . . By 10 o'clock, we were in the open sea. Our detention had lasted a year and twenty-five days."[163] *Diana*'s movement from her anchorage had been observed almost at once, and signals passed between HMS *Proserpina* and surrounding ships. But no vessel gave chase.

What course was Golovnin to take? He had no choice but to continue east towards Australia, but obviously there could be no call at Sydney. British officers would hold *Diana*. It was prudent in the circumstances to avoid even those waters that were regularly crossed by British shipping in the South Indian Ocean or around Australia. Provisions had been accumulated in *Diana*'s hold for weeks before her flight from Simon's Bay, and there were ample stores of water. Golovnin resolved to circumvent Australia by taking an unusually southerly and unfrequented track, then heading straight across the Tasman Sea. Avoiding British ports and settlements, he would revictual, water, and rest his people at a suitable Pacific island, then continue on his way towards the Eastern Carolines and Petropavlovsk. He accordingly went south to 41°S, then headed east.[164] Van Diemen's Land was passed by mid-July.

Before leaving Kronstadt, Golovnin had been supplied with charts and published works reckoned to be of future use to him on the Pacific crossings that his mission called for. He had not been issued with a library of *Voyages* and maps like that provided for *Nadezhda*, five years earlier, by the Academy of Sciences, the naval ministry, and Company directors.[165] Still, *Diana* had a useful store of *Voyages* aboard, including several by Cook and his associates on three Pacific expeditions.[166] Golovnin's decision to revictual at Cook's "Port Resolution," Tana, must be viewed within the context of the English-language works that bore immediately up on Cook's Second Voyage—that performed in *Resolution* and *Adventure* from 1772 to 1775. It is plain that that decision was arrived at on the basis of familiarity with Cook's own narrative, *A Voyage towards the South Pole* (London 1777) and with that of Cook's young German naturalist George (or Johann Georg Adam) Forster (1754–94). Forster's own *Voyage Around the World*, printed in London in the same year at Cook's, had since been published twice in German, as well as in French extracts.[167] But, as observed, *Diana*'s captain did not need such French translations. It is certain, even so, that the original (London) edition of Cook's narrative, with its deliberate description of the British call at Tana from 6 to 25 August 1774, in the course of which the Tannese were hospitable,[168] was complemented in *Diana*'s wardroom by a copy of a recent Russian version of that *Voyage*. More precisely, it was complemented by a tolerably accurate translation of the French version of Cook's own narrative, the *Voyage dans l'hémisphère australe* (1778) of Jean-Baptiste Suard (1733–1817).[169]

Lieutenant Golovnin's ability to use the English text, it will be obvious, removed the likelihood of *his* receiving faulty information from the Russian text eventually published in 1796 by the younger Golenishchev-Kutuzov.[170] Choosing Tana Island as *Diana*'s victualling stop, the Russians were completely unaffected by Bougainville's 1771 description of diseased New Hebrideans—as the British were to call them—at Aoba in the centre of the archipelago.[171] It has been argued that *Boudeuse* and *Étoile* had, by misfortune, found a specially "afflicted section of the population" of those islands on their brief visit of May 1768; and that the other "Cycladeans" were not comparably marked by "running scabs" and "dreadful sores."[172] However that may be, it is significant that, once again, the French Pacific record made no dent on Russian practice. Golovnin paid heed to Cook, not Bougainville, despite the fact that Bougainville had offered data on Maewo, Malekula, Pentecost, and other islands in the cluster to be visited.[173] Of Pedro Fernandez de Quiros's impressions of the people and resources of the Hebridean island he had found in April 1606, Espiritu Santo, Golovnin was wholly ignorant. The Spanish government had authorized no published record of the Quiros-Prado-Torres expedition.[174]

What did Cook's and Forster's 1777 narratives say about the Tannese and their island that encouraged Golovnin to look on Tana as a promising revictualling place? As the value of the Golovnin material on Tana rests in essence on collation with the Cook-Forster material of 1774, so does the value of the latter rest on proper understanding of the British stay at Tana and of Cook's New Hebridean exploration as a whole.[175] HMS *Resolution*, it must first be borne in mind, had come to Bougainville's "Great Cyclades" by way of Niue and Vatoa ("Turtle Island") in the Fijis, to extend and test the French discoveries of May 1768.[176] Cook duly spent six weeks in July and August 1774 on an exhaustive running survey of the archipelago's main island, first examining Maewo, Raga, Ambrim, and Aoba in the east, then passing slowly through the centre of the group and so to Tana, Erromanga, and Efate in the south.[177] The expedition spent two busy weeks at Tana, then resumed its northward cruise back to Efate, finally sailing away from the New Hebrides at the beginning of September.[178] Early contacts with the natives, first at Malekula in the northwest of the archipelago, had been discouraging: the islanders had treated British landing parties with suspicion and overt hostility.[179]

Despite the Forsters' deepening impatience with his caution and his officers' exhaustion, Cook manoeuvred, tacked, and pondered for a fortnight before settling on Tana as his local base.[180] He saw the likelihood of bloodshed and was anxious to avoid it. *Resolution* edged into the "small snug bason [sic]" of Uea[181] on 5 August, with a cautious yet impatient company. Nerves remained considerably strained until she left, every encounter with the Tannese being pregnant with dangerous misunderstanding. Once at least, despite Cook's best intentions and the natives' recognition of his firepower, there was a near tragedy ashore. Johann Reinhold Forster, never noted for his patience, clashed vociferously with a Tannese who, he claimed, had been misleading and deceiving him over the naming of an island nutmeg tree. Charles Clerke, second lieutenant, intervened and ordered Forster to the ship.[182] Another day, a sentry shot an islander. The sheer numbers of potentially aggresive and continuously armed natives ashore and round the ship wore tempers thin. A guard was kept by day and night, lest Paowang, or Pawyangom, who seemed to be a "Man of consequence,"[183] should lose even that measure of control over his countrymen that he possessed.

To the extent that Cook's and Forster's narratives reflected these persistent tensions and acknowledged that the Tannese were a warlike people (intertribal strife was as unmistakable in 1774 as when *Diana* came),[184] they offered scant encouragement to Golovnin. There was another way, however, to interpret Cook's and Forster's *Voyages*: the British had perforce been on their guard and had, at times, been inconvenienced by thronging warriors ashore, but they had taken on abundant fresh supplies (yams, sugarcane, plantain, fresh fish, and coconuts), had watered adequately at a pond no more than twenty yards inland,[185] and had controlled the situation. Russians too could mount an armed guard and, having taken full precautions, take on water and provisions. Kruzenshtern's "Marquesan Orders" to *Nadezhda*'s company at Nuka Hiva (1804) could be adapted as required. And *Diana*, like *Nadezhda*, had a store of trading articles and trinkets, though of course she carried fewer, as a warship on her way to Petropavlovsk with supplies, than had *Nadezhda* on a broadly scientific and commercial expedition.[186]

Golovnin was much in need of drinking water, victuals, and rest by late July 1809. His men had been at sea for seven weeks. The situation militated against academic interests of any sort. Nevertheless, it is unreasonable to suppose that Golovnin was unaware, as he coasted north to Tana, of the many scientific opportunities that lay before him. Forster's *Voyage* was especially suggestive: there were areas of botany, linguistics, and geology in which the Russians might deliberately complement the work of Cook and the two Forsters. As for anthropology, it was a word unknown to Cook and Golovnin; but it was hardly possible not to heed contributions to the study of Pacific Islanders in Forster's *Voyage*, and to contributions Golovnin might make. He was an able linguist, had already shown interest in non-European peoples, such as Negroes in Jamaica,[187] and was thorough in his work. He and his people complemented Forster's Melanesian studies energetically, once *Diana* had the necessary water and supplies aboard.[188]

The Russians sighted "Anattom" (Aneityum), the southernmost New Hebridean Island, on 25 July 1809 at 6 AM. Erronan, now often called Futuna, was observed within two hours from the crosstrees; by midday, *Diana* stood within two miles of Aneityum's centre on the southwest side.[189] Large crowds of islanders were visible ashore, beyond a reef, and many brandished spears. None, initially, seemed ready to make contact with *Diana* by canoe, but in the end two men did paddle out, shouting and pointing to an inlet half-concealed by the reef. They did not venture to approach *Diana* closely but continued to encourage her to move inshore. The inlet and the fact that Cook had made no landing on the island tempted Golovnin to stay.[190] His situation was tricky, however; food and water were required urgently and accidents could not be chanced. He took advantage of a southeast wind to move at once to Cook's "Port Resolution," Tana Island, west of Erronan. By dusk, the flickering volcanic flames of Mount Yasur on the southeast side of Tana served the Russians as a beacon. The volcano, as they knew, lay near the harbour. Golovnin entered Uea Bay at 9 AM, 26 July.[191]

The place, which had occasionally been illuminated in the night by flames erupting from the active Mount Yasur, to the Russians' fascination, was extremely beautiful. The bay was edged by mountains clad with jungle, and its waters teemed with fish. From time to time, volcanic rumblings were heard like distant gunfire, and ashes drifted in the air. First contact with the Tannese, who had gathered on the shoreline, was established by *Diana*'s pilot, Andrei Khlébnikov. Two natives met his cutter by canoe, and took a little Russian linen and assorted beads as payment for a dozen coconuts.[192] Along the shore, men yelled and waved green branches as a sign of peace, while others simultaneously brandished spears, heavy clubs, and bows and arrows. Like *Nadezhda* in Taio-hae Bay at Nuku Hiva in 1804, *Diana* was encircled by a crowd of native craft within a minute of her dropping anchor. In their midst there sat Gunama, the chief who was to play for Golovnin the role that Paowang had played for Cook in 1774. Gunama promptly understood the words that, in this moment of initial probing, Golovnin and Rikord read from J.R. Forster's *Observations*—Tannese words for water, swine, breadfruit, and coconut.[193] The Russians landed and, despite misunderstandings—Golovnin was reckoned to be called Diana by his hosts—barter ensued. The Tannese wanted iron, knives, and Russian clothes, and offered foodstuffs which did not include the *buga* (swine) that Golovnin had hoped for. Recollecting goats or cattle that *Resolution* had been carrying, Gunama asked for swine with horns, but this time Golovnin could not oblige.[194] At Golovnin's insistence, Tannese warriors laid down their weapons or, at least, withdrew some distance while the visitors, well-armed and watchful, examined Cook's watering pond. It proved to be a dirty semi-bog. Still, Golovnin brought *Diana* to the south side of Uea Bay and, that same afternoon, her company made ready for a watering and wooding expedition. Golovnin was given one small piglet as a gift, in exchange for presenting Gunama with scissors, beads, and needles. Next day, the Tannese helped *Diana*'s sailors to drag water casks from pond to shore. Meanwhile, other Russians bartered systematically for foodstuffs, took the basic astronomical and naval readings to confirm Cook's fix, or worked aboard the sloop herself. Midshipman Moore, an accomplished mimic, gathered words. His list, regrettably, was lost during his captivity at Matsumae in Japan in 1812.[195] Much to his credit, Golovnin himself had noted down some fifty Tannese words or phrases, which he published in St. Petersburg in 1816.[196] Overall, the Russian company showed more self-discipline at Tana than *Resolution*'s had.

So usefully begun, the Russian visit to Uea Bay continued pleasantly, to mutual advantage, on 27 July. Golovnin was welcomed by Gunama at his hut and given fresh coconut milk. The Tannese elder was presented with a coat to which assorted coloured ribbons, hooks, and buttons had been sewn, and with a motley comic turban made on Golovnin's instructions. Other chiefs (*teregi*) from the area, who wanted to be treated like Gunama, also left with Russian clothing. All were satisfied. In four days, the Russians had obtained more than a thousand coconuts, more than a hundredweight of sugarcane, plaintain, and breadfruit, and approximately 230 lbs of yams. *Diana*'s firewood and water stores were ample, and her company had washed and dried their clothing, traded steadily, and even rested. Tannese visitors aboard the sloop were numerous but well-controlled by Russian muskets. They remembered the firearms and cannon of Cook's *Resolution* or, more probably, had heard of their effects. Like their request for "hogs with horns," their attitude towards *Diana*'s falconets and carronades proved that Cook had been remembered.[197] To sustain their pleasant humour and to foster trade for foodstuffs, Golovnin distributed mirrors and paint among the islanders. More than a bucketful of oil paint was splashed and daubed over their bodies. In conjunction with the little mirrors, the results produced a fever of excitement and experiment.[198]

Recognizing that the time had come to leave for Petropavlovsk, Golovnin invited Chief Gunama and his elder son, Iata, to dine in *Diana*'s wardroom. Both declined strong spirits, wine, and even most of the prepared dishes that were served. Iata ate cooked fish with great reserve. The Russians did not understand the Tannese attitude to food.[199] Gunama claimed that he was full and had no appetite; the Russians gracefully accepted his excuse.

Despite its brevity, the Russian visit to Uea Bay ("Port Resolution") was fruitful, in practical and scientific terms alike. A single day had brought in "forty feet of sugarcane," ten lbs. of yam, 435 fresh coconuts, and figs.[200] *Diana*'s pilot and assistant pilot, Khlebnikov and Srednii, had surveyed Uea Bay efficiently by cutter. Tannese weaponry and other artefacts had been acquired in some quantity. The size and physical condition of the local population had been calculated. Evidence of local warfare, social structures, navigation, husbandry, and diet had been found; and note was taken of Gunama's and his people's clothing, body ornament, language, and temperament. No more could reasonably be expected of a naval company which, on departing from the Baltic, had anticipated no such visit; which had reason on arrival in Uea Bay to pay attention to provisionment and watering above all else; and which was anxious to arrive at Petropavlovsk by September, while the seas were safe for shipping. In itself and, more particularly, in conjunction with the British evidence of 1777, Golovnin's sojourn at Tana plays its part in Melanesian and, of course, New Hebridean anthropology.

*Diana* weighed anchor at dawn on 31 July. The wind being extremely weak, Gunama and a half a dozen other islanders came out to her, to barter one last time and to express a grief that Golovnin thought genuine.[201] Their journals filled with data, and their minds with recent memories, the Russian officers at least were even now assessing Tana as a future port of call for other vessels on the longer eastward route around the world to Petropavlovsk. Golovnin spoke for them all in 1816 when he concluded that, despite its ample natural resources, Tana Island was inferior in almost all respects to Sydney, New South Wales, as a resting and revictualling place for Russian vessels on their way to the Pacific settlements. Specifically, the islanders had not—at least in winter, when *Diana* had arrived—shown any readiness to barter hogs or fowl; had acknowledged that supplies of sweeter water than the swampy pond could offer at Uea Bay were fairly inaccessible to shipping; and had given evidence of being dangerous, albeit not to Russians.[202] Golov-

nin himself would have preferred to call at Sydney, but political developments had stopped him doing so. As it turned out, no other Russian vessel
called at Tana in the early nineteenth century.

The death from fever of *Diana*'s second carpenter, Ivan Savél'ev, within
an hour of her sailing from Uea Bay, was a depressing augury of coming
troubles. Trouble came, not on the passage to Kamchatka, but on Golovnin's
examining the Japanese-exploited Kurile Islands (Etorofu, Kunashiri).
Golovnin, Moore, and Khlebnikov were taken captive by the Japanese and
held two years.[203] Golovnin and Khlebnikov returned to European Russia
overland, by dogsled, reindeer, horse, carriage, and barge. They reached St.
Petersburg on 3 August 1814, exactly seven years after they had left it.[204]

Golovnin steered due north from Tana, passing six miles due west of
"Emir" (Aniwa) Island, seen by Cook on 5 August 1774.[205] When Eromanga's southern tip, Point Pilbarra, was sighted, he adjusted course towards the
east, then headed north once more—so passing east of all the northerly New
Hebrides (Map 2). The 169th meridian soon brought him north to Tikopia, a
particularly isolated island with a peak 1,200 feet above the sea. Its elevation
and solitude combined to make it an effective signpost for a vessel like
*Diana*, which was northward-bound and in the southeast trade winds belt.[206]
Golovnin was to be followed through these waters in the far east of the Santa
Cruz Islands, where land specks like Fataka and Anuta (Edward Edwards'
"Mitre Isle" and "Cherry Isle")[207] served as comparably elevated signposts,
by at least two other Russian ships during the early 1800s—*Apollón* (Lieutenant Stepan Khrushchev) on the passage north from Sydney to Kamchatka in June 1822,[208] and *Amerika* (Captain Ivan von-Schants) along the same
route in May 1835.[209] Other ships, such as *Elena* (Lieutenant V.S. Khromchenko) and *Krotkii* (Captain L.A. Hagemeister), passed no more than 6°
east of Anuta, on their run towards Kamchatka or the northwest coast. For
them, in 1829, Rotuma was the marker in an empty waste of ocean.[210] From
Anuta to Rotuma is about 500 miles, but that distance is small within the
oceanic context. The Pacific stretches 13,000 miles in Rotuma's latitude.
Anuta and Rotuma lay astride and slightly eastward of the Russian Navy's
highway to the North from New South Wales. Russian contacts with the
Polynesian people of Tuvalu (Ellice Islands) were predictable, given the Russian shipping pattern of the period.[211] That pattern, which *Diana* and *Neva*
had set together, called for summer navigation east of the New Hebrides and
west of Fiji, in longitudes approximately 175°–180°E.

Losing the southeast trade wind on 6 August 1809, in latitude 7°S, Golovnin moved NNE, passing a little out of sight of Arorae. Captain Patterson of
the *Elizabeth*, whose track of one month earlier *Diana* intersected, had
observed that little island southeast of the Gilbert Archipelago as he, too,
pressed up north towards the modern Kingsmill Islands.[212] Golovnin crossed

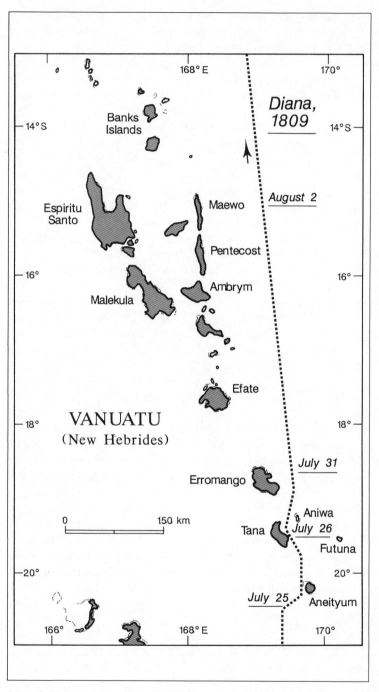

Map 2  Vanuatu (the New Hebrides), showing *Diana*'s route of 1809

the Equator, moving slowly out of Melanesian waters, in longitude 168°70′E. Cutting across the Marshall Islands, he arrived at Petropavlovsk on 25 September 1809, 792 days since he had sailed from Kronstadt roads.[213]

# 2

# VASILII MIKHAILOVICH GOLOVNIN'S ACCOUNT OF THE RUSSIAN VISIT TO ANEITYUM AND TANA (1809)

Golovnin's first published account of his experiences in the New Hebrides appeared in 1816, in the St. Petersburg journal *Syn Otechestva* (*Son of the Fatherland*, no. 31:177–200; no. 32:217–33; no. 33:3–23). It was based on his journals of 1809, on *Diana*'s log, and on other materials written by Lieutenant Rikord and possibly by Navigator Khlébnikov and others aboard. The delay had resulted from his captivity by the Japanese (1811–13); he, Khlébnikov, Midshipman Moore, and four of *Diana*'s seamen were seized on Kunashir, one of the Japanese-controlled Kurile Islands, in retaliation for raids made in that area by two young Russian naval officers, G.I. Davýdov and N.A. Khvostóv, in 1807. With minor alterations only, the 1816 text was reprinted as Chapter 3 of Golovnin's "abridged memoirs" of his voyage, *The Voyage of the Russian Imperial Sloop-of-War "Diana" from Kronstadt to Kamchatka in 1807–1809* (St. Petersburg 1819). Pages 139–246 of that work, that is, the conclusion of Chapter 2 ("Passage from the Cape of Good Hope to Tana Island") and Chapter 3 ("A Stay at Tana Island and Observations on It"), form the basis of the following translation, the first into English. Note has been taken, however, of more recent editions of Golovnin's text, notably in the 1864 omnibus *Works and Translations (Sochineniia i perevody Vasiliia Mikhailovicha Golovnina*, St. P., 5 vols.) and in the "two expeditions edition" of 1961, that is, the Soviet edition of the narratives of the Golovnin voyages to the Pacific in *Diana* (1807–9) and *Kamchatka* (1817–19). Finally, note has been taken of Golovnin's remarks on *Diana*'s passage from Cape Town to Tana as published, in official format and with hydrographic emphases, in *Proceedings of the Admiralty Department* (*Zapiski Admiralteiskago Departamenta* 1815, Pt. III), some nine months after his return to the capital. The original manuscript of Golovnin's *Voyage* on which both the 1816 and the 1819 "Tana sections" rested, that is, the holograph of "Puteshestvie Rossiiskago Imperatorskago shliupy Diany iz Kronshtadta v Kamchatku v 1807, 1808 i 1809 godakh," has been lost. An early copy, however, with corrections in the author's own hand, is preserved at TsGAVMF – the Central State Naval Archive of the USSR in Leningrad – under the reference *Fond* 7, op. 1, *delo* 11.

Golovnin's account of the Russians' visits to Anelgowhat Bay on the southwest coast of Aneityum and to Uea Bay (Port Resolution), on Tana's southeast shore, so rich in ethnographic data, has largely slipped through the literature. Even such serviceable works as G. Turner's *Nineteen Years in Polynesia* (1861), J. Inglis's *In the New Hebrides* (1887), C.B. Humphreys' *The Southern New Hebrides* (1926), and, among more recent scholarly studies, Jean Guiart's *Un Siècle et demi de contacts culturels à Tanna* (1956) fail to mention Golovnin's account. The Russian ethnographic data are considered separately here (Chapter 3). Not one makes even passing reference to ethnographic data brought to Europe by the crew of *Diana*.

Because Golovnin himself saw the importance of collating his remarks on Tana and its people with related observations in George Forster's *Voyage Round the World* (1977, Vol. II) and placed a series of comparisons of Forster-Cook and Russian data in his work, it has been deemed useful to restore Forster's originals where pertinent.

THE GOLOVNIN TEXT

At dawn, when the island of Anattom [Aneityum] came in sight, we also glimpsed Tana, directly ahead, from the cross-trees [see Map 3]. The island was conspicuous by the smoking volcano of which Captain Cook makes mention in his *Voyage*.[1] At 7:30 AM, Erronan [Futuna] became visible to our lookout, off to the NE.[2] Approaching the island of Anattom [Aneityum] at 9 AM, we could see smoke in numerous places – a sure sign that the island was inhabited. I ordered the Russian flag to be flown from the topgallant mast. It was at this moment that we observed a reef extending from the southern coast of the island in question westwards, and, at its centre, an islet [Inyog Islet].[3] The island was covered with green trees, which included palms and coconut palms. Not long afterwards, we also observed that behind the reef, that is, between it and the actual island, lay a stretch of calm water which natives were even then crossing in their craft.[4] (The term canoe is applied to such craft, and to the craft of all native peoples indeed, when they are hewn out of a single trunk.) Some of these canoes were making their way along the shoreline, but others were right in the breakers.[5] The closer we came, the more natives we spotted there.

By noon, we stood some two miles off the centre of the southwestern coast

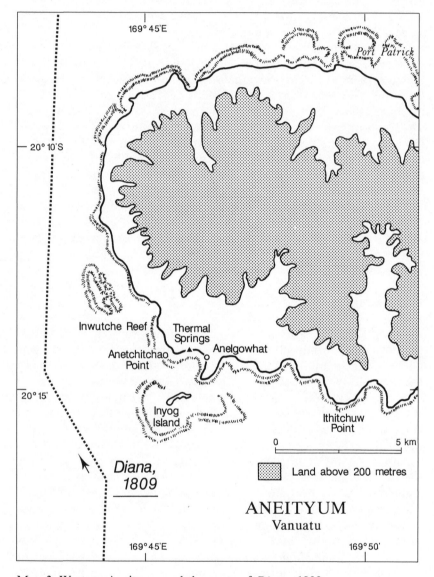

Map 3  Western Aneityum and the route of *Diana*, 1809

of the island of Anattom [Aneityum].[6] We could see a considerable number
of people ashore. They were naked[7] and were running about with extremely
elongated spears in their hands.[8] These they shook, though whether in menace or in order to invite us to draw still closer we cannot now say. I gave an
order that, in response to their signs, our people should hoist a white flag on
a long pole. The natives withdrew from the shore, however. Next, we saw
about a half a mile away from us a small canoe with support-beams or
outriggers; there were two natives aboard. ("Outrigger" is the term applied
to the two poles which protrude to one side of a canoe and which have a little
pole attached to their extremities. Dragging through the water, this pole
stops the craft from capsizing, as it would unquestionably tend to do without
such a device.)[9] Taking off canvas, I immediately ordered that we steer
towards this canoe, and that white kerchiefs be waved in various parts of the
ship. The natives, however, paddled away from us and towards the shore,
shouting something and pointing with their paddles at a small inlet behind
the reef [Anelgowhat Harbour]. When we resumed our course and put on
more sail, though, they turned back and came after us again. Once more we
moved towards them, but once again they hastened away from us, shouted
out, and pointed at the land. The bodies of these natives were a glossy black
and they were quite naked apart from narrow cloths tied round the waist.[10] A
white, elliptical figure of some sort hung at the chest of one man,[11] who,
placing one hand on that chest, held a paddle with the other and indicated
the shoreline. I believe he was trying to say that we should approach the
shore by the aforementioned inlet. Certainly, the little harbour had a capti-
vating aspect. It lay, as I have suggested, at the centre of the island's southwestern coast. And I would gladly have visited this island, the more so
because Cook did not do so;[12] but ignorance of the provisions that we might
or might not find there, of the natives' temper, and of the existence of a
nearby source of fresh water, all obliged me to prefer the known to the
doubtful and proceed at once to Port Resolution [Uea Bay], as Captain
Cook named the harbour in question after his own ship.[13] Tana was not far
off and I trusted to reach Port Resolution that same evening. Our situation
demanded that we reach Kamchatka that autumn without fail, and so haste
was very necessary. We passed by the northwestern point of Anattom [Anei-
tyum] at midday . . . and a steady following wind from the SE bore us quite
swiftly towards Tana, under a clear sky [see Map 4].

Tana Island's northern tip became visible at 6 PM, bearing 26°NW from us
. . .[14] but the impossibility of proceeding until the light was stronger eventually forced us to postpone our arrival in harbour till the morrow. So we hove
to, under small canvas, at 7 PM. That night proved to be a very dark one,
under cloudy skies, but the volcano of Tana, throwing up great flames,
served us as a beacon. We knew from Captain Cook's account that the

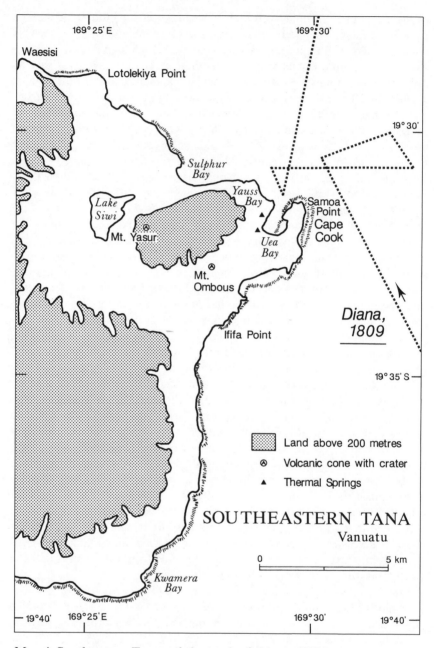

Map 4  Southeastern Tana and the track of *Diana*, 1809

volcano lay near the harbour, so we could set our course by it. The eruptions of this fiery mountain had a majestic appearance indeed, and weary though we were from our daily duties, we hesitated to leave the deck, whence we could admire so beautiful and yet so terrible a natural scene. All in all, the day had been most pleasant despite our having spent it hard at work.

Just as soon as it was light enough on the morning of July 26, that is, at 7 AM, we moved under a gentle northeasterly breeze towards the southeast shore of Tana, in order to examine the entry to Port Resolution.[15] Since we had no chart of the harbour, and since a bay was opening up to our right that was quite large enough to accommodate shipping [Yauss Bay], we made for it along sandy shores protected by a reef on which breakers hurled themselves with frightful force.

Many black and naked islanders, meanwhile, were running along that shore. All, from youngest to oldest, were armed with long boar-spears and clubs.[16] They made various signs to us and waved, apparently in invitation. Having moved some way along this coast, however, we realized that what had seemed a bay to us was in truth an inlet encircled by reefs. We tracked and moved north; but the wind suddenly died away and the swell began to push us towards the reef itself. . . . We clearly saw our ruin . . . but at the most fraught moment, the wind sprung up as before from ENE. . . . Such is the life of a sailor! His fate rests on a gust of wind. Passing by an underwater rock with which the reef in question terminates, we saw a bay that extended some distance. The natives ashore pointed to it, so I lay to and sent Navigator Khlebnikov ahead in the cutter to examine it.

As soon as the ship's cutter arrived in this bay, two natives went out in a canoe to meet it. They held in their hands a green branch, the usual sign of peace among the Pacific Islanders. Mr. Khlebnikov was kind to the natives, presenting them with a few beads and towels of unbleached linen,[17] in return for which they offered him thirteen coconuts. Returning to the sloop, Mr. Khlebnikov had this to report on the harbour. It appeared to stretch a mile across from north to south and extended inward perhaps a half-*versta* [1,750 feet]. It was seven or eight fathoms deep, with a fine sandy bottom. It was exposed only to northerly winds. Even though we did not yet know for certain that this was the bay called Port Resolution by Captain Cook, I decided to enter it. We did so at 9 AM and dropped anchor, to the loud and joyful shouts of a great crowd of islanders who had assembled on the shore or in their craft around us. Once we were inside this bay, we compared its layout with that described by Mr. Forster in his *Voyage*.[18] We were quickly convinced that it was, as we had hoped, Port Resolution. Astronomical determination of our latitude confirmed this.[19]

I must observe straightaway that, even on our arrival at Tana, we did have sufficient water left on board to see us through to Kamchatka. In the event,

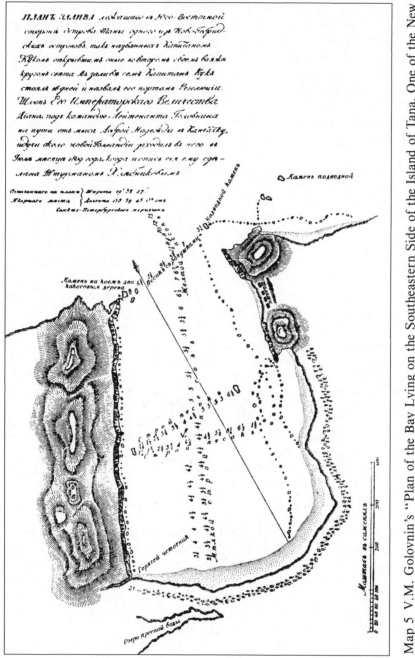

Map 5  V.M. Golovnin's "Plan of the Bay Lying on the Southeastern Side of the Island of Tana, One of the New Hebridean Islands," 1809

we proved unable to get naval provisions there; but I was hoping to reprovision with vegetables, fowls, and hogs,[20] and to build my crew's strength up, lest scurvy appear among them. For that reason, I also wanted to learn what I could about the natives of this island, which not a single modern navigator had visited since Cook's time. (D'Entrecasteaux had sailed within sight of these islands, when in search of La Pérouse, but he had made no landing.)[21] Nor, in all likelihood, had any European navigator but Quiros even seen the place before Captain Cook.[22]

Among the natives surrounding us in their craft was one elder, Gunama by name. By various signs, this man gave evidence of his friendly intentions and offered us his services.[23] To make our own needs known to him, we for our part now had recourse to the account of Captain Cook's voyage written by Mr. Forster. Finding among the small word list there the local names for things that we needed,[24] we tried them out on the natives, who repeated them, accompanying the words with various body movements. Gunama very quickly understood us when we said *tevai* [*te wai*], meaning water, *buga* (hog), *niu* (coconut), *emer* (breadfruit), *ani* (to eat), *nui* (to drink), and so forth. First, he showed us the place where we could water. From the location of the place, it was evidently that very source used by Cook's ships when they had watered here.[25]

I wanted to take a preliminary look at the place, so at noon I landed with two armed boats. Gunama came out to me in his canoe as soon as I left the sloop's side. On my return, I invited him to step on board and he in fact came on deck without hesitation. On the water, he had been bold and talkative, admiring our clothes and everything else his eyes happened to rest on. Now, I asked him the names of the surrounding islands. He understood my gestures and named the islands exactly as Mr. Forster has them in his narrative; Tana, Anattom [Aneityum], Eromanga, Irranan [Futuna], Emir [Aniwa].[26] I attempted, for my part, to explain to Gunama that we had come from afar and belonged to a populous and powerful nation called Russia. The name of my vessel, I explained, was *Diana*. But try as I might to get these ideas across, I failed: from all my words, all my body movements and gesturings he extracted only the notion that I was called Diana. Even this discovery, however, delighted him, and he immediately stood up and yelled "Diana!" to all his countrymen in their canoes surrounding us. "Diana!" he shouted, pointing at me. Seeing this, they all repeated the word at the top of their voices, pronouncing it excellently. . . . It is under that name, I imagine, that they remember me today.[27]

Gunama wished to know if we had any women aboard. Learning that we had not, he laughed loudly and indicated, by various highly explicit and all too intelligible signs, that women are essential for a certain purpose, which he also indicated. He talked a great deal on this occasion and seemed to be jesting at our expense, either wondering how we could live or even perpetuate our kind without women, or laughing at our diligence and nervousness in concealing our wives from them, if in fact we were doing so. But the inadequacy of our communication had meanwhile led me, too, into error. I asked Gunama for hogs, presenting him with assorted gifts, e.g., knives and scissors and beads, and also showing him some rather better articles with which I would be quite prepared to pay him for swine. He understood me perfectly well and, pointing at his own fingers, promised to bring me ten animals. Then he pointed at the cutter in which we were approaching the shore where he lived. I concluded that if we brought the cutter to his dwelling place, he would then exchange ten hogs for the articles I had just proposed. It turned out that he was actually offering me ten hogs for the cutter itself, which was the best of our rowing boats and with which I would not have parted for anything. Understanding that I would not exchange my cutter for ten hogs, Gunama then requested a *buga* with horns for each hog he gave us. *Buga* meant hog; and he made the horns with his fingers. He obviously meant cow, ram, or goat, which he had possibly seen on Cook's ship.[28] Since these natives have no quadrupeds among them other than swine and mice, they call all others *buga* too. This was the only incident that showed us that these people had indeed had dealings before with Europeans. It showed, too, that they had some knowledge of the action and effect of guns. For pointing at ours, the natives made evident by sound and gesture that the terrible and death-dealing arms were known to them. (When Captain Cook had sent his boats ashore here for the first time, the natives had launched an attack. Suspecting hostile intent in time, Cook ordered the cannon primed on his ships ahead of time; and a volley of cannonballs passing by the natives' ears and into the woods instantly scattered them and so alarmed them that they never dared launch an attack thereafter.[29] It was most likely that we ourselves were now being kindly treated by the natives as a result of that most efficacious means of bringing them to reason.) There were certainly no indications that any other European vessels had visited here at any time, nor did we find the natives in possession of the most trifling European article, even though Cook himself had distributed a quantity of objects, notably iron tools.[30] Finally, these natives did not know a single European word.

After these negotiations with Gunama had been concluded, we made our landing and were met by several hundred armed men. Having both muskets and rifles with us, though, we did not fear them but went straight onshore. We had told Gunama to instruct his countrymen not to come up close to us unless they had first placed their arms in the bush; and he had instantly carried out our request. As a result, many of the natives had thrown themselves into the bush, put their weapons down there, and returned empty-handed. Perhaps a majority, though, held onto their clubs and arrows and stood a little way off.[31] I looked over the place where we were to water and saw that it was indeed the one that Cook had used. It was the most enormous bog, strewn with muddy islets and covered with shrubs. Part of this bog, which bore a likeness to a pond, extended to within a quarter-*versta* [290 yards] of the shore on which we stood. There, the water was rather deeper though still pretty opaque and even dirty. Cook himself had complained of these deficiencies. I asked the natives if they had not better water and they replied that there was indeed better water up in the hills, but that it was far. So we were forced to be content with what was available here by the shore. I then presented the more affable of these natives with various trifles and obtained, in return, several coconuts and other plants.[32]

Between 2 PM and 3 PM this day, we moved closer in towards the south end of the bay where we would take on water.[33] The rest of the day was passed in working on the sloop: it was already late to start putting off boats for water. On this first day, we had bartered for 114 coconuts, two bunches of plantain, and yams weighing twenty-one and a half pounds.[34] In addition, Gunama brought me a 29-lb. pig as a gift, gratis, in the evening. I gave him, in return, some small scissors, a few sailmaker's needles, and some beads. But the caution which must always be taken when dealing with savages obliged me to take certain necessary measures. To this end, I gave the following orders to my company, in written form:

In Port Resolution, Tana. 26 July 1809

During the sloop *Diana*'s stay in Port Resolution on Tana Island, and in all other harbours on islands of the Pacific Ocean which are inhabited by native peoples and which our situation may permit us to visit, the following instructions will apply:

1. So that the natives may be obliged to furnish us with fresh provisions, neither officers nor members of the lower deck shall be permitted to barter for anything other than fresh provisions. Once we have stowed sufficient of these, I shall indicate the fact, and each man may then buy or exchange whatever he may wish on his own account.

2. No man shall barter foodstuffs for himself, and all foodstuffs obtained by purchase or barter shall be taken for the common store and divided equally among the crew. In this way, we shall ensure that those whose duties keep them constantly occupied in the sloop and who therefore have no leisure for barter with islanders, shall receive the same quantity of fresh foodstuffs as those men with more time from shipboard duties.

3. Lieutenant Rikord shall supervise bartering.

4. While in the roadstead, officers will not keep watch during the day. Only the naval cadets shall do this. At night, all shall stand watch, as at sea.

5. At night, the watch shall be armed as per standard regulations for boarding and the watch shall also adhere to signalling regulations.

6. Midshipman Moore and Midshipman Rudakóv shall attend to shore work in turn.

7. The naval cadet whose week it is to attend to the distribution of provisions shall watch and ensure that none of the fresh supplies brought from shore shall be given to the sick without instructions from the surgeon, and then only in the quantity prescribed by him.[35]

The weather remained clear, with only occasional clouds, right through 27 July, and the wind remained very gentle from the SE. At 6 AM, I duly sent our armed boats ashore for water and wood, accompanying them myself in the cutter. We were met by a small number of natives. Soon however their numbers swelled. They came towards us with wooden spears, arrows, and small clubs; but they then placed nearly all their weaponry in the bush and, approaching us empty-handed, treated us in friendly fashion. Many volunteered, indeed, to drag our water casks along (each cask held 4½ to 5½ bucketfuls), and we rewarded them with two beads for each cask taken aboard. They were perfectly content with this pay. We actually took the water and wood aboard at about noon, returning to the shore after our lunch. By then, there were even more islanders assembled than earlier, but they met us like old friends and again assisted us in our watering and wooding. Even though the natives' manner was so friendly, however, we were very careful, and all our people were armed except the men actually working. We returned to the sloop again at about 4:30 PM. Officers had various duties while ashore, each doing what had been assigned to him. One supervised the work itself, another organized a human chain, a third bartered with the natives for foodstuffs, a fourth took astronomical readings, and a fifth collected words in the local tongue. This last duty was performed by Mr. Moore, that luckless officer who was afterwards in captivity with me among the Japanese.[36] Moore had a marvellous way of expressing himself through pantomime, and by that means he was able to compile quite an extensive list of words in the language of Tana. It was lost, alas, during our subsequent captivity. On this second day, we bartered for 250 coconuts, 175 lbs. of yams, 66 feet of sugarcane, and four bunches of plantain.[37]

Towards evening, we moved across to the eastern side of the bay, to the residence of our friend Gunama.[38] His hut differed from the others only in point of size, however, and it proved to be quite bare. One can only suppose that these people had carried all their belongings off into the woods, for fear that we might take a fancy to them and carry them off for ourselves. Even those articles that we ourselves gave them, it may be noted, were all out of sight the next day. The suspicious Tannese had even driven into the woods their own hogs, whose excrement, however, we saw around their huts.

As is well known, the peoples of the Pacific Ocean regard us Europeans as poor tramps roaming the seas in search of sustenance. The Tannese were very likely afraid that we would discover that they had plenty of hogs and would then decide to settle among them. Captain Cook, like us, had failed to obtain much livestock from them.[39] When we visited Gunama, though, he did receive us kindly, having earlier met us right at the shore, and he did regale us with coconuts which he had a boy of ten or twelve fetch down from a palm in our presence. We marvelled at the ease with which the boy climbed up the tree, which was growing at an angle of at least 60° from horizontal, walking up it as if he were on the ground and holding on only by his hands. We were equally surprised by the strength of these people's teeth: to get the milk from coconuts, we ourselves had to split the nuts open with an axe, or smash them with a large stone. But these natives bit through the coconuts in a second, as easily as we might have dealt with an ordinary small nut.

Gunama pointed out to us his two sons. One was a boy of about 14, named Iata; the other, aged perhaps ten, was called Kadi. Together with these two sons and escorted by five or six other islanders, Gunama walked with us along the shoreline. He was not willing, however, that we should approach their cemetery, which lay in the bush, and so we looked at it only from afar. In the same way, he prevented our going round to the northeastern cape of this bay. Forster records that he, too, was prevented from going there, and that the natives threatened him, suggesting that if he did, he would be eaten.[40] We ourselves were not warned in this manner; but our hosts certainly did not want us to go there and we did not argue the point. After distributing a number of presents among Gunama, his children, and others present, we set off back to the sloop at sunset. The night of 28 July was excellent, so I ordered my men to wash their linen, in turns.

At dawn next day, we again set out in our boats to water and cut wood. Navigator Khlébnikov and Assistant Navigator Srednii did not accompany us now, since they were engaged on a survey of the harbour. The wind remained as before, but the weather worsened, with clouds and occasional rain. The boats returned to the sloop with water casks and wood around midday, and put off once more after a meal had been taken. The natives received us kindly on this day, as previously, not attempting to conceal articles from us and certainly not trying to attack us in an overt fashion. We were beginning to feel a degree of confidence in them now, though, truth to tell, we had greater faith in their fear of our firearms than in their good qualities. We knew well enough that they had tried to attack Cook's boats, though they had since been more peaceable: they had seen the effect of cannonballs fired from a ship, as I have mentioned. We ourselves, when we went shooting,[41] went in groups of only two or three and went quite far from the shore.[42] We were then met by many natives, some of whom would accompany us to show us places where birds might be had; but they offered us no insult. It was only our guides indeed who did cause us some annoyance, for supposing that our muskets could kill at any distance, they ran ahead of us like crazed men, yelling at the top of their voices and scaring off the birds. And when the latter settled again, these natives would point them out when they were scarcely visible – and then wonder that we did not shoot them all! We, for our part, did not want to make it obvious to the natives that our firearms could not in truth cause harm at any distance, so we found ourselves obliged to pretend that we had not spotted the birds or had thought them not worth shooting. We were equally careful to conceal from them the fact that our firearms needed to be reloaded, they supposing that one could fire away continually. The discovery of *that* secret might have led to our ruin.

It was on this day that I recognized that our Gunama was chief, not of the whole island, but only of a part of it. It happened as follows: the previous evening, Gunama had been greatly taken by my jacket, and more especially by its shiny buttons, since I had not taken the precaution of having them covered by little bits of cloth. (I had actually taken that step with regard to my arms, and the hilt and setting of my sword, my pistol, and my rifle had all been sewn up in blue material, lest their gleaming should entice the natives and cause them to demand those things of mine.) Gunama had several times expressed the wish to own my jacket, though. I was unwilling to part with an article so necessary to me, so I pretended that I had not understood him but gave orders that by morning a hospital-style robe should have assorted ribbons sewn onto it, particoloured though it already was, and moreover that as many brass buttons, hooks, and other trifles as possible should also be sewn onto the garment. I also ordered the manufacture of a hat like a turban, of white cloth, ornamented with various multicoloured bits of material that our tailor had at hand. And, now donning this ludicrous attire, I went ashore. The magnificence of my apparel at once captured the attention of the islanders, and they cried out, *Evvau!*, and gazed at my raiment.[43] Gunama, who could not keep his eyes off this gown, forgot all about my jacket; and wherever I went, all pointed at me with their finger and said, *Arromanu, Arromanu!*, meaning, "The chief"![44] Gunama eventually brought himself to ask me if he might possibly have this garment. I refused for a while, explaining that such items were very costly and that I needed them. Finally, though, I agreed to let him have them, as a special mark of friendship, and removing hat and gown, I placed them on him. The natives again shouted, *Evvau!* and surrounded Gunama who, forcing his way through the throng, marched proudly up and down the shore. But three or four other men approached me and requested similar garments, explaining that they too were *teregi* or chiefs, just like Gunama, and in no way inferior to him. And to support their claim to rank, they showed me a small bird's feather, stuck in their hair. It was lucky that the gift in question had not been expensive, in fact; and, not wishing to aggravate these men, I now ordered that each should have a similar robe made for him, only not as splendidly embellished as the one Gunama had received. This one incident apart, we never observed any jealousy among them, and it seemed to us that in general these natives were very friendly towards one another. They would stroll about in parties, their arms round each other or holding hands, and should any man be doing something and need help, others would willingly lend him assistance.

We saw no battle among these people and heard no argument. But it may very well be, of course, that they fight natives from other islands and perhaps from other regions of Tana Island too. I happened to notice that one man had an arrow wound in the groin, but I could not gather from what he said how he had come by it. The sheer quantity of their clubs, spears, arrows, etc. is certainly evidence in itself that they are familiar with warfare. Though the men treated each other in a friendly manner, I may add, they showed no consideration for their womenfolk, and we could clearly see that their women were in fact despised and even enslaved. All the heavy work was performed by women.[45] On this day, we acquired by barter 289 coconuts, 50 figs, 16 lbs. of yams, a bunch of plantain, and 36 feet of sugarcane.

The weather remained calm and clear till 10 AM on the 29th. Then a wind sprang up from the NE, the sky clouded over, and rain fell. For as long as it remained dry in the morning, we dried our flags, the many colours and quantity of which produced a marvellous effect on the natives. Day by day, the latter were now evincing more trust towards us, gathering around the sloop in their canoes in very large numbers. They gazed at the flags, not lowering their eyes, and repeated their usual exclamation of joy or wonder, *Evvau!* Our kind behaviour towards them and the gifts that we had distributed finally won their trust completely. On the first day of our call, they had scarcely dared to approach the sloop and we had proved quite unable to coax them on board, but now they were constantly visiting us. Everything they saw on board produced inexpressible wonder in them; but most of all, they liked our mirrors and the sounds of the bell. The mirrors had the same effect on these people as they do on animals who, on first seeing their own reflection, seek another animal behind the glass.

The Tannese love to paint their faces but have no colours other than red, black, and a crude white. Curious to see if they would also like other hues, I had some of them paint their faces with all the colours in my paint box. Hardly had they shown themselves to their countrymen, their mugs thus beautified, before all were yelling *Evvau!* and throwing themselves onto the sloop and asking to be similarly painted. I would certainly not have had enough paint to satisfy their desire in my own paint box, so I ordered that their faces should be daubed with oil paints available and at hand. Even this caused mighty satisfaction – we could hardly beat off all the natives indeed and managed to conserve only one bucket of paint!

While these natives were on deck, rum was being issued. It was being poured from a barrel into a little keg. I offered the islanders a little rum in a tumbler, but they smelt it and declined, saying *abo, abo,* meaning "bad, no good."[46] Then, mentioning *kava*, they showed by signs that that beverage of theirs produced a trance. After awhile they did take a little of the rum into their mouth, but it was immediately spat out.

Gunama and his elder son, Iata, were among our visitors and we invited them both into the cabin to eat with us. After a certain amount of trouble, we did manage to seat them at the table and on chairs. They wanted to sit on the deck. They sampled our dishes, but they did not want to eat them proper-ly. They did not, however, say that the food itself was bad or that they disliked it. They merely declined on the grounds of *tabu-rasissi*, that was, "stomachs full already." Iata ate only a little cooked fish, nor would he try even that before he had cleaned away the skin and convinced himself that the fish had been caught in this very bay. This shows, I think, that they either feared we had spoiled the fish or considered our food, so to speak, unclean and liable to defile them.[47]

When this meal was over, I went ashore with Gunama. I wanted very much to find out if his people had any articles left behind by Captain Cook. I certainly saw none. On this day though I did see an old man with a small piece of an old, thick bolt, such as *Diana* herself did not have. Supposing it to be a memento of Cook's visit to this island, I offered the old man a small knife for it; but he would not trade it. I added scissors to the offer, but still he was unimpressed. Finally, I also offered a towel and several other objects besides; but nothing would induce that stubborn old man to part with a bit of iron that was of no use to him. I concluded, on the basis of his years and conduct, that he remembered Cook and was holding on to the article as a keepsake. I was wrong. I afterwards learned that the bolt had been taken on board at the Cape of Good Hope and had served as a door stopper. Seaman Stupin had taken it ashore here in hopes of exchanging it for some rarity or other, and had given it to the elderly native. If the latter *had* surrendered the bolt to me, I would have preserved that bit of old iron like a treasure and presented it to our government, by mistake, together with all the other curiosities from Tana! (One wonders how many treasures like this bolt are in fact preserved in our museums and curiosity cabinets!) On this day, we obtained from the natives 435 coconuts, 10 lbs. of yams, 40 feet of sugarcane, three bunches of plantain, 130 figs, and a breadfruit.[48] A steady wind was blowing from the NNE on the night of 30 July, with light cloud cover.

At 6 AM next morning, we went ashore in the boats for a final time to wood and water; but at 8 AM the wind grew stronger and it poured with rain. Because the wind blew almost directly into the harbour, a considerable surf was whipped up by the shore, which put our rowing-boats in some danger. Lieutenant Rudakov, who was in command of the boats, saw the risk and sought assistance from the sloop in good time. Aid was given. On returning to the sloop, Lt. Rudakov told me that he and his men had indeed been at some risk: the cutter had very nearly been capsized by the surf and he had been forced to have all the water casks then in her heaved overboard. It was fortunate for us that the local natives were now well disposed toward us. There had been several hundred of them on a nearby shore and, far from taking advantage of our misfortune to harm our people, they had plunged into the sea, fished out the casks, handed them back, and then helped the oarsmen to pull out from the surf.[49] Shortly after noon, the wind died down, but rain continued to fall until evening, when the sky finally cleared. Lightning was still to be seen, even then, far off to the NE.

That same evening we went to the shoreline to fish, following the advice of islanders who had assured us that many fish would have been driven by the winds into the bay. And the natives themselves helped us to cast and drag a seine net. We were not too successful, for we caught only two fish. Knowing from Forster's account that there is a poisonous fish in these waters,[50] we asked the islanders if we might eat even the two we had caught. They all said yes, but then one small boy, evidently wishing to joke at our expense, pointed at the two fish and cried, *abo, abo!* ("no good"). All the others, meanwhile, were yelling *ani, ani!* ("eat, eat!"), and pointing at their own mouths. The boy smiled after a while and indicated that the fish were indeed edible. The natives were treating us in the most friendly fashion now, not only causing us no harm whatsoever but also causing us no anxiety. To the contrary, they were doing what they could to be of service to us. At first, as seen, I had permitted no man to barter with the natives for rarities, hoping thereby to oblige the natives to bring out more foodstuffs than they would otherwise have done. But now, since we had acquired from our hosts all the fresh supplies that they seemed disposed to furnish us with, I allowed all my people to barter for curios as they wished. The natives willingly parted with their arms for our trifles. It was only their clubs that they were not too willing to give up, those weapons being made of extremely hard wood known as *casuarina* and consequently requiring much time in the making.[51]

We observed that, in their trade with us, the Tannese – who were exceedingly fond of all finery – preferred shining knick-knacks to useful items, the utility of which we nonetheless demonstrated to them. At midnight, the wind swung round to the WSW, gusty: it blew straight from the volcano which is not more than five miles away. Every night hitherto, the volcano had erupted and sent up flames, but this night we saw no flames, even though dull sounds like distant thunder were audible.[52] The wind bore a very fine ash onto the sloop. . . . We were ready to leave by now. The necessary amounts of wood and water had been stowed; we had bartered for as many plants and edible roots from the natives as was possible; and it was plain that the islanders were not willing to part with any of their hogs or fowls whatever. So, having no reason to delay, we weighed anchor at 5:30 AM next morning, on 31 July, and moved out of the harbour.

As soon as the natives saw that we were indeed leaving, a great cry of *Evvau!* resounded along the shores around us. The wind, dying away, gave Gunama, his sons, and four or five of his fellow countrymen time enough to come out to us. On drawing near the sloop, they cried repeatedly, "Diana! Diana!", and pointed to our previous anchorage. Then, coming nearer still, they started to howl and to hum something, and wiped away tears – tears that were flowing unfeignedly from their eyes. As a present, Gunama had brought me out a yam root weighing no less than 16½ lbs.; we gave him a few things in return. Then, the wind springing up again, the sloop resumed her former course and began to leave Gunama behind in his canoe. The natives continued to wave at us, though, and Gunama repeated, in a pitiful voice, "Diana! Ah, Diana!" Such was the sensibility of these savages: they cried and shouted for as long as we remained within earshot.

Our parting with these new friends of the Pacific Ocean was not, in all honesty, too hard for us, even though their cries and tears did touch us. But scarcely had we left this bay before we were struck by a misfortune that did strike closer to our hearts. At 7 AM, our carpenter's mate, Ivan Savel'ev, died of a fever. . . . I was initially inclined to remain a few hours longer in harbour, so that we could bury our dead comrade ashore. Then I considered the matter further and thought it certain that we should not be able to conceal the gravesite from the islanders there, since they would be watching our every move. They would see that we had left a corpse behind, I reckoned, and would most likely exhume it, in order to get at the clothing, etc. Perhaps they might even consume the body, if the Forsters' suspicions of their cannibalism were fully justified.[53] (I shall return to this topic.) So I resolved not to bury Savel'ev ashore. At 11 AM, we set a course NE under a westerly wind and clear sky.

Alone among recent navigators, as I have mentioned, Captain Cook had visited the New Hebrides before us. He had been in "Port Resolution" sixteen days in August 1774. The naturalists Forster, father and son, who had been with Cook, made various observations on Tana Island and its inhabitants, with some of which I am not in accord, though we found most of the Forsters' comments to be just. I will here allude to what the younger Forster has to say on those subjects, merely adding my own observations to his.[54]

Regarding the reception given to the English by the Tannese, Forster expresses himself thus:

> Having brought the ship to an anchor, we were well pleased to see the natives coming off in their canoes from different parts of the bay, and paddling round about us at a little distance. Their behaviour was at first very irresolute; though all were armed with spears, clubs, bows and arrows. One or two came close to us, and sent a yam, or a coconut, upon the deck, for which we made them presents of our goods. . . . (II:262)

We in *Diana* experienced precisely the same reception. The natives were armed in the same way, and one individual among them presented us with a branch of the plant known as *kava* [*'awa*],[55] which grows abundantly nearly everywhere among the Pacific Islands. (The natives make an intoxicating drink from its roots, of which they are very fond.) This was obviously done as a gesture of friendship and peace. I ordered that the branch should be tied to our mainsail shrouds, an action that gave the natives much satisfaction.

> In a few moments (adds Forster), the number of canoes encreased to seventeen; some of them contained twenty-two men; others ten, seven, five and the smallest only two; so that the number of people about us exceeded two hundred. (II:262)

Such a large number of craft never approached us at any time, nor did we ever see a canoe that could have held so many.[56] On the other hand, we did see numerous craft that contained only one man. "They pronounced several words to us from time to time," continues Mr. Forster, "and seemed to propose questions." We experienced the very same thing.

> We had hung a net overboard astern (says Forster), containing salt meat for dinner, which the sea water was to freshen, as we did every day; one of the natives, an old man, seized this net, and was about to detach it; but being called to, he instantly desisted. However, another shook his dart at us on this occasion, and still another adjusted an arrow to his bow,

taking aim by turns at different persons on the quarter-deck. (II:263)

The natives stole nothing from us and never attempted to remove any object from the sloop. Nor, for that matter, did we ever observe that they meant even to take advantage of our negligence if they could, or hoped to take something away, save on one single occasion. This was once when there were many natives assembled ashore and one man wanted to remove a hoop from a water cask. The natives never threatened us, and they seemed to us neither severe nor angry.

> One of them (continues Forster) offered captain Cook his club and, having agreed to take a piece of cloth for it, it was let down into his canoe. However, he had no sooner received this cloth, than he took no farther trouble to fulfill his agreement. . . . (II:269)

With us, the natives never tried on anything of the sort. It often happened that a man regretted a deal, having exchanged a weapon, a club particularly, for some trifle or other that had caught his fancy suddenly. It was sometimes even clear that a native repented of a decision. But no man ever demanded back an object that he had earlier bartered away or tried to return some article of ours to us.

Of the opposition shown to the English by these natives, who apparently numbered about nine hundred at that time, when Cook's men attempted to land on Tana Island, Forster has the following to say:

> Captain Cook ordered a musket-ball to be fired over their heads, in order if possible to frighten them away . . . but one of them, standing close to the water's edge, was so bold as to turn his posteriors to us, and slap them with his hand, which is the usual challenge with all the nations of the South Sea. . . . (II:272)

When we ourselves landed for the first time, to get water, there were more than a thousand people on the shore. We were surrounded by them, and they all carried some kind of weapon with them. Yet they showed no inclination to attack us and always moved aside or even sat down when we asked them to do so. Cook ordered that stakes with ropes tied between them should be driven into the ground on either side of a track leading from the shoreline to the pond where he was to water, thereby forming a passageway twenty-five or thirty fathoms wide along which his people might pass in safety; and he forbade the natives to cross the limits established by these ropes. I did not make use of such precautions because they seemed unnecessary. Cook had also insistently requested that the natives lay down their weapons: some had obliged him, while others would not. We, for our part, did not demand this from the islanders because we always had *our* weapons in our hands (only at the start did we ask the natives with arms not to stand close to us); but after a while, when the Tannese had come to trust our peaceable intentions, they freely put their own weapons down in the bush and approached us empty-handed. Forster adds that the English "often offered to purchase their arms, but the natives constantly refused to part with them." Matters were different at the time of our own visit. The Tannese traded every kind of weapon they possessed as soon as they spotted something they really liked. At the beginning, as I have said, they were rather reluctant to barter away their clubs. But in due course, they became ready to trade even with clubs.

> One of them (says Forster) disposed of a cylindrical piece of alabaster, two inches long, which he wore as a nose jewel. Before he delivered it, he washed it in the sea, whether from a principle of cleanliness or not, we could not determine. . . . (II:274)

I myself acquired a number of such objects,[57] but the natives were not so polite or cleanly. For taking the sticks from their nasal cartilage, they left us to wash them off or not, as we might choose.

During the English visit, some of the natives had danced and, even while doing so, threatened with spears. Other natives, who were standing quietly by, had watched the dance in question. From the start to the finish of our own stay in "Port Resolution," the natives never threatened us in any way; nor did they give the notion that the weapons they did carry were for possible use against us in particular. Some of these natives had exchanged names with the English. They did not offer to do this with us. Perhaps lack of time prevented our acquiring the necessary degree of friendship with them. For names certainly *are* still exchanged, as a mark of friendship, on all the South Sea Islands.

Mr. Forster has this to say of the outward appearance and the physique of the Tannese:

> They are of the middle-sized stature, but many among them may be reckoned tall. Their limbs are well made, and rather slender; some are likewise very stout and strong; but those beautiful outlines, which are so frequent among the people of the Society and Friendly Islands, and of the Marquesas, are rarely to be met with at Tanna. I did not observe one single corpulent man among them; all are active, and full of spirit. Their features are large, the nose broad, but the eyes full and in general agree-

able. The colour of their hair is black; however, we observed some which had brown or yellowish tips. It grew very thick and bushy, and generally frizzled. . . . They almost go perfectly naked; but, true to the general characteristic of mankind, they wear several sorts of ornaments. (II:274–75)

Having examined the islanders whom we met and compared them with those thus described, I find Forster's description to be quite an accurate one in all respects, and I have nothing to add. I merely note that we did not chance to meet with a single individual with an evil physiognomy or with anyone having light brown or reddish hair. There is one point on which I am not entirely in accord with Mr. Forster, though. He writes that many of the islanders have a swelling around the eyes, ascribing to this their custom of sitting in smoke. This swelling, according to Forster, makes the natives incline the head back, to bring the eye into line with an object they wish to see. I myself observed no such deficiency in the natives of Tana, whose ornaments Mr. Forster describes in these terms:

They dress their hair after the following method: they take a quantity, not exceeding a pigeon's quill in thickness, and wrap it in a thin thread or ribbon, made of the stalk of a bindweed, so that only a small tuft remains at the end. All the hair on the head is disposed in exactly the same manner, so that they have several hundred *queues*, three or four inches long, standing on end. . . .Most of them also wear a thin stick or reed, about nine inches long, in their hair, with which they occasionally disturb the vermin that abound in their heads. A reed set with cock's or owl's feathers, is likewise sometimes stuck in their hair as an ornament. (II:275–76)

I can confirm that it is precisely thus that the Tannese do wear their hair, young and old alike following the same style. They do indeed often disport sticks ornamented with, or more precisely hung around with, feathers, as embellishments. We acquired a few such sticks from them by barter. I myself did not observe that they use the hair-stick to scratch the head, nor did I ever see them using any other implement for the purpose.

A few of them (continues Forster) also wear a cap made of a green plantane leaf, or of matted work, on their heads. Some twist their beard into a kind of rope, but the greater number leave it in its natural form. They usually bore an aperture through the nasal cartilage between the nostrils and wear a cylindrical stone, or a bit of reed, half an inch thick. The ears are pierced with a very large hole, in which they wear a number of rings of tortoise-shell, or of a piece of white shell an inch in diameter. Round their neck they sometimes pass a string to which they fasten a shell, or a small cylindrical piece of green nephritic stone, resembling that which is common at New Zeeland. On the left upper arm, they commonly have a bracelet made of a piece of coco-nut shell, either curiously carved, or plain and polished. . . . Some of them wear a belt, or sash, of a kind of coarse cloth, made of the inner bark of a tree. . . . Paints are reserved for the face: they are red ochre, white lime, and a colour shining like black lead; all these they mix with coco-nut oil, and lay on the face in oblique bars, two or three inches broad. . . . Incisions are chiefly made on the upper arm and the belly, and supply the place of punctures. They cut the flesh with a bamboo, or a sharp shell, and apply a particular plant, which forms an elevated scar on the surface of the skin. . . . (II:276–77)

All of the above description we found to be very just and accurate; indeed, one could hardly give a more faithful picture of the body ornamentation of these people. I myself observed all the ornaments mentioned and all, excepting the greenstones, were offered to me in the course of barter. With that sort of ornament, though, the natives were *not* willing to part, even though I offered them knives, scissors, flints, piece of cloth, and other things. One must suppose that the stone is a rarity among them, obtained only with difficulty. After this green-coloured stone, the thing they prized most was tortoise-shell. It seemed to us that it was usual for the Tannese to paint their faces. On the first day of our visit, quite a number of them offered us as gifts prepared colouring substances which were in daily use, i.e., those mentioned by Mr. Forster; and they wanted me to paint my own face with them. I thanked them for their goodness but tried to explain that the paints were superfluous until such time as I reached my home, when I could use them and play the dandy among my own countrymen. As I said above, the natives proved exceedingly partial to our paints, and we duly daubed them. When they caught sight of themselves in a mirror, they went into frenzies of delight, laughing, leaping about, and shouting.

Mr. Forster records that the males of Tana conceal that part of the anatomy which modesty obliges us to conceal in almost every country of the world, and do so in the same manner as do the people of Malikolo [Malekula] Island, i.e., they make a covering from the leaves of a plant resembling ginger, conceal their genitals, pull the covering up, and tie it to a thread round the belly which is secured round the waist. The description offered by Mr. Forster on this subject is perfectly just:

Boys, as soon as they attain the age of six years, are already provided with these leaves, which seems to confirm what I have already observed in regard to the Mallicollese [Malekulans], viz., that they do not employ this covering from motives of decency. Indeed it had so much the contrary appearance, that in the person of every native of Tanna or Mallicollo [Malekula], we thought we saw a living representation of that terrible divinity, who protected the gardens and orchards of the ancients. . . . (II:277)

I have an observation to make here. I did not see six-year-old boys in such coverings, and even boys of eight and ten ran around naked. Boys aged fourteen or more wore the coverings like adults. Moreover, I have excellent proof that the garment in question was, indeed, being worn from motives of modesty, despite Mr. Forster's remarks. Returning from a hot-spring once with Messrs. Khlebnikov and Srednii, and walking along the shore, we came upon a group of natives, some of whom had just that moment emerged from the water and so had not managed to put anything on.[58] Catching sight of us, these men instantly covered their private parts with their hands and moved off to one side. Having turned away from us, they then put on the covering piece, and came back towards us. Mr. Rikord offered one of them a gift that would have been rich indeed to him, in exchange for such a cloth; but the native covered his face with both hands, when he understood the proposition, laughed, and ran off.

Mr. Forster thus describes the weapons of the Tannese:

The weapons which the men of Tanna constantly carry are bows and arrows, clubs, darts, and slings. Their young men are commonly slingers and archers, but those of a more advanced age make use of clubs or darts. The bows are made of the best club-wood (*casuarina*), very strong and elastic. . . . Their slings are made of coco-nut fibres, and worn round the arm or waist; they have a broad part for the reception of the stone, of which the people carry several with them in a leaf. The darts or spears are the third sort of missile weapons at Tanna. They are commonly made of a thin, knotty, and ill-shaped stick, not exceeding half an inch in diameter, but nine or ten feet long. At the thickest end they are shaped into a triangular point, six or eight inches long, and on each corner there is a row of eight or ten beards or hooks. These darts they throw with great accuracy, at a short distance, by the help of a piece of plaited cord. . . . (II:278–79)

This description of the Tannese weaponry is perfectly correct: we found the arms just as recorded by Mr. Forster. I acquired some by barter. Regarding the force with which the natives hurl these spears, Mr. Forster says that he saw one thrown ten or twelve yards into a picket only four inches in diameter, and with such might that the spear's jagged end went right through it. None of us witnessed anything like this. Forster further asserts that the arrows would fly eight or ten yards with much accuracy but since the natives fear to snap their bows, they seldom stretch them back to the maximum extent possible. Consequently, says Forster, the arrows have little effect at twenty-five or thirty yards and are not very dangerous. I found this observation to be just. Of the natives' skill with their weaponry, Forster adds this:

> The boys ran before us, and gave us repeated marks of their skill in warlike exercises. They slung a stone with great accuracy, and made use of a green reed, or stiff grass, in lieu of a dart. They had attained to such perfection in throwing the latter, that . . . it entered above an inch into the hardest wood. (II:317)

We ourselves never observed any such degree of perfection in spear-throwing, and I must further confess that the last part of Forster's assertion here strikes me as highly improbable.

> The clubs (continues Forster) are reserved for close engagement, and every grown man carries one of them, besides some of the missile weapons. They are of four or five different shapes. The most valuable are made of the *casuarina*, about four feet long, straight, cylindrical, highly polished, and knobbed at one end. One knob is round but the other, with which they strike, is cut into the figure of a star, with many prominent points. Another sort of club is about six feet long. . . . A third kind is about five feet long and has a flat piece, eight or ten inches long, projecting at right angles. A fourth is exactly like this, but has one of these flat blades on each side of the handle. Lastly, a fifth is simply a piece of coral rock, about eighteen inches long, and two in diameter, rudely shaped into a cylinder. (II:279–80)

Time has evidently produced no changes in the weaponry of these folk. In 1809, we found their arms exactly as here described and managed to obtain several specimens of each kind by barter. The most esteemed weapon is certainly the large club made of *casuarina* wood, for which the Tannese always demanded several objects they particularly liked, and which they sometimes altogether declined to trade away. They would barter away their other arms for mere bagatelles. Mr. Forster writes that no Tana Islander walks abroad without his weapons, and this is true. During our own stay, they were always armed, old men and even ten-year-old boys included. But it is very probable, after all, that the presence of such alarming guests as the English and ourselves had obliged them to be very cautious and not to let go of their weapons.

Of Tannese women, Forster says this:

> We saw but few women on this day, and those who appeared kept at a great distance from us; however they all seemed ill-favoured, and of smaller stature than the men. The young girls had only a string tied about the middle, with a little wisp of dry grasses fastened to it, before and behind; but those of a maturer age wore a short petticoat made of leaves. Their ears were hung full of tortoise-shell rings, and necklaces of shells fell on their bosom (II:280). But they were so nervous, that if we only fixed our eyes upon them, they instantly ran away, to the great entertainment of the men. We observed some of them which had a smile on their countenance, but in general they looked gloomy and melancholy. (II:286)

Our own observations fully confirmed all of this. At first, the women were certainly timorous and shy, but subsequently they did mingle in crowds, with men, and stopped fearing us. Many of the women seemed lively and gay, in fact, later; and boys were bold enough to laugh and joke with us. In another passage, Forster writes:

> All those who carried loads were women, whilst the men walked on unconcernedly without any incumbrance, except their arms. It should appear from this circumstance, that the people of Tanna are not yet arrived at that advanced state, which distinguishes the natives of the Society and Friendly Islands. All savage nations have the general character of using the other sex with great unkindness and indignity. . . . (II:292)

We observed the same phenomenon: even ten- or twelve-year-old boys would frequently threaten or shove women, and all heavy articles, such as firewood and domestic implements, were invariably carried by women while we were at Port Resolution. Elsewhere in his narrative, Forster says that the English saw more women on another day, most of whom were married. These carried their children on their backs in satchels made of matting.[59] We ourselves saw the Tana women with their offspring on their backs, as described. Whether or not they had acquired the offspring through cohabitation with a single man, we were unable to ascertain. When we asked by signs if a couple were man and wife, they would reply that they were living together, but they gave no indication how long this had been so. With regard to the natives' behaviour towards the English, Forster has this to say, among other things:

When we offered one of the natives some beads, or a nail, or a piece of ribbon, he would not step forward to take it. They desired us to place the proffered objects on the ground. They would then take it up in a leaf, not touching it with the bare hand. . . .(II:267)

The natives never acted in this way during our stay, taking everything offered straight in the hand, which was bare. This would seem to show that, on encountering Europeans for the first time, the Tannese had feared to be, so to speak, contaminated by them; and that, having learned from experience that the objects left them by the English caused no harm, the islanders did not fear us in 1809. Forster also writes:

One young man . . . told us his name was Fannokko, and enquired for our names, which he endeavoured to remember. . . . He sat down to dinner with us, and tasted of our salt pork, but did not eat more than a single morsel of it. He also tasted a little wine after dinner; but though he drank it without shewing any dislike, he did not choose to take a second glass. His manners at table were extremely becoming and decorous; and the only practice which did not appear quite cleanly in our eyes, was his making use of a stick, which he wore in his hair, instead of a fork, with which he occasionally scratched his head. (II:287–88)

It is the fact that the Tannese like to ask names and attempt to memorize them. They pronounced many of our own names quite well, and a few other Russian words besides. During our own sojourn there, the Tannese wanted to eat nothing of ours. Gunama's son Iata, when at table, ate only a tiny morsel of grilled fish. Whatever he might be offered, he declined with the phrase, *tabu rasissi*, that is, "full stomach!" Even the fish, I think, he consumed only because it had been caught in his presence and he knew what it would be like. Our Iata was similarly decorous at table, eating his fish with a fork, moreover, as he had no stick through his hair.

Forster writes that the islanders wanted the English to leave Tana as soon as possible, and that the visitors were obliged to show, by fingers, how many days the ships would remain. This information calmed the natives. The Tannese seemed differently disposed towards us, wishing us to stay longer. Elsewhere, Forster makes it plain that the natives had then feared the English, whose very voices alarmed them as they wandered through the bush. One or two natives were heard blowing on conch shells in the plantations through which the English were passing. Among many peoples and especially in the Pacific Ocean, observes Forster, that would be a signal of danger, made to warn other natives in distant villages. Navigator Khlebnikov and I walked far from the shoreline into the woods, and natives met us there; but they showed no alarm on this occasion. We saw some of the large shells used to give danger signals, in fact acquiring some by barter. Much though the Tannese had feared the English at first, one must note however, they subsequently grew more intimate with them than they ever did with us. And without in the least envying the good fortune of the English in this regard, I will just insert here, in Mr. Forster's own words, something about the civility shown to them:

> They became so familiar at last as to point out some girls to us, whom from an excess of hospitality not uncommon with uncivilized nations, they offered to their friends with gestures not in the least equivocal. (II:345)

Forster writes further that the Tannese did not greatly value iron implements, preferring trifles that could become ornaments, especially Tahitian material, New Zealand greenstone, and shells with mother-of-pearl or nacre. What they mostly prized, though, was tortoise-shell. We experienced the same thing: when we showed the natives the use of iron tools, they marvelled and wanted to have some; but they soon forgot about them, preferring shining trifles that could serve as ornaments. They would even suspend little knives, scissors, and needles to their ears, or hang them round the neck. Tortoise-shell remained their most prized article for as long as we stayed at Tana, and we ourselves turned tortoise-shell pieces into rings for them. Our locksmith was able to perform this work precisely to their taste.

Mr. Forster suspected these natives of cannibalism:

> In the afternoon we landed, we walked along the seashore towards the east point, where natives had prevented our going two days before. . . . As we were going to cross the point and proceed along the shore beyond it, fifteen or twenty natives crowded about us, and begged us with the greatest earnestness to return. We were not much inclined to comply with their demand, but they repeated their intreaties, and at last made signs that we should be killed and eaten. . . . They showed, by signs, how they killed a man, cut his limbs asunder, and separated the flesh from the bones. Lastly, they bit their own arms. . . . We had reason to suspect that some place of worship was concealed in the groves. (II:299–301)

Navigator Khlebnikov, Dr. Brandt, and I walked towards the point of which Forster speaks here, and walked along the shoreline moreover; but the natives met us kindly and were unarmed.[60] Gunama was chief in the nearby village, if one may so designate a few huts collected together. We came to the point itself, and would have gone on and round it. The natives dissuaded us, however, repeating the words, *abo, abo*, which they had used on previous occasions when something had displeased them. However, they neither threatened us nor made any pantomimes to indicate the killing and eating of people. Not wishing to argue the point with the natives for the sake of sheer curiosity, we did not discuss the matter long and left them in peace. We were allowed to approach a number of huts in this locality and to peer in. This provoked no signs of resistance or dissatisfaction. I may say that the huts were so low that a person could hardly sit up straight in them. They had a side entrance and were all empty. It is possible, even probable, that the Tannese had previously carried all their belongings off into the woods and hidden them there, as a precaution. As far as the singing mentioned by Forster is concerned, we listened attentively each morning but never heard any. If the natives had been singing during our stay as they had during the English ships' visit, we should most certainly have heard it, for *Diana* was anchored nearer to the point in question than the English vessels had been, and the weather was calm for the most part. At dawn, a perfect silence reigned in the valley and in the bay itself.

Mr. Forster observes of the Tannese language that many words demand a heavy aspiration and guttural pronunciation, but are filled with vowels and so easily uttered. Of the songs of Tana, he writes that they struck him as well-rounded and pleasanter than the songs of other Pacific Islands he had visited. The songs sung on Tana, he adds, also had a greater range of notes than did the airs of Tahiti or Tonga. The language spoken at Tana was certainly far from unpleasing to our ears, and some words had a pleasant sound. We ourselves could pronounce them pretty well. Forster's remarks on this subject are just. As for the actual songs, I myself only once heard a native singing, which he was doing of his own accord and without our asking. His voice was not unpleasant. The song sounded sad or, as our peasants might put it, mournful, and the words, *emio, emio* were reiterated many times.[61]

Of the Tannese chiefs or elders, Forster has the following to say:

> We found a very old decrepit man sitting on the bench, whom we had never seen before. Many among the crowd told us his name was Yogai, and that he was their *areekee*. . . . Near him sat another person, who might have passed for an old man, if he had not been in company with the former. The rest of the people told us he was the son of Yogai, and named Yatta. (II:337–38)

The natives pointed out to us a number of elders or chiefs of various districts of Tana, also naming the places of which they were chiefs; but they always called these individuals *teregi*, not *ariki*. Gunama, our acquaintance, was one of these *teregi*. His son was also named Iata or Yatta. Possibly the word signifies a rank and is not a proper name.

In view of its geographical location, Tana Island could well serve as a port of call for vessels bound for Kamchatka from the Cape of Good Hope, were it not for one failing, of which I shall speak. I may say in passing that this route is certainly the most convenient and the shortest one to Kamchatka. I have in mind not only actual distances but also favourable wind, helpful currents, and certain other factors. When *Diana* took that route out, we were not certain that it was free of dangers, but we ascertained for ourselves that the dangers are non-existent. Ships may proceed safely if they will follow *Diana*'s route as closely as possible. Sweet water, wood, and foodstuffs are all better obtained at Port Jackson, however, than anywhere else. Hostilities with the English did not permit me to do so, of course. Port Resolution in Tana is safe from the winds. One has merely to be careful in selecting an anchorage, since there is a coral bottom in many places and coral can easily cut through a hawser. The harbour is easily recognizable by the volcano standing nine or ten *versts* to its north.[62] The mutual locations are best appreciated from a map [see Map 5].

We came to Tana in the month of July, which is the equivalent of January in our Northern Hemisphere; so one might say we arrived in mid-winter. Because of Tana's position in the Pacific Ocean, however, its winter is very much hotter than our Russian summer. Indeed, the local summer differs from winter only in that it rains quite frequently. While we were there, Tana offered a fine abundance of coconuts but few yams, breadfruit, bananas, and little *Arum esculentum* [yam] and sugarcane. For some of these the season was already over, for others it had not yet begun. In season, the island must assuredly be full of such natural products: we saw extensive plantations of bananas and fig-trees by the grove,[63] all protected by wooden palings. Mr. [Johann Reinhold] Forster, I may mention here, records that he saw a two-foot high stone wall around a plantation. I saw no stone walls.

The only animals we saw on Tana were swine.[64] Dogs, numerous on other Pacific Islands, are absent here. Forster records that when the Tannese saw a dog on deck, they called it *buga*, that is, "hog," which is proof enough in itself that they had not seen such a creature before. (Captain Cook left a dog and a bitch on Tana, but we could not make out from the natives what happened to them.)[65] Forster adds that the English saw fowls around every hut, as well as well-fed swine, and bats in the woods, and a fleeing rat along a path. I saw only one single piglet and one chicken, which the natives had brought out to barter. I saw no rats or bats whatsoever. Nor did we spot any pigeons, though Forster saw several sorts,[66] as well as other bird species such as flycatchers [*mukholovki*], creepers, and parakeets.[67] In fact, I saw only six species of bird in all. Mr. Forster writes further that the waters around Tana are filled with fish of many kinds, and that the English used seines to catch mullet, Brasilian pike, dart-fish, Cavalgas, parrot fish, sting-rays, toothless rays, angel fish, sharks with sucking-fish attached, and dolphins, not to mention various kinds of mackerel.[68] We ourselves proved less fortunate. On the last day of our stay, the wind was very brisk from the ocean but then died away. I then went ashore, and natives assured me there were plenty of fish about. We drew a seine-net several times but we caught only two fish and a pair of small round crayfish. One of the fish was very large and unknown to us. The other was, I think, of the sort called Ten-pounder by the English in the West Indies.[69] Shells were certainly quite scarce along the shores of Tana and the natives in fact obtained shells from other islands, as they explained to us by signs. Forster made the same observation. The English had also caught many eels in the pond where Cook's ships watered. We did not try to catch eels and I must confess, to my shame, that I had not read that part of Forster's narrative in which he touches on the subject. We neglected to catch eels out of ignorance: with our nets, we could quite easily have done so. My negligence in this regard may serve as a warning to others. One must carefully read all accounts of a place to be visited.

In the main, Tana cannot be said to be such a good shelter for the mariner, at least in the months of July and August. There was simply not much produce available then, and the natives will not barter away their swine or fowls for anything. Forster complains of the fact. The English, he says, offered to exchange an iron axe for a hog, but the Tannese would not listen to the proposition and did not sell a single hog to the visitors. The Tannese likewise saw our axes in use every day, and again marvelled at the extreme utility of the implement. However, they offered us only weaponry and products of the country for axes, as they had before. They gave us neither swine nor even fowls. Mr. Forster thought that the Tannese would in time understand the advantages that could be drawn from iron tools. He put it thus:

> European goods were in no repute; but as we left a considerable number of nails and some hatchets among them, the durability of the metal will soon teach them to hold it in high esteem, and it is not improbable that the next ship which may happen to visit them, will find them fond of iron-ware and eager to barter provisions for it. (II:364)

How mistaken Forster has proved! *Diana* was the very next ship to call at Tana after Cook's, but we saw no trace of European articles, no nails, and no other pieces of iron. Only the horror evinced by the natives when they looked at our cannon proved their earlier acquaintance with Europeans. They wondered at our iron tools and they wanted to have some, but they would offer only trifles in exchange, certainly not their hogs or fowls, which are the most necessary articles for a mariner that the island can furnish.

The other inconvenience to which mariners coming to this particular island will be subjected is that arising from a shortage of fresh water. In a hot and unpleasant climate, they will be obliged to take water from muddy ponds. The water there is stagnant. And even during our own short stay, the pond we were using began to stink so badly that we all preferred the old water brought from the Cape of Good Hope to that, supposedly new, but actually stagnant water. But most important of all for the mariner is the fact that the intolerable summer heat of these parts may subject a crew to fatal illnesses resulting from noxious vapours, e.g., from the bogs and ponds with which the woods surrounding Port Resolution are full. It would seem that such vapours might well give persons unaccustomed to the climate and its vagaries a fever like the yellow fever, which annually kills so many Europeans in the West Indies.[70] I may also mention, in connection with local inconveniences, the nearby volcano itself. Our decks and masts were literally covered with ash, for hours on end; and so was the very coastline. On the final day of our stay, the wind blew from the north and directly from the volcano. The natives themselves put us on guard, warning us not to face the eruptions. They showed, by signs, that the fine dust could cause eye illness.[71]

The principal foods of the Tannese, it appears, are plants of various sorts. Some, such as breadfruit and yams, they bake. We several times acquired such foodstuffs ready-cooked and found them very tasty. The Tannese also make a kind of pie using bananas, Caribbean cabbage, coconuts, and other ingredients. Not knowing how they had been made, even so, I could not bring myself to swallow more than two or three mouthfuls without shuddering. My imagination kept suggesting to me that the same methods had been used in their preparation as in that of the strong drink prepared from *kava* roots. The natives of many Pacific Islands chew those roots well, then spit them out into a vessel which, filled with chewed roots, saliva, and a little water, is left standing some time. The intoxicating drink results from this revolting compound. Mr. Forster himself had liked these Tannese pies. He calls them puddings and, on obtaining one from a woman, praises the culinary skill of the Tannese females, supposing that they make them.[72] I cannot say for certain, for my part, if men or women concoct these pies.

Only the chiefs and people of advanced years, one may think, eat swine and fowls.[73] At least, this is suggested by way the Tannese prize such livestock. They all eat wild birds, though, as was indicated to us by signs. They showed us how birds are caught: there is a special sort of arrow for birds, as for fish. Mr. Forster writes that when the English caught fish in their seine nets, the natives would invariably ask for some. It was evident that this fishing method was familiar to them. I myself saw them with a net, albeit a very small one, and acquired it by barter. The Tannese also consume the flesh of shellfish, some of which they twice brought to me.[74]

The Tannese are certainly behind the natives of the Society, Friendly, Sandwich, and Marquesas Islands in the manufacture of their necessary artefacts. Their most essential article, I suppose, is their canoe, and that is very crudely fashioned. A long tree trunk, roughly hollowed out, forms the basis of the Tannese craft. One or two planks are then attached to the sides by means of rope woven from coconut fibre. The rope is simply pushed through knotholes in the timber.[75] Paddles too are very unskilfully made and have a clumsy look. Their sails, according to Forster, are nothing more than little triangular pieces of bast matting, with one point upward. We ourselves did not see a single craft with a sail while we were in Port Resolution. We did spot a couple, however, that were approaching the coast a little further north than the bay. We thought they had crossed from Emir [Aniwa] or Erromanga. The sails on those two craft looked exactly like those described by Forster.[76] The best work of the Tannese is undoubtedly their clubs which, even though made of extremely hard wood, are well finished, especially when one bears in mind that shells are used in lieu of other tools in their making. They also have a variety of musical instruments consisting of four, six, or eight pieces of reed, bound together in order of length. Forster records that he saw one of eight pipes.[77] We obtained a few by barter. The pipes are moved along the lips and, as the player blows, an awkward whistling is produced. Other artistic products of the Tannese are tortoise shell rings, bast bags,[78] and a few other coarsely worked objects of small size.

With reference to the number of natives on Tana Island, Mr. Forster writes that it could not have exceeded 20,000. I do not see how he could possibly have determined that: it is impossible to count a savage people living scattered in the woods and hills over a quite considerable area. And the natives themselves are incapable of counting in hundreds, so they cannot well have told Forster how many of them were there. He must have taken very uncertain, if not chimerical, data as the basis for his estimate of the island's total population. It is in the same manner that Forster determines the populations of all other islands inhabited by native peoples. It is, indeed a common enough habit of academics to speak by guesswork on matters that cannot be ascertained for sure.[79]

Of the natives of other islands lying adjacent to Tana, Forster says that one individual among the Tannese was certainly from Erromanga. The man seemed to be speaking another language, and the Tannese spoke it to him; he appeared not to understand theirs. The English saw no special features in his physiognomy that could have distinguished him from the Tannese. His clothing or, more precisely, his body ornamentation was just like theirs, and his hair too was short and curly. The man was of a cheerful and lively disposition and seemed more inclined to amusement, perhaps, than did the Tannese. Of Emir [Aniwa] Island, Forster says that he was unable to establish whether or not it is inhabited. We discovered that it is, and we saw natives of that island at Tana, as well as one man from Anattom [Aneityum]. Had the Tannese not told us this, however, we would not have been able to distinguish those persons by facial features or attire, so much were they all alike. Nor did we detect any difference of speech. The Tannese treated us very kindly, and they treated these other men kindly too. The latter seemed to have come to Tana on some particular business,[80] did not much concern themselves with us, and looked at us without evident surprise. As I mentioned earlier, the list of Tannese words that was compiled by the late Mr. Moore was lost, by some accident, at the time of our captivity in Japan.[81] I am therefore able to include here only the few words that I myself noted down in one of my notebooks:

| | |
|---|---|
| *meri* | sun |
| *vennoa* | earth |
| *tassi* | sea |
| *nima* | hut |
| *tewai* | water |
| *azor* | volcano, fire |
| *nessen* | rain |
| *adeta* | canoe, craft |
| *togos* | fire, burns |
| *kanari* | shell |
| *taski* | plantain |
| *ruk* | sugarcane |
| *emer* | breadfruit |
| *naik* | bananas |
| *nui* | coconuts |
| *kava* | kava roots |
| *nuk* | yam roots |
| *tanasago* | war hatchet |
| *tarif* | sling |
| *teregi* | chief |
| *arromanu* | chief |
| *arroman* | man |
| *bran* | woman |
| *buga* | hog |
| *mianu* | bird |
| *namu* | fish |

| | |
|---|---|
| *kaio* | long feather |
| *tegi naboi* | coconut shell bracelet |
| *abo, abo* | bad, no good |
| *oa, oa* | yes, good |
| *kavas* | woman's skirt |
| *nau* | musical (reed) instrument |
| *nep* | large club |
| *nufanga* | bow |
| *tanarop* | basket |
| *kazasiva* | cord used in casting spears, sling |
| *nitei* | arrow for shooting a man |
| *paga* | axe with shell blade |
| *kanauka* | fish hook |
| *kari na arroman* | to kill people |
| *kari menu* | to kill birds |
| *kari naumui* | to catch fish |
| *agurei* | sit down! |
| *araga* | come over here! |
| *aburi* | to sleep |
| *ani* | to eat |
| *nui* | to drink |
| *tabu rasissi* | stomach is full |
| *sina* | his name is (pointing at a person) |

*Evvau!* or *Ibau!* was the exclamation the Tannese invariably made when they had seen something new to them or something that made them marvel. They used the same exclamation when a thing pleased them or when they wanted it. Differing tones and gestures imparted different meanings to it. Wishing to convey wonderment, they would exclaim *ibau!*, snapping their fingers and leaning the body forward. If they disliked something, they would grimace as a European might on spotting something revolting.

I will conclude my observations on Tana here by cautioning all those mariners who may chance to visit it that, notwithstanding the natives' friendly behaviour towards us, the visitor should not blindly trust in their peaceable disposition. For it is extremely likely that only fear of our many firearms had the effect of restraining the Tannese from attacking us; and, enticed by the quantity of our articles that were dazzling to them, they would surely have attempted to kill us and possess themselves of the ship, I suspect, were it not for our armed strength. It is for this reason that the natives should be left believing that cannon and firearms can indeed kill at any range, just so long as a target is in view, and that such weapons can be used in a moment and without preparations. With these considerations in mind, I never allowed my people to reload in the natives' presence or, at least, insisted that they reload in such a way that the natives could not observe the process. In these circumstances, it is good to have double-barrelled guns.


As I have said, it was at 11 AM on 31 July that we took our departure from Emir [Aniwa] Island, the SW extremity of which then bore approximately six miles to our NE. We then steered north and held as close as practicable to the meridian of Petropavlovsk-in-Kamchatka, to save time. The map showed that route to be strewn with islands, most discovered by seventeenth-century voyagers who had lacked the means of precisely determining their geographical positions.

# 3

# THE ETHNOGRAPHIC RECORD

## HEALTH, DIET, AND HUSBANDRY

Golovnin found the people of Port Resolution to be strong and healthy in their prime. They were, in general, slender and agile. Some were stout and some were relatively tall, as Cook's people had found. Numbers of Tannese "volunteered, indeed, to drag our water casks along," and others on another day happily "plunged into the sea," fished out numerous casks that had been jettisoned from *Diana*'s launch, then helped the Russians "pull out from the surf" along the Enekahi (west) side of the bay, by pushing hard. They were a muscular and energetic people. In the Russians' view, the local women were "despised, even enslaved"; but they were adequately nourished and able to perform the heavy labour the men imposed upon them. Women always carried "heavy articles," such as "domestic implements" and firewood, and younger married women frequently had infants on their backs in plaited "satchels." The agility of Tannese youths was demonstrated by ascents of tall coconut palms, to which they held by hands alone, by weapons practice, and by work performed in heavy seas. The Russians saw at least the bow and arrow being used during their stay (as well as evidence of recently inflicted arrow wounds).

In general, Port Resolution natives seemed untroubled by disease or illness. Low huts examined by the Russians at Samoa village, on the east side of the bay, gave proper shelter from the rains when necessary.[1] And, unpleasant though the Russians found the swamps behind the large watering pond, the local populace was not in fact subject to fatal illnesses resulting from the region's "noxious vapours." Golovnin was no geologist and pardonably failed to appreciate that the volcanic ash, so heavily laid down around the bay and to its west, drained surface water, so the area was relatively safe against malaria (hence the heavy concentration of Tannese around that bay). Golovnin had travelled widely but had never seen a countryside like that of the Yenkahe system of volcanoes on the southeast side on Tana. On the bay's east side, Samoa village sat on dark pleistocene tufa; to the west were jumbled piles of basaltic lava interspersed with hot sulphuric springs and awesome gashes in the rock. In fact, the pyroclastic apron to the east and thick caldera outflows to the west were not a threat to human health; and Golovnin was wrong to fear yellow fever on the island.

On the other hand, the ashes that provided healthy drainage and in which enormous yams would grow did pose a threat to human sight. *Diana*'s decks and masts were thickly coated by the windblown, gritty ash from Mount Yasur. Still, the Russians saw no evidence of ocular myopathy or heavy eyelids such as Cook's people had noted; nor did Golovnin see any "swelling round the eyes," ascribed by Forster to the Tannese habit of sitting for extended periods of time in smoke. The local people's teeth, too, struck the Russians as particularly sound: they bit through coconuts as Europeans crack a walnut.

In Golovnin's opinion, the Tannese diet was entirely adequate and based on plants rather than meat. In season, there was evidently a sufficiency of yams and breadfruit, sugarcane, and numerous varieties of figs, bananas, and coconuts. The latter could be had year round. The Tannese baked their breadfruit and their yams in earthen ovens and had, indeed, some culinary skills. The Russians sampled "pies" of mixed ingredients, as Forster had described them.[2] Golovnin's short word list offers hints at the particular varieties or sorts of foodstuffs he was given in July, Tannese mid-winter.[3] Of the fifty words or phrases therein, no less than sixteen bear immediately on the Russians' major purpose at Port Resolution: getting food and water (see section on language below). "Pies" or "puddings" were a staple of the Tannese and the Erromangan diet till the first part of the present century, and "Carribbean cabbage," as the Russians term *tampoli* (a variety of edible hibiscus) was in use in 1900 as in 1809.[4] It was apparent to the Russians that the Tannese treated hogs as a variety of wealth. They were correct to think so, but they had too little time and information to appreciate the quantities of swine that were in fact on Tana. Nor did Golovnin (or Cook) know that the animals were destined for the ceremonial of the reciprocal exchanges feast, and not available for barter to themselves.[5] The Russians rightly saw the Tannese as authorities on bird-catching and fishing, taking maximum advantage of their knowledge, though with limited results. The Tannese knew precisely where to find the birds required for the pot, and had "a special sort of arrow" for the purpose. Fish, their largest source of protein, were both speared and netted. Golovnin obtained a net of modest size for the imperial collection in St. Petersburg.[6] Large quantities of shellfish, too, were eaten. Kava (*Piper methysticum*) was familiar to Chief Gunama and his people.

Coming as they did in late July, *Diana*'s company could not expect to find abundant breadfruit or a great supply of plantain on the island. What they purchased (see below, section on Tannese-Russian trade and intercourse) in the way of plants and tubers was a tolerably accurate reflection of the cycle of the Tannese diet. Figs and coconuts were plentiful in winter; there were yams in modest quantity; and plantain was not readily available. There would be meat at feasts after the Russians' own departure.

Golovnin says nothing of the "slash-and-burn" technique which, almost certainly, had been employed by local men a month or so before *Diana* had arrived. It is apparent, even so, that when he walked beyond the bay and saw "extensive plantations of bananas," he was not hampered by undergrowth or scrub. The local husbandry was following its pattern: there were "fig-trees by the grove," and all were carefully surrounded by a paling. Swine and fowls were being raised, but not for trade as understood by Golovnin.

Gunama's gifts were modest, by New Hebridean as by Russian standards. Golovnin received a 29-lb. piglet: swine were "rolling in their fat" ashore.[7] He was presented with a yam weighing a little more than 16 lbs. in a locality where certain yams grew ten feet long and weighed perhaps 200 lbs. in season.[8] Golovnin himself well understood that Chief Gunama had not wanted Russian ironware enough to give his choicest trading articles for it, but that the island "must assuredly be full" of useful plants (in proper season) and by no means poor in animal resources.

CLOTHING AND BODY ORNAMENT

Aneityumese and Tannese islanders did not go naked. Men and boys in puberty covered their genitalia with leaves, held in position by "a thread around the belly," as described by Forster, Cook, and other visitors of 1774. The Russians held that Tannese males wore the covering for modesty and were ashamed of total nakedness. They noted boys of eight and ten who did go absolutely naked and, in that respect, their information differed from Forster's. Girls likewise had string around the waist, from which a bunch of grasses fell in front, and more behind.[9] The older women wore a skirt or petticoat whose length reflected their maturity. The Russians also saw the Tannese sash or loincloth; capes, however, are conspicuously absent from the Golovnin account. When *Resolution* had been present, and the weather had been similarly blustery and rainy, older women had made use of shoulder "mats".[10]

Golovnin observed the Tannese hair style of plaited strings or queues, hundreds of which, tied up by fibre, stood on end across the scalp.[11] And as in 1774, the nine-inch hair stick was common.[12] Golovnin suggests that it was not the mark of chiefly status, as the British had implied, but rather was the ornament of men in general. The Russians spotted many reeds or sticks carefully "hung around with feathers, as embellishments." As Golovnin's own word list indicates, these sticks were *kaio* plumes, with white feathers from cocks or from other birds.[13] Beards continued to be plaited into rope, in 1809, and skin was cicatrized by cutting, not tattooed, in the traditional New Hebridean manner.

The Aneityumese and Tannese made extensive use of colouring or "painting" substances. Seen from *Diana*'s deck, the people of Anelgowhat were "glossy black" from application of a black lead preparation. Much was brought from Erromanga. Numerous Port Resolution natives made habitual and heavy use of "red, black, and crude white" substance on the face especially. They willingly tried other colours, which the Russians could supply. The Golovnin account provides no detail of patterns, colour mix, or emphasis.

As for the Tannese use of ornament, the Russians saw the full classical range in 1809, in use exactly as the British had recorded it. The Russians purchased nose sticks, earrings, and heavy necklaces. Earrings of tortoise shell were highly prized, and Russian objects such as little knives and scissors were adapted by the islanders as ear ornaments. The Tannese were impressed by shining articles, notably implements and mother-of-pearl shells. Their estimation of the latter was a function of the scarcity of shells. The Tana reefs are not conducive to conchology today, nor did they offer shells to natives in the past.[14] Like nephrite, shells were commonly imported by the Tannese.

Nephrite ornaments, in fact, were those the islanders were least willing to trade away to Golovnin. Not even shiny implements or foreign cloth tempted Gunama and his men to part with one small cylinder of "the New Zealand greenstone," which had actually come from North New Caledonia.[15] Such nephrite pendants held the pride of place among the ornaments in use around Port Resolution. Next came rings of tortoise shell. Apparently less value was attached to white *tridacna* shell, ovals of which were worn both at the chest (as at Anelgowhat when *Diana* passed) and from the ear. Coconut shell bracelets were observed worn on the upper arm, as when the British had arrived. In short, the local repertoire of body ornaments had undergone no notable change since *Resolution* had departed from the bay.

TANNESE-RUSSIAN TRADE AND INTERCOURSE

Golovnin insists upon the friendly, even joyous welcome he was given by the people of Port Resolution when, completely unannounced and unexpected, he descended on them from the sea. One is aware of the possibility that he is writing to an audience and so intent on placing Russian-native dealings in as generous a light as possible. There are, regrettably, no other printed narratives or manuscripts available with which the Golovnin account might be compared. It is clear, nonetheless, that *Diana* was hospitably received by representatives of that same group, then settled on the east side of Port Resolution (locally, Uea), who had welcomed Cook in 1774. That group was almost certainly the Karumene tribe with whom, not fully understanding the political significance of all his actions, Cook had first made contact on arrival. Then so happily embodied by the Forsters' Pawyangom (Cook's Paowang),[16] that tribe had—not unreasonably—viewed itself thereafter as allied with Cook's own people. By the same token, the natives on the west side of the bay, with whom the British had connections slightly later, had been conscious of their own lack of priority. Those Enekahi people had, indeed, regarded Cook and all his fellows as potential enemies. Gunama put out personally from a shore which Golovnin does not describe, but which was evidently on the bay's east side, to re-establish the connection with a company of white-faced foreigners whom he regarded, *a priori*, as not dangerous to him. He could not know that *Resolution* and *Diana* had been sent by different "tribes" of Europeans. From the very first, accordingly, he offered evidence of "friendly intentions and offered services."

If he himself had not seen Cook during his boyhood, he almost certainly had heard tell of Cook's extraordinary military powers and connections with the Karumene people. Golovnin was the unwitting beneficiary of Cook's relations earlier with the local populace. Of local tribal tensions of the period, the Karumene and their Warumene allies on the east side of the bay were intermittently at war with the more numerous Enekahi to the west and with the powerful Kasurumene people near Mount Yasur.[17] It was obvious to Cook, and to the Russians, that hostilities did occur: Golovnin saw arrow wounds and stores of weaponry. Whatever local conflict had existed in the days and weeks preceding *Diana*'s arrival, however, was suspended. Tannese warfare was in any case sporadic and hostilities were often broken off with few mortalities. Taken together with the obvious potential that the newcomers now offered would-be traders, and to chiefs especially, the dreadful memory of European gunfire had in itself affected the position of the Enekahi warriors—to what extent became apparent when the Russians landed, not near Samoa village, but in Enekahi territory where the Cook watering pond was situated. And Gunama and his people were not only left in peace by recent rivals to their west; the Enekahi also provided friendly competition for the Russians' trading goods, once it was plain that Golovnin was not an enemy. Because the Russians were continually armed with foreign weaponry, whose strength the Enekahi understood, it proved considerably easier for Golovnin to roam towards the slopes of Mount Yasur than it had been for Cook's associates. There is indeed no indication that the Russians understood how ill-disposed the Enekahi might have been towards them, since their native intermediary Chief Gunama had his residence and base east of the bay (Samoa village). Nor, excusably, could Golovnin have known that his arrival from the south would cause a rapid northward influx of potential chiefly traders. It is plain from his account that, like *Resolution*'s coming, *Diana*'s very presence drew some influential "foreigners"—Kwamera-speaking chiefs or men of rank—from further south.[18] Thus, Port Resolution's population (and Gunama's neighbours) gained a different and temporary aspect as a consequence of Golovnin's own presence. All, however, kept the peace, as was expedient.

The Russians straightaway stated the objects of their visit: food and water. By doing so, they calmed Tannese fears. As was reasonable in the circumstance, many islanders nevertheless removed their personal belongings from their huts, lest Russians take them to their ship. But, all in all, relations with the fabulously wealthy foreigners were cordial. The Tannese brought down foodstuffs and were handsomely rewarded. They traded honestly, albeit not for swine as Golovnin had hoped, and showed no menace to their guests. During the Russians' five-day stay, the following supplies were stowed aboard:

| Day | Plaintain | Coconuts | Yams | Sugarcane | Figs |
|-------|-----------|----------|----------|-----------|------|
| 1 | 2 | 114 | 21 lbs. | 0 | 0 |
| 2 | 4 | 250 | 175 lbs. | 66' | 0 |
| 3 | 1 | 289 | 16 lbs. | 36' | 50 |
| 4 | 3 | 435 | 10 lbs. | 40' | 130 |
| Total | 10 bunches | 1088 | 222 lbs. | 142' | 180 |

In exchange for these foodstuffs and for ample drinking water, Golovnin offered a range of Russian manufactured goods, including "unbleached linen towels," cloth and clothing, scissors, knives, flints, beads, brass buttons, sailmaker's needles, mirrors, and assorted paints. Clothing and shining trinkets were preferred by Chief Gunama to the Russians' ironware. As the visitors were disappointed by the lack of hogs for barter, so the Tannese were deceived in hopes of getting *Diana*'s launch or even cattle. Golovnin perceived correctly that supplies of basic foodstuffs were declining by the third day of his stay. Figs and coconuts alone seemed likely to continue to be plentiful. He therefore readied for departure on 30 July. Besides the foodstuffs mentioned, *Diana* left with many local artefacts, including clubs and javelins, reed pipes and conch shells, nose sticks, *kaio* plumes, colouring pigments, and body ornaments. Some Russian goods were earned by local men, such as for payment for their labour in the watering and as assistants on a bird shoot. Other manufactured articles were offered to conspicuously "affable," obliging natives. Most, however, went to Chief Gunama.

Notwithstanding their extreme respect for Russian firepower and their friendliness towards the Russians, Chief Gunama and his people were unwilling that their visitors should walk to certain places on the bay's east side (modern Cape Cook). The British had been similarly stopped. Ile Pou, at the cape's northern extremity, was certainly off limits to the Russians. So too was a sacred area nearer Samoa village, termed a "cemetery" by Golovnin.[19] The Russians saw no reason to insist on seeing either place, so peace was preserved.

A virtue of the Golovnin account is that it shows what influence Cook's visit to the area had had, or, more precisely, how that influence survived after thirty-five years. The people settled round Port Resolution had remembered, first, the terrible effect of British cannon; second, large edible quadrupeds; and third, the fact that Cook had traded heavily. No objects left by Cook were to be seen in 1809, nor were the Tannese much impressed by Russian iron. Golovnin had been expecting evidence of greater British influence in the immediate vicinity.[20]

WAR AND TRANSPORT

Both at Anelgowhat and at Port Resolution, Golovnin was met by well-armed warriors, whose frequent inter-tribal conflicts he himself was very likely interrupting. Northwest of Port Resolution, Tannese boys and men were armed with "long boar-spears and clubs." And when the Russians made their first landing inside the bay, others were similarly armed or carried bows and arrows. Many warriors declined to place their weapons on the ground or in the woods, as they were asked. Next day, again, "all carried some kind of weapon with them." None, however, made overt threats or seemed menacing to Golovnin, whose men were also armed continuously and alert. Nor, by the third day of his visit, were those warriors reluctant to exchange even the polished hardwood clubs that they particularly valued for the Russians' goods. In this respect, they showed less nervousness than had their local predecessors at the time of Cook's arrival.

Golovnin saw every kind of Tannese weapon that the British had described: long spear or javelin, reed dart, coconut fibre sling with stones, clubs large and small, and Hebridean bow and arrow. Spears were released, with dreadful force, with the assistance of a becket that was looped around the forefinger. They were often nine or ten feet long, tipped with a jagged point. Like Forster, Golovnin saw arrows shot and recognized their limited effect beyond a range of thirty yards. Boys demonstrated archery and spear-throwing for the Russians' benefit. They seemed to fear that their bows would snap if stretched too taut. Their bow and arrow were essentially a Melanesian weapon: bows were termed *nufanga* (modern *nefane*), arrows aimed at men—*nitei*. In addition, Golovnin observed the special Tannese throwing stone, the *kawas*, smooth and shaped like a scythe stone. It too features in his word list.[21]

With regard to club varieties, the Russian evidence adds little to the evidence provided by the Forsters. Five were still in use in 1809, including one stout throwing club based on the pointed Erromangan *telughomti* and a coral cylinder. To judge by Golovnin's suggestive word list, one large club was called a *nep* while *tanasago* was a "war-hatchet," that is, George Forster's third club type, an adze-like weapon with "a flat piece, eight or ten inches long, projecting at right angles, which . . . is formed with a very sharp edge."[22] It is significant that of the fifty words in Golovnin's vocabulary, seven have to do with war and form the largest single word group after words describing foodstuffs and the elements. The Tannese way of life had local warfare as its backdrop.

Local warfare was essentially a land-based undertaking. War canoes were not in evidence, and Golovnin was unimpressed by Tannese shipbuilding and seamanship. Most dugouts in Port Resolution were extremely crudely fashioned by the local shell-blade adze, or *paga*, which the Russians saw in use, and carried one or two men only. Such canoes, of hollowed breadfruit trunks, were fitted with an outrigger and simple wash strake ("planks are then attached . . . by means of rope woven from coconut"). Paddles were comparably crude.[23]

The Russian evidence suggests that some or all of the canoes that Cook had seen at Tana, which had carried twenty men with ease, had come from nearby Aniwa or Futuna. Certainly the craft that Golovnin saw looked ill-suited for long inter-island crossings and were obviously used for in-shore fishing. None had sails. On the other hand, the Russians did see sailing craft approaching Sulphur Bay or its vicinity, under a NE wind, and thought it probable that they were coming from Aniwa to the east. Tannese canoes lacked any mast, "bast matting" sails being guyed by fibre cordage to the sides, with the result that they could sail only before the wind. Aniwan or Futunan (Polynesian) craft could make the passage west to Tana and return, even in winter, when both Cook and Golovnin had chanced to come.

LANGUAGE

The people of Port Resolution spoke, and speak, a language called Kwamera. It is one of six surviving languages on Tana. In the early 1800s, there were more.[24] Approximately one Tannese in ten was a Kwamera speaker.[25] When assessed in 1971 by the Australian linguist, Darrell Tryon, the Kwamera tongue was spoken by 1,100 people in an area from Port Resolution down to the south (Kwamera) coastline, and around the island's west side to Yankwaneneai village. There were two main dialects. That is essentially true today.

Kwamera-English dictionaries do not exist, nor have other Tannese languages been studied in a comprehensive manner. Consequently, pioneering works like those of R.H. Codrington (1885), A. Hagen (1889), and S.H. Ray (1893) are still consulted by the student of New Hebridean languages. It follows that Golovnin's Tannese material, taken together with the word list collected on Cook's second voyage (1774), is significant for Melanesian language studies as a whole, for Tannese studies in the Austronesian context, and above all for the theorist of Polynesian back migration.[26]

> Approximately four to five thousand years ago, the major groups of islands in Melanesia were settled by Austronesian (Oceanic) speakers. As the speakers of this Oceanic language dispersed, their language began differentiating, thus giving rise to the tremendous linguistic diversity found in the area today. . . . Around 1000 BC, a Central Pacific language group began breaking up into the Fijian and Polynesian groups which are ancestral to the languages spoken today. To this general scheme must be added the westward migration of Polynesian speakers, in the last two thousand years or less, back into Melanesia and settling the outliers such as Anuta, Tikopia, the Duff Islands, etc. . . . [27]

As observed, Futuna and Aniwa were inhabited, when Cook arrived, by islanders of Polynesian ancestry. Those people, who were seafarers (and whose descendants' language has been studied very recently by J.W. Dougherty), had sailed west to Tana periodically for several centuries by 1800.[28] Tana's northeast point lay only thirteen miles southwest of Aniwa and was plainly visible. The British had believed that both canoes found in Port Resolution and a reddish-yellow hair tint, to be observed occasionally on Tannese men, indicated that Aniwans or Futunans had been present as a genetic, cultural, and economic influence on Tana's eastern shores for generations. Russian evidence lends weight to that hypothesis. Not only did the Russians see Aniwan sailing craft coming to Tana; they also encountered several Aniwans whom Gunama had hospitably received, and left a record of such Polynesians' cumulative influence on the Kwamera language spoken by their hosts.

Although a Melanesian language, Kwamera had absorbed numerous

Polynesian words. Some of these words figured in Golovnin's short word list, for example, *tevai* [*te wai*], water, naik [*navaiki*], a banana variety, *niu* coconut, *mianu* [*manu*] bird, and (perhaps) *teregi* [*te ariki*], chief. Others were cognate with the Sie language forms of Erromanga, to the north, for instance, *emer* [Sie: *nemar*], breadfruit variety, and *tassi* [*tas*], the ocean. Both as a control for J.R. Forster's Tannese word list and particularly as a source of terms not present in the Forster list of 1778, the Russian word list merits notice.

*Part Two*

THE RUSSIANS AND FIJI

# 4

# PREPARATIONS FOR THE BELLINGSHAUSEN VISIT, 1820

BACKGROUND: I.F. KRUZENSHTERN AND EARLY EUROPEAN CONTACTS WITH
THE FIJI ISLANDS

Kruzenshtern was the essential human link between the British expeditionary experience of Oceania and Russian naval practice in the early nineteeth
century. It was, significantly, as a scholar and hydrographer, not as a seaman
who had personally visited Fiji, that he performed that service. As he
focused the attention of his countrymen on the Marquesan and Hawaiian
archipelagoes in Polynesia, by describing *Nadezhda*'s and *Neva*'s visits to
Nukuhiva and the Kona coast in 1804, so, slightly earlier, did he direct
attention to the Fiji Archipelago. Busy though he was as the commander of a
major expedition with commercial, scientific, and political objectives, Kruzenshtern found time to study parts of Oceania that were, in 1804–6, of
purely academic interest to Russia. One such part was eastern Melanesia.
He was actually studying the early Dutch and British contacts with Fijians
*while at sea* aboard *Nadezhda* (1804–5). The results were offered in a journal
published at St. Petersburg's Academy of Sciences, within the context of a
hydrographic survey of the voyages of *Heemskercq* and *Zeehaen* (1642–43),
Able Janszoon Tasman's and Frans Jacobszoon Visscher's first great voyage
of discovery.[1]

Even in his early service years, the young Lieutenant Kruzenshtern had
shown particular awareness of the importance of hydrography. While serving with the British as a Russian Volunteer from 1793 to 1797 and while
sailing to and living in Bengal and China from 1798 to 1799, he had recognized that—to the obvious misfortune of innumerable sailors—even recent
charts of eastern waters and especially of Oceania were riddled with alarm-

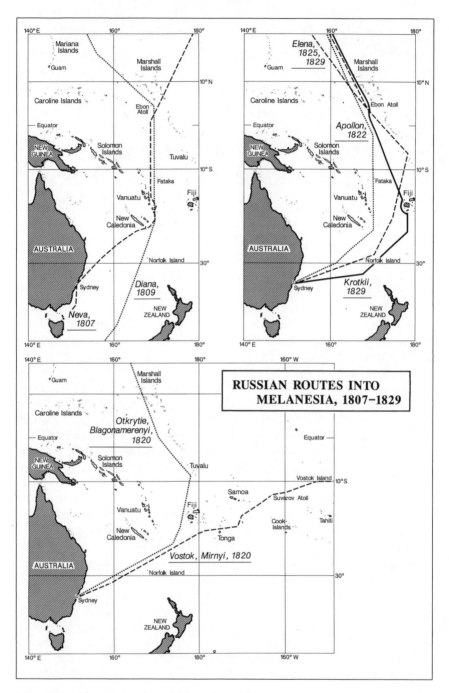

Map 6  Russian routes into Melanesia, 1807–29

ing errors. His attention was repeatedly directed to the problem while he
served, with much distinction, in the British frigate *Thetis* (Captain Alexander Cochrane) in a Halifax-based squadron then (1794–96) commanded
by George Murray.[2] Cochrane's second lieutenant was George Tobin
(1768–1838), who had sailed with Captain William Bligh (1791–93) to the
West Indies and Tahiti.[3] Kruzenshtern encouraged Tobin, barely eighteen
months his senior, to reminisce about his passages to India and Oceania,
about the celebrated Bligh, and more especially about the latter's skill as a
dead-reckoner. Bligh had hired Tobin as Lieutenant in *Providence* (1791)
while still composing his account of an extraordinary passage in *Bounty*'s
launch (1788), across the Fiji Islands and to Dutch Timor.[4] The famous
mutiny was fresh in Bligh's and Tobin's memories alike when, eighteen
months after the publication of Bligh's *Voyage to the South Sea* (1792),
Tobin, Kruzenshtern, and others in *Thetis*'s wardroom were discussing it.
The book was known to everyone. It was impossible to read it, to learn about
entire groups of hitherto unknown Fijian Islands (modern Ngau and Nairai,
Viti Levu, Koro, the Yasawa Islands, Mota, Vatganai), and not appreciate
the shortcomings of Aaron Arrowsmith's Pacific charts.[5]

Kruzenshtern continued to collect materials on the discovery and true
positions of the Fiji Islands, and of other archipelagoes in the Pacific, not
deliberately to be sure or as a matter of priority but incrementally, before his
own expedition. By 1801 he was familiar with Captain Wilson's *Missionary
Voyage to the Southern Pacific Ocean* (London 1799) and with *Duff*'s contacts in the Exploring Isles (modern Vanua Mbavalu) of September 1797.[6]
He had become acquainted, even earlier, with Captain Henry Barber's
bloody contact with inhabitants of the Yasawa group in April 1794 as he was
bringing the trader *Arthur* up from Sydney, New South Wales.[7] Barber's
tracks and Kruzenshtern's had intersected more than once even by 1800,
when the Russian took a passage from Canton to London in, by curious
coincidence, HMS *Bombay Castle*.[8] (Tobin had seen service in her also.)
*Arthur* was Madras-based. In August 1797, Kruzenshtern met shipmasters
and government officials there who were certainly familiar with Barber and
the trading operations which, for three years by then, had brought his vessel
to the Russian northwest coast of North America.[9] Again, Barber and Kruzenshtern were in Canton within a few months of each other.[10] Which report
of *Arthur*'s touching at the Fiji Islands Kruzenshtern had read is far from
clear: the original report, published in India, had been reprinted several
times by 1800 in Calcutta, New England, and Europe.[11] What is pertinent is
that the facts of *Arthur*'s contracts in Fiji, like those of *Duff*, and *Bounty*'s
launch, and Tasman's ships, were all at Kruzenshtern's disposal when, in
1804, he came to Oceania himself.

Following are extracts from his study of the Dutch discoveries in Oceania,
printed in 1806, that focus on Fiji:

On 6 February 1643, in Latitude 17°19'S, Longitude 201°35'W [sic], eighteen or twenty islets were sighted, all surrounded by rocks and reefs. Tasman called the islets Prince Willem's Islands, and the reefs—Heemskercq Reefs. The islands have been examined very seldom, even to the present time. Many ships have passed through that dangerous archipelago, however, without pausing. These include the English vessel *Arthur*, from which in 1794 Captain Barber saw six similar clusters, actually stopping at the largest. (The natives, who are assuredly cannibals according to their neighbours, the Friendly Islanders, fell on Barber and forced him to leave.) Captain Wilson of the missionary ship *Duff* likewise entangled himself in such islands, in 1797, as far as Latitude 16°30'S, Long. 180°40'E, striking on a coral reef. The most southerly of those islands would appear to have been those which Captain Bligh had discovered in 1789, named after himself, and asserted to lie in 19°15'S, 182°E. In 1792 also, Bligh's course took him through those isles.

It is indeed a great pity that Captain Bligh's two voyages were not both published: for Bligh has proved one of Cook's associates who has done great honour to him, as a teacher. Rare though they are, those qualities that distinguish the eminent seaman, and which Cook possessed, would appear to be possessed also by Bligh. Captain Tobin, that most skilful and knowledgable officer in the English naval service, who made a voyage with Bligh as second lieutenant and with whom I myself served for several years on end, would always speak to me most admiringly about his former commander. Tobin did not conceal the fact that Bligh had indeed been strict. . . . On his second voyage, Bligh held his course right through the highly dangerous Fijian Archipelago, whose savage natives attacked him. To the NE of the Cyclades, he discovered that cluster of isles to which he gave the name, Sir Joseph Banks' Islands. Sailing along the southern coast of Louisiada, he later passed the Endeavour Straight, which is a most risky one, through which nobody had passed since Cook himself in 1789 [sic]. Captain Maitland, of the American ship *Ann and Hope*, came upon many more of these islands in December 1799, calling them, in entirety, the Land of Liberty. Friendly Islanders [Tongans] call the natives of these islands, Fidies [sic]. I do not think that all the aforementioned island groups can very well, as several maps now suggest, be joined together in a single group. . . .[12]

Using the excellent small library and chart collection placed aboard *Nadezhda*, in the weeks before she left the Baltic (1803), Kruzenshtern retraced Tasman's and Visscher's movements from New Zealand to the southern Tongan outlyers and so to what are now the Ringgold Islands and Nanuku Reef.[13] He was perfectly correct to state that, notwithstanding an increased volume of European shipping in that area, the many reefs and islets south of (modern) Nggele Levu on the northeast fringe of Fiji were essentially uncharted in the 1800s. Kruzenshtern's allusion to the islets "named after himself" by Bligh is, in reality, to Yangasa Levu and the cluster to its west. The "Cyclades" northwest, not northeast, of which Bligh saw the Banks Islands, were Bougainville's Northern New Hebrides: his name for them, retained here by Kruzenshtern, was shortly to be pushed into oblivion by Cook's.[14] "Louisiada" is the archipelago extending SSE from Papua New Guinea.

Kruzenshtern's overview of European and American discoveries in Fiji was a first step in the process of acquainting Russian officers and others with that archipelago. It was by no means error-free. *Duff* did not, in fact, touch on a reef described by Bligh, nor was Endeavour Strait first passed by Cook ten years after his own demise, as contended in the article! Such slips do not detract from the importance of the paper as a sober and well-balanced introduction to the subject, and indeed to the "savage" and "dangerous" Fijians, for Russian readers. As for Kruzenshtern himself, he saw the paper as a sketch to be employed, with other sketches, in draughting a thoroughly reliable and comprehensive study of the physical conditions and geography of Oceania. He was to labour on that magnum opus, which appeared as *An Atlas of the South Sea* (1823–26) with long appendices, for twenty years.[15]

THE EXPEDITION: PREPARATIONS AND ARRIVAL

*Nadezhda* and *Neva* had been entrusted with a range of political, commercial, scientific, and maritime tasks. Thereafter, Russian vessels sailed to the North Pacific Ocean with less numerous and better-focused aims. As *Suvórov* (Lieutenant Mikhail P. Lázarev) went on an economic-cum-strategic mission to the ever-hungry outposts of the North Pacific rim (1813–16),[16] *Riurik* (Lieutenant Otto von Kotzebue 1787–1846) made for Oceania and Arctic latitudes with scientific and strategic aims.[17] Now, in the post-Napoleonic years of peace, the ends of empire and science coincided, at least where European navies were concerned; and this was recognized as fully by Sir John Barrow, now Secretary to the Admiralty Board in London, as by Kruzenshtern's superiors at Kronstadt.[18]

No one, argued Barrow, could contend that the discovery of Kotzebue Sound in 1816, on the far northwestern edge of North America, had no strategic or political significance.[19] Had Kotzebue forced *Riurik* into the navigable northern passage that his influential patron, Count N.P. Rumiántsev, still believed existed, then whatever purely scientific objects the lieutenant might have had would have been quite beside the point. The whole complexion of the China trade would have been altered overnight. In any case, the search was on again for that desired and commercially most crucial passage to the Orient from Europe through the ice, with all its promises of glory and of gain.[20] It was clear that the Russians were not idling. "It would," wrote Barrow testily, "be mortifying if a naval power of but yesterday were to complete a discovery in the nineteenth century which was so happily commenced by Englishmen, in the sixteenth."[21] The House of Commons sympathized. A large reward was duly offered for the finding of a navigable seaway. The heroic age of English Arctic exploration had begun— the age of Scoresby, Franklin, Parry, and the Rosses. But as Kotzebue's Arctic probe had spurred the British to fresh efforts in the North, giving employment to distinguished naval officers who otherwise might well have been ashore and unemployed, so did these efforts in their turn provoke an even grander Russian undertaking.[22]

The time had come, it was agreed in June 1818, for the Russians also to win laurels and political advantage from a voyage of discovery in Cook's tradition. It was hardly thinkable not to persist where Kotzebue and his men had done so well: Russia had economic and strategic interests in chilly northern waters off Chukotka, to the north of Bering Strait, and now in Kotzebue Sound. Yet failure there could not be balanced, as for England, by success in Asia, Africa, and Australia. The Russian Navy lacked the ships, though not the officers or seamen, to attempt repeated distant seaborne expeditions.[23] Such was the essential argument that led to adoption of the notion of a two-poles expedition (mid-November 1818).[24] While one small squadron sought a navigable passage in the North linking Pacific and Atlantic tidal waters, another squadron would investigate the farthest South where, since Cook's return in 1775, no work whatever had been done. In Antarctica, if anywhere, Russians might match the work of Cook. Thus did the Bellingshausen-Lazarev Antarctic expedition (1819–21) both arise from and itself develop political, professional, and scientific tendencies that had been evident earlier in Russian naval ventures in the North Pacific area. Indeed, the Russian double polar expedition—*Vostok* and *Mirnyi* to the South, *Otkrytie* and *Blagonamerennyi* through Bering Strait and northward—was, in essence, an imperial response to mounting international pressures to which Englishmen and Russians had contributed alike. And as the mounting double expedition bore the stamp of Cook's activities of forty years before (and of his followers, from Clerke to Kotzebue, in the Arctic), so too did its very form. Part of the legacy that Cook and Kruzenshtern had jointly left the Russian fleet by 1806, it has been emphasized most justly, bore directly on the science of ethnology.[25] That legacy proved highly valuable when, in August 1820, and towards the end of an extensive winter cruise through Polynesia (Tuamotu Archipelago, Tahiti, Tonga), *Vostok* (Captain-Lieutenant Faddei F. Bellingshausen) and *Mirnyi* (Captain-Lieutenant Mikhail P. Lazarev) traversed the Lau Group of Fiji, sighting Ono and its

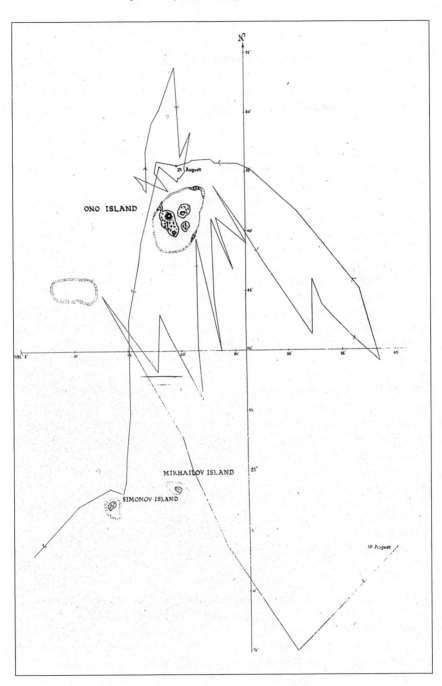

Map 7 Bellingshausen's track around Ono-i-Lau, 19–21 August 1820

outlyers, en route to Sydney, New South Wales.[26] Ethnographically, the Russian pause at Ono on 20 August 1820 was by far the most important one by Europeans in the nineteenth century.

From the beginning, Kruzenshtern himself had shown lively interest in the proposed Antarctic enterprise. He had composed long memoranda on the subject, having first been offered command of it himself.[27] (He had declined, citing ill health.) He had advised the naval minister, de Traversay, on personnel, logistics, and routes. He found himself in a position to renew Cook's scientific legacy in Russian settings, and did so to the best of his ability, commending Captain V.M. Golovnin, late of *Diana*, as commander of the "Southern Division" being formed.[28] It would have been a strange coincidence had Golovnin, the only Russian officer (apart from ex-subordinates) to have encountered Melanesians (Tana Island, 1809), been given *Vostok*. But he was unavailable for duty in Antarctica, being away with *Kamchatka* on the Russian northwest coast. Under the circumstances, Kruzenshtern then spoke for Bellingshausen, who had sailed in *Nadezhda* as a midshipman in 1803–6 and whose career he had followed with approval. "Our Navy," he suggested, "is of course rich in both competent and enterprising officers. Of all those known to me, though, only Golovnin might be compared with Bellingshausen."[29] Traversay at first demurred. If an old *Nadezhda* hand were given the command, there were more senior former lieutenants to consider, such as Makar Ivanovich Ratmanov. But like Kruzenshtern, Ratmanov pleaded sickness now, quickly declining the position which in March 1819 went to Bellingshausen by default. It was a happy accident for South Pacific and particularly Lauan and Tahitian studies.

Faddei Faddeevich (by baptism, Fabian Gottlieb) Bellinsgauzen or von Bellingshausen (1778–1852) came of a distinguished Baltic family long settled on the Isle of Oesel (Saaremaa) off Esthland or the Russian Baltic province of Estonia.[30] Like many of their rank and situation, Bellingshausens had since 1711 served the Russian Crown but had become impoverished. Specific service prospects were inherent in the very time and place of Captain Bellingshausen's birth.[31] For Baltic Germans whose estates lay in Estonia, the naval base of Reval (modern Tallin) was a magnet.[32] As a consequence of those political advantages which they in any case enjoyed as representatives of an élite long and well favoured in St. Petersburg, and of their attitude towards the service life, a high proportion of such officers— including Kotzebue, Bellingshausen, Krusenstern, Wrangel, and Lütke— reached high rank and wielded great and lasting influence within the Navy.

Bellingshausen was enrolled in 1788 in the imperial *morskoi kadetskii korpus* (Naval Corps) at the age of ten, and as a cadet sailed to England. As a midshipman, he served on frigates in the Baltic Sea (1797–1803). Such was his competence in nautical astronomy and in hydrography that in 1803 he was recommended by Rear-Admiral Petr I. Khanykov, his commanding officer, to Kruzenshtern and so participated in the Russian expedition round the world led by him. As a midshipman and, later, junior lieutenant in *Nadezhda*, Bellingshausen has no say in how the Russians would relate to Polynesians when, on 7 May 1804, they entered Taio-hae Bay on Nukuhiva in the Washington-Marquesas Islands.[33] He was conscious, even so, of the significance of that first Russian landing on a South Pacific Island and, moreover, of the soundness of his captain's attitude towards it.[34] First, the ship must be supplied with fresh foodstuffs and drinking water; later, bartering for native artefacts might be encouraged.[35] Day by day, through peaceful trade, paddles and staffs, adzes and nets, fans, necklaces, and other articles were gathered, sketched, described, and stowed as Bellingshausen watched.[36] And Kruzenshtern successfully avoided those misfortunes the inherent possibility of which had troubled him upon arrival in the islands: theft and sexual familiarity leading to pointless complications and fatal retribution by the gun. In 1820, Bellingshausen followed Kruzenshtern in his alert and somewhat prudish, but unquestionably sensible, approach to all these matters.[37]

Kruzenshtern thus had served as a human link, for youthful officers like Bellingshausen and the brothers Otto and Moritz Kotzebue, who were also in his ship, between the present and the world that Cook had known. Lieutenant Bellingshausen, as it happened, was not sent off to England as a Volunteer with the British Navy, like his future second-in-command in Oceania, Lieutenant Mikhail Petrovich Lazarev. Lazarev spent from 1804 to 1808 in British ships and territories, travelling extensively and planning Russia's role in the Pacific and the East.[38] It was experience that served him well: by June 1813 he had command of *Suvorov* and was bound for Sitka. It was the first of three Pacific voyages (1813–16, 1819–21, 1822–25) during the course of which he played his part in strengthening an Anglo-Russian maritime entente that even Kotzebue's unforeseen successes in the Arctic could not ruin.[39]

Long before he took command of *Vostok* and *Mirnyi* in 1819, Bellingshausen had enjoyed a reputation for reliability at sea that linked him with Pacific exploration and with Cook. First in the Baltic with the frigate *Mel'poména* in 1809–10, then with *Flora* and *Minerva* on the Black Sea station where for months he was engaged on taxing coastal survey work,[40] he had evinced great coolness under pressure. When appointed to the Southern expedition, "he was forty years of age and in the flower of ability and strength."[41] "It would," writes Hunter Christie, "be invidious to compare Cook and Bellingshausen. Cook has well been called incomparable; but no pioneer ever found a worthier disciple and successor to carry on the work which he began."[42]

Reaching Kronstadt from the south of Russia (May 1819), to supervise the readying and lading of his vessels, Bellingshausen made it plain that he intended to gather "native curiosities" in Oceania. Considerable quantities of broken iron hoop, buttons and gimlets, knives and scissors, beads and mirrors, and a fair supply of cotton bales, ticking, and chintz and calico material were stowed for large-scale barter later with Pacific islanders.[43] He was more fortunately placed that Cook had been in that respect: *Vostok* and *Mirnyi* were both larger craft than Cook had had, *Vostok* being a vessel of 900 tons, *Mirnyi*—a slow-sailing but roomy transport of some 530 tons unladen. "*Endeavour* was a relatively small vessel whose cargo-space considerably limited the amount of bulky ethnographica that could be taken back. Again, the primary task of Banks and Solander was natural-historical study."[44]

Matters augured well already, from the standpoint of ethnography. In 1803–6 Bellingshausen had encountered native peoples in the South Pacific basin and Kamchatka and had studied them attentively. He now had orders from the Admiralty to "pass over nothing new, useful, or curious" and to pursue investigations "in the broad sense, with regard to any matter that may widen any area of human knowledge."[45] All his officers were to assist the German naturalists named to *Vostok*, Karl-Heinrich Mertens (1796–1853) and Gustav Kunze (1793–1851), botanists and doctors both, "whenever feasible."[46] His expedition had no mercantile object, no specifically commercial end, to draw his energies or time away from science and discovery. Nor were his officers and gentlemen of science lacking interest in fields far removed from those supposedly their own. His twenty-five-year-old astronomer, for instance, Ivan Mikhailovich Simonov (1794–1855), was clearly interested in ethnology as well as physics and geodesy.[47] Among the several particularly versatile lieutenants in his ship were Arkadii Leskóv, who was to visit Oceania again aboard *Moller* (1827–28), and the future Decembrist, Konstantin Petrovich Tórson.[48] Finally, *Vostok* carried an able artist, Pavel Nikolaevich Mikhailov (1780–1840), a graduate of the St. Petersburg Academy of Arts, to whose considerable skills we are indebted for a record of the Russo-Lauan meeting of late August 1820.[49]

Mertens and Kunze literally missed the boat at Copenhagen where, in mid-July 1819, both were expected to present themselves.[50] Their absence only heightened the significance of Simonov's and Bellingshausen's interest in native peoples. Both *Vostok* and *Mirnyi* spent the best part of a month in Portsmouth, making ready for a crossing to Brazil and thence Antarctica. New sextants, telescopes, chronometers, and other instruments were bought in London, where a meeting was arranged with the already aged Joseph Banks.[51] The Russians left for Rio de Janeiro on 26 August. In Brazil, too, all went well. Finally moving south, the Russians saw South Georgia Island on 27 December. By 28 January 1820 they were twenty miles or less from what is now called Princess Martha Land. They turned aside, but three weeks later they were once again in sight of land or, more precisely, ice resting on land. This was Antarctica. The expedition pressed on east, remaining south of 60°S for a full quarter of the circuit of that line of latitude. At last, in April 1820, they moved up to New South Wales where the governor, Lachlan Macquarie, proved hospitable.[52] Well rested and provisioned, Bellingshausen and his people left Port Jackson on 23 May 1820 for a cruise across the Low or Tuamotu Archipelago. They reached it almost four weeks later after unexpected visits to Queen Charlotte Sound, New Zealand,[53] and a planned visit to Rapa, in the Austral Islands. Finally, they set about the business of discovery in Polynesia. Bellingshausen's skills were soon rewarded. On 10 July, he gave the first certain record of Angatau in the Tuamotu cluster. On 13 July, he discovered Nihiru, on 15 July Katiu, on 16 July Fakarava, on 18 July Niau, and on 30 July Matahiva. Then, on 1 August, Bellingshausen gave the first solid report of Vostok Island in 10°5'50"S, 152°16'50"W.[54] The island still carries that name.

Well satisfied with six weeks' running survey work in an indifferently charted part of Polynesia, Bellingshausen turned his thoughts once more to Sydney and Antarctic waters. Southern spring approached, and he was anxious to continue hydrographic work begun a year earlier. He made accordingly for Sydney, crossing first the Northern Cooks (Rakahanga, Pukapuka), then the Vava'u group of Tonga.[55] On 19 August 1820, three uncharted islands were observed. The first two were very small and low, six and a half miles apart, the position given for the more easterly being latitude 21°1'35"S, longitude 178°40'13"W. Named after *Vostok*'s artist Mikhailov, this was Tuvana-i-Tholo; the other islet, off to the northwest and named for Simonov, was Tuvana-i-Ra. Both struck the Russians as potentially most dangerous, and *Vostok* herself, came close to ruin on "Mikhailov Island."[56] The third, far larger island proved to be a little reef-fringed cluster and was actually Ono-i-Lau, in latitude 20°39'S, longitude 178°40'W. The Russians thus came to the southeasternmost islands of the widely scattered Fiji archipelago. They could not know that they had been preceded there by the *Bounty* mutineers, in the little launch *Matavy*, on 28 June 1791.[57] Those mutineers, who had drifted west in HMS *Pandora*'s tender for at least a month before landing (most happily for them) at Mana on the eastern side of Ono,[58] had not only lacked the urge to do a little basic scientific work, but had also left no solid, published record of their call. It fell, accordingly, to Russians to present Ono-i-Lau to the Eurocentric world.

# 5

# THE RUSSIAN RECORDS OF THE LAUAN VISIT, 1820

INTRODUCTION

The narrative record of *Vostok*'s and *Mirnyi*'s call at Ono-i-Lau is, by early nineteenth-century and Russian standards, very adequate. We have published accounts by Bellingshausen himself, by his versatile young scientist Ivan Mikhailovich Simonov (1794–1855), by Pavel Mikhailovich Novosil'-skii, midshipman in *Mirnyi*, and by a literate and sharp-eyed seaman in that same vessel named Egor' Kiselëv. (See Bellingshauzen 1960:317–34; Sementovskii 1951:163–66, 185, 258.) Unfortunately, manuscript materials relating to the 1920 visit have not yet been fully studied by the Soviet historians and others who, alone, have means to track them down in state-directed archives. It is virtually certain that such primary materials *are* in a range of larger manuscript repositories, most in Leningrad: every officer aboard a Russian naval vessel in the South Pacific Ocean in the early 1800s was required to maintain a daily journal and moreover, at the voyage's conclusion, to surrender it to the imperial authorities (the naval ministry). Besides the two sober commanders, Bellingshausen and his second-in-command Mikhail Lazarev, a dozen "officers and gentlemen" arrived at Ono. They included Captain-Lieutenant Ivan Zavadóvskii, five lieutenants (Ignat'ev, Leskov, Torson, Annenkov, Obernibésov), three senior midshipmen (Demidov, Kupreiánov, Novosil'skii), Surgeon Galkin, Surgeon Iakov Berkh, and Simonov, who among other roles fulfilled that of astronomer. All wrote accounts of their experience in Melanesia with *Vostok* or *Mirnyi*. So, most probably, did other seamen in positions of responsibility, for instance, pilots (Il'in and Poriadin), clerks, and mates. Few of these visitors to Ono, to be sure, were *savants* or men of science in the Bellingshausen mould. The point is that numerous, intelligent observers did leave records of their visit. The majority no doubt promptly surrendered those accounts (and other documents besides) to Bellingshausen, who exploited them when drawing up his own official narrative. Thus certain passages from Simonov's or Novosil'skii's records of events at, say, Ono-i-Lau are paraphrased in Bellingshausen's text.

Even the use of several officers' reports and notes, however, and their later reappearance in a narrative composed by the commander did not guarantee that they would see the light of day. The fate of source materials on Oceania depended on the overall success of the entire mission as perceived by the imperial authorities; and many factors might produce a "failure" verdict on a naval enterprise. The 1822–25 Vasil'ev-Shishmarev venture, for example, was completely overshadowed by Bellingshausen's Southern enterprise, though much material Vasil'ev and Shishmarev gathered of relevance to Melanesian studies and Australia might have been printed by the Russian naval ministry. In short, several journals by participants in Bellingshausen's expedition lost their chance of publication, in an era of suspicion and political repression. Some at least must be supposed to hold some interest for Melanesian studies. Recent Soviet historians such as Ostrovskii, Lipshits, Kuznetsova, and Shur have insisted on this fact in published papers (see Bibliography). I discuss these matters in the first part of this survey of the Russians in the Great South Sea (Volume One: *The Russians and Australia*).

Suffice it to note here that documents by members of the Russian Navy's 1819–24 double polar expedition are still being discovered. In October 1948, the journal kept by Aleksei Petrovich Lazarev, lieutenant in the sloop *Blagonamerennyi*, was recognized in the provincial archive of Smolensk. Well-edited and annotated, it was published two years later. By the 1960s, in TsGAVMF (the Central State Archive of the Navy of the USSR, in Leningrad) was being searched by V.V. Kuznetsóva, who believed it must contain other materials by Lazarev's companions. In particular, she looked for documents by men who later prospered in the service, such as the captain of the sloop *Blagonamerennyi*, Gleb Shishmarev, and Midshipman Nikolai D. Shishmarev, his nephew. (Gleb attained flag rank; Nikolai became a commodore.) Kuznetsova found and reported on the midshipman's neglected journal (see Bibliography). More recently, the Soviet historian of the Hawaiian Islands, Daniel D. Tumarkin, has pursued the path that Kuznetsova took. Among his own finds in the central naval archive have been 1820–21 materials by Bellingshausen's counterpart on the Pacific-Arctic enterprise, Mikhail N. Vasil'ev, and by Lieutenant Roman Boil' [Boyle] of *Otkrytie*. They were reported in *Sovetskaia Etnografiia* in 1983 (see Bibliography, under Tumarkin).Probably further discoveries of primary materials relating to the South Pacific peoples will be made by those whose academic interests lie far

away—in South America, for instance, or Antarctica. *Vostok* called, after
all, at both those continents during her voyage round the globe; and as the
work of Soviet Antarctic specialists has drawn attention to materials of
value to the Melanesian student, so has that of recent Soviet historians of
Chile and Brazil. In this connection, special mention must be made of V.N.
Sementovskii, L.A. Shur, and B.N. Komissarov (see Bibliography), all of
whom worked in their turn in the archival storehouse that is Leningrad.

BRIEF OBSERVATIONS ON THE RUSSIAN TEXTS

Bellingshausen's observations on the people of Ono-i-Lau were recorded
daily in stiff-backed navy journals. He was instructed to ignore nothing new,
useful, or curious in any area of knowledge and accordingly spent many
hours on the journals which, he knew, would be examined by his service
chiefs. Small wonder that his prose was sober. He was forever navigating
between the Scylla and Charybdis of frivolity and tedium. In the end, he had
from 1822 to 1824 in which to polish observations made, often at night and
in discomfort, while in Fiji.

Had he wished to do so, Bellingshausen could have "rearranged" events
and altered emphases. There are good reasons for believing that the changes
that he did make to his 1820 journal were essentially stylistic. In the first
place, he was honest and punctilious by nature. Torson's sudden fall from
grace, for instance, did not cause his ex-commander to deny, even in writing,
that his services at sea had been distinguished—or indeed that an Atlantic
islet had been named for him. Nor, in the second place, *could* Bellingshausen
easily have rearranged whole patterns of events in the Pacific with impunity.
Although the writings of his own former subordinates were temporarily in
his possession, there were witnesses to almost all the scenes that he
described, and some had influence. And some, notably Simonov, were outside the pale of naval discipline by 1822.

Ten notebooks were submitted to the naval ministry by Bellingshausen in
April 1824. They contained his narrative in copperplate: he wrote methodically and in a small, elegant hand. In another submission the same month, he
requested that the Crown finance a first edition of 1200 copies of his work.
Nothing happened. Months went by. Frustrated, Bellingshausen finally
composed a lengthy memorandum on the matter of his voyage to the recently
created Naval Scientific Committee of the Naval Staff. Perhaps the government would print 600 copies of his work, at least? Committee chairman at
the time was Vice-Admiral Loggin Golenishchev-Kutuzov who, in early life,
had spent much time translating Cook. He viewed the problem sympatheti-
cally. Orders were given for 600 copies of the narrative to be published at the
state's expense.

At last, after a final set of problems with officious editors (Messrs. Nikol'-skii and Chizhov) had been overcome in Bellingshausen's absence, (he was serving on the Danube), his account was printed in 1831. *Dvukratnye izys-kaniia . . . (Repeated Explorations in the Southern Icy Ocean and a Voyage Round the World in the Years 1819 to 1821)* appeared in two volumes, supplemented by an *Atlas* that contained the work of Pavel Nikolaevich Mikhailov, the expedition's artist, and a set of nineteen maps. A whole volume of correspondence on the controversial issue of editing Bellings-hausen's manuscript, dating from August 1828 to 1831, remains in TsGAVMF (Departament Morskago Ministerstva, Delo Uchonogo Kom-iteta, No. 20). The manuscript itself has long been lost. It was, in conse-quence, impossible for either A.I. Andreev or E.E. Shvede, the respective editors of the 1949 and 1960 Soviet editions of the Bellingshausen narrative, to do more than reproduce the 1831 text with efficient annotations and assorted complementary materials. The following translation of the Bellings-hausen passage dated 19–22 August 1820 (or the "Lauan Passage") is based on Chapter 5 of the original St. Petersburg edition.

Of the two accounts of his encounters with the Lauans by Ivan M. Simo-nov presented here, the first, printed in 1822, is based on text of the astrono-mer's "extraordinary" (that is, public) lecture of 7 July 1822. That lecture, which was given at the University of Kazan', Simonov's alma mater, was entitled "A Word on the Successes of the Voyage of the Sloops *Vostok* and *Mirnyi* Around the World." It was grounded on notebooks he had kept during the voyage but was popular in tone. The university itself printed the somewhat polished speech in pamphlet form. It was presented to a new, Soviet audience in 1951 by Dr. V.N. Sementovskii, in the documentary compendium, *Russkie otkrytiia v Antarktike . . . (Russian Discoveries in Antarctica in the Years 1819–1821*, pp. 31–47). The source of the following translation is pages 41–42 of that edition.

Simonov's *Vostok* notebooks and writings were exploited more than once over the next few years. They comprised the heart of an amusing set of letters, for example, that he sent to Baron Franz von Zach (1754–1932) for publication in the latter's periodical, *Correspondance astronomique, géogra-phique* (Genoa 1818–26). Simonov and Zach, former director of the large Seeberg Observatory at Gotha, shared common astronomical and geodesic interests. Then, in 1823, Simonov himself reviewed and edited his South Pacific "letters." They were published, in a slightly altered form, in *Journal des Voyages, ou Archives géographiques du XIXe siécle* (69 cahier, July 1824, 5–26), under the heading, "Précis du Voyage de Découvertes . . . dans l'Océan Pacifique et dans les Mers Australes." Parisians thus had the chance to read about "King Fio" and the Ono Islanders ten years before their own Dumont D'Urville provided first-hand French material about the Lauans of

Toyota and Matuku in his *Voyage de la corvette "L'Astrolabe"* (Paris 1834, Vol. 4, pp. 424–29). The "Précis" was later translated into Russian and appeared in the periodical *Severnyi arkhiv* (St. Petersburg, 1827: Vol. 8: "Izvestie o puteshestvii . . . ," or "Information on the Voyage of Captain Bellingshausen of 1819–21"). To recapitulate: the primary materials served as the basis of a public lecture, which was printed, and of letters sent to Zach which, having first been fused into a single narrative, were printed in Genoa, re-edited and then published in Paris, and eventually brought back to St. Petersburg in Russian (1827).

But what of Simonov's original material itself, that is, the notebooks kept aboard *Vostok*? As it was natural that he had wished to draw immediate advantage from his voyage and to speak to influential people in Kazan', where he was to make a brilliant career as a scientist, so also it was natural that by the later 1820s he should focus his endeavours on his science. His career was already prospering. By 1830 he was enviably placed as both professor of astronomy and corresponding member of the (then as now) conservative Academy of Sciences. He had in any case produced his printed "Word," to leave some record of the voyage round the world which was the major intellectual and physical adventure of his life. He left his notebooks as they were, reviewed them, sorted them, postponed the thought of publishing them. Finally, in 1846–48, he thought about likely publishers of an account like his, and, on the basis of his holograph, composed a narrative in twenty copybooks. But time ran out in 1855; Simonov died without completing his manuscript, "The Sloops *Vostok* and *Mirnyi*, or the Voyage of Russians in the Southern Icy Ocean and Around the World." It remained in the possession of Kazan' University's Main Library, where today it is preserved as MS 4533. The "Lauan Passage" below is from Chapter 7 of that manuscript, headed "Plavanie v Tropicheskikh Predelakh Velikago Okeana" ("A Voyage in the Tropic Zones of the Great Ocean"). I thank Dr. A.S. Gur'ianov, Director of the Main University Library in Kazan', for granting me access to it.

The fourth passage translated here, by Midshipman Pavel M. Novosil'skii of *Mirnyi*, is taken from a book published anonymously by him in 1853: *Iuzhnyi polius: iz zapisok byvshego morskago ofitsera* (*The South Pole: From the Memoirs of a Former Naval Officer*, St. Petersburg). Midshipman Novosil'skii typified the younger officers chosen by M.P. Lazarev for the Pacific enterprise, by his abilities and breadth of interests. A graduate of the Imperial Naval Cadet Corps, he returned to it in 1822 as an instructor in astronomy and calculus. In 1825 he was transferred at his own request to the Ministry of Public Education. He pursued a not uncomfortable dry-land career, finding time in mid-life to keep up interests in polar exploration and to polish up the journal of his youth.

That journal, like the Bellingshausen holograph of 1824, was almost certainly recovered by its author and cannot, as a result, now be consulted. It is fairly plain, however, from both textual and circumstantial evidence, that Novosil'skii did not print his journal as originally written. The 1853 text is a smoothly flowing narrative, replete with comments and reflections that could only have been made after the expedition's end. Again, derivative material is used to lend more substance to the book, though not, most happily for Fiji studies, in its "Lauan Passage."

It is certainly regrettable that Novosil'skii edited his journal. On the other hand, the orderly and chronological arrangement of material in 1853 suggests that Novosil'skii's emendations to his journal were stylistic, not substantive, in their nature. Certainly, the "Lauan Passage" (dated 20 August 1820 in the Sixth Part, "Russkie Ostrova—Otaiti," of the 1853 text) follows logically after an entry on Vava'u (Tonga Islands), which *Vostok* had passed and *Mirnyi* had hurriedly surveyed four days before. Numerous paragraphs begin with dates. Thus is the 1820 journal to be glimpsed in, or behind, the printed text. The "Lauan Passage" is produced on page 258 of Sementovskii's compendium, *Russian Discoveries* (Moscow 1951); it is immediately followed by a section marked "30 August, nameday of the Sovereign Emperor. . . ," referring to the death of Seaman Blokov.

Finally, I offer a translation from the journal kept by Leading Seaman Egor' Kiselev of *Vostok*, found in the ancient town of Suzdal' in the later 1930s. It was published in the travel periodical *Vokrug sveta* (*Around the World*) in 1941 (no. 4:40–43), by Iakov Tarnopol'skii. Unfortunately, Tarnopol'skii made "improvements" to the 1820 narrative and the resultant text left much to be desired. The manuscript, entitled "Pamiatnik prinadlezhit matrozu 1 stat'i Egoriu Kiselevu . . ." (Journal Belonging to Seaman First Class Egor' Kiselev, Who Was on a Distant Voyage in the Sloop *Vostok* in 1819–1821"), was reprinted with a good deal more textual fidelity by A.I. Andreev in 1949. Andreev's compilation of primary materials, entitled *The Voyage of the Sloops "Vostok" and "Mirnyi" into Antarctica in the Years 1819–1821*), complemented his edition of the Bellingshausen narrative, also of 1949. Crude though it is, the journal is the work of an intelligent, observant man and is indicative of the high calibre of seamen on *Vostok* and *Mirnyi* at that time. Andreev's text was borrowed for inclusion in the Sementovskii compilation, and appears there on pages 179–88. The "Lauan Passage" is on page 185.

THE TEXTS

*Ivan Mikhailovich Simonov (1822)*

Excluding the Tahitian group, we found in all these regions only one island that was unknown before our arrival.[1] Its natives were distinguished from their neighbours by a particular gentleness, perceptible in their very appearance as in the trusting way they came onto our ship. This island lies not far from the Friendly Islands and is called, by its inhabitants, Ono. We were there forty-eight hours and a few of the island's elders spent a night aboard the sloop, which was something not one of the peoples we had earlier encountered had ever agreed to do.[2]

Fishing is the principal exercise of the South Pacific Island peoples, and on that business they occasionally sail to places far removed from their own in extremely long and narrow craft. In order to prevent these from capsizing, they fasten outriggers to one side.[3] They also have double canoes. Every man seated in such canoes paddles for himself, with a small paddle. At Ono, we found some quite large craft which moved under sail, the sails being constructed of reed mats.[4] Those particular islanders fish with wooden, bone, and shell hooks. Those natives who had had previous contact with Europeans would seek pearls, though by no means in large quantities.[5]

Among the handicrafts of these Ono Islanders are manufacture of matting and of a sort of material that is beaten out from tree bast. The resultant stuff is white, though they sometimes die it yellow by means of a colouring substance obtained from one species of fern, or produce red tones by application of fern leaves smeared with another substance. The latter is extracted from the berries of a plant called *matti* by the Tahitians,[6] or from another leaf which these natives themselves call *to-u*.[7] The mats are spread over the ground and sat upon, while the material is used to cover up certain parts of the body.

Our passage through such interesting regions as these would, however, have been far more pleasant had the scorching heat of the sun not wearied us, and had the submarine coral reefs surrounding the islands we encountered not presented us with many dangers. It was while we were near Ono Island, rather late one evening, that we suddenly caught the sound of waves, to which we were unaccustomed. On looking carefully around, we spotted the foam of great waves smashing against a coral reef.[8] The peril was not more than a quarter of a mile away.

## Ivan Mikhailovich Simonov (1840s)

Next day, we were close to the island of Ono. A double canoe under sail soon approached the side of our sloop. Speaking strictly, it was two long, narrow craft, the sides of which were bound together with boards.[9] This double canoe was surrounded by many small craft, one of which was actually first to reach our ladder. The two men seated in it came up onto *Vostok* most trustingly, to be received by us with great friendliness. They had brought us out coconuts, bananas, and other fruit, as well as roots, for which we recompensed them generously.

Everything plainly indicated that the natives of *this* island, Ono, had never seen Europeans. If our first two visitors did, in fact, board the sloop boldly, this was because one of them had earlier made the acquaintance of Europeans while in the Friendly Islands. The name of that native was Paul'.[10] A native of the island of Tonga or Tongatabu, he had been carried hither to Ono by a storm and had subsequently won the good opinion of the people and the confidence of their king. He was quickly followed up onto the sloop, however, by other islanders, including two sons of the local king, who came out on a double canoe. An hour later, the *turan* [*turaga*] or ruler of Ono, whose name was Fio, himself came out to visit us.

On the arrival of the King, Paul assumed the duties of master of ceremonies and there unfolded an interesting ceremony of mutual introductions between the *turan* [*turaga*] and the captain of our sloop *Vostok*. Paul seated the two men facing each other on the deck and surrounded them with the king's suite.[11] Fio then ordered a branch of a coconut palm to be brought from his canoe. The branch had two unripe nuts on it. Fio handed this branch to Paul, who held it aloft, sang some song or other very sonorously, and clapped his hands and struck his thighs. The members of the royal suite then joined in, striking their hands and thighs in the same way. At the conclusion of the singing, Paul started to break off from the branch those offshoots bearing no fruit, at the same time repeating certain words that were incomprehensible to us. After this, all the natives present began to sing, clapping as before. Finally, everyone stood up and our guests walked up to us to greet us by touching noses, in the manner accepted throughout Polynesia.[12] This whole scene took place on our quarterdeck. Our captain then led *Turan* [*turaga*] Fio down into his own cabin, to present him with some red flannel, a medal, a saw, several axes, and various other articles. Our native guests set off home from the sloop quite late. Fio himself, Paul, and one other islander, though, who also belonged to the king's suite, remained aboard to spend the night with us. Paul visited my own quarters.

In order to entertain our guests with something quite remarkable for them, Captain Bellingshausen now ordered a few rockets to be fired off in front of them. The natives were at first completely taken aback by the suddenness and brilliance of the spectacle, expressing their wonder orally and by bringing their palms sharply up against the mouth, thereby producing a sound something like, *Avavava, A-va-va*. . . .[13] At the moment when the rockets crackled and exploded, Fio held the captain's coat. The sensation of amazement having passed, and the feeling of alarm alone remaining, our guests asked us to halt the spectacle forthwith.

Fio and his two retainers dined with us with pleasure, then went off to sleep in the captain's own quarters, where mattresses with pillows and bed-sheets had been prepared for them on the floor. But their slumbers were brief and disturbed. That day and that night, as on all others during our passage through the tropics, I was making hourly observations of the rise and fall of the mercury in our barometers. And since the latter were lying in the captain's cabin, where the aforementioned bedding had been prepared for our guests, I was going in there at the beginning of each hour. Every time I appeared in the night, my little lamp in my hand, the natives leapt up and muttered something in their own language. It was very understandable that they should sleep poorly. Many and worrying reflections were doubtless troubling Fio, making him ponder on what he had witnessed the previous day and evening. Doubtless, he was also wondering if he had acted wisely in trusting these quite unknown and very powerful newcomers. The natives remained in their disturbed state, at all events, until morning came. Shortly before sunrise, when I went to check the air temperature outside the sloop by means of a thermometer suspended on the quarterdeck, I met them on the upper deck. Still, while Ono Island remained in sight, our guests calmly walked about the quarterdeck and stern, blankets thrown over their shoulders like Roman togas. They had simply taken the blankets. Captain Bellingshausen let them keep their (improperly acquired) mantles.

At sunrise, other islanders came out to us again, this time in seven sailing craft and thirty-six paddled canoes, to the number of about two hundred. And on this day we acquired many rare things by barter: various sorts of weaponry, the martial emblems of chiefs,[14] white and coloured stuffs,[15] large shells. Many of these articles were better finished than their counterparts on Tahiti. As had the island's king, so also did all our other guests invite us ashore with unfeignedly friendly intent, assuring us that *there* we should receive a live hog, *buaga* [*vuata*], which appeared to be the most valued article of trade on these isles, for every piece of glass we gave. Spring, however, was already approaching and our captain, who had carefully calculated the time required for the investigations that still lay ahead of us, was anxious to set a course for Port Jackson, where the sloops might be made ready for our final survey in the Southern Icy Ocean.[16]

At Ono Island, we saw for the last time a native people new to us. On our subsequent voyaging we encountered many islands, to be sure, and discovered not a few new ones, but all those other islands proved to be uninhabited. Having had dealings with natives of islands scattered across the vast expanses of the Pacific Ocean, we had already observed that they were distinguished one from another not only by skin tone, but also by artificial factors, so to speak. Undoubtedly, the principal external point of difference between the peoples of different islands lies in tattoo. Properly to observe differences in designs produced on the human body itself, it is necessary to range very widely and, in the course of travel, to accustom the eye to those patterns which distinguish not only one tribe from another tribe, but also one class of people from another class on the same island. Other, rather more noticeable indicators of differences between peoples in different places may be subsumed, as in Europe, under the heading of fashion. For certainly fashion penetrates even the primitive life styles of the unenlightened nations of the regions of Oceania.

Among the Ono Islanders, fashion concentrates itself in hair style—for want of clothing. King Fio's hair, which was in tight curls and may very well have been naturally curly, was worn *à la Titus*. His son's hair was divided into little bunches tied at the scalp with threads, the ends of the bunches being brushed up all over the head save at the back, where locks descended to the shoulders.[17] A downy flower had been threaded into his hair over the right temple. Some individuals had their hair cut very short at the sides and on top, but allowed it to fall in even curls or little ringlets[18] from the temples and back of the head. This coiffure was complemented by powder, more-over—powder applied more fancifully than in France, for it is multico-loured, red, yellow, and a light blue. And besides all this, natives had often thrust wooden combs or foot-long shell pins horizontally through their hair at the back of the head.[19] Both the combs and the hairpins were so worn that the hair could be combed but the coiffure not disturbed in the process. Some individuals wore necklaces made of small shells threaded on laces of human hair. Yet others wore ground pearl shells, threaded on similar laces, like a circle of medals. Many wore mother-of-pearl shells in bracelet form on their arms, above the elbow. The lower part of the ears of all Ono Islanders had large slits, through which had been inserted sizeable pieces of shell, perhaps an inch and a quarter thick and two and a half inches long. As a result of this, their earlobes hung down quite hideously.[20] The most morbid custom obtaining almost throughout Oceania, however, is the removal of a finger in memory of deceased close relatives. On Ono, we saw many men with missing little fingers.

We took our leave of the gentle and friendly natives of Ono at 9 AM on 22 August, pushing off from the sloop's side both King Fio himself and the combed and powdered Polynesian marquises who surrounded him. Once their narrow craft were clear of us, we gave the wind liberty to fill our sails; and quite soon we were drawing level with that same coral reef which had recently enough threatened to destroy us. . . . By 2 PM, we were passing to the west of Mikhailov and Simonov Islands.[21]

*F.F. Bellingshausen*

By 8:30 the next morning (20 August), we found ourselves not far from a continuous above-water reef. It was SE of an island, which it surrounded to varying distances.[22] Then we caught sight of natives ashore, some of whom were coming out to the reef in a number of craft. So tremendous was the surf breaking over this reef that it was impossible to have any communication with these islanders; so I soon turned into the wind with the object of circling around this island. I meant to send a boat ashore if the natives came out to us. In the event, it was not until 11 AM that we were able to weather the northern stretch of the reef encircling this isle.[23] We then hove to and awaited the islanders in their canoes. Two came out under sail, all the rest being paddled. As soon as a couple of craft were alongside the sloop, we again filled our own sails.

These craft had outriggers on one side only and each brought three men. A pair of natives came aboard our sloop at once at our very first invitation and, when we showed them some kindness, were not backward in making our further acquaintance and in making themselves at ease.[24] One of these craft, in which one islander had stayed behind, was drawn sideways on by the sloop's considerable wake and capsized, the rope by which it was secured having broken. As a result of this, I was obliged to lie to once again and put off a boat to rescue the native and bring the canoe in tow again. The man's companions, now on board the sloop, did not concern themselves about all this in the least, indeed, became quite merry on observing their fellow countryman floundering in the water. It was not long after this before the natives were coming out in large numbers, all boarding the sloop. A few of them were chiefs, and to these we gave presents, placing medals around their necks. They attempted to initiate barter. We repaid them liberally for all their trifles—for we did not expect to find other inhabited islands on our route to Port Jackson and we were bound thence for the Southern Icy Ocean where, because of the climate, there could be no natives. I asked the chiefs, who had come out to us in double canoes with sails, to present certain gifts from us to their king, who had remained ashore. And I am certain that the islanders, who showed complete honesty in their trade, unfailingly carried out my instruction in that regard.

It was shortly after this that we discovered that two sons of the king were actually among the chiefs present. I led them to my quarters, put medals round their necks as had been done earlier for other natives, and gave them additional special gifts: a piece of red material apiece, a large knife, a mirror, and several iron craftsman's tools each.[25] It was to them that I entrusted the gifts meant particularly for the king ashore. They assured me that he himself would soon be paying us a visit. One native, who had come out to us accompanied by his own sons, remained with us quite some time. We learned that his name was Paul' and that he was one of the royal retainers. He was from Tangatabu [Tongatabu] whence, together with a few of his own countrymen, he had been carried by a storm to this island, whose natives had shown him goodwill.[26]

When the royal canoe did come out, Paul' led me up to our stern and pointed out the king for me. Fio, as the king was called, proved to be a man of about fifty, of large stature. His skin was tattooed only on the hands, indeed, on the fingers, there being very small spots at the joints. His hair was greying slightly and was painstakingly tended, like a wig. His face and body were swarthy in colouration, and his eyes were black. Like all the South Pacific Islanders, he had a narrow girdle tied around his middle part.

Once the king had come on board the sloop, he and I greeted each other by touching noses. Then, at Fio's request, I and Mr. Zavadovskii[27] sat down with him on the quarterdeck. Paul' and one other native, an elderly man, also sat, and we thus formed a small circle apart. Next, on Fio's orders, a coconut branch with two green nuts on it was brought up from his canoe. He took this branch and handed it to Paul' who, holding it aloft by the end, began to sing[28] loudly. Half-way through this song, two natives joined in and then all clapped their hands and thighs. Paul' next began partially to break each shoot of the branch, pressing it up against the main branch itself. Every time he broke and bent a shoot, he uttered certain words in a singsong voice. At the conclusion of all this, everyone again broke into song and started to clap their hands as before. This action doubtless betokened friendship, for the islanders were clearly attempting in every possible way to show us their amicable disposition.

I led the king into my cabin, placed a silver medal round his neck, and gave him a saw, several axes, iron and glass vessels, knives, mirrors, pieces of calico, and various needles and other such trifles. He was delighted to have these things, immediately ordering that they be taken ashore in his canoe. He had already observed to me that he had earlier received my initial gifts to him, that is, the gifts sent by his sons. Fio next took tea with us. Everything he saw was new to him, so he examined everything with attention.

On 21 August we bartered with these islanders for various weapons that they had, e.g., pikes, cudgels, smaller clubs, and something resembling a rifle butt.[29] All these articles had been skilfully ornamented with carving. We also obtained, by barter, a broad spade, carved and then painted with some dry white substance.[30] Such spades were apparently the property of chiefs alone; they are perhaps marks of their distinction. Besides this weaponry, we also acquired cloth, combs, hairpins, various ornaments made from shells, pieces of yellow colouring matter which rather resembled the so-called *shizhgel'*,[31] cords skilfully woven from human hair, various other cords of coconut fibre, and other things. Provisions with which the natives supplied us included taro, yams, coconuts, breadfruit, certain kinds of root other than yam, a sort of potato, sugarcane, and both cultivated and mountain bananas.

Drawing nearer the shore at 2 PM, we saw on a hillside some good-sized, downy trees in the shade of which a village lay spread out.[32] The dwellings were externally like those of Otaiti [Tahiti], only a little lower. Almost all the adjacent islets seemed to be cultivated and must be fertile.[33]

The natives themselves resemble the Tahitians in many ways. They adorn the head in this manner: all the hair is divided up into little bunches which are then tied at the roots with a very fine thread. The upper ends of these bunches are combed with much care, and the resultant head of hair looks rather like a wig.[34] Some of the islanders put a yellowing colouring substance on the hair, too; and we saw a few individuals who had tied and combed (in the fashion just described) only the hair at the front of their head. The hair at their temples and at the back hung down in tight curls.[35] Many had thrust into their hair, always horizontally and on one side only, hardwood or turtleshell combs[36] or turtleshell pins, the latter being up to a foot long.[37] These islanders use these hairpins when at their coiffure, lest the effect be spoiled.[38]

The natives' necks were decorated, for the most part, with well-cleaned mother-of-pearl shells, braids of human hair on which small shells had been threaded, or necklaces made of shells rather like bugles.[39] In the right ear, they place a cylindrical piece of shell approximately 1¼ inches thick and 2½ or 3 inches long, as a result of which the right ear lobe was appreciably longer than the left on those natives we saw. On their arms, above the elbow, they wear rings likewise fashioned from sizeable shells. Such hair styles and ornaments of course give these people an unusual appearance; but it is not an unattractive one. I noticed that many of them had only four fingers on each hand, the little finger having been cut off in memory of the death of a very close relative. In general, we found the islanders cheerful in disposition, frank, honest, trusting, and inclined to be friendly. There is no doubt that they are also brave and warlike, for that is indicated by the many wounds on their bodies as by the quantity of weaponry that we were able to acquire by barter.

In the last *Voyage* of Captain Cook, it is mentioned that Cook heard while at Tongatabu that an island called Feise, whose natives were highly warlike and courageous, lay three days' thence to the WNW.[40] Captain Cook actually saw two men from Feise Island, indeed, and wrote of them: "One of their ears hangs down almost the shoulder; they are skilful in handicrafts, and the island they inhabit is a very fertile one."[41] I have no doubt that the island we ourselves were now visiting was in fact Feise, for everything Cook ~te about the island in question corresponded with what we found here, ~t the natives called it Ono and were ruled by a king named Fio. ⁊assed from father to son, though, it is hardly surpris- Tongatabu should have called Ono Island itself—Fio.

For on the Friendly Islands too, the names of kings are transmitted from father to son. The present king there is named Pulago, as were his predecessors.[42]

With the approach of night, all the islanders returned to the shore, but the king stayed behind with Paul' and the other chief, awaiting his own canoe. It did not come until the following morning. Our guests dined with us aboard and imitated us in all processes involved in the taking of supper. When it was completely dark, I ordered that a few rockets should be fired off. At first, our natives were much alarmed and while the crackling continued the king actually held on to me firmly. When they saw that the rockets had been fired only for their entertainment and were quite harmless, they gave full expression to their amazement by exclamations and by trilling in a loud, drawn-out manner, frequently striking their lips with their fingers. What engrossed them most of all, though, was our artificial magnet which attracted iron. They laughed particularly when a needle put on a sheet of paper would follow the magnet when the latter was under that paper. We prepared hospital-style mattresses for all our guests, in my cabin, for the night, also readying bed-sheets, one per man, so that they could cover themselves. At first, they did in fact all lie down; but they slept poorly and were incessantly leaping up and coming up on deck.[43]

The island itself was not visible, because of the darkness. I separately asked the king and each of the other natives where it lay. Having first glanced at the sky, they made good estimates of the positions of Ono and the other islands. For during the evening, they had observed on which side of Ono we were holding course. It is clear from this that they have some understanding of the movements of heavenly bodies. They must have, indeed, in order to calculate time or to recognize numerous lands in the event of long voyages to the Fidzhi [Fiji] or Friendly Islands. Paul' told us that to the west of Ono lay another and larger isle called Pau, and to the WNW another called Laketo.[44] At what distance the latter lay from Ono, we could not make out from what he said.[45]

We learned the following words of the islanders' language:

| | |
|---|---|
| *kavai* | a kind of potato |
| *puaka* | hog |
| *seli* | small knife |
| *ambu* | coconut |
| *koli* | dog |
| *maluk* | butt-like weapon |
| *eikolo* | bone |
| *leru* | finger ring |
| *atoku* | hairpins |

| | |
|---|---|
| *sakiun* | patches |
| *saitazh* | scissors |
| *tariga* | ear |
| *kummi* | beard |
| *falua* | land |
| *kanikin malum* | spade, weapon |
| *glandzhi* | sticks |
| *malum* | weapon |
| *ambalemato malum* | spear |
| *maida malum* | variety of club |
| *eivodi* | paddle |
| *sun-siup* | bent club |
| *amasi* | material, cloth |
| *e-amba* | bast matting |
| *itakoi* | bow |
| *manau* | arrow |
| *buli-gon-go* | porcelain shells |
| *ediba* | pearl shell |
| *vallo-a* | human hair braid |
| *avango* | vessel, canoe |
| *vakko* | nail |
| *a-rfeno* | yellow paint |
| *a-spoa* | cock |
| *mona* | hen |
| *eolu-Alatolu* | 3 stars of Orion |
| *eolu-vullo* | moon |
| *minako* | good, well |
| *alinsangu* | hand |
| *induti* | finger |
| *autu* | nose |
| *nrako* | mouth |
| *ambachi* | teeth |
| *aianri* | brow |
| *amata* | eye |
| *ame* | tongue |
| *aulu* | hair |
| *akokupo* | fingernail |
| *beri* | foot, leg |
| *andaku* | back, spine |
| *ambuka* | fire |

Throughout the night, we remained in one position by making short tacks.

At first light on 22 August, we stood in for land again and at sunrise the natives put out to sea towards us in seven sailing craft and thirty canoes under paddles only. Ten men or more sat in the sailing canoes, while the other craft carried three or four persons. The natives now brought us a quantity of beautifully made weapons, assorted ornaments, and large shells into which they blew in the event of a sudden assembling of the people or as a summons to battle.[46] They also brought out various cloths resembling printed material, checked and red or coffee in tone, extremely fine. The finest of all, however, were white and were about the size of a handkerchief.[47] We had not seen stuffs of such quality on Otaiti [Tahiti]. And so skilfully and beautifully folded were these small kerchiefs that, having once unfolded them, we could not refold them in the same way.

Among the sailing craft that came out to us was the king's, in which were conveyed, as gifts for us, two hogs, coconuts, taro roots, and yams. I gave the king other presents in return for all this, furthermore giving his elder son a large carving knife, a pistol, a little powder, and some bullets, and demonstrating how the firearm should be used against an enemy. At the same time, I gave the king and several other islanders orange and other seeds, showing how they should be planted in the earth. The natives seemed well pleased with all these gifts also and promised to sow the seeds, which, I doubt not, they later did. On the shores of their island, we saw cultivated kitchen gardens where, most likely, they were growing taro, yams, and so forth.

The islanders willingly took everything we gave them, to be sure; but in the end they preferred knives and scissors over everything else, including our axes. They persisted in calling to us to join them ashore. We declined, however, since there was no obvious point in putting a boat ashore without a naturalist and, if we had in fact dropped anchor, we would inevitably have lost days. For we would first have been obliged to find a safe passage through the coral reef to the anchorage. And the approach of spring in the Southern Hemisphere did not permit me to lose time, given that I wished to spend a longer period than before[48] at Port Jackson to replace the bowsprit support which had become quite untrustworthy for a voyage in the high southern latitudes.

Ono Island actually consists of several small and hilly islets, the largest of which is some 2½ miles long and 1½ miles broad. All the islets are, so to speak, encircled by a coral wall rising above sea level in some places but broken here and there on the north. It is from this side that canoes put out.[49] The coral wall itself lies on a NE-WSW axis and is about seven miles long. Its centre lies in latitude 20°39′S, longitude 178°40′W. Gently sloping areas of the islets in question are cultivated or covered by various sorts of tree, including the coconut palm.

On 23 August at 9 AM we said farewell to King Fio, with whom I had become quite friendly in a short time, and he set off for the shore. Having sent all the other natives off the sloop, I then gave orders for their canoes to be pushed off from our sides. But the natives hung onto our stern line, letting go only when the increased headway of the sloop forced them to, the wake driving one canoe hard up against another. One craft actually capsized; and at this, the natives finally ceased to hug our side.

One of the young islanders wanted to stay on our sloop and I had agreed to take him with us; but he insisted that we take his companions also and I could not agree to that, for fear that they would not withstand the extreme Southern clime. I set a course for Mikhailov and Simonov Islands,[50] with a view to fixing their true positions. Passing along the west side of Ono Island, we spotted from the crosstrees that same surf from which we had speedily turned away on the evening of the 19th, so escaping obvious peril. I held my course towards these breakers in order to examine and determine the position of the actual bank,[51] so preserving future mariners from inevitable disaster at night. We passed the bank, which makes a lagoon, at 11 AM . . . I named it *Beregis'* [Beware].

## Pavel Mikhailovich Novosil'skii

On the night of the 19th, *Vostok* very nearly ran onto the surf surrounding a coral bar—we barely managed to wear ship before striking the reef itself. The least delay could have meant the sloop's ruin. On the morning of 20 August, our two ships were soon approached by two sizeable sailing craft and by several smaller ones which were being paddled. The natives came right up to us without the slightest hesitation, then came up on deck. We learned from them that an island right by us was called Ono. The natives resembled those of Otaiti [Tahiti] and were naked except for a narrow girdle. They had divided their hair into numerous bunches, tying each bunch around with slender threads and then, as it were, beating up the upper ends. Into this magnificent coiffure, which looked like a wig, they had thrust long pins made of turtleshell; and with these, they were continually combing their hair. Round their necks they wore pearl shell necklaces and round their arms—rings also of shell. The islanders proved to be a gay people and soon made friends with us. Their king, named Fio, and one of his sons boarded *Vostok* and even passed a night there. The captain was generous with gifts for his native guests, who were persistently inviting us to spend some time ashore with them. We were obliged to hasten on our way to Port Jackson, however. Ono Island lies in latitude 20°39'S, long. 178°40'W. . . .[52]

## Leading Seaman Egor' Kiselev

On 12 August we sailed past two small islands. There was stunted woods with bushes. No people. Also known to nobody. Then, on the 20th, we found a very rich and very big island, they called it Tarunar.[53] Masses of savages there, but the people was very mild. As many as twenty boats came out to us, full of people, and they brought presents out to us in them: sugar cane and wild pigs and mussels-shells and pearls.[54] At this place, our captain presented seven men with bronze medals on copper chains. . . .[55]

# 6

# OBSERVATIONS ON THE RUSSIAN
# NARRATIVES AND DRAWINGS

Brief comments are offered here on the ethnographic evidence provided by the "1820" Russian narratives and illustrations, as opposed to that inherent in the Lauan artefacts from Ono held in Leningrad (MAE) or in Kazan' (the Simonov Collection"; see below, Chapter 7). Although the evidence of artefact and written and/or illustrative record is, of course, part of a single whole, and therefore mutually complementary, it is convenient to comment on the artefacts themselves within the pre-established context of a survey of the narrative materials. Attention is directed here to the evidence of Russian-Lauan contact; Lauan physical appearance, body ornament, and diet; language; weaponry and social order.

Bellingshausen's narrative was an official, public document presented with the government's approval and at state expense. Its author worked under constraints that neither Simonov nor Novosil'skii felt, when, rather later, they returned to notes and journals of their voyage. Both the latter furthermore had semi-popular accounts in mind when, in the forties and the fifties, they approached their publishers.[1] Novosil'skii in particular made more extensive use than Bellingshausen had (or even wished to) of local colour and journalistic method. Attitudes and facts may thus be altered in response to market needs, and distinctions *are* inherent between books written for public entertainment and enlightenment and formal documents. While bearing this in mind, however, we may reasonably think (see Chapter 5 above, pp 101–13) that the sum of Russian texts and illustrations gives a generally accurate impression both of what the Russians saw and thought at Ono and of *what was truly there*. Because the texts describe the same events, phenomena, and individuals, they are essentially self-focusing, each bringing others into sharp perspective. That perspective is again enhanced by adoption of the "mutual interpretation method" (written records plus the literature based on fieldwork) that such ethnologists as H.E. Maude, A.R. Tippett, and N. Lurie commend.[2] That approach has been adopted in this section.

RUSSIAN-LAUAN CONTACT

## Russian Arrival and "Discovery"

*Vostok* first made contact with the Ono group, and so with the Fijian Archipelago, at Tuvana-i-Ra, shortly after 2 PM on 19 August 1820. Tuvana-i-Tholo was also sighted, from the sloop's topmast lookout, within minutes. *Mirnyi* was then some little distance away to the south. Both islets were low but covered with coconut palms and perhaps a mile in length; both were encircled by reefs at least one mile across, on which a white surf broke forbiddingly. Bellingshausen approached them not with landing in view but in order to chart them (running survey). As he did so, at approximately 3 PM, Ono-i-Lau was seen lying low on the northern horizon. Bellingshausen sailed nearer Tuvana-i-Ra, which he named for *Vostok*'s artist, Mikhailov, and past Tuvana-i-Tholo, which he named for his astronomer, Ivan M. Simonov. It seemed to him, as it had seemed to General Lachlan Macquarie, his obliging host in New South Wales five months earlier, that arts and sciences as represented by the draughtsman and astronomer could thus be linked within a context of humane discovery.[3] Today, though, native names are used, not Bellingshausen's. As the chart published in 1831 suggests, the two small islands stand along the northern edge of a reef platform some six miles across. Both are twenty-two nautical miles (40.7 kilometres) distant from Ono-i-Lau.[4] The Russians thought them uninhabited.

By 5 PM, the running survey of the Tuvanas being complete and the SE wind still steady, Bellingshausen moved off on a course to NW. To proceed directly to Ono-i-Lau was not feasible. Night fell. False fires were lit aboard *Vostok* and quickly answered by *Mirnyi*, now sailing to her west. At approximately 9 PM, the *Vostok* had a near escape from destruction on Vuata Ono ("Beregis") Reef. That coral barrier, lying eight miles SSW of Ono-i-Lau, was barely visible in nighttime and was very nearly Bellingshausen's graveyard.[5] *Vostok* withdrew towards the south and an extremely watchful night was passed. By 8 AM next morning, both ships were well in sight of the "continuous above-water reef" surrounding Ono-i-Lau. The reef was visible, writes Bellingshausen, southeast of that island group. Therefore the Russians stood off Mana Islets and the natives glimpsed ashore, some three miles off, were on the southern half of Onolevu, largest of the three volcanic fragments of the ancient, long-breached crater, Onolevu, Doi, and Davura, that comprise Ono-i-Lau's interrupted "inner ring." This was the windward shore, on which the villages of Nukuni and Lovoni stand today. Because most strangers came to Ono from the Tongan side with the prevailing winds, the main village of Onolevu had, since ancient times, stood on its eastern shore.[6]

Bellingshausen's future hosts had seen him coming. Since the larger hill of Onolevu, Delailoa, is 113 metres high, and even the more gentle southern eminence, called Nawamaji, rises more than 60 metres, we may think that Ono Islanders had been examining the spectacle of *Vostok*'s and *Mirnyi*'s sails since an early hour. And among them, as we know, was one person at least, the so-called Paul', who had had personal experience of European vessels and connected them with useful trade. It was the visitors' good fortune that he did not link them promptly and exclusively with gunfire and slaughter.[7] If the Ono Islanders themselves knew of such giant ships by hearsay, as was practically inevitable given *Bounty*'s tender's stay of June 1791 and growing Lauan-Tongan contacts, they too failed to connect them, at first, with death. Bellingshausen was probably indebted to his mentor, Captain Cook, for this desirable turn of events. Ono-i-Lau's closest neighbour, fifty-four miles north, is Cook's "Turtle Island" or Vatoa, seen and visited in 1774; and far from firing on the terrified Vatoans, Cook had left them nails, medals, and one or two knives.[8] Various versions of the story of *that* seaborne apparition at Vatoa, we may reasonably suppose, had reached Ono-i-Lau before Bellingshausen's birth. The Ono Islanders "gave preference to knives and scissors over everything" aboard the Russian sloops and were particularly pleased to be presented, like the natives of Vatoa half a century before, with bronze medallions.[9]

It was while *Vostok* and *Mirnyi* were beating up the southeast side of Onolevu that the islanders came out towards the reef by Mana Islets in a number of canoes. The Russians rightly judging that the high surf on the reef made closer contact with the natives "quite impossible," and that a better anchorage must be discovered, Bellingshausen headed north and round the reef. Thus far, he had unwittingly repeated the performance of the *Bounty* mutineers in the little tender *Matavy*, who had similarly headed north from Mana Islets to the reef's northern extremity, the Lauans keeping pace within the island group's lagoon.[10] The Russian vessel's movements might have made men unfamiliar with European ship-handling uncertain of their object. Still, the Ono Islanders moved towards the boat passage just west of the Yanuya Islets and, in due course, Bellingshausen saw the place. We may regret the intricacy of that passage for, to judge by Bellingshausen's narrative, he would have put a launch ashore if native craft had made their way beyond the reef by 10 AM, and his account would have been ethnographically the richer. On the other hand, we must be grateful that the Lauans' attitude and conduct, when at length they reached *Vostok* off the Yanuya Islets, led the Russians to prolong their call at Ono by a day.

*First Contact by Yanuya Islets: 20 August 1820*

Having weathered the northern rim of the Ono-i-Lau reef at approximately 11 AM, Bellingshausen and Lazarev both hove to and waited. They were soon approached by a *ndrua*, a large double canoe under sail, and by several smaller paddled canoes. The latter all carried three or four men apiece, and had outriggers on one side.[11] A second double canoe joined the first alongside *Vostok* after some minutes, once the Russians' friendly motives seemed apparent. The Russian texts do not mention speeches addressed to them from a canoe, as in southern and central Polynesia, or of weapons in the craft approaching them.[12]

Despite a brisk easterly wind, the first Lauan craft to reach the Russians had no sail but was paddled by two or possibly three islanders. That craft came up to *Vostok*'s rope ladder. *Mirnyi* stood slightly further out. The Russians beckoned to the Lauans to board *Vostok*, which two natives did at the first invitation and without evident fear. One of the pair clearly had had previous dealings with Europeans. The example and reception aboard of this man, the Tongan Paul', encouraged other Ono men to emulate him. They, however, were obliged to wait some minutes as the sloop was under way again: Bellingshausen thought it best to limit further, noisy contact until the natives' friendly attitude was obvious and information had been gleaned about their island. "Everything" at all events, "plainly indicated that the natives of this island, Ono, had never seen Europeans" (Simonov). In fact, some natives who were youths in 1791 might have survived to witness the Russians' arrival.

At this juncture, with Paul' and another native aboard, the Russians took a welcome opportunity to demonstrate their friendly disposition. A paddling canoe was drawn across *Vostok*'s wake and, while sideways on, capsized. Not appreciating Lauan stamina and expertise in water, Bellingshausen saw a crisis that did not exist: he sent a boat to "rescue" the capsized but sanguine islanders and brought the small canoe in tow. The Ono Islanders meanwhile took a long look at the Russians in the launch. The process of establishing connections on a human plane advanced another stage. *Vostok* hove to again and other Lauan craft approached her.

Other islanders now boarded *Vostok*, among them "two sons of the local king," who had been watching from a nearby *ndrua*. Soon, numerous Ono men were boarding her and all was cordial, though Russian seamen were alert and fully armed. The Russians had no difficulty distinguishing degrees of social rank among their visitors: chiefs had arrived in state and were deferred to by the commoners. No islander, however, felt constrained from bartering at once for white man's goods (*vavalagi*) to the extent that he was able, and the Russians proved obliging. Girls and women are conspicuously absent from the Russian texts describing these events; none, it appears, left the shore. Once the "king's sons'" special status had been recognized, the Russians reinforced it by removing them from other natives' sight, then, in the captain's quarters, giving them not only bronze medallions but also other special gifts including Russian iron tools, mirrors, and knives. King Fio was promptly offered even grander gifts. Though Bellingshausen might employ the word *korol'* (king) smilingly, he took no action, now or later, that was likely to reduce the royal power.[13] Paul' was acting as intermediary between the Russian chief and Lauan king even before the "royal craft" came through the passage in the reef out to *Vostok*. At Bellingshausen's own request, Paul' led him onto the sloop's stern deck and pointed Fio out. Perhaps an hour had elapsed since Paul' had come aboard.

Fio, the "*turan* or ruler of Ono" (Simonov), boarded *Vostok* unhesitatingly and greeted Bellingshausen, as by implication from the Russian texts the other islanders had not, by touching noses. Paul' then assumed the duties of master of ceremonies, he and Fio both believing that a certain ceremony was important in the novel circumstances. Bellingshausen and the officer commanding *Vostok*, I. Zavadovskii, whom Fio rightly treated as an "elder," were asked to be seated on the quarterdeck away from common seamen, whether Russian or Fijian.

The Russians were most favourably struck by "a particular gentleness" in the Ono Islanders, "perceptible," it even seemed to Simonov, "in their very appearance." They were trusting, cheerful, and (according to Novosil'skii) even "gay."

*The "Ceremony of Introduction"*

Bellingshausen took his part in Lauan ceremonial when, Paul' and one other elder having been brought onto *Vostok*'s main deck, he accepted "trifles," coconuts, and other foodstuffs from their hands. He failed, understandably, to recognize the full significance of Paul''s initial actions; and he failed to distinguish them from barter, which took place almost immediately afterwards. What was a "curiosity" or "trifle" to a European officer might well have socio-political, if not religious, meaning to a Lauan. Paul' and his companion had been sent to Bellingshausen as a visiting paramount chief; and that companion was almost certainly of chiefly rank himself. The chief's sailing craft could have outpaced that in which Paul' and his associate had reached *Vostok*. It was by Fio's will that Paul''s small craft had reached her

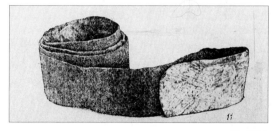

PLATE 1

*upper*  "Natives of Tana," from H. Robertson, *Erromanga*, 1902
*lower*  Thick tapa belt, from Port Resolution, Tana, 1809;
held at MAE, Leningrad:  No. 736-288.  340 by 7 cms

PLATE 2

*clockwise*  L.A. Hagemeister; V.M. Golovnin; I.F. Kruzenshtern; Iu. F. Lisianskii

PLATE 3

Ivan Mikhailovich Simonov, circa 1822

PLATE 4

Lauan *masi* (material) in the
"Simonov Collection" at Kazan'.
State University Museum,
Nos. 160-35-36

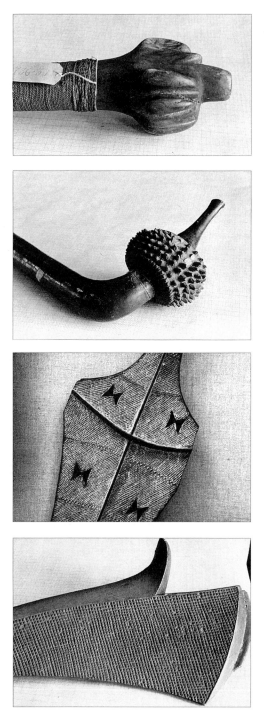

PLATE 5

Specimens of four Fijian club types, collected at Ono-i-Lau in August 1820, MAE, Nos. 736-12, 17, 21, 34

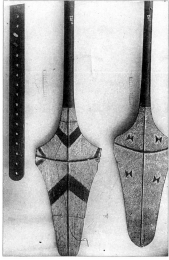

PLATE 6

Overview of two Lauan spade clubs, Nos. 736-16-17

PLATE 7

Details of club 736-12
(upper pair), 736-17, and 736-21
("pineapple club" head)

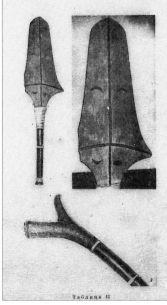

Таблица II

PLATE 8

Details of Lauan spade clubs at
Kazan' University Museum, Nos.
160-17-19, from SMAE, 30 (1974)

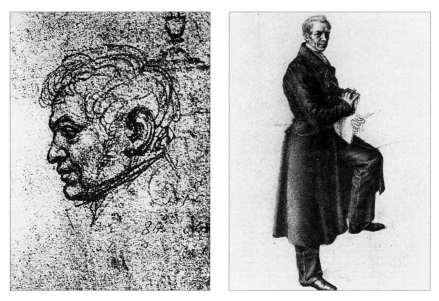

PLATE 9

F.F. Bellingshausen; P.N. Mikhailov (self-portrait, from State Russian Museum, Leningrad)

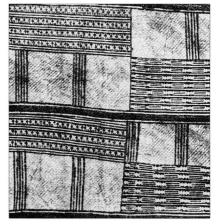

PLATE 10

*left* Detail of *masi* stuff from Lau, 1820, MAE 736-12

*above* Detail of face of Lauan *kinikini*, 1820, MAE 736-17

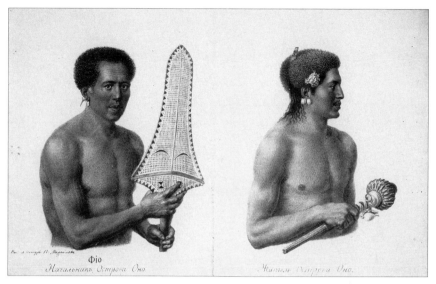

PLATE 11

Portraits of Ono Islanders, by Pavel N. Mikhailov, from Bellingshausen, *Dvukratnye izyskaniia: atlas* (St. Petersburg, 1831)

PLATE 12

M.N. Vasil'ev; G.S. Shishmarev

PLATE 13

Russian sloop-of-war of the Otkrytie-Kamchatka class

PLATE 14

Anuta Island viewed from the west

first, with a *tambua* to be formally presented to the unknown chief. Paul', it seems, did not make much of the initial presentation, being mightily preoccupied with what he saw aboard the giant craft. Nevertheless, a form of public presentation and acceptance of a symbol had occurred. The true interpretation of that symbol is debatable, but it appears that the *tambua* of the coconut-palm branch implied benevolence and welcome. Paul' 's and Bellingshausen's ceremony was, or very strikingly resembled, that traditionally called *thavu-i-kelekele* ("the raising of the anchor"). That *Vostok* had not dropped anchor permanently was immaterial to Fio and his envoy; what had meaning was the giant craft's intention to make contact and, it seemed, remain awhile.

Fio's own arrival on the sloop involved the Russians in a further ceremonial event. This was, in essence, Ono's welcome for a visiting paramount chief who had accepted a preliminary offer (brought by Paul') and who, by implication, had also accepted the suggestion that he stay.

The "Russian chief" had not yet decided whether to anchor; but in any case Fio was justified, given the visitors' behaviour, in assuming that the "Russian chief" would land. This second ceremony, it is ventured, was a form—adapted to the odd, indeed unprecedented situation in which Fio found himself—of the Lauan ceremonial *i-luva ni tawake* ("undoing the pennant on the chief's canoe"). Bellingshausen had lowered his sails, or at least some of his sails, not conceiving that the action had specific connotations for the watching islanders, such as acceptance of *tambua* and a willingness to land in peace.

The Russians' ignorance of Lauan etiquette and language posed a problem for the king's master of ceremonies, Paul'. And for the student of the Bellingshausen visit with the king, there is the unrelated problem of the Russians' inability to recognize and/or record the true significance of what occurred. Nevertheless, a few brief speculative comments will be ventured. When a *tambua* was about to be presented to a visiting high chief in former times (and Ono culture was in 1820 wholly unaffected by the *vavalagi*), the respected individual among the local group who was to make the presentation uttered words of preparation and warning. The formula used was brief but promptly recognized by Lauans. One was very likely used aboard *Vostok* but Bellingshausen did not recognize it. Even had Zavadovskii been his own master of ceremonies, as the Tongan Paul' seemed to have wished he were and almost, for the purposes of ceremonial, did pretend was the case, he would not have recognized it either. Consequently, Paul' was bound to act *as if* the suitable responses had been made. He then proceeded on his own initiative, placing the two chiefs on the deck apart from men of lower rank, facing each other and encircled by a suite.

The *tambua* now to be presented, the coconut branch frequently used in Lau instead of *yanggona* bowls or *masi* cloth, meanwhile was in Fio's large canoe beside the sloop. On his orders, it was brought to the deck. He took the branch, with its two unripe, green nuts, and gave it formally to Paul', who held it high and by one end. Paul' then sang or chanted a song or formula with emphasis. Next, he placed it on the deck and clapped his hands and thighs as a token of appreciation of the king's presenting the *tambua* to his mighty guest. Elders joined in. The song or chanting ended. Paul' picked up the branch again. He began, says Simonov, "to break off from the branch those offshoots bearing no fruit." Bellingshausen, who was obviously closer, paints a rather different picture, and informs us that the offshoots were not broken, they were merely bent up hard against the stem. The "certain words" uttered by Paul' alone included a brief, stylized speech of welcome to the Russians, mentioning the king and the branch's recipient. The Lauans then stood up and all touched noses with those Russians whom they recognized as "elders." Strict attention was always paid to the requirements of social rank and decorum.[14]

Bellingshausen rightly understood this ceremony as a friendly one. His attitude towards his chiefly hosts foreshadowed that of later British royal visitors to the Fijian archipelago. The point is underscored by C.K. Roth, who comments that "apart from the mark of goodwill intended in every presentation of *tambua*, it was frequently the vehicle for a request. . . . Nowadays [1952], the implicit request is merely one for a reciprocal show of goodwill.[15]

## Gifts and Barter

Bellingshausen failed to recognize the full importance of the (second) *tambua*, as, a little previously, he had failed to appreciate the non-commercial meaning of the first. It is apparent though that Ono Islanders who reached *Vostok* some minutes after Paul', "a few" of whom were chiefs, did wish to barter. It is unclear from the Russian texts whether they or Bellingshausen started an exchange of goods, but one inclines to think the Russians acted first. To men of rank they offered "gifts, placing medals round their neck." The Lauans offered trading goods almost at once and "were repaid for all their trifles."

Trade had soon been complicated, though, by Bellingshausen's asking Lauan chiefs to take prestigious presents to their king, who was ashore or still approaching *Vostok*. Fio thus found his initial *tambua*, sent with Paul', oddly reciprocated. In the first place, the response implied that there were requests he had never made (for foreign artefacts and weapons). Second, his important visitor remained at sea despite acceptance of *tambua* and a partial lowering of sails. Finally, the European goods were wonderful; and several

Ono-i-Lauans had received red cloth, mirrors and knives, axes, and other iron tools. The visiting high chief's behaviour was unusual, but he was evidently friendly. Fio though it proper to approach his visitor in person.

Now occurred a further obfuscation of the lines between the categories "gift" and "barter ware." As seen, the Russians only roughly understood the meaning of the ceremonies on their deck, but having taken the *tambua*, the Russian chief had broken protocol by not proceeding to the shore in his canoe but, as it were, showering presents on the donor. Such exchanges as took place in Captain Bellingshausen's cabin should, by Lauan etiquette, have taken place ashore. The Russian axes, knives and mirrors, glass vessels, and other articles given to Fio were immediately *sent* ashore, where they should have been.

Next morning, Russo-Lauan bartering proceeded on a wider scale. As the Russians had presented many handsome gifts already, and in view of the extreme desirability of some of them, Fio felt bound to offer no less handsome articles. Prominent among the "1820 Ono" artefacts now held in Soviet museums are a number with chiefly connotations or associations, such as Fio was alone likely to offer *vavalagi* like the Russians: *kinikini* [spades] and very elegantly finished *totokia* [clubs].[16] Clearly, Fio played a large role in the gift exchange and barter on the morning of 21 August 1820. His example would have strengthened the desire that his people in any case must have felt to take advantage of the Russians' presence in order to exchange even their best, most prized possessions for such articles as scissors, knives, and mirrors. Thus, the Russians soon acquired not just specimens of many kinds of weaponry, but first-rate specimens in duplicate.

The Russians recognized their elegance and beauty and, more significantly, the esteem in which the Ono Islanders held some of them, notably *kinikini*. Bellingshausen thought such articles were "the property of chiefs alone," probably "marks of their distinction." In Simonov's opinion, many of these well-carved objects were "better finished" than their counterparts at Matavai Bay, Tahiti, where *Vostok* had been lately. In sum, the circumstances favoured rapid acquisition of a relatively sizeable collection of the weaponry in use on Ono in the early nineteenth century. The Russian visit must significantly have depleted the reserves of certain sorts of chiefly artefact on Ono at the time. If the Soviet collection is in fact *not* representative of local weaponry on Ono in the early 1800s (which unquestionably it is not), it is because of the superior embellishment of many items in it, such as *totokia*, *sali*, and *gata* clubs, and of a lack of cruder cudgels.

Twenty-second August saw continuing and equally confused barter and gift exchange, but now the Russians themselves were responsible for the confusion. Both sides were apparently untroubled by the social or political significance of the interpretation the "other side" might be placing on events and/or specific articles. But Bellingshausen *chose* to view specific articles sent out by Fio as a set of "royal gifts" (two hogs, coconuts, taro, yams) and to regard his own response in a political and altogether non-commercial light. His attitude was influenced by his associations with, and knowledge of, the European social systems of his day, not by knowledge of Melanesian practice. He could simply not have known what status Fio had attached to these new "gifts" or whether any quid pro quo were being looked for. Under the circumstances, the dividing line between pure trade and princely interchange became, if not invisible, then indefinable.[17]

By Cook's standard, the Russians bartered extensively at Ono. Both *Vostok* and *Mirnyi* carried ample stores of trade goods, and other island calls had not been anticipated on the passage down to Sydney. There was certainly no need for Bellingshausen to surrender other ethnographica and so make room aboard *his* ship for Lauan artefacts, as in another age Cook had been virtually forced to give up *tapa* from Tahiti when he had stowed Maori "Clothing, Weapons, Ornaments," and other things.[18] The Ono Islanders acquired in considerable quantity what Bellingshausen and his second-in-command, Mikhail Lazarev, were willing to offer them: tools, iron, cloth, and ornaments. And, as they had in other parts of Oceania, the Russians also gave what they supposed would benefit their native hosts and incidentally, might be of future use to other Europeans in the area. Such articles included orange seeds. The spirit of the later eighteenth-century Enlightenment was at work, preserved by Russians in another age. Not once while in Fijian waters, one might add in this connection, did the Russians strive to gain any political advantage from their overwhelming strength. Like Kruzenshtern in 1804, they sought only the currency of knowledge and, perhaps, a little glory. It is certainly regrettable that Bellingshausen had no botanist on board, for if he had, he would no doubt have made a landing. One is grateful, on the other hand, for Simonov's good sense and ethnological discrimination during bartering for Ono artefacts, collecting duplicates, for instance, and evincing keen awareness of the importance of technique (see below, "The '1820 Ono' Artefacts," 197–202).

Initially, the Ono Islanders gladly took everything the Russians offered, including articles they had neither seen before nor perhaps even heard about. Cook's longboat had left nothing but a knife or two, nails, and medals on Vatoa; nor, to judge by Russian evidence, had European goods arrived on Ono from the Tongan Islands independently of Paul' or in his craft.[19] Had any Russian seen a European article, or evidence of some familiarity with ironware, he likely would have mentioned it. Within a single day, however, Fio's countrymen were giving preference to knives and scissors over everything the Russians offered. Probably they remembered knives described by the Vatoans or others who had visited Vatoa or other places where Cook and his compatriots had been. At all events, they immediately appreciated the great utility of knives as implements-cum-weapons.

Among the articles acquired by the Russians at Ono-i-Lau on 20–22 August 1820 were the following:

weapons—"pikes, cudgels, and smaller clubs": *kinikini, sali, gata* clubs; throwing clubs;
implements—human hair laces; vegetable fibre cords;
material—*masi* barkcloth; *i sala* "turbans"; "various cloths, checked and red or coffee in colour"; matting;
ornaments—hardwood and turtleshell hairpins and combs; "various ornaments made of shell"; pieces of turmeric colouring (*rerega*);
musical instruments—*davui* conch;
foodstuffs—two hogs; taro; yams; coconuts; sugarcane; "sweet potatoes"; "cultivated and mountain bananas."

In return for these, and for drinking water and fresh fish in very modest quantities, the Russians left bronze and silver medallions, large and small knives, scissors, pieces of rough red flannelette, lengths of calico, saws, axes, iron and glass tableware, vegetable and fruit seeds, woollen blankets, copper chains, a pistol, a little powder, a few bullets for the gun, needles, little mirrors, and assorted beads.

The Lauans persistently invited the Russians to land on Ono, incidentally offering clues to local scales of commercial value, such as "assuring us that *there* we should receive a live hog . . . for every piece of glass we gave" (Simonov). The Russians caught these clues but, not being traders, did not raise the exchange value of glass or knives accordingly. It was clear that the Ono Islanders prized their hogs. Bellingshausen was, indeed, disappointed in his hopes of getting livestock by barter.

PHYSIQUE, HEALTH, BODY ORNAMENT, AND CLOTHING

*Physique*

"The natives," reports Novosil'skii, "resembled those of Otaiti." Bellingshausen concurs: "The natives themselves resemble the Tahitians in many ways," one being physique. In general, the Ono Islanders struck the Russians as large, well formed, and rather muscular. Fio was "a man of perhaps fifty, of large stature." He was "swarthy," but the Russian adjective *chernyi* (black), applied to other South Pacific islanders, is not used by Bellingshausen or his officers in describing the Ono people. Russian narrative and pictorial data, in sum, support N. Gabel's contention that Polynesian physical characteristics were pronounced in South and Central Lau in those localities to which Tongans (and possibly others) had migrated or had been driven by the elements in the past.[20] Fio and his sons, at least, were tall, with clear-cut features tending towards the aquiline,[21] and certainly had the lighter skin tone Lauan commoners might have expected of their chiefs. "Many of the present chiefly families [of Lau] trace their descent from strangers who sailed or drifted from distant islands. . . . Strong Polynesian influence, both physical and cultural, is evident in Lau; this was contributed mainly by visiting parties of Tongans, many of whom . . . even settled permanently.[22] Paul' had followed a traditional, time-honoured route of Tongan mariner-adventurers, northwest and west, to Lau.[23] Fio honoured him and had—to judge by Russian evidence—accepted him as an important chief of Ono. Given the looks and antecedents of the male chiefs of Ono, local women's underprivileged position (reflected by their absence from encounters with the Russians), sits well with Polynesian patriarchal views.[24]

## Health and Diet

The Russian texts have nothing to say about women on Ono. Male islanders appear to have enjoyed abundant foodstuffs and a relatively varied diet. No diseases were apparent to the Russians, nor were sickly or deformed persons in evidence.

Unlike most other islands of Southern Lau, Ono produced, and still produces, fine yam crops. June and early July were traditionally harvest-time for yams, so the Russians came when they probably were abundant. Since the Russian texts do not mention the quantities or relative proportions of the foodstuffs the Ono people offered, one cannot say how large a part the yam played in their trade, or in the local people's diet. It is clear, even so, that yams were eaten in considerable quantity on Ono and were supplemented both by taro and by breadfruit.

Coconuts were also an important article in local diet and economy, being employed as food and drink and as a major source of good plaiting material and sennit. Fifty years ago, when Laura Thompson was engaged in fieldwork on Lau, Ono enjoyed the reputation of producing "the best flavoured coconuts" in the entire region.[25] Lauans made their sennit, by tradition, from *niu ni mangimangi*, but the coconut judged most succulent were *niu ndrau*. Both sorts grew on Ono in the early contact period, as they do now. The Ono Islanders do not, however, seem to have had coconut-based oil on their bodies while the Russians were there.

The visitors were also offered wild (or "mountain") and at least one sort of cultivated banana. Breadfruit, sugarcane, and manioc, combined with plantain and bananas, would have supplemented yams to produce a large, nutritious food supply. The Ono people had, besides, both fish and shellfish, the occasional edible turtle, and of course the hogs (*puaka*) that they failed to present to Bellingshausen. Pork was prized by Fio's people; nor, it seems, did Fio, Paul', or other islanders object to eating meat aboard *Vostok*.

Also included in the Bellingshausen word list are both *koli* (dog) and *a-spoa* (misreading for *a toa*, fowl). Both dogs and fowl were patently familiar to Fio's people, who no doubt consumed the latter as *i thoi*, or to supplement other foodstuffs. Dogs were not commonly eaten by the Lauans.

In general, the Ono Islanders seemed healthy to the Russians, who record neither the ravages of leprosy (*sakuka*) nor (the skin disease called) yaws.[26] It is exceedingly improbable, though possible, that Bellingshausen and his people would by August 1820, after months in Oceania and frequent contact with Pacific Islanders, have looked on yaws as battle wounds (which *were* in evidence, or vice versa).

## Body Markings and Distension

In Lau as elsewhere in Fiji, in former times, girls commonly were tattooed on upper thighs and buttocks before puberty.[27] Boys were not tattooed, though males did endure the "tattooing tooth" (*mbati*) rather later and on other body parts than upper thighs, buttocks, and genitals. Fio alone is specifically described as having "particoloured skin," at finger joints, that is by his knuckles. These "small spots," however, were unquestionably keloids, or small raised cicatrices; Lauan chiefs did not indulge in deep tattooing in the Maori or Marquesan manner.

Conversely, most did submit to certain mutilations of the hands and ears, more specifically, to the amputation of a little finger joint or joints and earlobe-slitting and distension. Both these practices were seen by Bellingshausen and his men in 1820. *Vostok*'s artist, Pavel N. Mikhailov, has left us two portraits of Ono men, Dovili (Fio's son) and Tutenberi (Plate 11) wearing reel-like ear ornaments in the distended (right) earlobe.[28] In both cases, the ornament is unmistakably a well-carved cylinder of sperm whale tooth (*sau-ni-daliga*.) Such plugs, the size of which reflected chiefly rank or priestly status, were traditionally treasured (like the whale tooth itself) by Lauan chiefs.[29] Those being worn by Dovili and Tutenberi, which were at least *two* centimetres in diameter, were relatively modest by the standards of the early 1800s. Some were as much as twice that thickness. Like their "king," both chiefs long before had submitted to the bamboo-slitting process of the lobes, and had enlarged the perforation systematically by insertion perhaps of a barkcloth roll or plantain leaf, in hopes of passing unimpeded into Bulu, the Fijian afterworld. Those who had shirked such

mutilations could not run the dreadful gauntlet of the waiting and malevo-
lent *kalou loa* spirits.[30] Fio's portrait shows his wearing, not a *sau-ni-daliga*
plug, but what appears to be auger shells and/or a spurred whale tooth
ornament.[31]

### Coiffure

The Ono Islanders' hair was, in 1820, almost always "divided up into little
bunches . . . then tied at the roots with a very fine thread" (Bellingshausen).
The islanders were highly conscious of their hair and paid it much attention.
Simonov thought that fashion had been developed at Ono in the hairstyle
because for obvious climatic reasons they had little need of clothing for
protection. Certainly, the Russians saw impressive heads of hair, with cascades of *tobe* ringlets.[32] To compare Mikhailov's sketches with contemporary drawings of more northerly Fijian chiefs, however, is to recognize the
strength of Polynesian physical or ethnic influence in Southern Lau. Considerable though the dressed coiffures of some of Fio's people evidently were, he
and his son Dovili and the chief called Tutenberi all had relatively short and
wavy hair. Comments by Fergus Clunie on these matters bear primarily on
the elegant and dandified Dovili: "In the Lau Group, where a higher proportion of Polynesian ancestry in the population left many people with less
frizzled, wavier hair, shorter styles were more commonplace, often accompanied by curtains or cascades of *tobe* ringlets. . . . These fashionable, long,
often tasselled ringlets were sources of vanity and pride.[33] Dovili's *tobe*
ringlets fell perhaps six inches to the neck. Fio himself had short and greying
hair.

Another Ono man drawn by Mikhailov, named Salogo, whose hair is
similarly wavy and unfrizzled, wears a loose fringe round a clipped tonsure.
The fringe, on the Mikhailov original still held in Leningrad, is shown dyed
bright yellow, while the central part is reddish like the top and front of
Tutenberi's hair.[34] It is significant, in this regard, that Simonov should mention local use of pulped *vetau* (*Mammea odorata*) as a dying agent. Likely it
was used by Fio's people on their hair as on their barkcloth. Bellingshausen
makes it evident that turmeric (*a rerega*) was in use as a conveniently port-
able and widespread yellow dye. As for the light blue tone observed by Simonov on certain islanders' coiffures, it had long been in the Lauan
repertoire.[35] Ono men of rank, it seems, made heavy use of yellow grated
sandalwood, as their hair powder.

Among other articles worn in the hair and observed in 1820 were ornamental combs of polished tree fern wood and turtleshell; *i milamila* (head-
scratching skewers); (*i geu*) (slivers worn at the back of the head); and bright

red flowers by the right ear.[36] Conspicuously missing from the Russian texts
are *kabikabi* (flower wreathes) and *vau kula* (headbands).

## Barkcloth

The Russians found Fio and his people clad in the traditional range of
Lauan winter clothing. Barkcloth was abundant and was offered for barter
in various forms. Bellingshausen acquired "white and coloured stuffs," that
is, dyed and undyed *masi* ("girdles"), and *i sala* (headdresses). The latter, of
fine, white cloth, protected the coiffure.[37] Lauan *masi* struck the Russians as
resembling European printed cloth, at least on sight. Much at Ono was
"checked, and red or coffee" in hue. Woven cords (*waloa*) or, in Bellingshausen's word list, *vallo-a*, were frequently dyed black.

Impressed by the quality and fineness of the Ono *masi*, the Russians
acquired some by barter off Yanuya Islets. They cannot now be identified
among the Leningrad collections of "pre-1828 Fijian" barkcloths.[38] From
the Soviet museum records, though, it is apparent that the Lauan cloth
brought to St. Petersburg in 1822 by Bellingshausen or by Lazarev was not
the earliest Fijian *masi* to be delivered to the Navy or Academy of Sciences.
Three or more pieces of *masi* had arrived in 1809. They are today in MAE's
Collection No. 737 as items 11, 12 and 34.[39] Though their provenance was
studied by the Russian anthropologist Piotrovskii, who was struck by the
suggestive fact that other cloth from Oceania with which they had been kept
since 1809 had been presented or perhaps sold to the *Kunstkamera* by
Johann Reinhold Forster, Cook's companion on the second voyage
(1772–75), it cannot be said with certainty from whom that cash-conscious
savant obtained the barkcloth samples. They were not, at all events, of
Lauan make. Varying from ten to seventeen metres in length and forty-two
to sixty-seven centimetres in breadth, the strips are composite and ornamented with assorted geometrical designs (rhomboids, triangles, parallels),
and dyed dark red or terracotta brown.[40]

## Fishing and Canoes

Ono-i-Lau was abundantly supplied with foodstuffs. Fio's people, by extension, were considerably less dependent on the products of the sea for sustenance than were Fulangans or Kambarans, for example. In itself, this fact
decreased the likelihood that Bellingshausen's hosts would have been fishing
when he visited in the Southern winter. Other factors must be kept in mind
as we survey the Russian evidence for fishing. Russians' presence at the
island would have halted much food-gathering activity, including fishing,

which was largely woman's work in any case and was conducted less from vessels than with nets from shore. As seen, the Russians had no dealings with the females of Ono. That being so, their texts, not surprisingly, contain no reference to fishing nets despite allusions to the very fibre cords from which, traditionally, fishing nets were made. Nor, for that matter, are there references to the Lauan fish trap (*toni kana*) or of stupefying fish.

Together with the comment that he saw numerous little sailing craft, Simonov's remark that Ono Islanders fished "using wooden, bone, and shell hooks" clearly indicates that men did fish at sea using the hook-and-line *siva* technique. Fish-spearing was usually men's work in the Lau Group. Even fishing for certain kinds of fish outside the reef such as bonito using composite shell hooks, was barred to Lauan women. Ono men were expert swimmers, as the Russians emphasize, and were accustomed to inter-island voyages in craft well suited to some types of deep sea fishing. They habitually fished beyond the reef for extra food as well as sport. The Russians make no mention of turtle fishing or indeed of turtle fishermen, though Fio almost certainly had one or more of them in service.[41] On the other hand, the Russians saw assorted ornaments with turtleshell components. In 1820, Fio had authority over Vatoa (Turtle Island), though possibly he recognized a limit to his right even to turtles caught at Ono-i-Lau.[42]

Most of the canoes seen by the Russians at that island cluster were of modest size and build and used for (very local) transport and/or fishing, not for warfare. Indeed, the visitors saw no evidence of seaborne warfare in the area. They did see three basic types of craft in use at Ono: paddling canoes or *waqa vothe*; single sailing craft with sides raised up by planking for a deck and with a solid outrigger, that is, canoes called *thamakau*; and considerably larger double craft, with two unequal hulls, connecting beams, platform, and large mat sails, called *ndrua*.[43] The latter were apparently reserved for the use of chiefs. All three varieties of craft were used beyond the reef, such were the wonder caused by Russian sloops and the determination of the islanders to have prolonged and frequent contact with their visitors.

Both the paddled dug-outs and the small sailing canoes that met *Vostok* carried three or four men only. Sailing craft were heavily outnumbered by the common dug-outs. On the other hand, at least two twin canoes (*ndrua*) were in evidence. At sunrise on the second day of Bellingshausen's visit, seven sailing craft put out towards the strangers, in the midst of thirty smaller paddled craft. Simonov increases Bellingshausen's thirty to three dozen, incidentally suggesting that 200 islanders came out aboard them. Bellingshausen's figures give us slightly less, perhaps 175. Given the likelihood that men from every district of the cluster would, by now, have made their move towards the sloops, it is obvious that population estimates might be advanced—with proper caution—on the basis of those figures.

Fio appears to have sailed on the same *ndrua* more than once while Bellingshausen was at hand. The latter writes particularly about "the royal craft." But Simonov and Novosil'skii agree that even smaller *thamakau* were of no mean size. The craft in question, with their ponderous "reed matting" sails (Simonov) that demanded such attention and which rotted so depressingly when wet,[44] were major articles of ceremonial exchange in former times. Suitable hardwood for building such craft grew well on Ono, though perhaps in smaller stands than on Kambara, to which Tongan chiefs sent many carpenters and workmen by the early 1820s. Simonov's "reed" sails were of the lateen type, made of pandanus strips sewn together with sennit of the sort wrapped round the shaft of the Kazan' Museum's heavy *kiakavo* (see below, "The I.M. Simonov Collection," 150–85). Partly as a consequence of its geography ("the route to Ono is considered the most difficult in Lau"),[45] Ono had traditionally and consistently produced fine navigators. Russian evidence confirms not only the islanders' dexterity and fearlessness in choppy waters, but also their acute sense of direction. Twice at least before the Russians' eyes, Ono-i-Lauan craft capsized beyond the reef, but all such incidents were treated with hilarity. At least one islander thought seriously of embarking with the Russians in *Vostok*, hoping his countrymen would voyage with him.

As the Russian evidence confirms, the Ono Islanders were highly skilled at estimating their position and direction by the stars.[46] One notes with interest, in this connection, that the 1820 Bellingshausen word list offers "three stars of Orion" (*Eolu-Alatolu*) "moon", and "paddle." Fio and his countrymen aboard *Vostok* had clearly sought and named that constellation as they calculated Ono's own position in the dark; once having fixed Ono-i-Lau or, more accurately, Onolevu, they could also make fair estimates for other islands known to them including—necessarily, in view of its political importance in the Lau Group—Lakemba. Lifelong seamen, they had all "noted on which side . . . we were holding course" a little earlier, before the light had gone. Uncertainty about the whereabouts of Onolevu, furthermore, disturbed them greatly. While the island was in sight, they strolled quite calmly on the Russians' quarterdeck and stern. Among the other islands named that night was "Pau," which allegedly lay west of Ono and exceeded it in size. Perhaps a typographic error in the first Russian edition of the Bellingshausen narrative produced this "Pau" from the original form "Bau," where, as Paul' the Tongan certainly knew well, the *vavalagi* had for years been getting sandalwood. More probably, the Russians caught an echo of the rising strength of Mbau off the coast of Viti Levu, and recorded it unwittingly.[47]

Juxtaposition of the themes of pearl-seeking and fishing in the Simonov account seems to indicate that Fio's people sought the pearl mussel, *a civa* or, in Bellingshausen's rendering, *ediba*, from canoes whose length and narrowness impressed the Russians as, in 1903–6, they would impress the British scholar and administrator Basil Thomson. Thomson makes remarks in his study of Fijian social usage, *The Fijians* (1908) which have relevance to Fio's and the Russians' intermediary Paul', within the context of canoe-building and Lauan navigation:

> Occasional intercourse between Tonga and Fiji had taken place for per-haps three or four centuries . . . but it was not until later in the eighteenth century that it became regular. The Tongans steered for Lakemba, where they took part with one or other of the factions that happened to be at war . . . built themselves new war-canoes in Kambara of *vesi*, a timber very scarce in Tonga, and set sail for their own country. But not a few stayed behind, and gradually a little colony of Tongan-speaking half-castes established itself on all the principal windward islands. . . . From 1790 to 1810 it had become the custom for Tongan chiefs to voyage to Fiji in their clumsy *tongiaki*, join in native wars, and take back as their portion of the loot Fijian *ndrua*. . . .[48]

WEAPONRY AND SOCIAL ORDER

## *Lauan Weapons*

The Russians acquired weaponry throughout their stay at Ono. Most Fijian clubs in the impressive MAE Collection (Leningrad), if not all seventeen of them, may be supposed to have been taken to St. Petersburg in 1822 by Bel-lingshausen.[49] On 21 August 1820, it is plain, the Russians took on "pikes, cudgels, and small clubs," as well as *culacula* and at least one *kinikini*. Next morning, the natives again brought out "a quantity of beautifully carved weaponry." Pavel Mikhailov drew some of it aboard the sloop without delay, including two multi-barbed fighting spears, four long *motodua* (barbless "pikes" or javelins), a four-pronged chiefly *saisai*, two Lauan bows (*dakai*) with their arrows (*a gasau*), and, for good measure, assorted *sali*, *gata*, *culacula*, *bulibuli*, *totokia*, and *bowai* clubs.[50] Fio's son Dovili he positioned with a flange-headed or fluted throwing club, *i ula tavatava*, in his hand (Plate 11). It was as varied and intriguing an assortment of Fijian weapons as the Russians could have hoped to find on a single island. Of the common Lauan weapons of that period, indeed, only the *vunikau* and *gugu* clubs and slings were not in evidence on Ono, though the visitors could hardly know it. Well might Bellingshausen comment that, despite his kind reception by the islanders, he had no doubt that they were warlike. In itself, the very quantity of weaponry available for rapid barter made it plain that, as a rule, the Ono

Islanders had weapons. Nor did the fact of their surrendering much weaponry to foreigners, to get what might perhaps never again be so available to them, imply that war was not expected to recur. The situation that the Russians had created by arriving was unique; it would, in retrospect, have been remarkable only had Fio and his countrymen *declined* to give the Russians first-rate weapons in exchange for iron tools, mirrors, and knives.

The Russians were impressed by the considerable care with which the weaponry of Ono had been made and decorated. Manufacture of such weaponry, they recognized, certainly was seen as necessary; but it provided scope for an aesthetic urge as well. It appears that most or all the weapons offered on 21 August were carved; most, moreover, were more elegantly finished than comparable arms seen by the Russians at Tahiti. *Kinikini*, among other things, were decorated with a white colouring substance, likely well-burnt coral lime. Such "painting" made the deeply carved design stand out emphatically, thus indicating to everyone that the possessor of the "broad spade" was a chief or man of status. Bellingshausen was the first to view the Lauan *kinikini* as "the property of chiefs alone . . . perhaps signs of distinction." Simonov, however, more explictly suggests that they had social, ceremonial, and military significance and functions. They were, as he expresses it, the "martial emblems" of a Lauan chief. Like European field marshals' batons, they were weapons only incidentally or in extremes, but they could certainly *be* used in an extremity.[51]

Fio and his elders trusted Bellingshausen's peaceable intent to an extent that seemed remarkable to Simonov. No other South Pacific Islanders had been prepared even to stay aboard *Vostok* all night. Several times, however, Simonov's and other Russians' texts bring William Lockerby's (1808-9) account of the Fijian character to mind. "In peace," wrote Lockerby after his stay with the Fijians, they were "mild and generous towards their friends." In warfare, they were "fearless and savage to the utmost degree."[52] As noted, Bellingshausen found the Lauans frank and friendly but saw evidence of martial inclinations or, at least, of clear fighting capabilities. A number of the men seen off Yanuya Islets had scars or healed wounds, and the quantity of weaponry was obvious. "By the beginning of the nineteenth century," as Fergus Clunie notes, most parts of Fiji were "enmeshed in treacherous plots, intrigues, murders and raids. . . . Heavy clubs, spears, and other weapons accompanied the wary Fijians even on short walks beyond the village."[53] The total absence from the scene of females is readily explained in terms of Lauan expectations that, occasionally and especially when strangers were about, special women would be abducted. Captain Cook had learned at Tonga that the people of "Feise," whom the Russians had, quite properly, identified with Fio's people and Fijians generally, were very "martial."[54]

The abundance of fine weaponry at Ono reinforced the Russians' view that Ono *was* part of "Feise," but it is not emphasized in Russian narratives. This too may be explained by Russian knowledge of the Cook account and the resultant expectation that the natives west of Tonga must be warlike. Whether or not Ono-i-Lau had hereditary weaponmaking specialists (*matai-ni-malumu*) as a special class or family or in the retinue of Fio is unclear from European records of that period. It is plain, in any event, that in the early 1800s chiefs like Fio could command a large and serviceable arsenal of weaponry. What was not made on Ono could be purchased to the north, where "the principal occupation of the men not on the war path was, precisely, the manufacture of . . . implements of war."[55]

For symmetry, aesthetic reasons, or perhaps recalling and reflecting the traditional cross-swords arrangement of the European martial past, Mikhailov gave pride of place in his important study headed "Weaponry of the Inhabitants of Ono Island" (Plate 3a here) to Lauan bows. In fact, as Russian texts themselves confirm, the bow and arrow was by no means then the essential instrument in Lauan warfare. The club, in its assorted forms, was paramount in 1820 as before. Here Bellingshausen's word list is particularly helpful. A number of the words heard and noted refer to Lauan weapon types, such as *eikolo* [*a ikolo*], throwing club; *malum* [*malugu*], curved club, *itakoi* [*dakai*], bow, *ambalemato* [*bale*], barbed spear, plus [*moto*], single-pointed spear. Paul Geraghty comments here (see below, "Linguistic Evidence," 139–46) on the importance of such data notwithstanding basic difficulties of interpreting the Bellingshausen Russian-language narrative. Fully one-quarter of the 1820 word list echoes military life, with its insistence on such articles as spears, clubs, sticks and knives, bows, arrows, and the like. Nor can such words as "scissors," "fire," "bone," "canoe," or "paddle" be divorced from incidental but reasonable military associations. War, in sum, looms large in Bellingshausen's evidence. Since language is the dress of thought, we may suppose that it loomed similarly large in local thought. No doubt the Russians as officers had professional and well-developed interests in weaponry and asked the names of island objects that were brought out to their sloops. But it was obviously Lauans who had brought them and pointed out their features in the first place.

Clubs, then, would appear to have formed the best part of the arsenal of Fio and his people, especially perhaps of Fio and the other chiefs and elders. Of the clubs taken to Russia, many had been in Fio's or other chiefs' hands in 1820. These included, as mentioned, *kinikini* and at least one *totokia* battle hammer. But the spear, too, was common and evidently had been in use recently by Fio's people before the Russians arrived. They do not mention a spear-hurling cord or stick, however, almost certainly because they saw no "pikes" or spears being hurled. Among the spears illustrated by

Mikhailov are a four-pronged *saisai* and a long *sa musumusu* (second from bottom, Plate 5). The latter, with its shaft skilfully pierced and designed to snap on impact, leaving inches of the hardwood tip embedded in its victim, is rare today.[56]

Several weapons feature in Mikhailov's illustration but are missing from the catalogue or *opis'* of the Leningrad museum (MAE); other articles, including bamboo knives and *bale moto*, likewise missing from the Soviet Fijian collection today, are plainly mentioned in the 1820 narratives.[57] A few drawn by Mikhailov at Ono and completed subsequently are identifiable among the weapons held in Leningrad.[58]

Among the "large shells" that the Ono Islanders brought out to barter were *davui*, heavy conches blown, as Bellingshausen puts it well, "in the event of a sudden assembling of the people or as a summons to battle." Bellingshausen could not know that such large shells were also blown in other, peaceful situations, for example at the close of a successful turtle hunt.[59] Since everything Bellingshausen knew about the shells derived from Paul' or other islanders, it is obvious that they themselves had linked such shells with warlike preparations, not with food.

Several *kinikini* were among the large spatular clubs brought to St. Petersburg in 1822, many or all of which are now in MAE's Collection No. 736.[60] That so many specimens of an essentially adopted, non-Fijian sort and shape of club should have been found on Ono underlines the strength of local Tongan influence in 1820. Of the twenty-three such articles examined by the scholar William Churchill during the First World War, not one was thought by the Fijians to have been of local provenance and of Fijian workmanship. They had, in fact, been made by Tongan craftsmen based in Fiji.[61] Russian evidence suggests that *kinikini* were, in 1820 Ono, much in view as chiefs' emblems. As for Fio's readiness to give the Russians finely carved and finished clubs, which possibly had lengthy histories themselves as well as socially significant associations for himself and Ono Islanders in general, it is itself some indication of the *mana* that the "Russian chief" possessed in Lauan sight. If one assumes that at least some of Fio's clubs were new, these comments by the writer A.R. Tippett are illuminating: "Quite apart from techniques, two psychological factors lie behind the production of a finely produced Fijian club. First, there is the honor of producing a work worthy of high praise . . . and second, there is the readiness to give away the finest craftwork to the person of high rank without recompense. . . . For a *koroi* or a *visawaqa* (titled warriors) to handle a club was to charge it with *mana*."[62] Bellingshausen unquestionably was viewed by Fio's people as a man of rank and, since he voyaged in a massive ship with many "platforms," guns, and "pennants," also of exalted military status.

## Firearms and Rockets

The Russians speculated that Fio and his countrymen had never handled European guns nor seen or heard a naval rocket. When they had first boarded *Vostok*, as seen, the Lauans had evinced no nervousness about heavy guns, as Maoris had done some ten weeks earlier in Queen Charlotte Sound; nor did they point at them, gesticulate, or shout out, "pu!" Vatoa Islanders had not been close enough in 1774 to get a good look at the British vessels' armament, nor had they heard a cannon fired. Paul' the Tongan quite likely had heard a European or New England gun but, like the Ono Islanders, was unperturbed by those aboard *Vostok* and *Mirnyi*. "Gun" does not feature on the 1820 word list. All these facts support the Russians' supposition that their hosts, apart from Paul', had never dealt with Europeans. Bellingshausen's Lauan guests aboard *Vostok* were, not surprisingly, alarmed by the dramatic sight and sound of naval rockets. (Were the rockets shooting stars, or little spirits, or the souls of slaughtered men?)[63] By flutttering their fingers by their lips, in their amazement, they produced a sound like *a-u, a-u!*—a traditional Fijian cry put up by the recipients of presentations.[64] Fear outlasted wonder, and the pelasure that the spectacle produced was quickly gone.

Next day, the "Russian chief" presented Fio's elder son, Dovili, with a pistol, demonstrating how the powder and the bullets also offered should be used against an enemy. No doubt the pistol's strictly military significance in local warfare at that time was small. As Joseph Waterhouse observed even in 1886, prestige continued to attach to clubs and killing by the club; and clubs were crucial in the warfare of the area a half a century after the Bellingshausen visit.[65] "Prince" Dovili would in any case quickly have used up his little store of ammunition (if rain had not already spoiled it). What was significant about the pistol was, of course, its effect of strongly reinforcing the recipient's own *mana* on the island. In Lau, as in Fiji generally, *koroi* were not merely warriors, nor mere weapons that had killed numerous men; men and arms alike were, in the words of Tippett, "*mana* repositories and *mana* transmitters."[66] Fio's son gained something very valuable from the chiefly *vavalagi* when the pistol and its strange accoutrements were offered to him publicly. He was affected by the cultural, not by the military, significance inherent in the action. There are even grounds for thinking that the Ono Islanders would have been predisposed to reverence the firearm once Bellingshausen and his men were gone from sight.[67] Unconsciously, as well as consciously, the Russians acted in a way that would have tended to enhance the chief's power.

## Authority

Fio enjoyed, if not absolute, then at least very great authority on Ono. Russian evidence shows that he had access to supplies and weapons and could mobilize many canoes and men whenever he desired. "The nobility in Fiji had peculiarly high social status; so high that it probably resulted from a semi-divine character that was bequeathed to them from ancient times."[68]

Paul, and others at Ono-i-Lau, spoke of Fio as *turaga*, which Simonov interpreted as "ruler." The Fijian word has indeed, as Hocart stresses, several possible interpretations.[69] Even so, there is no question but that "chief" is the essential meaning. Paul' defined his own social and political position with proper reference to Fio, and to him alone. He and the king's sons had been sent, on the Russians' arrival, by the "king." As royal envoy, to employ a Western term, and as the bearer of *tambua*, the opening gift, Paul' fulfilled the duties of the herald (*mata ni vanua*). His behaviour on *Vostok*'s quarter-deck or "platform," when the "king" came out, supports remarks by Wallace Deane to the effect that royal heralds had considerable power as the spokesmen for *turaga*. ("Some *mata ni vanua* had great influence and were always the spokesmen of their chiefs in every important ceremony."[70] Of the ceremony on *Vostok*'s deck with "King Fio," Paul', and other men of rank, it in some ways resembled formal kava ceremonies in the Tongan manner. As on such occasions, the *turaga* sat with Paul' (*mata ni vanua*) on one hand and an honoured elder (*matapule*) on the other. As on such occasions, furthermore, they kept their distance from *kaisi*, common people, and created an *alofi* circle (chiefly retinue). Simonov's use of the term "suite" was particularly apt. Again, a branch of unripe coconuts (*i vono ni vanua*) was formally offered to the *vavalagi* chief. Fio took central place among the *alofi* as of right.

Russian evidence reflects a social system fully capable of dealing with an odd, indeed, unprecedented situation. Bellingshausen himself had of course produced that situation, the parameters of which he understood. One indication of a communal response was the reaction of a Lauan youth whom Bellingshausen had agreed to take along to unknown lands: "he insisted that we take his companions also." Another was the great number of islanders afloat and bartering with Russians simultaneously. Given the language barrier with which the Russians and their hosts had to cope as best they could, the Russian evidence of Lauan social structure is considerably richer than it might have been. Again, Pacific studies benefit from the deliberate and academic attitude towards their work taken by Russian naval officers in Oceania throughout the age of sail.[71]

PAVEL NIKOLAEVICH MIKHAILOV'S LAUAN DRAWINGS

*Mikhailov's Instructions and Approach*

Pavel Nikolaevich Mikhailov (1786–1840), official artist on the Bellings-hausen-Lazarev Antarctic expedition, was the son of a successful actor whose collapse and death reduced his children's opportunities for social or professional advancement. However, strings were pulled, so that at the age of nine Mikhailov was enrolled at the St. Petersburg Academy of Arts, where he remained, under the eye of its director, the grandee A.N. Olenin, until 1807.[72] The Academy was his essential base and spiritual home throughout his life. Among the medals he won at the conclusion of his studies in 1806–7 were two for artists drawing scenery and the facades of buildings.[73] Both award-winning paintings gave promise of the landscapes that afterwards lent great charm to many of his ethnographic studies undertaken as the artist in *Vostok* (1819–21), such as of natives of Brazil and New South Wales.[74] He became a member of the Academy and at the age of twenty-nine made a fine portrait of Count Fedor P. Tolstoi. In 1819 the Academy itself commended him to the attention of the naval ministry as a would-be artist on a voyage round the world. He was appointed to the Southern polar venture and immediately fell within the pale of Navy discipline. Specifically, he was to follow these instructions.

> The draughtsman [*risoval'shchik*] shall make drawings of all noteworthy places visited, and shall likewise portray native peoples and their dress and games. . . . All portfolios of whatever kind, all descriptions, and all sketches, etc. will, at the conclusion of the voyage, be handed to the Divisional Commander, who shall submit them all without exception to the Emperor through the naval minister, on returning to Russia. . . .[75]

Like Stepan Kurliandtsev of *Nadezhda* (1803–6), Emel'ian Korneev of *Otkrytie* (1819–21), and Mikhail Tikhanov of *Kamchatka* (1817–19), all dispatched from the Academy of Arts to Oceania with naval squadrons, Mikhailov was to strive for accurate representation, to avoid embellishment of what he saw, and not to trust to memory.[76] He followed his instructions faithfully, returning to St. Petersburg with several hundred watercolours, pen sketches, pencilled roughs, and other drawings.[77]

Conscious of his supplementary instructions from the Academy of Arts, Mikhailov sketched many of his subjects both full-face and in profile. That was standard Russian practice on an expedition to which Navy and Academies alike contributed. When time was lacking, as at Ono, he deliberately drew or painted one subject full-face, such as Fio, another man in profile, such as Dovili, thereby maximizing ethnographic value. In the proper eighteenth-century tradition, he expended time and energy on the precise depiction of arms and ornaments. But, knowing he would certainly be able to draw Ono Island weapons later (they were stowed aboard *Vostok*), and that he would not see other South Pacific Islanders before returning to Australia, he took great pains over the half-dozen figures that survive.

## The Lauan Studies

Mikhailov was conservative in his use of drawing paper. After all, he could not buy a fresh portfolio at will in Oceania or in Antarctica. Consequently, each page of his original portfolio (now held in the Drawings Division of the State Russian Museum in Leningrad) is used to the full. Only two pages were devoted to the Ono stay, but they contain ten Lauan heads. One page, No. 54 by Mikhailov's 1820 pagination, contains the following five waist-length studies: (1) furthest to the left, "Fio, Chief of Ono Island"; (2) Fio, head only, seen from the left; (3) "Tutenberi," a bearded male facing half-right, with reel-like ear ornament and large shell chest ornament; (4) "Paul'," uncoloured; and (5) "Dovili," a son of Fio, facing right, with a flower over the right ear and *tobe* tresses over the neck. Page No. 55 offers five more Lauan faces, some quite roughly done but others practically completed. One is of another bearded man, Salogo, with red-dyed hair at the back; two others are preliminary sketches of an islander with corn-coloured and reddish hair, facing left. Mikhailov learned the names of all his subjects, and recorded them in pencil which is now extremely faded, either over or beneath his drawings. Mixing Latin and Cyrillic letters, he produced the name forms described above or something very close to them. (Dovili might conceivably be read as Dovli, for example.) The deliberate positioning of Fio's index finger on inverted ornamental triangles on his *kinikini* would suggest that, as the orders and artistic instincts of the artist all required, Bellingshausen's draughtsman had employed his early training as a portraitist. Conversely, it is evident from the entire group of Lauan portraits that Fio and his countrymen had all been drawn in such a way as to facilitate transmission to the European world of basic scientific data: body ornament, physique, hair, artefacts, expression, colouring. Mikhailov's work had, after all, the same significance and function as photography in later times.[78]

## Subsequent Use of Mikhailov's Lauan Studies

On his return to Russian in August 1822, Mikhailov entrusted his original portfolio to Bellingshausen, as required by his orders. As is obvious from Bellingshausen's warm letter of commendation to the naval ministry that very month, the Navy was entirely satisfied with Mikhailov as a naval draughtsman. His work was soon returned to him and, for the next twelve months and more, Mikhailov laboured to complete his "expeditionary portfolio." Eventually, in 1823, he presented a coloured album to the naval ministry, for use in illustrating Bellingshausen's narrative which, as he knew, was almost finished. The album, a set of aquarelles with white lead tincture, would have brought Fio and other Ono Islanders to the attention of the educated public had the Bellingshausen voyage been produced without delay. However, it was not used for seven years.[79] At this point, Mikhailov sent several sketches, possibly all copies of originals (but arguably not), to *Vostok*'s former astronomer, Ivan M. Simonov, on loose sheets.[80] Thirty finished aquarelles, meanwhile, had been handed to another, younger man at the St. Petersburg Academy of Arts, Ivan Pavlovich Fridrits (1803-60), to be lithographed. They were to illustrate the Bellingshausen text and to be published at the state's expense. Fridrits, who had been at the Academy for nine years and had studied under Nikolai Utkin, set to work. The results were barely adequate: much detail and tonal contrast was, unfortunately, lost. But so, more seriously, was the government's benevolence towards the project of producing an account of Bellingshausen's voyage. Like so many other publishing and academic projects of the period (late 1825), Mikhailov's suffered from the anti-autocratic demonstration and attempted coup called the Decembrist Revolution (14 December 1825). Konstantin Petrovich Torson, one of Bellingshausen's own lieutenants in *Vostok*, was implicated in the rising and arrested on the orders of Emperor Nicholas I.[81] Suddenly all plans to publish Bellingshausen's works were put on hold.[82] At last, in 1827, the tsar gave orders for 600 copies to be printed, with a separate and serviceable *Atlas*.[83] Once again, Mikhailov's plates were readied for the press.

On active service on the Danube now, Russia and Turkey being once again at war, Bellingshausen could not check the printer's work or copy-edit it. The editing was done by an officious bureaucrat named Apollon Nikol'skii and, after his dismissal for constant cavalier treatment of submitted texts, by a librarian named Chizhov.[84] Happily for Melanesian studies, only very minor damage was inflicted by Nikol'skii on the Mikhailov-Bellingshausen record of *Vostok*'s and *Mirnyi*'s brief Fijian stay. The *Atlas* appeared, as a supplement to Bellingshausen's long-awaited *Dvukratnye izyskaniia* (*Repeated Explorations in the Southern Icy Ocean . . .*), in August 1831. Besides nineteen maps, it contained some forty-seven studies by Mikhailov. The original portfolio of 1819-21, then held in Admiralty storage, was in due course handed to the State Russian Museum's Drawing Section (*Otdel risunka*), where it is kept (reference R-29001-29308) with a portion of Mikhailov's later work as *Moller*'s artist on her voyage round the world in 1826-29. Some of the finer studies of the *Moller* period date from a stay at

Honolulu (6 December 1827–9 February 1828).[85] *Moller* did not pass through Melanesia. As for the finished album which, as seen, Mikhailov presented on the basis of his earlier portfolio, it was identified by the historian A.I. Andreev in the late 1940s and is now kept at the State Historical Museum in Moscow. It is in good condition. Other "1820" copies, and a few originals, are in the State Historical Museum of the Estonian SSR (Eesti NSV Riikliik Ajaloomuuseum) in Tallin; but the great majority of these are of Alaskan or Kamchatkan subjects.[86]

When, in 1949, the Soviets produced a new edition of the 1831 account of Bellingshausen's voyage, they included an inadequate and sorrily produced collection of Mikhailov's 1820 work. Production standards were considerably higher ten years later when the maritime historian E. Shvede began his work on a revised and annotated third edition. Included in that work were a sketch of Ono-i-Lau from the sea (facing p. 304); "Fio, Chief of Ono Island" and "A Native of Ono Island" (identified by the artist as Dovili, facing p. 305); "Natives of Ono Island" (the figure on the right being identified as Tutenberi); and "Weaponry of the Inhabitants of Ono Island" (also facing p. 384).

Mikhailov was unable to re-establish himslf in the capital on returning to European Russia for the second time in 1829, and spent much energy struggling for a pension from the Crown. He spent his final years in a fellow artist's rooms in St. Petersburg and died of tuberculosis on 12 September 1840. His Lauan sketches are among the earliest by any European and bear witness to his conscientiousness and skill.[87]

THE LINGUISTIC EVIDENCE (by Paul Geraghty, Suva)

*Introductory Remarks*

This is a brief study of the Ono-i-Lau word list which appeared in Bellingshausen's narrative, *Dvukratnye izyskaniia . . . ,* published in St. Petersburg in 1831. The circumstances of its compilation are both clear and obscure. We know that it was drawn up on *Vostok*, just off the island group of Ono, in the space of two days in 1820. But we do not know exactly who compiled it (Bellingshausen writes of "we,)" nor do we know precisely who the Lauan informants were ("the natives"). Moreover, the original manuscript has long been lost. These circumstances make interpretation more difficult. Fortunately, there are linguistic techniques which, when combined with knowledge of the contemporary language of Ono-i-Lau and of other Fijian tongues, will enable us to supply not only the form and meaning of most of the words recorded, but also missing details of the 1820 circumstances of the compilation.[88] In applying these techniques, we assume that the list is accurate and consistent, within limits set by the linguistic and other preconceptions of the Russians. We find this working hypothesis to be, on the whole, well justified.

*Published Word List*

Bellingshausen's Ono word list is reproduced below with its entries numbered, for ease of subsequence reference, with Ono words italicized and with original glosses translated into English.[89]

| | | |
|---|---|---|
| 1 | *kavai* | kind of potato |
| 2 | *puaka* | hog |
| 3 | *seli* | small knife |
| 4 | *ambu* | coconut |
| 5 | *koli* | dog |
| 6 | *maluk* | weapon resembling the rifle's butt end |
| 7 | *eikolo* | bone, ivory |
| 8 | *leru* | finger-ring, armring |
| 9 | *atoku* | hairpins |
| 10 | *sakiun* | pay, reimburse |
| 11 | *saitazh* | scissors |
| 12 | *tariga* | ear |
| 13 | *kummi* | beard |
| 14 | *falua* | land |
| 15 | *kanikin malum* | spade, weapon |
| 16 | *glandzhi* | sticks, batons |
| 17 | *malum* | weapon |
| 18 | *ambale-malo malum* | spear |
| 19 | *maida malum* | club variety |
| 20 | *eivodi* | paddle |
| 21 | *sun-siup* | bent club |
| 22 | *amasi* | material |
| 23 | *e-amba* | bast mats |
| 24 | *itakoi* | bow (weapon) |
| 25 | *manau* | arrow |
| 26 | *buli-gon-go* | "porcelain" shells |
| 27 | *ediba* | pearl mussel |
| 28 | *vallo-a* | braid or lace of woven hairs |
| 29 | *avango* | vessel, canoe |
| 30 | *vakko* | nail (iron) |
| 31 | *a-rfeno* | yellow paint |
| 32 | *a-spoa* | cock (bird) |

| | |
|---|---|
| 33 *mona* | hen |
| 34 *eolu-alatolu* | three stars of Orion's Belt |
| 35 *eolu-Vullo* | moon |
| 36 *minako* | good, well |
| 37 *alinsangu* | hand, arm |
| 38 *induti* | finger |
| 39 *autu* | nose |
| 40 *nrako* | mouth |
| 41 *ambachi* | teeth |
| 42 *aianri* | brow |
| 43 *amata* | eye |
| 44 *ame* | tongue |
| 45 *aulu* | hair |
| 46 *akokupo* | fingernail |
| 47 *beri* | foot, leg |
| 48 *andaku* | spine, back |
| 49 *ambuka* | fire |

## Interpretation of the List and of Ono-i-Lauan Sounds

Bellingshausen's account of drawing up this word list suggests that the words spoken by men of Ono, in the Ono language, were recorded by five native speakers of Russian who employed Russian morphology and Russian semantics. An examination will follow here of how Russian speakers might be expected to have interpreted Ono-i-Lauan phonology and semantics. More than half the entries are derivable from Ono words as predicted. Ways will then be suggested to account for the majority of the remaining entries.

Unless a compiler of words is a language expert, such as Cook's Anderson, he will segment and transcribe sounds heard according to the phonetics of his native tongue, and not haphazardly. We do not know precisely how the two languages in question here were pronounced in 1820; we assume that they were pronounced much as they are now.[90] We also ignore the fact that Bellingshausen spoke German in infancy since, first, he spoke excellent Russian and, second, he was not the sole compiler of the list. (The most diligent collectors most likely were Ivan M. Simonov and his assistants from among the two sloops' lieutenants.)

Most sounds in the Ono language have direct phonetic equivalents in Russian: *p, t, j[tʃ], r, k, b[mb], d[nd], z[ndz], dr[ndr], q[ng], f, s, m, n, l.* The three remaining consonants—*v, co,* and *gn*—do not occur in Russian and so might be transcribed as any phonetically similar Russian sound that occurs in the same environment. The qualifier is important, as word-final high vowels (*i* and *u*) in Fijian are often devoiced after non-prenasalized stops before word-final high vowels and may be perceived as being word-final. To a Russian, voiced obstruents before a voiceless vowel would be perceived as voiceless. The Fijian glides *w* and *v* have no phonetic equivalents in Russian. Given that Fijian *y* is frequently more mid than high, possible transcriptions would be: Russian phoneme *v*, *u* for Fijian *w*, and Russian phonemen *i*, *ie* for *y*.

## Russian Interpretation of Ono Meanings

The non-linguist will classify meanings as well as sounds in the way to which he is accustomed. And since semantic categories in Russian and Ono Fijian do not always coincide, it is to be expected that—even though the Russians and islanders had the same object or action in view—the meaning of the word given may be more or less specific than the meaning inferred. This discrepancy need not necessarily be due to first-language influence; for instance, the enquirer may point to a man, hoping to elicit the word for *man*, and be given the man's name—but clearly it often is a result of such influence. An example is (4) on Bellingshausen's list. A Russian speaker had recorded the Ono word for what, in his language, was simply a *coconut*. In Russian, as in English, the term was an indivisible semantic category. In Fijian, however, there are many variety and growth stage names; it happened that the one under enquiry was *a bu*—one at the stage when it was filled with sweet liquid. Assuming that Ono words were interpreted in August 1820 in accordance with Russian phonology and semantics, we arrive at the following initial hypotheses:

| Entry number | Ono word | Meaning |
|:---:|:---|:---|
| 1 | *kawai* | kind of yam, similar in shape and taste to a potato |
| 2 | *puaka* | pig |
| 3 | *isele* | knife[91] |
| 4 | *a bu* | immature coconut, suitable for drinking |
| 5 | *koli* | dog |
| 6 | *malugu* | kind of curved club |
| 8 | *leru* | trochus shell |
| 13 | *kumi* | beard |
| 17 | *malugu* | kind of curved club |
| 20 | *a ivoce* | paddle |
| 22 | *a masi* | bark cloth |
| 23 | *yaba* | mat |

| 27 | *a civa* | pearl mussel |
| 28 | *waloa* | cord stained black |
| 29 | *a waqa* | boat, vessel |
| 30 | *ivako* | peg, nail |
| 36 | *vinaka* | good or well |
| 38 | *iduci* | index finger |
| 39 | *a ucu* | nose |
| 40 | *draka* | mouth |
| 41 | *a baji* | teeth |
| 42 | *a yadre* | forehead |
| 43 | *a mata* | eye, face |
| 44 | *yame* | tongue |
| 45 | *a ulu* | head, hair |
| 48 | *a daku* | back |
| 49 | *a buka* | firewood |

## Extending the Hypothesis: Misreadings

In the absence of Bellingshausen's original manuscript, we are dependent upon the first published version of his word list. One problem with any such version of a word list is, of course, that misreadings are likely to have occurred—more likely, moreover, than in narrative passages, where editors and typesetters alike may use their knowledge of the language to resolve troublesome ambiguities in cursive script. A clear indication of this problem may be seen in the Russian text preceding the Ono word list, where the name of a larger island WNW is given as *Laketo*, whereas the reference was obviously to *Lakeba* (*Lakemba*). We might expect the Russians to have written Lakemba or Lakembo, but for reasons discussed below, what they probably heard was "Lakepa," which was subsequently misread in St. Petersburg and printed as Laketo. The following five entries in the 1820 word-list are all readily explicable as simple misreadings:

| Entry number | 1831 form | Misreading for |
|:---:|:---|:---|
| 9 | *atoku* | ataku (*a taku*, turtle shell) |
| 16 | *glandzhi* | mandzhi (*gazi*, truncheon-like club) |
| 31 | *a-rfeno* | a-ryeryeno (*a rerega*, turmeric) |
| 32 | *a-spoa* | a-toa (*a toa*, fowl) |
| 37 | *alinsangu* | alimangu (*a ligaqu*, my hand) |

The Russians, then, heard not *Lakeba* but *Lakepa*, and recorded what they heard. Similarly, the even larger island to their west was apparently not heard as *Bau*, but as *Pau*. The 1831 narrative explains these discrepancies: the informant off the Yanuya Islets was no Fijian but Paul' the Tongan. As a Tongan speaker, Paul' probably would not have distinguished between plain and prenasalized obstruent pairs such as Fijian *p* and *b*, pronouncing both as *p*. He would also, we think, have pronounced both *t* and *d* as *t*, and moreover have pronounced *l* intervocalically as a sound more closely resembling *r*. If we amend the working hypothesis here to allow for the fact that some Ono words in the Russians' list were provided by a Tongan or Tongans resident there, the following three additional entries are explained:

| | | | |
|---|---|---|---|
| 12 | Tariga (ear) | Tonganized: *tariga* | Ono: *daliga* |
| 14 | Falua (land) | Tonganized: *fanua* | Ono: *vanua* |
| 24 | Itakoi (bow) | Tonganized: *takai* | Ono: *dakai* |

In addition, entry no 34, *eolu-alatolu*, contains an unmistakably Tongan element: *alatolu* is Tongan for the three stars of Orion's Belt, of which Polynesian navigators traditionally made much use on long-range voyages.

*Discussion of Remaining Problems*

The remaining entries in the 1820 word list are problematic, and are considered, very briefly, below.

7   *Eikolo* (bone, ivory). The form is derivable perfectly from Fijian *a ikolo*, throwing club; some such clubs had ivory inlay. The word thus may have been offered in response to the Russians' having pointed at such inlaid work on an artefact.

10  *Sakiun* (pay, reimburse). The Ono word for "to pay" is *sauma*. Possible *sauma* was recorded and became illegible; alternatively, see below here under 47.

11  *Saitazh* (scissors). The modern Ono word, *ijoji*, is entirely different from this form, and no Ono sound could properly be transcribed by *zh*. Again, see 47 below.

18  *Ambale-mato malum* (spear). All three elements here are weapon names: *bale* (barbed spear), *moto* (single-pointed spear), and *malugu* (curved club). The Russian enquirer would appear to have pointed at a particular item in a collection of local weaponry and elicited the names of those weapons closest to him or most prominent.

19  *Maida malum* (club variety). Perhaps Fijian: *maii da malugu*, that is, "that is a *malugu*."

21  *Sun-siup* (bent club). This description may apply to the curved mace

with a spiked head and beak known, in Bauan, as *totokia*. The old Ono name for the weapon is unknown. This was conceivably a drastic misreading in St. Petersburg of a manuscript rendering of *sokisoki*, the porcupine fish (*Diodon sp.*), which is a plausible name for the *totokia*. The entry is a most difficult one.

25 *Manau* (arrow). Probably derived from *gasau*, meaning arrow, for which *masau* might have been expected. The problem is how a Russian came to mishear or, more likely, misread *c* (the form of the Cyrillic 's') as *n*. If a misreading, the cause might have lain in the writer's spacing of Cyrillic "a" and "n."

26 *Buli-gon-go* ("porcelain" shells). Probably *buli qaqua*, "white cowry, *Ovula ovum*." There appears to be no record of this term in use on Ono, but it was recorded by Neyret (1935) from an unstated location in eastern Fiji. This particular shell was used in the decoration of chiefly houses, canoes, bowls, and so forth, and is attached to the *ikolo* throwing club. The transcription is a little odd: *bulingangau* would be expected, but see no. 46 below.

33 *Mona* (hen). This was possibly a rendering of the Tongan *moa*, with an interfering *n*. It may alternatively have arisen from a misunderstanding which itself derived from differences in semantic categorization. Fijian languages have a single term for the fowl *Gallus gallus* (in Ono, *toa*), whereas English and Russian have terms for male and female birds. The first specimen the Russians pointed to was perhaps a cock, for which the term *toa* was accepted (entry no. 32). Expecting the term for the female bird to differ, they then pointed at a hen, and would not accept the word *toa*. They then perhaps pointed to the distinguishing features, including the much less prominent crest; and the Lauans may have offered the word for "brain," *mona*, which was duly accepted and recorded.

34 *Eolu-Alatolu* (three stars of Orion). *Alatolu* is Tongan for the three stars in question; *vullo*, in entry no. 35, is a predictable and easily explained transcription of Ono *vula*, meaning the moon. *Eolu*, however, remains enigmatic.

46 *Akokupo* (fingernail). The modern Ono word for finger- and toenail is *taukuku*, but older people are said to have used the term *kukutau*. The misreading of Cyrillic *o* for *u* is *not* an expected one; neither can *o* be predicted for *au*. Since this occurs also in no. 26, however, possibly *au* was perceived as *o* in some environments (perhaps when not carrying full stress: see no. 25).

47 *Beri* (leg, foot). *Beri* is an expected Cyrillic transcription of *bere*, which is a northeast Vanualevu word for a footprint. Ono is said to have been settled from Loa, close to the northeast Vanualevu language area, and does share a few words with Vanualevu rather than Lau; so it is possible

that *bere* is an old Ono word. If so, either its meaning had altered to "leg
or foot," or the islanders saw the finger as pointing to a wet footprint on
*Vostok*'s deck, rather than to a human foot.

CONCLUSION

As a record of the language of Ono in the early 1800s, the Bellingshausen
word list tends to confirm the impression gained by reading the linguistic
works of Christian missionaries in Lakemba fifteen or twenty years later:
that, despite the massive cultural changes of the last 150 years, the languages
of Lau have been remarkably stable, with only slight tendencies to replace
Lauan with Standard Fijian vocabulary, as witnessed, in the Russian word
list, by nos. 10 (*iselekoji*, "scissors"; now *ikoji*), and 46 *kukutau* ("finger,"
"toe"; now *taukuku*).

The great majority of the words recorded in 1820 were Ono words.
Some, however, were plainly Tongan or, at least, were Tonganized Fijian.
Here the linguistic evidence stands with the 1820 evidence of physical traits
to emphasize the *heavy* influence of Polynesian settlers in southern Lau.

# 7

# THE ARTEFACTS FROM ONO IN KAZAN' AND LENINGRAD

GENERAL REMARKS

Artefacts from Ono-i-Lau are among those held in the Fijian sub-collections of the I.M. Simonov Collection at Kazan' State University Main Library, Kazan',[1] and the Peter-the-Great Museum of Ethnography (now MAE) of the Academy of Sciences of the USSR, in Leningrad. The latter has evolved from, and still uses, the ancient halls and artefact collections of the eighteenth-century *Kunst-Kammer* [Russian: *Kunstkamera* of the Academy of Sciences]. Both institutions also hold Fijian artefacts of other provenance, acquired earlier or later. It is basically with the Kazan' and Leningrad "pre-1828" collections that this section is concerned, that is, with articles brought to St. Petersburg in Russian naval vessels in the early nineteenth century. Those are, at MAE, Collections No. 736 and 737, and in Kazan', Collection 160. The Fijian artefacts in MAE Collection No. 737 are officially described in the museum inventories as having been transferred to the Academy of Sciences' old "cabinet of curiosities" (*Kunstkamera*) from the Admiralty's own museum, in the year 1809.[2] There are reasons for believing they had actually been acquired in the year 1782, together with some three dozen Tahitian and Hawaiian objects, from an individual connected with James Cook, possibly Johann Reinhold Forster, the splenetic German naturalist.[3] All three articles—fine specimens of barkcloth—had apparently, therefore, been in St. Petersburg a quarter century before the *Kunstkamera* acquired them; nor, even then, were they displayed in public view. None was of Lauan manufacture. Lauan artefacts in MAE's Collection No. 736 and in Kazan's Collection No. 160, on the other hand, were indisputably brought back from Ono by the Bellingshausen-Lazarev Antarctic expedition. And the texts here translated make it possible to venture where and when specific objects were acquired. More than that, narrative evidence permits us to propose in just what circumstances, and/or in exchange for what imported goods, specific objects were obtained. Taken together, the Kazan' and Leningrad collections form the largest and perhaps the most significant assemblage of artefacts from early Ono in the world. Some of those artefacts have major scientific interest. The evidence of artefact and written records are not only mutually complementary, but also reinforce each other's ethnographic strength while compensating for their weaknesses, such as the want of crudely made and common articles in daily use in 1820.

COLLECTING PROCESS

For all its shortage of specifically non-naval scientific expertise, the Bellingshausen expedition was in general far better placed than any venture led by Captain Cook had been to form collections of Pacific Island artefacts in situ. In the first place, Bellingshausen and his officers were highly conscious of, and interested in, the peoples of the South Pacific Ocean and had read about them widely, as the pioneers, Cook's people, had not. To judge by Bellingshausen's version of that section of the Cook-King *Voyage* (London 1784) in which islanders from Fiji were alluded to, he had perused the rather less than literal translation of that work made by his subsequent professional supporter in the Russian Naval Staff, Loggin I. Golenishchev-Kutuzov.[4] He was certainly acquainted with the works of George and Johann Reinhold Forster, who had both sailed with Cook to Melanesia. In the second place, sufficient time had passed by 1820 for the Rousseauesque approach to "savage peoples" to have vanished among members of the Russian fleet at least, if not among the educated Russian public. Bellingshausen, for his own part, insisted that the Russian Crown's approach towards such peoples should at all times be benevolent but also commonsensical: "On despatching this expedition, His Imperial Majesty had in mind the widening of our knowledge of the terrestrial globe and the acquainting of native peoples with us Europeans and vice versa."[5] His behaviour while at Ono was as rational as it was soberly inquisitive, but here, too, he was considerably better placed than Cook or Bougainville had been, for he was late upon the scene and so had precedents to follow where relations with the South Pacific peoples and the gathering of "curios" and "native products" were concerned. Cook had arrived in Oceania with "Toys, Beeds, and glass Buttons" to barter for provisions and, if any were left over, "curiosities."[6] *Vostok* and *Mirnyi* carried quantities of trinkets and their officers set out intending to exchange some, if not all, of them for native artefacts. Again, "the use of professional artists, adopted by Banks and Cook on the *Endeavour*, had become standard practice. . . . Now, the nascent science of ethnography made extensive use of draughtsmen to assist in the description of material."[7] The Russians came to Ono pre-disposed and well equipped to barter:

> In order to induce the natives to treat us amicably and to allow us to obtain from them, through barter, fresh supplies and various handmade articles, we were furnished at St. Petersburg with such things as were calculated to please peoples still in an almost primitive state, viz.:

| | | |
|---|---:|---|
| Knives, miscellaneous | 400 | |
| Knives, garden size | 20 | |
| Saws, one-man | 10 | |
| Saws, cross- | 10 | |
| Chisels | 30 | |
| Gimlets | 125 | |
| Rasps & files | 100 | |
| Axes | 100 | |
| Scissors | 50 | |
| Flints, steel | 300 | |
| Small bells & whistles | 185 | |
| Fringes, mixed shades | 60 | *arshin* |
| Striped ticking | 100 | *arshin* |
| Tumblers | 120 | |
| Wire, copper | 100 | lbs. |
| Wire, iron | 80 | lbs. |
| Horn combs | 250 | |
| Needles, various | 5000 | |
| Rings | 250 | |
| Garnets | 5 | strings |
| Beads, small & large | 20 | strings |
| Wax candles | 1000 | |
| Mirrors, various | 1000 | |
| Red flanelette | 218 | *arshin* |
| Kaleidoscopes | 24 | |
| Vegetable & fruit seed | 100 | lbs. |

> etc., etc.[8]

*Vostok*'s astronomer, Ivan M. Simonov, played an important role in the collection of Fijian artefacts in 1820, as is evident both from his narrative and from the artefacts now in Kazan'. Numerous members of the two sloops' companies, however, plainly bartered for such artefacts; and few of those would have been equally aware of the importance of acquiring objects that were broadly representative of local culture.[9] Fio's people, on the other

hand, failed to offer certain workaday utensils and materials of poorer manufacture to their unexpected guests, whose ship might leave at any time.

On returning to St. Petersburg in August 1821, the members of the Bellingshausen-Lazarev Antarctic expedition were specifically required to submit all
native artefacts in their possession, or collected by them, to the Russian
government. The matter had been dealt in the fifteenth section of the third
set of instructions sent to Bellingshausen (June 1819): "All collections of
objects of every kind . . . shall, at the conclusion of the voyage, be entrusted
to the Divisional Commander, who shall present them all, without exception, to His Majesty the Emperor through the naval minister."[10] It is unlikely
that these explicit orders were deliberately flouted, but unlikley also that the
South Pacific artefacts passed "without exception" from the two ships' companies into official hands. Moreover, artefacts may well have been discarded
while the sloops were at sea in 1820, as Hawaiian artefacts had been discarded as a nuisance by the crew of *Neva* in 1804.[11] Clearly, artefacts were
brought from South Pacific Islands by *Vostok* or *Mirnyi* which were never in
the Admiralty Department Museum in St. Petersburg, and Lauan artefacts
may well have been among them. As for Simonov, we must suppose that—in
his circumstances at the expedition's close—he did in fact part, for a while,
with the South Pacific artefacts he had acquired. At the time, he had an
academic and professional career yet to make and was, to that extent, unable
to antagonize imperial authority.[12] Probably he had in any case no serious
objection to the naval ministry's retaining his collection, almost certainly on
a temporary basis. Thirty-seven South Pacific artefacts, most of them duplicates of others that were staying in St. Petersburg, were duly handed back to
him; by 1822 they had been sent, boxed up with books and precious scientific instruments likewise intended for his use at the provincial university
recently founded in Kazan', by heavy ox-cart heading slowly via Moscow,
for his youthful alma mater.[13] They were there and awaiting his attention
when, in 1824, he returned from study leave in France and Austria.[14] From
those thirty-seven objects grew Kazan' State University's Museum of Ethnography of modern times, "a major academic and research institution with
valuable collections, in total more than 5,000 objects, from peoples in all
parts of the world."[15] Since their accession in Kazan', seven articles in the
original assemblage have been lost: Collection No. 160 accordingly now
consists of thirty items.

Scientifically, it remains a precious one, as one of the earliest such collections from Oceania. . . . It has certainly great value for study of a Pacific

Island culture not yet destroyed by colonialism, and presents interest in a second respect. Many of its constituent artefacts have parallels, that is, analogous pieces, in the oldest collections of the Museum of Anthropology and Ethnography in Leningrad, also from Oceania in the first quarter of the nineteenth century. The fact opens up various possibilities for comparative study.[16]

Soviet interest in the Simonov Collection at Kazan', as in the South Pacific artefacts at MAE in Leningrad brought by *Vostok* and *Mirnyi* (1821), increased dramatically in 1948 and in the context of political arrangements for Antarctica. Such claims as Moscow might pretend to have to any say over the future jurisdiction or indeed the exploitation of Antarctica were, after all, wholly dependent on the Bellingshausen sightings of that continent and, in a broader sense, on Bellingshausen's Southern work of 1820–21. Suddenly, Soviet officialdom and the Academy of Sciences grew keenly interested in those primary materials—accounts, reports, and letters, charts and specimens of any sort—that had arrived aboard *Vostok* and *Mirnyi* and had for decades lain untouched in dusty drawers. At Kazan' State University, attention was immediately given to the Simonov Collection and unpublished narrative (MS 4533) headed, "The Sloops 'Vostok' and 'Mirnyi,' or, A Voyage by Russians in the Southern Icy Ocean and Around the World."[17] Urged on by fear, in those last years of Stalin's reign, numerous leading academics and assorted printing houses did their utmost to support the State position on Antarctica. Even in 1949 much primary material was offered to the public—and the Western world—which bore on real and alleged Russian discoveries and triumphs in Antarctica in 1821. This included eyewitness accounts by officers and men aboard *Vostok* and *Mirnyi*,[18] and a Soviet edition of the Bellingshausen narrative of 1831. In a preface to a second compilation of such narratives printed in Moscow in 1951, *Russkie otkrytiia v Antarktike v 1819, 1820, i 1821 godakh* (*Russian Discoveries in Antarctica in the Years 1819-21*), the historian A.I. Solov'ev spelled out the need for such activity:

Resting on their historic right and struggling against all effforts by aggressors and instigators of a new war to turn Antarctica into a base for airborne operations, the Soviet peoples cannot regard with indifference the imperialists' attempts to resolve questions regarding Antarctica without their own participation. . . . On 7 June 1950, the Government of the USSR sent to the Governments of the USA, Great Britain, France, Norway, Australia, Argentina and New Zealand a memorandum concerning the form of government of Antarctica. . . . The text . . . drew attention to a resolution of the General Assembly of the Geographical

Society of the USSR of 10 February 1949, in which the Society stressed the extreme significance of discoveries made by Russian mariners in Antarctica. . . .[19]

Rejecting Western claims to any "slice" of the Antarctic pie, Kazan'-based scholars soon produced their own (first) contribution to the "struggle": N.I. Vorob'ev, E.P. Busygin, and G.V. Iusupov, all of Kazan's Faculty of Physical Geography, produced a paper for the Geographical Society in Leningrad entitled, "The Ethnographic Observations of I.M. Simonov on the Islands of the Pacific Ocean."[20] It not only offered prints of certain artefacts in Simonov's Collection and, indeed, of the complete glass cabinet containing most of it, as it appeared at that time;[21] it also commented on Lauan articles and, on the basis of the printed *Word Regarding the Successes of the Voyage of the Sloops "Vostok" and "Mirnyi"* (1822),[22] on Simonov's ethnography in Lau. In particular, notice was drawn to his awareness of fishing methods and equipment, to the barkcloth specimens held at Kazan', and to "the special marks of dignity" associated with Pacific Island chiefs, including Fio, in the early 1800s. Incidentally, we learn that one such "mark of dignity" at least, a *kinikini* now numbered 160–17, which Simonov had doubtless bought from Fio or his sons the year before, was in 1821 of special interest to Mikhail Magnitskii (1778–1844) in his capacity as minister of church affairs and public education. Magnitskii, an extreme reactionary who was to recommend closure of the youthful university he was inspecting, wrote a special memorandum on the meaning of such artefacts, indeed.[23] He wished to use Simonov's papers and such artefacts as "the insignia of chiefs" to prove that peoples everywhere approved the principles and practice of autocracy. The Lauan *kinikini* was particularly drawn to the attention of Magnitskii's local tool, named Gorodchaninov, who wrote an arch-reactionary article, "Regarding Natural Autocracy Among the Savages." "Thus," write the Soviet ethnographers indignantly, "would representatives of the autocracy in Russia seize at any possibility of pointing to the 'natural' origins of power held by those supporting serfdom."[24] Simonov's fine *kinikini* was among the first Fijian artefacts to be efficiently described by Russian scholars: it was studied and described by B.F. Adler in 1916.[25] Vorob'ev's and his colleagues' own paper of 1949 was followed, barely nine months later, by Ivan N. Aleksandrov's article, "Professor I.M. Simonov, Participant in F.F. Bellingshausen's Expedition to Antarctica" (Kazan' 1950).[26] Thus, unpredictably, have politics been useful to ethnography and in particular to South Pacific studies.

Building on their predecessors' work, two younger Soviet ethnographers, V.R. Kabo and N.M. Bondarev, looked at the Simonov Collection with a fresh critical eye from 1972 to 1974. The resultant description, "I.M. Simonov's Collection from Oceania," appeared in Leningrad in 1974.[27] The following is based on that description:

1 (Kazan' 160–15)   Pearl-oyster shell, with edges slightly toothed; one edge now broken. There are two small, round apertures in the shell's upper half, which was clearly used as an ornament. From Ono Island.

2 (Kazan' 160–17)   Chief's staff made of hard, heavy wood, paddle-shaped. The blade is covered on both sides with carved rectangles and diamonds. The patterns are placed asymmetrically round the two principal intersecting lines, which stand out in relief. Both faces are also ornamented with half-moons which, on one half of the paddle's suface, are placed symmetrically to each other. On the other half, a half-moon is balanced by a diamond. The principal lines, standing out in relief, divide the blade's surface into two equal pairs. The shorter line passes through the protruding side edges of the staff, one of which is broken off. Dimensions: length 61 cm, width 18–28 cm. The handle is oval in cross-section, polished smooth, with a slight thickening at the end. Where blade meets handle, there is rattan lashing (ten lashings around). There are two further rattan "rings" at the handle's lower end; the handle is 53 cm long and 5 cm in diameter. The overall dimensions are: length 115 cm, breadth 28 cm. From Ono Island.

    A very similar staff is illustrated by P.N. Mikhailov, Ship's Artist with the Bellingshausen-Lazarev expedition. It is held in the hand of Fio, chief of Ono Island. Another such staff is represented in another of Mikhailov's drawings, among various examples of Fijian hunting and ceremonial objects and weapons. I. Simonov writes of Fio himself in his memoirs. Such staffs or paddles served as the insignia of chiefs in Fiji (see B.F. Adler, "A Mark of Distinction from Ono Island," in *Izvestiia Obshchestva Arkheologii, Istorii, i Etnografii*, Vol. 29, Kazan' 1916: 253–59).

    Analogous staffs are held in one of the oldest collections at the Miklukho-Maklai Institue's

Museum of Ethnography, as Nos. 736–14, 736–15, 736–16, 736–17, 736–18, and 736–19. They differ only in their ornamentation. Evidently the embellishment of each staff was distinctive and was intended by the carver to be so, though certain elements of the ornamental pattern are recurrent.

3 (Kazan' 160–19) Staff club made of dark yellow wood. A single piece of timber was used. Surfaces are smoothly polished. One end is butt-like and reminiscent of an ancient musket. This split part is covered with ornamental dots, which give way to notches lower down the spur. The dots comprise diamonds and rectangles or, sometimes, merely zigzagging lines. Five rattan lashings are spaced out over the staff. The end opposite the butt-like division thickens out a little. Length overall: 96 cm; length of handle covered with decorative dots, 21 cm. Clearly from Ono, since an object just like it is depicted in one of P.N. Mikhailov's illustrations. MAE has other staffs like it: Nos. 736–11–13 and 736–22–30.

4 (Kazan' 160–11) Wooden comb, consisting of 20 separate, sharpened teeth. The upper, narrow part has been tightly bound with yellow and black threads. which alternate, made from vegetable fibres. The comb widens toward the other end. Length 10.5 cm; width 3–5 cm. Analogous combs from New Caledonia are held in one of MAE's oldest collections, and were gathered on Captian Cook's last expedition (Nos. 505–22–23).

5 (Kazan' 160–20) Staff club, made of dark yellow wood; round in cross-section and well polished. Upper end bound, 6 cm from the end, with threads of vegetable fibres, light and dark brown, glued down. Overall length 120 cm; diameter 4.5 cm; this object and 160–19 were evidently chiefs' insignia.

6 (Kazan' 160–22) Bamboo stick, 61 cm in length, 1.5 cm in diameter. The whole surface is covered with a carved geometrical ornament, which is finely done. Both ends have been slightly sharpened.

7 (Kazan' 160–23) Bamboo stick, 50.5 cm in length, 2.2 cm diameter; one end has been sharpened, ornamented with carving, and separated from the remaining length

of the stick by a twine binding resembling a ring. This itself is wrapped around, externally, with red thread.

8 (Kazan' 160–24) Spear, of heavy and very dark wood. The haft is in two sections, glued together. The length of the tip is 21 cm. There are 14 rows of thorns, carved from the same piece of wood as the upper haft. Each row has 5 teeth, steadily diminishing in size towards the tip. The length of the haft's upper part is 143 cm, and of the lower—118 cm. The overall length of the spear is thus 261 cm; maximum diameter 3.2 cm, minimum—1.2 cm.

9 (Kazan' 160–25) Spear, light in weight, dark in colour; consists of two sections glued together. At the upper end are 5 rows of thorns, carved from the same timber as the haft. Each row has 8 teeth; 4 are broken in the first row, one in the second row. Length of the haft part with thorns—62 cm. Lengths of the haft's upper and lower parts: 143 & 107 cm; overall length of the spear 250 cm. Maximum diameter 3 cm. A spear like this, and like 160-24, may be seen in P.N. Mikhailov's illustration of Ono Islanders' weaponry.

10 (Kazan' 160–35) *Masi*; rectangular piece, light brown in tone; 230 by 225 cm. At both ends there is bordering, 44.5 cm. wide, showing a complex ornament of geometrical patterns (triangles, parallel stripes, crosses), of white, black, and brown colours. Fairly soft and fine stuff.[28]

## LAUAN ARTEFACTS IN LENINGRAD AND THEIR SIGNIFICANCE

Perhaps two dozen Lauan articles, gathered at Ono, are today in the Peter-the-Great Museum of Anthropology and Ethnography in Leningrad. The twenty-one acknowledged items are, without exception, clubs. They are described below in Appendix A. There are, besides, assorted ornaments and spears, some of which may well be Lauan, though the Soviets describe them carefully as "Melanesian; provenance unknown,"[29] The ethnographic value of this Leningrad collection is considerably heightened by the presence, in Kazan', of complementary material from Lau. Of those artefacts, as of the Maori artefacts at MAE and in the same collection (No. 736), one can say with confidence that provenance is certain.[30]

The St. Petersburg Academy of Sciences' Fijian artefacts provoked no

academic interest during the nineteenth century, though they were certainly
examined, from the 1880s onward, by a growing stream of visitors. The mere
existence of that basically unrepresentative imperial collection, on the other
hand, encouraged Russians with the necessary means to make donations—
both of money and of artefacts—and to enhance it. One such Russian, who
was perfectly familiar with its Fijian section, was the eminent ethnologist
and anthropologist N.N. Miklukho-Maklai (1846–88). Another, of the
younger generation, was the most successful travelling collector to leave
Russia for the South Pacific Ocean in the first years of this century, V.V.
Sviatlóvskii (1871–1927).[31] Both, aware of the weaknesses of the St. Petersburg Fijian store of artefacts, presented objects, not from Ono, certainly,
but calculated to redress the main imbalance in that store as it existed in
their period. Miklukho-Maklai's Fijian offerings were registered by the
Director of the *Kunstkamera* in 1886 and now form part of MAE's Collection No. 168.[32] Sviatlovskii's, collected in the course of an exhausting South
Pacific tour, reached St. Petersburg in 1907–8.[33] It was in Honolulu, on 3–5
February 1908, that he completed plans to visit Suva and obtain such local
items as he could.

Parts of his correspondence with Vladimir V. Radlov, then Director at the
Museum, now MAE, were published in 1974 and throw interesting light
both on the Suva trade in local curiosities as it had grown by 1908 and on
Sviatlovskii's own relations with Sir E. Imthurm, then Governor of Fiji.[34]
Those relations were particularly civil, and as a result the Russian gained
permission "for objects representative of the Fijian life-style to be sent to the
St. Petersburg Museum for the cost of transport only, lest they all need to be
dragged off back to Suva."[35] Fifteen artefacts from Fiji went by steamer to
St. Petersburg. They included wooden vessels, *masi* (barkcloth) specimens,
ceramic ware, and a whale-tooth *tambua*.[36] The three fine specimens of
single-layered, fringed white *masi* were described by L.G. Rozina, also in
1974.[37] Today, 1908 acquisitions are in three MAE collections: Nos. 1198,
1352, and 1432[38] and illustrate precisely those activities and areas of culture—ritual and games, fishing and cooking—which, for reasons given earlier, the 1820 visitors could *not* examine. Thus did emphases within the 1820
artefact collections find an echo in the serious collecting of the early 1900s.
Nor have echoes died away even today: Soviet visitors to Fiji since the early
1970s have taken pains to make complete verbal descriptions of the artefacts
they have seen.[39] The latter lists honour the memories of Bellingshausen,
Simonov, and Cook.

# 8

# ENVOI: RUSSIAN SHIPPING IN THE FIJI ISLANDS, 1820–35

GENERAL REMARKS

Between 1820 and 1835, five Russian ships passed by or through the Fiji Islands on their northward passages from Sydney to the Russian North Pacific settlements of Petropavlovsk-in-Kamchatka, Unalaska, Kodiak, or Sitka (Novo-Arkhangel'sk in Alaska).[1] All had made the eastward voyage from Brazil, across the South Atlantic Ocean, south of Cape Town, through the South Indian Ocean, to Australia.[2] Four of the five vessels were Navy sloops or transports, one—*Elena* (Lieutenant Vasilii S. Khrómchenko)—was a small Russian-American Company ship with naval officers and crew.[3] The Navy ships, which cut through Melanesia in the course of complex, multi-purpose voyages of exploration, scientific investigation, and provisionment, were *Otkrytie* (Captain-Lieutenant Mikhail N. Vasil'ev), *Blagonamerennyi* (Captain-Lieutenant Gleb S. Shishmarev), *Krotkii* (Captain-Lieutenant Leontii A. Hagemeister), and *Amerika* (Khromchenko again and Captain Ivan I. von Schants).[4] Of the four, two crossed the region twice: *Elena* (1825, 1829) and *Amerika* (1832, 1835). Thus Russian ships passed by or through the Fiji Islands seven times in fifteen years. No landings were attempted, but a good deal of hydrography was undertaken. The results remain in Leningrad, predominantly in the Navy archives and unpublished to this day.[5]

Predictably, given their northern destinations and knowledge of prevailing winds in season, the commanders of the five vessels crossed the Fiji archipelago at the same time of the year, over a spread of eleven weeks. All were anxious to exploit the southeast trade winds to the maximum, so shortening the northward passage to the northern settlements. *Otkrytie* and *Blagonamerennyi* skirted the Fiji Islands earliest, in early April 1820; and *Amerika* came latest, in June 1832.[6] Other common factors, too, produce an aspect of homogeneity in Russian visits of the period. No Russian ship arriving off the Fiji Islands, for example, urgently needed water or supplies: all had been handsomely provisioned in Australia. No ship had special orders to investigate the islands, yet the seven visits all produced at least a running survey of the lands observed. Again, no vessel lacked intelligent and highly trained observers who, moreover, were required, as mentioned, to keep journals by the Russian naval ministry itself. Several officers who passed the Fiji Islands in the first four days of April 1820, as participants of the Vasil'ev-Shishmarev Arctic venture,[7] later tried to publish narratives of their experiences on the basis of the 1820 journals. Among them were Lieutenant Aleksei P. Lazarev of *Blagonamerennyi*, and his friend Lieutenant Pavel I. Zelenoi of *Otkrytie*. A third man, Karl A. Gillesem (or Hulsen), midshipman in A.P. Lazarev's own sloop, after almost thirty years' delay did bring out a personal account of his experience of Oceania.[8] It is a disappointing effort, from the standpoint of Fijian studies.

Nicholas I's known lack of interest in publications of accounts of North or South Pacific ventures proved a problem, as was seen, even for Bellingshausen, whose important narrative came out only in 1831 and in a small edition. Mikhail N. Vasil'ev, commander of the Northern wing ("Division") of the two-pronged polar venture, never did produce a printed narrative. But then, his literary interests were weak.[9] Such first-hand narratives as *were* eventually offered to the Russian reading public had, with few exceptions, been retained by the imperial authorities for decades. Thus, Evgenii Berens' record of *Krotkii's* cruise of 1828–30 was published long after his death, in 1903.[10] One unusually early publication of an officer's description of a pass along the Western Fiji chain was that of August 1840, when Vasilii Zavoiko's exercise in travel literature found its way into the bookshops of St. Petersburg.[11] Zavoiko's *Impressions of a Seaman* offered cameos from *Amerika's* second (and final) cruise through Melanesia—that of 1835.

Aleksei Petrovich Lazarev (1791–1862) was one of three brothers in the Navy, all of whom saw mid-Pacific waters. Andrei, the eldest, came with *Ladoga* in 1823.[12] Mikhail came three times, with *Mirnyi* (1814), *Suvorov* (1820), and *Kreiser* (1823–24).[13] Aleksei was more the courtier than Mikhail or Andrei. Nonetheless, he was on active naval service until the latter part of 1828, when politically oppressive clouds had already darkened his prospects for continuing promotion in the fleet.[14] The fate of his account well illustrates how, in a larger way, the fate of source materials depended on the overall success of an entire voyage as perceived by the imperial authorities. Various factors might produce a "failure verdict" on a naval enterprise, so militating against the likelihood of publication of its records at the State's expense. Vasil'ev's venture in the North Pacific was completely overshadowed by Bellingshausen's great success in Antarctica. Again, the presence of future Decembrists in *Vostok*, *Kreiser*, and *Apollon*, all three warships in the Pacific in the early 1820s, turned the tsar against such officers as Aleksei P. Lazarev and even his commander, G.S. Shishmarev.[15] Aleksei Lazarev wrote his account of *Blagonamerennyi's* voyage on the basis of his own journals in 1821–22 or shortly after. He strove to see it published until August 1830. The original, in copperplate and leatherbound, was "found" in 1948 and published two years later.[16] Passages relating to Fiji appeared on pages 159–61.

*Blagonamerennyi's* APPROACH TO FIJI, 2–5 APRIL 1820

Well provisioned and with rested crews, the sloops *Otkrytie* and *Blagonamerennyi* left Sydney in mid-March and made for Norfolk Island in company. Vasil'ev wished to pass south and east of the Tonga group, but strong easterly winds forced him to change his plans.[17] By 28 March, both sloops were heading for the Lau Group of Fiji, with the aim of leaving Tonga to starboard. Foul weather and high winds forced another change of route within three days; Shishmarev proceeded in the general direction of Kandavu. Even at a distance of a hundred miles, Viti Levu caused the wind to blow erratically to the discomfort of the Russians, some of whom were very queasy. Every day brought sharper squalls and less consistent winds.[18] At last, on 3 April, the skies did clear; there was heat lightning but winds blew steadily SE.

> That night, though, the weather was foul. At about 3:30 AM on the 4th, we saw something like a little fire away to the WSW. All hands came up. Upon examination, we saw that it was indeed a fire, but not very near. We doubted if it could well be a fresh discovery, though, as the Americans and the English were often calling at the Fiji Islands to get sandalwood. We consequently supposed that many ships must have been on this course. Still, we looked intently awhile and convinced ourselves that we had, in fact, sighted a fire. Laying on the port tack, we hove to, then moved close-hauled to the SE. Continuing thus till 5 AM, we moved on the starboard tack to the NW and then went W, to see the isle on which a fire had burned in the night. . . . The horizon was gloomy, but still far clearer than it had been by night and we would assuredly have seen an island, if one had existed. . . .[19]

*Blagonamerennyi* was reckoned to be ninety-six miles WSW of "the Fijis" at 3 AM on 2 April. "The Fijis" must be assumed, in context, to mean Viti Levu and the immediately adjacent islets. Despite the conditions, the sloop

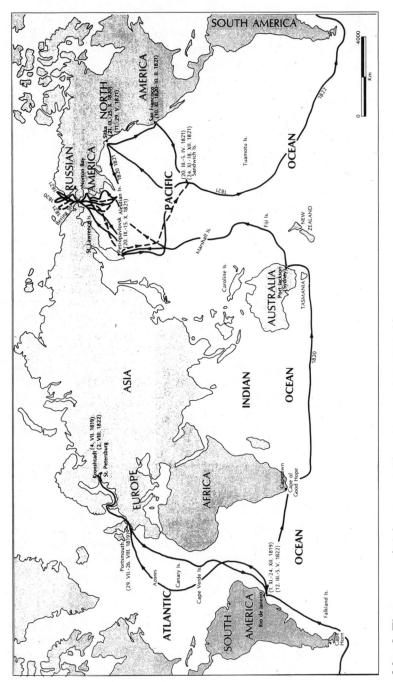

Map 8 The voyage of *Otkrytie* and *Blagonamerennyi*, 1819–22

was making at least five knots, on a northerly course. It follows that when fire was apparently spotted, forty-eight hours later, *Blagonamerennyi* was already NW of the Yasawa Group. No land exists southwest of the sloop's likely position at that time; but the Russian text refers, three times, to (shipping) lights or fire (*ogni, ogon'*). The text itself provides a clue: at Honolulu, twelve months later, the Russians learned about the activities of Captain Allen of the whaler *Maro*, and of other ardent whalers from New England ports, who were expanding the hunt south to New Zealand and as far west as Japan.[20] Apparently a whaler's brick-based cauldron for the rendering of blubber had caught the Russians' eye during the night.[21]

THE COMPANY VESSEL *Elena*'s TWO PASSES BY ROTUMA ISLAND, 1825 AND 1829

The Russian-American Company vessal *Elena* twice passed within a few miles of Rotuma on her passage north from Sydney to Alaska (Novo-Ark-hangel'sk). On both occasions, the commander—Pavel Chistiakóv in 1825, Vasilii Khrómchenko in 1829—approached deliberately near to check chronometers.[22] The geographical position of Rotuma was believed to have been accurately fixed.[23] The Russians reckoned its position to be latitude 12°30'50", longitude 178°54'E. Their longitudinal fixes were surprisingly erroneous, Rotuma's true position being 177°05'E.[24] Like Anuta (Cherry Island) to its west, observed by Captain Edward Edwards in August 1791 as he searched for *Bounty* mutineers in HMS *Pandora*, Rotuma was particularly useful as a signpost for the Russians passing northward.[25] It was isolated, had a high volcanic crater (840' above the sea), and had a most distinctive shape.[26] Like both Fataka and Anuta, finally, it figured prominently on the crucial sheet of I.F. Kruzenshtern's *Atlas iuzhnago moria* (*Atlas of the South Sea*, St. P. 1823). Dissatisfied with the assistance given South Pacific mariners by such cartographers as Aaron Arrowsmith (1750–1823) and José Espinosa,[27] Kruzenshtern since the early 1800s had been collecting first-hand data for inclusion in his great Pacific atlas. Prominent among his sources for the Fiji Islands were, inevitably, William Bligh of *Bounty* fame and George H. Hamilton, *Pandora's* Scottish surgeon. Bligh's own *Voyage* to the South Sea had appeared in June 1792 (and been imported to St. Petersburg immediately); Hamilton's account of the *Pandora's* cruise had come out nine months later, at his own expense, in Berwick, Scotland. Kruzenshtern, and other Russians after him, including Chistiakóv and Khromchenko, accepted Hamilton's and Edwards' name for their "discovery": Grenville Island.[28]

Unlike Chistiakov in 1828, Khromchenko in 1829 felt predisposed towards experimenting with a new and shorter route from Sydney to the

Russian Northwest Coast.[29] It seemed to him, as he perused the logs and journals of Efim Klochkóv, Vasilii Golovnin, and other Russians who had crossed the Southwestern Pacific to that coast, and as he weighed his own experience aboard *Riurik* (1816) en route from Penrhyn Island to the Marshalls,[30] that a good deal of time and effort might be saved by sailing east from New South Wales to the longitude of, say, Suvorov Island (163°30'W), which the Russians themselves had sighted by chance in 1814.

> Proposing to reach the settlements on the American coast by the very shortest course, he accordingly planned to proceed eastward from New Holland without going north and crossing the parallels of the Friendly or Society Islands. . . . By this means, he planned to use the southeast trade winds to greatest effect; for the wind would not back up, on crossing little islands, and he could enter the empty expanses of the Great South Sea. . . . The failure of the trade wind prevented this and obliged Lieutenant Khromchenko to take another route. . . . *Elena* traversed the Tropic of Capricorn in lat. 172°30'E.[31]

Steering almost due north past Matthew Island, first sighted by Captain Thomas Gilbert (1788),[32] Khromchenko passed the Yasawa Group on 5–6 May, then altered course to NNE. Rotuma came in sight on 8 May, was carefully surveyed, and passed within a range of fourteen miles.[33] Khromchenko's and *prikazchik* [clerk] Vasilii Kashevárov's logs[34] and journals were submitted at the voyage's conclusion to the Company's main office in St. Petersburg. *Elena* was a Company-owned ship and they themselves were on secondment to it. Their logs and journals were in due course, in 1830, made available to Loggin Golenishchev-Kutuzov of the Russian Naval Staff and to the Hydrographic Depot of the naval ministry. A brief but factual account of *Elena*'s voyage to the Northwest coast was printed by the government in 1832,[35] "Puteshestvie . . . sudna Eleny," *Zapiski Uchonogo Komiteta Morskago Shtaba*, Vol. 9:304–12.

NAVAL TRANSPORT *Krotkii* OFF KANDAVU AND NAVITI ISLANDS, 1829

By chance and not design, the naval transport *Krotkii* (Captain-Lieutenant L.A. Hagemeister, who was sailing on his third Pacific voyage) passed Rotuma barely three days after *Elena*, on 12 May 1829.[36] Hagemeister had left Sydney days before his colleague, Khromchenko.[37] Whereas *Elena* had been pressing north from Norfolk Island to the southern tropic, though, *Krotkii* had deliberately moved NE to cross that tropic practically due south of Viti Levu (178°02'E). Hagemeister, furthermore, had thought to do a little survey work among the Fijis as he passed. While reprovisioning and resting

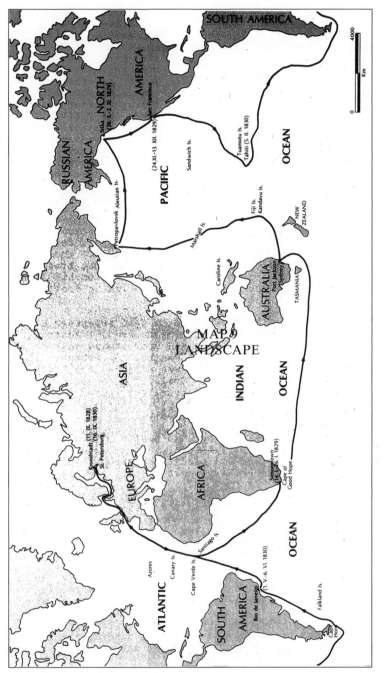

Map 9  The voyage of Gagemmeister on *Krotkii*, 1828–30

in Sydney, he heard of the investigations made two years before among the Fijis and the Loyalties by Captain Jules Sébastien Dumont D'Urville of *L'Astrolabe*.[38] The French, it seemed, had put their largest efforts into central Melanesia. Hagemeister resolved to pass "along the western fringe of the Fiji or Viti Islands. Having examined these, he would determine the latitude and longitude of Hunter or Farewell Island,[39] with which the Fiji Group ends to the north."[40]

Kandavu Island to the south of Viti Levu had been seen by Bligh (1792) but not described by him.[41] New England seamen too, notably Captain Bentley of the *Ann and Hope*, had seen the place but left no serviceable record for a foreign navigator.[42] Hagemeister sighted it (7 May 1829) from the SSE, and then spent two days surveying it and fixing its position astronomically.[43] His fix, at longitude 177°58′E, latitude 19°07′S, was accurate within some sixteen minutes longitudinal. His data coincided well with those of J. Dumont D'Urville who, in his time, had called the island "Candaboque."[44] Here are extracts from the narrative describing *Krotkii*'s passage through the Fiji Archipelago by Midshipman (later Vice-Admiral) Evgenii Berens, which appeared finally in 1903:

> On the evening of 6 May, we had spotted Maivul Island [Kandavu], southernmost of the Fijis, which had surprised us not a little as we were forty miles distant. It was seen, of course, because of its very considerable height. The isle is correctly indicated on the chart as regards latitude and longitude. But these isles are, in general, little described and it is supposed that there are many among them which are still entirely unknown to us. Up to the present, only the Americans have been visiting the Fijis, taking away cinnamon, cloves, and nutmeg, *inter alia*. There is, in fact, a harbour on Maivul, where their vessels put in. On 7 May, quite a large quantity of sugarcane floated around our ship. We succeeded in catching a few canes and raising them aboard. . . .[45]

The chart in question was, indubitably, Kruzenshtern's, based on Bligh's, Wilson's, and several New Englanders' materials.[46] The harbour was Galoa, on Kandavu's southwest shore, where Americans had been calling intermittently since about 1812.[47] The heights described from *Krotkii* rose immediately east of what is now Cape Washington, Kandavu's western point. They rise 800 metres above sea level and are perfectly visible from forty miles south.[48]

> By 8 May [continues Berens], we were passing along the shores of Naviti Island, the western side of which had never been described. It was our captain's intention, that being so, to approach the shore in question to

survey it; but the winds, blowing from NE several days consecutively now, drove us from the meridian of Naviti, the western extremity of which lies in latitude 17°01'S, longitude 177°08'20"E.[49]

*Krotkii* was passing the Yasawa Group, still heading north. Her path here intersected that of *Bounty*'s launch, with Bligh aboard, of 8 May 1788.[50] Bligh had, in fact, had neither energy nor opportunity to chart Naviti as he struggled west to safety. On 12 May 1829, the Russians crossed Rotuma's parallel. Altering course to WNW, they then pressed on to Ocean Island (which was not observed) and Ebon Atoll (Boston Island), in the Ralik Chain, Southwestern Marshalls.[51]

*Amerika*'S TWO PASSES WEST OF THE YASAWA GROUP

Like *Elena*, the three-master *Amerika* brushed by the Fiji Islands twice, in 1832 and 1835. Both times she was transporting mixed cargoes of naval stores and foodstuffs to Kamchatka. On the first voyage, she was commanded by Khromchenko, now on his third Pacific mission;[52] on the second, the commander was the Finnish-born Ivan Ivanovich von Schantz (1802–79).[53] On neither crossing did her officers make any contribution to contemporary knowledge of the Fiji Archipelago. On both occasions, on the other hand, the Russians showed their growing self-assurance in those waters, to the Fiji Islands' west, in which until recently they had been cautious. For the second passage, of 1835, we have not only Nikolai A. Ivashintsev's data, published in St. Petersburg in 1849, but also the particularly colourful Zavoiko narrative.[54]. Of the *Amerika*'s first passage, Ivashintsev has the following to say: "On 20 June 1832, the Russians crossed the Tropic of Capricorn, and next day they reached the parallel of Hunter or Fearn Island, easternmost isle in the New Caledonia Group. That island they left 270 miles to their west. . . ."[55] Hunter Island, spotted in 1798 by Captain Fearn, lay in longitude 171°50'E.[56] Khromchenko in 1832 must, then, have been in or near longitude 176°E as he moved north to Kandavu's latitude. Even so, no land seems to have been sighted until *Amerika* traversed the Ellices (Tuvalu) ten days later.[57]

Captain von Schantz had a particularly awkward passage east from Sydney in April 1835. The winds were contrary and strong. Zavoiko makes these terse remarks about the later northward push: "On 9 May, we crossed the Tropic of Capricorn: this was in longitude 178°21'31"E. Now, in the tropics, we suffered some five days of calms. Afterwards, by the Equator, there were rains and variable winds. We traversed the line, on 23 May, in 171°14'30"E."[58]

It is obvious from this that *Amerika* passed close by the Yasawa Group, west of Rotuma, so north towards Ocean Island. Shortly afterwards, the "Princess Group" was sighted (longitude 167°38′E, latitude 8°16′N), in the Eastern Carolinean Ralik Chain, skirted by Kotzebue and the *Riurik* in 1817.

*Part Three*

# THE RUSSIANS IN TUVALU
# (ELLICE ISLANDS)
# AND ANUTA ISLAND
# (EASTERN SANTA CRUZ GROUP)

# 9

# "DISCOVERING" DISCOVERED ATOLLS

## GENERAL REMARKS

Polynesia is frequently depicted on maps as an enormous triangle with Easter Island, the Hawaiian Islands, and New Zealand at its points. Numerous islands with a "mixed" or "pure" ethnic Polynesian population lie, however, west of the imaginary line that joins New Zealand and Hawaii; of these, all but a few had gained their Polynesian residents by 1800 when, in Johann Reinhold Forster's biting words, "the worst of Seamen" from St. Petersburg were planning their arrival "in a Sea where they are utter Strangers."[1] To include these Polynesian outlyers or, more precisely, islands with acknowledged Polynesian districts or communities, the line between New Zealand and Hawaii must be pushed west. Its bulge, thus overlapping Melanesia's hypothetical northeastern boundary, must certainly include Fataka and Anuta Islands (see Map 10), as well as what were formerly the Ellice Islands (now Tuvalu), and Futuna.[2] Russian vessels running north from New South Wales to Kamchatka in the early 1800s, all of which reached at least New Caledonia's (Vanuatu's) meridian before proceeding to the Southern Tropic, were traversing seas where meetings with such western Polynesians might occur. And they did occur, at both Tuvalu in 1820, 1829, and 1832 and Anuta in 1822. Russian records of those meetings, some of which are still unpublished, are of considerable ethnographic interest and form a chapter in the history of European-Polynesian contact.[3]

As observed above, the Russians made no fewer than seven passages across the western fringe of the Fiji Islands between 1820 and 1835, and all brought Russian companies, if not in sight of, then within a hundred miles of Rotuma Island (latitude 12°29'S, longitude 177°05'E), which they treated as

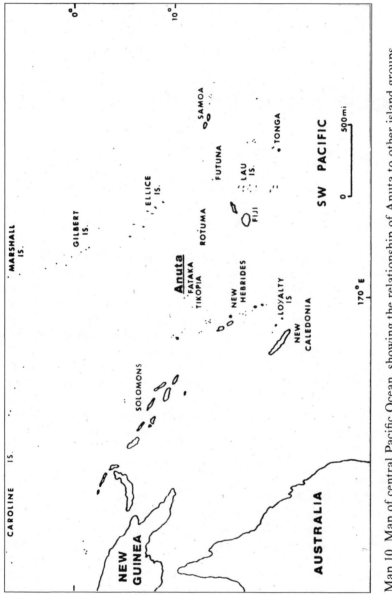

Map 10  Map of central Pacific Ocean, showing the relationship of Anuta to other island groups

a beacon.[4] Easterlies and/or southeasterlies prevail from March to June when all these crossings, by *Otkrytie, Blagonamerennyi, Elena, Krotkii,* and *Amerika,* were made. Through that entire portion of the southwestern Pacific Ocean, though, prevailing equatorial (warm) currents tend SW, that is to say, they flow towards and past Rotuma from Tuvalu. Such conjunctions of persistent wind and current in the waters west of Fiji (as in many other parts of Oceania) slowed sailing vessels heading north or east. The interruption of the trade wind by the Fijis, and Tuvalu north of latitude 8°S, worsened the problem. Typically, *Blagonamerennyi* crossed thirty miles of open ocean some days, but no more than eight or nine on others, as she struggled north past the Yasawa Group of Fiji between 6 and 12 April 1820.[5] Nine years later, *Elena,* too, was practically becalmed from time to time north of the latitude of Viti Levu on a course towards Rotuma. But to take proper advantage of prevailing winds and currents in the northern hemisphere and to cross the Marshall Islands with the least delay, it was essential not to drift west (south of the Line). Thus, even if a crossing of the Line in the vicinity of Ocean Island (longitude 170°50'E) were contemplated, as for instance by the careful Hagemeister of *Krotkii* in late May 1829,[6] it was important to press northward from Rotuma. Not surprisingly, Russian captains saw the islands of Tuvalu on their northeastern horizon and some were tempted to investigate them further.

The temptation to examine them was strengthened by assorted factors. First, even recent maps failed to show the scattered atolls—Funafuti, Nanumea, Nui, Vaitupu, Niutao, Nukulaelae, Nukufetau, Nanumanga, and Niulakita—either accurately or in their entirety.[7] The need for running surveys was self-evident. Second, the islanders themselves welcomed their visitors in 1820. Lastly, fruit and other foodstuffs might be offered to the visitor. That they were *not* brought out for barter with the Russians showed how seldom the Tuvalans had had intercourse—for good or ill—with Europeans. In itself, that circumstance struck Russian officers as worthy of research.[8]

TUVALU AND OTHER "DISCOVERED" ATOLLS

"Tuvalu" means "eight islands" in the local tongue. There are in fact nine islets in the cluster, but the ninth is uninhabited. The nine cover slightly less than twenty-six square kilometres, but stretch over a double chain of 668 kilometers.[9] Some islands are miniature clusters of a dozen, even twenty tiny islets, barely breaking through the waves.[10] Four of the nine principal islands—Funafuti, Nukufetau, Nui, and Vaitupu—are atolls; none has coral sandy soil rising more than five metres above the sea. As for the atoll vegetation, it is limited to coconuts, pandanus, breadfruit, taro, and bananas if one does not count extensive mangrove swamp. In sum, Tuvalu is a cluster of extremely small and poor atolls, rich in fish perhaps but lacking those resources which in other times had attracted the imperialist, far from early nineteenth-century commercial shipping routes: a low, neglected, unimportant archipelago.[11]

And yet, it had been visited by foreigners for centuries. Three centuries before the Russians came or slightly more, Samoan immigrants had come; perhaps two centuries before, Tongans had followed in waves.[12] By 1568, Alvaro de Mendaña and the Spanish had arrived. It is by no means certain which Tuvalan islands they observed and named "Isla de Jesus" and, in 1595 during Mendaña's second expedition, "Solitaria."[13] The weight of evidence seems to suggest Nui and Niulakita.[14] The Spanish finds were never publicly announced in any case, so that the archipelago effectively remained unknown until the late eighteenth century when Spaniards came again, led by Francisco Maurelle in *La Princessa*.[15] Maurelle, carrying papers from Manila to New Spain, left at the wrong time of the year for the normal North Pacific route and made an unsuccessful effort to traverse the South Pacific eastwards. On his detour from Tonga, he discovered "Gran Cocal" or Niutao, then "San Agostino," now called Nanumea.[16] Had the Spanish had their way, these finds would likewise have remained a Spanish secret, but by chance, Maurelle's account of his adventures in the South Seas was secured by the Frenchman, Jean François de La Pérouse, and it was published with the latter's *Voyage* in June 1798.[17] Thus, Russians knew at least about Maurelle's minor discoveries by 1800. Later British sightings, by the merchantman *Elizabeth* in 1809 for instance, were, of course, noted by Kruzenshtern but were not marked on Russian maps. It was as well that they were not: the "Sherson Island" seen by Captain Patterson of the *Elizabeth* was actually Nanumea.

The years 1819–20 brought the Europeans' leisurely discovery of the Tuvalu archipelago to an abrupt conclusion. Two ships, *Rebecca* (Captain de Peyster) and *Blagonamerennyi* (Captain G.S. Shishmarev) arrived off Nukufetau and the other major atoll in the cluster, Funafuti, within months of each other. The merchatman *Rebecca* was en route from Valparaiso to India when, at approximately 3 AM one day, she virtually ran aground on Funafuti. De Peyster counted fourteen low islands and keys and named them all, after his own financial backer of the time, Ellice's Islands. Next morning, he spotted seventeen more islets in a cluster forty miles northwest. These he named De Peyster's Islands. The position of their southernmost extremity he reckoned to be latitude 8°5′S, longitude 178°17′E.[18] This second cluster was Nukufetau. Motolalo Key, which was De Peyster's southern fix, lies in the given latitude and longitude 178°22′E.[19] Because De Peyster reached Bengal within a few weeks of the Russians' own departure from the Baltic, it is unlikely that they could have learned—even in Sydney by a vessel from

Madras—about his discoveries. The Russians had acordingly no reason to anticipate that land would be observed where it was sighted on 16 April 1820 from *Blagonamerennyi*'s fore-crosstrees.[20] They were justified, but wrong, in thinking that they had made a new discovery.

News of the so-called "Blagonamerennyi Cluster" reached St. Petersburg in August 1820 in despatches from Kamchatka. More specifically, it came in a report by Captain-Lieutenant Mikhail N. Vasil'ev to the naval minister, dated "Petropavlovsk Port, June 1820."[21] The material was handed on to Kruzenshtern, who thus had data on the cluster two full years before *Otkrytie* and *Blagonamerennyi* themselves returned to Kronstadt on 2 August 1822.[22] Those data were, of course, incorporated in his *Atlas* in 1823. Neither this, however, nor New England press announcements of the sightings made by Arend S. De Peyster, for instance, in the *Independent Chronicle* and in *The Repertory* (both of Boston) on 8–9 February 1820,[23] stopped assorted Europeans from "discovering" Nukufetau and Funafuti for themselves over the next several years.[24] Still, New England whalers like those on *Loper* of Nantucket were surprised in 1826 to come on Niutao ("Loper's Island"), Vaitupu ("Tracy's Island"), and the atolls to their north.[25] Here, to end this section, is an extract from the *Independent Chronicle*'s report dated 9 February 1820, used by Kruzenshtern together with the complementary report from Petropavlovsk by Vasil'ev, on the *Rebecca*'s sighting of 17 May 1819: "On the evening of the 17th May 1819, one of the people discovered a large fire. We hove to until daybreak, when another small low Island appeared above five miles under our lee; we past it close; it appeared cloathed with cocoanut trees, and doubtless is inhabited. . . . De Peyster's Islands lie in 181°43'W, lat. 8°5'S."[26]

Nukufetau is reckoned in modern publications to lie in 8°00'S, 178°29'E, the fix being, again, Motolalo Atoll on its southern tip. It consists in fact of some twenty islets situated on a reef of twenty-four miles' circumstance.[27] Archaeology confirms the Russian evidence of 1820, indicating that for centuries the cluster's main (or only) village stood near Savave, on its southwest rim. This was the rim past which the Russian vessels sailed at a distance of three-quarters of a mile (see Map 11).

RUSSIAN VISIT TO NUKUFETAU ATOLL, 17–18 APRIL 1820

*Otkrytie* and *Blagonamerennyi* struggled NNE from Rotuma from 9 to 16 April. After the 9th, *Blagonamerennyi* went ahead. The sloops remained in touch, however, using telegraphs at intervals.[28] Then, on the 15th, squalls and rains increased the distance and *Otkrytie* fell back from her companion ship, whose track was slightly eastward of her own.

Map 11 "The Blagonamerennyi Group of Islands" (Nukufetau, 1820)

At 7:30 AM on 17 April [recorded *Blagonamerennyi's* Second Lieutenant, Aleksei Petrovich Lazarev], Seaman Feoktist Potapov spotted from the fore-cross-trees a shore, straight ahead NW of us. It transpired that it was a cluster of eleven low-lying coral islands, all well wooded and joined by a reef. We were about fifteen miles from the most southerly of them. We signalled this at once to *Otkrytie*, which asked us which islands we took these to be. We congratulated *Otkrytie* on a fresh discovery, for such it certainly was, as according to Arrowsmith's chart the nearest islands, found in 1781 or seen by the brig *Elizabeth* in 1809, were at noon 176 miles off to our NW. Moving perhaps five miles closer in, we sighted a circle of water between islets joined by a coral reef.

These islands were indeed low and coral, and we observed on them abundant coconut palms, pandanus, and breadfruit trees. Not one of them was longer than a mile. Birds flew around us, but in very small numbers. We saw only one frigate bird and a few pelicans or boobies among them.

Meanwhile four craft had put out from the shore and were steering straight towards us. We slipped along the lee of the islands in order to survey them. Although *Otkrytie* was hove to, the islanders did not go up to her, since we were far closer than her to these islands, but continued to make for us. Wishing to see these natives, we ourselves now shortened sail and lay to.

Once the islanders had approached our sloop to within twenty fathoms, without however coming alongside, each one of us waved white kerchiefs or such greenery as there was on board the sloop, in lieu of the green branch which on other islands the natives take as a sign of peace. And by these gestures we indicated to them that they should come aboard; but it was all in vain. Captain Shishmarev then sent an officer in a boat to make the natives' acquaintance and to present them with pieces of hoop-iron and mirrors. When the officer came up to them, they did not quite move away; but it appeared that they did not wish to join him either. He, however, did get to one craft in which, as in the other three, sat four islanders. And they took hold of the oars of our boat and so kept together with it, without, evidently, fearing the sloop at all. They considered themselves so far away from her that her weaponry could not be used against them; even so, they were cautious with regard to the ship's boat.

Seeing our friendly disposition, the companions of these natives likewise approached us and made our acquaintance. As assurance of their friendliness, these islanders touched noses with our people, offending our sense of smell with the odour of coconut oil. The officer invited them onto the sloop and, showing them where they might board, himself returned to her. At first, the islanders seemed to be following him up with much rapidity; but suddenly they halted again and began to talk among themselves. They were unwilling to continue to voyage with us, even though we had thrown them a rope from the sloop. Such is the way of all natives when they visit strangers for the first time.

These islanders were all of middling size, well-shaped and tolerably full-bodied. Their faces were fairly attractive, a few being even handsome, though relatively darker than many other South Sea Islanders— though still not as black as Africans. Their skin tone was a dark chestnut, gleaming from their custom of smearing the body with coconut oil. They had girdles woven from coconut fibres at the middle, and from these hung ribbons that they had also made, multicolored but mostly red. The hair of the head was tied up in a bunch at the crown, with some resembling animals' tails hanging from it. White and orange-coloured flowers had been thrust into the hair itself; and almost all of them had white shells tied round the arms a little above the elbow. We received one such as a gift. As they drew near us, the islanders themselves showed a green branch as a sign of peace. It seemed to me that their bodies were not tattooed. Others, though, asserted that they had observed a few marks on shoulders. These natives' ears had been pierced and distended like those of many South Sea Islanders; but there was nothing in the lobes.

The craft of these islanders were of the very simplest and even of poor construction, consisting of a few planks sewn together with coconut fibre cords. They leaked so badly that those sitting in them were forced constantly to bail out water. They measured up to twenty feet in length, and were broad enough in the beam for one man to sit, that is, about a foot and a half. They had an outrigger on one side, identical stern and bow, and a triangular mat sail.

These natives' weaponry consisted of wooden pikes with crudely cut teeth. The crudeness was probably because the islanders seldom use their pikes and seldom wage war among themselves. We inferred this from their behaviour: on meeting us, they gave no evidence of insolence or hostility. Their conduct was, indeed, of the very friendliest nature. Everything we saw obliged us to suppose that they were a very peaceable people. They brought out nothing whatever in the way of produce, coconuts, etc.; nor had they any manufactures of any sort with them except for a single mat (carpet). Very likely, they had not come out to trade in any case but only wanted to look at us. Both from that fact and from their indifference towards the pieces of iron that we gave them, one can only conclude that they had not yet encountered Europeans and were still unfamiliar with iron, that metal that was so enticing for other natives of the Great South Sea. On the other hand, even the very smallest mirror would hold their complete attention. That Europeans had never before visited them was also to be concluded from the very fact that these natives, even having spotted our ships, were ignorant of mariners' needs and so brought us out no edible supplies despite their evidently having an abundance of them.

Seeing that it was impossible to persuade the islanders to come aboard the sloop by means of any pantomime requests, we merely presented those among them who were older with bronze and silver medallions, swung into the wind, and proceeded along the islands to make a running survey. We thought that the natives would perhaps board *Otkrytie*, if we ourselves left them, but they in fact headed straight home. *Otkrytie* also shortly swung into the wind and came after us.

At noon (17 April), being not more than a mile and a half or two miles south of the southwesternmost island by the compass, we determined its latitude and longitude. Passing along it, we then took a NNE course past the western side of the cluster, surveying it by both angles and bearings, at the same time noting positions of objects in one line of sight. I was frightened by a completely unexpected occurrence when we stood no more than three-quarters of a mile off the nearest island. Being on watch, I was making the survey of that same isle with the captain and navigator. This done, and when all the others had gone below to dine, I remained alone—and from the forecastle someone yelled, "Rocks ahead!". . . . I myself glimpsed two rocks which, plunging down into the depths, had doubtless been more alarmed by the sloop than we had been by them: for they were two whales that had been sleeping on the ocean's surface. . . .

At 4 PM, passing the northern islands in the cluster, we asked the commander of the expedition if we should regard these as a fresh discovery and were told, in reply, "If they have been seen by nobody, we shall call them the Blagonamerennyi Group." We thanked him for the honour shown us. . . .[29]

A second account of *Blagonamerennyi*'s meeting with the Nukufetauans is from the pen of her own captain, Gleb S. Shishmarev (1784–1835),[30] as submitted to Vasil'ev a week later (25 April 1820) and on the basis of his own and of his officers' impressions. That account, which offers details not present in the A.P. Lazarev report, was published by the Soviet historian A.I. Andreev in 1950. Here are extracts:

The savages we saw came up to us in four craft, to the number of sixteen men; all were of middling size and some were large, even, stout, and fairly handsome, of a dark brown hue. They wore at the waist a girdle made from coconut fibres, embellished with red ribbons of the same material. . . . Their coiffure was of hair pulled up towards the crown in a bunch and decorated with flowers. From the back of the head of some individuals, there fell several bunches of a brown colour that resembled wild beasts' tails. . . . There was not a single woman in the native craft which . . . had triangular sails sewn from matting. The mast was set at an angle of 30 degrees to the prow. It might be said, in general, that these people's craft are made far worse than are the craft of many South Sea Islanders. As they approached us, one of the savages held in his hand a green branch, no doubt in sign of peace. . . . Having drawn near, however, they were unwilling to come alongside the sloop, even though a rope had been flung to them, so I sent Lieutenant Ignat'ev out to them in our launch to give them iron and various trifles. The natives received Ignat'ev with caution but kindly, and touched noses with him in sign of amity. They looked at the iron and threw it aside without interest. Mirrors captivated them more than anything. They did ask Ignat'ev and the oarsmen for their forage caps and for the kerchiefs round their necks, but at the same time they acted in a most friendly fashion. They had nothing with them in the way of edible supplies or manufactures, however, apart from a few mats on which they were seated. Their arms were wooden pikes with barbs, very poorly carved, from which one may deduce that these people are very peaceable and make no great use of weaponry. Insofar as one can judge, from our very brief encounter with these natives, Europeans had never called on them before: this is suggested by their indifference towards iron, with which they seemed entirely unacquainted.

Being unable to persuade the islanders to come aboard my sloop, I swung into the wind, imagining that they would go to *Otkrytie* upon leaving us. With that in view, I refrained from presenting them with the medals that should have been presented to the chief. I observed no one among them who was a chief. . . .

Captain-Lieutenant Shishmarev.[31]

This report, dated 25 April 1820, was brought to Petropavlovsk-in-Kamchatka by Vasil'ev. It was forwarded immediately to St. Petersburg with a description of his voyage from Brazil to Petropavlovsk by Vasil'ev himself,[32] by courier sent from the Governor—Captain Rikord, who had sailed in *Diana* (1807-9) as V.M. Golovnin's comrade and second-in-command. Vasil'ev was not a fluent writer. Dour and deliberate, he seldom expanded on his basic theme: the progress of his ships around the world. Still, his June 1820 report, also published by Andreev as Appendix 17 to Aleksei P. Lazarev's *Zapiski* (*Memoirs*) in 1950, merits brief quotation here. It presents the Russian visit to Tuvalu in a rather wider context:

My intention had been to follow a route little used by other mariners, crossing the Equator between 170° and 180°W of Greenwich. When we had left Port Jackson, winds from E and NE had met us almost in the same parallel; and we had spent ten days in latitude 15°S, then eight days becalmed between the New Hebrides and Fiji. Clear weather made the heat intolerable, the thermometer indicating 25° Reaumur in the shade, and 22° at night; in the sun, it reached 33°. To everyone's pleasure, the trade wind from the east having been met on 17 April, I was informed by the sloop *Blagonamerennyi* that she could see land to the NE. And shortly after, we too sighted low sandy islands covered with sparse bush, directly ahead of us as we steered. These islands are not shown on Arrowsmith's chart, by which we were calculating our route. Coming up to them, we hove to at midday, in order to fix their latitude and longitude. By our reckonings, they lay in 8°00'S, 178°20'E. . . . The nearest islands on Arrowsmith's charts are the two islets called Avgustin [San Agostino or Nanumea] and Kakao [Gran Cocal or Niutao], seen from the brig *Elizabeth* in 1809 in latitude 6°S. It seems to me most improbable that an error of two degrees of latitude would have been made in the tropics, where the skies are almost always clear.

The isles that we found are inhabited. While we were hove to, natives went out to *Blagonamerennyi* in four craft; but they did not venture to go on board her, many though the signs of invitation might be. A sloop's jolly boat was put off to give these people presents. They paid no attention to iron, but they delighted in a mirror and liked our clothing very much. Still, they could not bring themselves to board our vessel.

These natives are dark brown in colour and go naked apart from a girdle. Their craft resemble those described for the Friendly Islands. Hastening towards Kamchatka as I was, I did not stop at this group to make a detailed survey. Indeed, we saw only the isles' southern and northwestern sides; on their eastern side, trees appeared now and then on the horizon. . . .[33]

As Vasil'ev largely depended on material supplied by Shishmarev, who had been nearer to the atoll, so the latter made good use in his report of oral comments made by First Lieutenant Ivan N. Ignat'ev, who had met the islanders. Brief though the meeting was, as seen, Ignat'ev noted much; he was a quick-witted and able officer who in 1828 served with great distinction in the Russo-Turkish War and reached flag rank.[34]

Vasil'ev's report cited here was accompanied by a general map of Nukufetau entitled "The Blagonamerennyi Group of Islands, Discovered by the Sloop *Blagonamerennyi* on 17/29 April 1820." It combined data gathered from both sloops, which took roughly parallel courses up the atoll's western side. From a point midway between Motolalo and Fale Atolls, the Russians coasted past the low Fale sub-cluster at a distance of perhaps a thousand metres. The sixteen islanders came out from that locality, most likely from the village of Savave. By 2 PM, standing due west of Teafua Pass into the large Nukufetauan lagoon, the men on both ships had an intermittent glimpse, through their British telescopes,[35] of palms growing from Vasamotu north to Funaota (see Map 12). They did not recognize Deafatule Pass but saw the mangroves to its north.

## THE ETHNOGRAPHIC EVIDENCE

The Tuvalu archipelago was settled from Samoa and from Tonga. The first Proto-Polynesians arrived perhaps 650 years ago. Their descendants are on Nanumea to this day.[36] Recent research suggests that Vaitupu was settled in the late 1600s and that Nukulaelae was settled still more recently from Funafuti.[37] There are numerous traditional accounts of these arrivals from the south and east, which certainly continued intermittently for centuries and go some way toward explaining major dialectic variations that occur within Tuvalu. Nukufetau—Land of the Fetau Tree—is considered by its people to have first been settled by a nameless Tongan and his five wives, whose descendants made a voyage back to Tonga to import coconut palms, then sorely lacking on the atoll.[38] As shown by the American ethnologist E. Burrows in his 1938–40 works on "culture areas," all Tuvalu islands except Nui (with its broadly Micronesian population) have a Polynesian cultural identity.[39] The Soviet ethnologist N.A. Butinov has suggested in a 1982 monograph that they should also be seen as falling comfortably in Burrows' "Western Polynesian Area."[40] And certainly the Russian evidence of 1820 lends weight to that position. For example, both triangular mat sails and undifferentiated low canoe prows and sterns, as seen off Fale by the 1820 visitors, are cultural features of the "Western" area.[41] The point is strengthened by Vasil'ev's own casual remark that Nukufetauan craft were much like "those described for the Friendly Islands," that is, Tonga.[42] Moreover, *Otkrytie* carried the Cook-King narrative (1784) of *Resolution*'s and *Discovery*'s voyage of 1776–80, as well as Loggin Golenishchev-Kutuzov's Russian version of it. Both provided details of Tongan craft seen by the British in the Haapai sector (May 1777).[43]

*Otkrytie* and *Blagonamerennyi* plainly had been observed some distance south of Motolala, which, writes Lazarev, the Russians saw some fifteen miles off or slightly less by 8 AM. The islanders accordingly had time to prepare for the visit. Still, at noon, the massive *paalangi* (strangers') ships were south of Fale, for the tip of which their Polynesian predecessors, too, had made in other times.[44] If any landings were attempted, it was reasonable

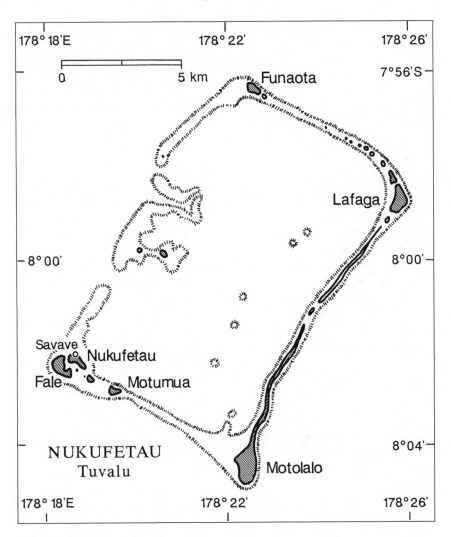

Map 12  Nukufetau, Tuvalu

to suppose, it would be there. The Russians, for their part, were very pleased but not surprised when four canoes put out from that locality.

These craft were four-man *vakakaiva* of the sort taken to sea and not employed in atoll fishing or for running local errands.[45] Twenty feet in length or more, they had for centuries been used in ocean fishing. Local specialists (*tufunga fai vaka*) had traditionally built them, of *fetau* (*Calophyllum inophyllum L.*) or, more commonly, of *pukavai* (*Pisonia grandis R. Br.*).[46] The simplicity and inferior construction of the 1820 craft points to the latter,

poorer timber—pawpaw or papaya wood, in English. As for Lazarev's coconut fibre cordage, it was evidently *kolokolo* sennit of a type Nukufetauans
had made for centuries.[47] James Haddon's and A. Hornell's seminal study of
*Canoes of Oceania* has a discussion of the context of Vasil'ev's and Lazarev's further remarks about Tuvalu craft: the "triangular sails sewn from
matting," the "mast set at an angle of 30 degrees to the prow," and the
apparent tendency to leak.[48]

Nukufetau is invisible to both its closest neighbours, Funafuti and Vaitupi
to the east; and from the other, northern atolls of the cluster, it is separated
by considerable expanses of water. Nonetheless, regular contacts were maintained among the islands, and the passing of such European vessels as *Elizabeth* in 1809 and of *Rebecca* only recently would necessarily have spread
them.[49] De Peyster's apparition would, of course, have had particular significance for Nukufetau, adumbrating the arrival of the Russians who
appeared, like the people of *Rebecca*, from the SSE, at the beginning of the
dry season, with giant sails, and with no desire to tarry. That Tuvalu Island-

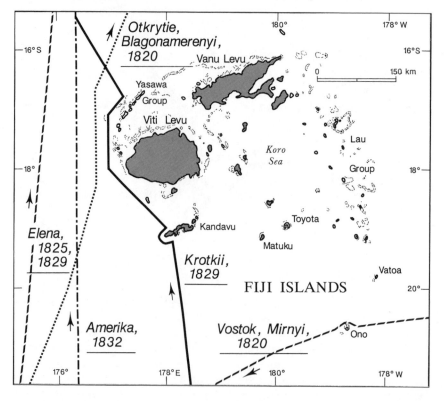

Map 13  Russian routes through the Fiji Islands, 1830–32

ers had no idea of the military power of such visitors, from Tongans or from other seafarers, does not seem plausible. For them, however, *paalangi* had not yet proved to be murderous. The Russians were accordingly approached with proper Polynesian ceremony, cautiously but civilly. Captain-Lieutenant Shishmarev records, suggestively, that he "observed no one amongst them who was a chief." It seems indeed that no *aliki* was at hand, and that the craft had left the shore under their own captains' command, that is, with local *tautai* (master fishermen) aboard.[50] Lieutenant Lazarev refers to "those among them who were older" (*byvshikh postaree*), which, suggesting as it does both middle age and some authority (in context), might appropriately be applied to *tautai*. No Nukufetauan made a speech of any sort, at least to judge by Russian texts. None of the sixteen men was obviously larger than the rest. Again, the inference is—absence of *aliki*.

The islanders met by the Russians were dressed in traditional *malo*. The red ornamentation was observed, at Nukufetau, by members of the Wilkes expedition in 1841.[51] The "girdles" seen in 1820 may well have been of pandanus leaf rather than coconut fibre. Topknots, the use of flowers in the hair, and the dying of hair bright red, were likewise traditional at Nukufetau as elsewhere in Tuvalu.[52] Like the Vaitupuans, the Nukufetauans enlarged earlobe apertures and inserted flowers, leaves, and smaller ornaments.[53] White shell necklaces and armbands were also observed by the Wilkes expedition: in terms of material culture, little if anything changed at Nukufetau between 1820 and 1841. Still, in the 1840s, tattooing was generally limited to the upper arms, upper chest, and shoulders—though some leg tattooing was also spotted.[54]

The specific variety of outrigger canoe seen by the Russians was in use at Nukufetau until very recent times. When examined by the German ethnologist Gerd Koch in 1960-1, it was known as *vaka fakakolota*.[55] The sail was still set on a mast "at an angle of 30 degrees to the prow" and was still made of triangular shaped *mekei* matting. Two other details in the Russian texts are suggestive: the "red ribbons" embellishing the natives' "girdles" and the gleaming darkness of skin tone. The former were perhaps strips of material of the variety worn, for centuries, over *titi nino* dance skirts by Nukufetauans. The latter anticipates remarks made by Captain Plaskett, of the New England whaler *Independence*, on visiting Niutao ("Smut Face Island") and Vaitupu in 1826-7. The natives, Plaskett claimed, would daub their faces with smut or soot, as well as coconut oil, to indicate their rank. This matter was investigated thoroughly in 1980 by the anthropologists Keith Chambers and Douglas Munro (see Bibliography, Chambers & Munro, 1980:177-8).

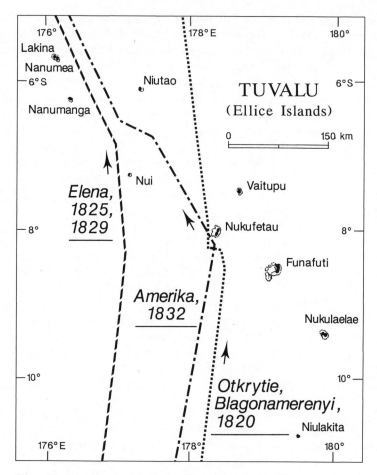

Map 14  Russian routes through Tuvalu, 1820–29

THE RUSSIANS AND "GRAN COCAL"

According to Lieutenant A.P. Lazarev, Nukufetau was lost to sight from *Blagonamerennyi* at 5 PM on 17 April 1820.[56] Winds were easterly and fairly steady, and the sloop made five to seven knots during the night. The next morning, at 6 AM, Vasil'ev signalled from *Otkrytie*, inviting Shishmarev and certain officers to breakfast on the flagship. Both vessels hove to at noon and, having eaten pleasantly in company, the gathered officers compared notes. They tried to reconcile their own supposed discovery with the material they had on little islands in the area. Apparently the best of that material was Aaron Arrowsmith's revised edition of his *Chart of the Pacific Ocean*, published (and acquired by the Russian naval ministry) in 1810. "At noon [writes Lazarev], Arrowsmith's chart showed that Manveble or Shevson's [sic] Island, seen by the brig *Elizabeth* in 1809, was 120 miles from us and NW 60°30'. . . ."[57]

"Shevson's Island was actually "Sherson's Isle," or Nanumea islet of Nanumea Atoll, so named by Patterson in 1809.[58] "Manveble" is, almost certainly, a printer's error. Patterson had failed to recognize Nanumea Atoll as Maurelle's "San Agostino," first encountered by the Spanish on 6 May 1781.[59] To track the Russians' northward progress of 17–18 April 1820 is, in any case, to see that they had passed just out of sight and to the west of Vaitupu and approximately sixty miles east of Nui (or Mendana's "Isla de Jesus."[60] Had Vasil'ev been able or inclined to go due north or NNE from the "Blagonamerennyi Group," he would have made a true discovery for Europe. Vaitupu was not known to Europeans, it would seem, until 1825 when it was sighted by the Yankee whaling captain Obed Starbuck in *Hero*.[61] As it was, the Russians missed the honour of discovery by seconds.

Now, the first edition of the "elephantine" *Chart of the Pacific* made by Arrowsmith (London 1798),[62] of which apparently the Russians had no copy, had not only indicated both Tuvalu finds of May 1781 ("Isla San Augustin" and "Gran Cocal"), but also had evidently done so on the basis of the log kept by Maurelle's chief pilot, Vasquez.[63] On that chart, "Gran Cocal" was placed at 6°06'S, 178°42'E, and "San Augustin" (Nanumea) at 5°42'S, 177°36'E. Upon reflection, Arrowsmith shifted both islands in the 1810 edition of his chart, "San Augustin" just over one degree westward to a point extremely near its true position, "Gran Cocal" to 5°54'S, 176°36'E. The seventy-odd miles that had previously separated them were thus reduced to about twenty-two miles.[64] Thus, by reacting to reports of *Elizabeth*'s "discovery" of 1809, did Arrowsmith initiate the process of identifying "Gran Cocal" with Nanumanga, incidentally erasing Niutao from his chart.

The true identity of "Gran Cocal" has interested scholars since, in 1960, Andrew Sharp asserted baldly that, en route to Nanumea, "Maurelle came to Nanomana [Nanumanga].[65] Of the subsequent and keenly argued controversy, to which H.E. Maude and K.S. Chambers made the largest contributions, it suffices here to say that it concluded with a general acceptance of the claims of Niutao to be "Gran Cocal."[66] What is significant within the "1820 Russians" context, obviously, is that nothing indicated to Vasil'ev and Shishmarev that Niutao lay ahead. And so, proceeding NNW toward another islet seen by Patterson in 1809, "Hope" in the Gilberts' southern sector (modern Arorae),[67] they failed to sight Maurelle's true "Gran Cocal"—again by seconds. Less persistent squalls during the crucial day would very likely have provided Kruzenshtern, through the Vasil'ev report and logs, with the material he needed to dispel the ever-worsening confusion.

As it was, he followed Purdy in equating "Gran Cocal" with "Sherson's Isle."[68] Retrospectively, it is apparent that in doing so he was suggesting that "Cocal" *was* Niutao, since that was the atoll actually sighted by the Spanish on 5 May 1781. Kruzenshtern stated his case in 1824, in his *Recueil de mémoires hydrographiques* (St. P., Vol. I:23–4).

That very year, the hydrographic situation was further disturbed by the visit to Tuvalu of the French vessel *Coquille* (Captain Louis Isidor Duperrey). Leaving Rotuma early in May 1824, Duperrey saw an island on the 9th which he believed to be Maurelle's "Gran Cocal."[69] As is clear from his fairly accurate report and fix, this atoll was, in fact, Nanumanga. Next morning, the French observed "San Augustin" or Nanumea, whose inhabitants attempted to make contact with them. (The canoes could not keep pace with *La Coquille*.)[70] Three published works offered descriptions of these French-Tuvalu meetings, incidentally reporting the position of the isle that Duperrey called "Gran Cocal." These were his own *Voyage autour du monde* (Paris 1827) with its accompanying *Atlas* (1825), and a *Mémoire sur les opérations géographiques* (1827).[71] According to the French, "Gran Cocal" now lay in latitude 6°5′33″S, longitude 176°20′E.[72] It was SSE from what Maurelle and Duperrey alike called "San Augustin," that is, from Nanumea. Duperrey's material, taken together with the celebrated *Chart of the Pacific Ocean* (1810) by Arrowsmith, John Purdy's "Tables of Observed Positions" (1816), Kruzenshtern's more recent *Atlas*, and assorted other printed works, confused the Russians when they reached Tuvalu for the second (1829) and third time (1832). "Gran Cocal" was clearly stated, in those published works, to lie in latitude 6°11′S, 6°5′S, even 5°54′S; nor had its longitude yet stabilized![73]

The captain of both transports that traversed Tuvalu on those later northward voyages was Kotzebue's former navigator on *Riurik* (1815–18), Vasilii Stepanovich Khromchenko.[74] In 1829, as seen, he was en route to Sitka as commander of the Russian-American Company ship *Elena*.[75] Three years later, he returned as the commander of *Amerika*, bound for Kamchatka with another load of naval stores, dry goods, and other articles for Company employees in the North Pacific settlements.[76] A fine sea officer of much experience, he was entrusted by the Company on both occasions with despatches and a cargo worth almost a half a million roubles.[77] Given liberty to choose his own route to the North Pacific settlements, he twice looked in at Portsmouth, England, Rio de Janeiro, and Sydney, New South Wales. Nor did similarities between the voyages of *Elena* and *Amerika* stop there: having twice been well received by the colonial authorities in Sydney, Khromchenko traversed Tuvalu twice and twice surveyed the Marshalls.[78] More than any other Russian of that period, he reinforced the elements of regularity, even routine, that were becoming obvious by 1825-27 in the Russian Navy's trans-Pacific service.

Leaving Sydney on 30 April 1829, Khromchenko passed Norfolk Island, then Rotuma Island (9 May), as he pressed on to the North.[79] Like Hagemeister in the Navy transport *Krotkii*, who was even then en route for Fiji, Khromchenko had left Australia with thoughts of French activity in mind. For Hagemeister, it was news of Dumont D'Urville's probings in the Loyalties that proved decisive where the choosing of a track through Melanesia was concerned, bringing *Krotkii* to Kandavu, Fiji on 8 May.[80] For Khromchenko, it was the Duperrey *Voyage* and *Mémoire*, of 1827, that exerted greater pressure. From Rotuma, he proceeded to the spot where, five years earlier, the French had found and charted "Gran Cocal" (lat.6°5′S, long. 176°20′E). Neither the French material nor Arrowsmith nor Kruzenshtern gave any reason to suppose land would be sighted on the way. For, though the fact that Mendaña had discovered that his "Isla de Jesus" in approximately latitude 6°45′S had long been recognized by chartmakers, that island had not yet ended its roamings on European maps. Nor was it possible for Arrowsmith, or anybody else, to fix its longitude.[81] As a result, Nui had vanished altogether—for the purposes of practical, commercial navigation— until the Dutch ships *Reigersbergen* (Captain Koerzen) and *Pollux* (Captain Eeg) had chanced upon it, on 14 July 1825.[82] (Nor, even then, did the supposed "Isla de Jesus" leave the map: in the 1840s there was still general uncertainty about the actual locations of Mendaña's sightings that produced double charting. Nui figured both as "Jesus" and as "Nederlandich" Island!)[83] News of the Dutch warships' discovery was very slow to reach St. Petersburg. Not until February 1826 was it reported in the press of Rotterdam; not until April was it broadcast to the English-speaking world.[84]

Khromchenko therefore was surprised and pleased when land was spotted from *Elena*'s masthead on 11 May, where none was indicated on his charts. He moved toward it, reckoned its position, fixed its highest elevation (eighty feet), and judged its breadth (half a mile). Though inhabited and thickly wooded, it did not offer a serviceable anchorage. Believing he had made a fresh discovery, therefore, Khromchenko named the island for his First Lieutenant, Baron Lorenz or Lavrentii von Loewenthal (in Russian: Lavrentii fon Levendal'),[85] and continued on to "Gran Cocal." By *Elena*'s reckonings, the island lay in latitude 7°13′S, longitude 177°14′E.[86] By Eeg's less careful reckoning, it lay in 7°10′S, 177°33′E. The actual position is considered to be 7°16′S, 177°10′E.[87] Khromchenko was thus correct to within about three miles in his fix, a quite commendable performance.

*Elena* steered north from Nui on 12 May. "Flocks of land birds were seen flying to the SW, but no shores were seen."[88] The flocks were evidently south of Nanumanga which, despite uncertain winds and sudden squalls, the Russians sighted on 14 May. With Duperrey's report before him, Khromchenko deliberately set about the business of surveying. The results were puzzling: even having duly compensated for the fact that Duperrey had reckoned longitude east of a line passing through Paris, not through Greenwich, he himself and *Elena*'s navigation-minded clerk V. Kashevarov fixed the isle of "Gran Cocal" in 176°13′E—seven minutes west of Duperrey's most careful reckoning. Nor did *Elena*'s latitudinal result confirm *Coquille*'s; and, again, the difference exceeded seven minutes. Khromchenko hove to, and reckoned Nanumanga's longitude with eight chronometers. He scarcely needed to emend his fix. Surprised that Duperrey had made such errors in the recent past, he moved off NNE.[89]

Returning to Australia (Port Jackson) three years later, in 1832, with the 660-ton *Amerika*, a fast three-master, Khromchenko set sail for Tuvalu on 10 June. From a position WSW of the Yasawa Group of Fiji on 25 June, he made directly for Rotuma and, from there, took a course a fraction eastward of *Elena*'s track of 1829. He wished to sight Nukufetau ("the Peyster Group").[90]

In his *Atlas* and hydrographic commentaries, Kruzenshtern had laid to rest Russian pretensions to have found that group for Europe. He had done so on the basis of De Peyster's own letter describing his discovery, as printed in the Boston press of February 1820.[91] Russian hydrography in Oceania was, by tradition, cumulative. Careful charting, for example at Hawaii, in the Washington-Marquesas Islands, and the Ratak Chain of Eastern Micronesia, much encouraged later complementary surveying work by other captains. Incidentally, such sets of visits to the same localities lent certain emphases to Russian science in the North and South Pacific, which are echoed by the strength of ethnographic and botanical collections held in Leningrad today.[92] Nukufetau was of interest to Khromchenko precisely for the reason that the Russians had themselves surveyed it. He proposed to build deliberately on their work. "On 28 June [writes the historian N.A. Ivashintsev], the transport approached the Peyster Group. From noon observations, that group was found to lie in latitude 8°0′23″S, longitude 178°21′25″E. Just before sunrise on 30 June, in latitude 6°30′S, a false sun was observed—a rare phenomenon in that zone. That same day, the *Amerika* passed within sight of the islands of Gran Cocal and San Augustin; she passed to their east. . . ."[93]

Again, Khromchenko's reckonings were more correct than those given by charts in current use: his latitudinal fix for Motolalo islet was twenty-three seconds more accurate than Shishmarev's of 1820, and his longitudinal, 1 minute 25 seconds.[94] *Amerika*, like other European vessels of the period, was long in sight of Fale islet and Savave village. Only Nanumea (or Maurelle's "San Augustin") and Nanumanga are aligned, north and south of one another, in a way that meets the Russian text's requirement. That text shows that those atolls were observed, off to the transport's west, within a space of hours. Khromchenko thus shows that, whereas Kruzenshtern had been contending that the vexing "Gran Cocal" was truly Niutao when he called it "Sherson's Isle," Duperrey had sighted Nanumanga—even though he wrongly called it "Gran Cocal."[95] Thus,unwittingly but usefully, did Khromchenko (who noted Nanumanga's true location as he passed) contribute evidence that Niutao *had* been seen from *La Princessa*, half a century before.[96]

# 10

# ANUTA ISLAND

VOYAGE OF THE ARMED SLOOP *Apollon*, 1821–2

The years 1820–22 marked the high point in the Russian-American Company's effort to supply its North Pacific outposts, with the Navy's aid, by ship and from the Baltic Sea.[1] That effort, which was shortly to be recognized as ineffectual and scandalously costly, was supported in the two-year period by half a dozen ships: *Kutuzov*, *Riurik*, *Elizaveta*, *Apollon*, *Kreiser*, and *Ladoga*.[2] Besides these ships, the naval brig *Aiaks* also sailed for the colonies, only to run aground off Holland; and *Otkrytie*, *Blagonamerennyi*, and *Borodino*, which had sailed from the Baltic in 1819, all reached Sitka in the fall of 1820. All ten vessels, four of which had been acquired by the Company directors for the North Pacific service, were commanded by reliable young naval officers and crewed by Navy seamen on secondment. All took different and sometimes interweaving routes through Oceania (except *Aiaks*, of course, and the no less unfortunate *Elizaveta*, which was sold at a disastrous loss in Cape Town).[3] All, by obvious extension, were potential witnesses to life and culture, trade and human intercourse in Melanesia. As it happened, *Apollon*, a 32-gun sloop bringing supplies to Petropavlovsk and with orders to conduct surveillance cruises off the coastline of Alaska,[4] was the ship to pass Fataka and Anuta close enough to meet the Polynesians there (14 July 1822).

Like *Otkrytie*, which had traversed Tuvalu twelve months earlier, *Apollon* (Captain Irinarkh Stepanovich Tulúb'ev) was a new ship of about 900 tons. She was the nucleus, at least, of a Pacific squadron; but initially Tulub'ev's orders emphasized the mercantile-provisionment dimension of his mission.[5]

Given liberty to choose his own subordinates, he took a surgeon, a lieutenant, and a group of hardened seamen who barely eighteen months before
had returned to Kronstadt with *Kamchatka* (Captain-Lieutenant V.M.
Golovnin) after a long Pacific voyage (1817–19).[6] Like *Kamchatka*, *Apollon*
carried 119 proven seamen. Like *Kamchatka* and *Otkrytie*, she called at
Portsmouth and Rio de Janeiro before going into higher southern latitudes.

But *Apollon*'s was not a happy voyage. First, she lost *Aiaks*, her companion vessel, then, crossing the North Sea in a storm, she proved alarmingly
unstable. Masts and spars were shortened, and in Portsmouth her stores were
hurriedly restowed. Finally, Tulub'ev fell a victim to consumption. He eventually died at sea on 31 March 1822 and was succeeded in command by
*Apollon*'s senior lieutenant, Stepan Petrovich Khrushchév.[7] Tulub'ev's
death was followed, nine months later, by that of his own nephew Aleksandr,
who had sailed in his sloop as midshipman. When *Apollon* at length arrived
at Sydney for provisions, water, and above all rest, Khrushchev was in
command. He stayed seventeen days and was received and entertained hospitably.[8]

Well rested and provisioned, the Russians left Port Jackson on 26 June
1822. Steering east toward Ball's Pyramid and Lord Howe Island, they
encountered variable winds. They crossed the Southern Tropic in longitude
169°25'E, almost 5° west of the 1820 Russians' crossing point but in *Diana*'s
1809 track.[9] To read Khrushchev's 1832 account of *Apollon*'s Pacific transit
is to recognize that he, like the unfortunate Tulub'ev, both admired and—in
naval matters—followed V.M. Golovnin. Like *Diana*, *Apollon* passed close
to Walpole Island SE of the Loyalties,[10] then pressed due north. Like Golovnin in 1809, Khrushchev headed deliberately for the southern edge of Captain Cook's New Hebrides. There, *Diana*'s and *Apollon*'s tracks crossed.
Whereas Golovnin had paused at Tana, Khrushchev pressed on until, on or
about 13 July, he once again crossed *Diana*'s track off Tikopia.[11] What
ensued is best described by *Apollon*'s "interpreter" (and most unlikely pas-
senger), Akhilles Pavlovich Shabél'skii.[12] A friend of the great poet Pushkin
and a student of the English language, of colonial administration, prison
systems, botany, and chemistry, Shabel'skii had received a first-rate education at the Tsarskoe Selo lycée outside St. Petersburg. A traveller by temperament, he was seconded to the Navy (1821), then appointed Second
Secretary at the Russian Mission (1825) in the United States.[13] There, as in
New South Wales and Upper California with *Apollon*, it was his business to
observe and to interpret for his seniors.[14] He was a man of much perception,
and his record of a visit to Anuta is the more significant for the compara-
tively terse nautical data that Khrushchev thought it his duty to provide.

AKHILLES P. SHABEL'SKII'S ACCOUNT OF A VISIT TO ANUTA

On the basis of the journal he had kept in *Apollon* throughout her mission, Shabel'skii in 1824–25 prepared a narrative account of his experiences. He completed it with some despatch, and it was published in St. Petersburg in 1826, as *Voyage aux colonies russes de l'Amérique, fait à bord du sloop de guerre l'Apollon, pendant les années 1821, 1822, et 1823*. Portions of that narrative appeared in St. Petersburg, in Russian, and with minor variations of the text.[15] The following is taken from pages 37–42 of the Shabel'skii *Voyage*.

Very early in the morning, on the 14th of that month, we caught sight of Mitre Island. It is composed of two large hills, joined by a promontory. On its northwestern side, one sees two conical rocks rising up. One of these rocks offers a phenomenon that one sees but rarely on circling the globe: wind and water, those two powerful destructive agents, have so exercised their forces on it as to aereate its summit and undermine it at the base. At present, that rock has a certain resemblance to a mitre, which perhaps led to that name being given to the whole island.[16]

The part of Mitre [Fataka] open to the effect of the prevailing wind is arid and bare of vegetation; but the rest of the isle is covered with the richest verdure. When we were alongside it, we were not more than half a nautical mile distant, and we distinctly saw that the sea breaks with great force against the eastern part of the island. Waves constantly brought in by the prevailing winds against the shores there have holed them at the base, forming deep caverns.

Being some eight nautical miles distant from Mitre, we sighted Cherry Island [Anuta]. These two isles had been discovered in 1791 by Edwards, captain of the English corvette *Pandora*. This was all we knew about them, for descriptions of them are nowhere to be found.[17]

As we passed Mitre, we saw very clearly that it was not populated, but on approaching Cherry we could make out a hedge that ran across the island and, soon after that, a man knocking coconuts. We were obliged to hasten on our way to Kamchatka, and so we could not land on this island, which appeared to promise a pleasant and interesting stop. But when we were some two miles offshore, we hove to because we saw coming out toward us fourteen natives in two outrigger canoes. They were making signs to us with pieces of their cloth, made of reeds, to which we responded by waving white handkerchiefs in the air. Having seen these peace signals, the natives approached our vessel with the greatest confidence. Then, when they were four or five *toises* (24′-30′) distant, several of them threw themselves into the sea and, despite the considerable coolness of the conditions, showed much agility in swimming.

From afar, their figures had a rather repulsive air. It was, above all, their long hair that gave them this appearance. Great was our astonishment, therefore, when they came on board our ship and we saw that they were men of considerable stature, with well-proportioned limbs and extremely regular facial features—features that bespoke the goodness of their nature. Setting foot on the ship, each one of these natives showed, by his expression, the amazement with which he was struck at the sight of so many objects that were novel to him; but each one also proceeded, immediately afterwards, to make us a gift of a few coconuts. One of them seemed to be their chief, for when that individual boarded us, he was supported by two of his countrymen; and when someone wanted to make an exchange with us, his permission was sought.

We started speaking to them with the aid of a dictionary of the New Hebrides language;[18] but they could scarcely comprehend us. As soon as we began to use a dictionary of the language of the Friendly Islands, though, compiled thanks to the efforts of Admiral D'Entrecasteaux,[19] all obstacles vanished. The first question we then put to them was, what was the island they inhabited called? They replied, in one voice, Anouta.

One can certainly suppose that these people have had contact with Europeans very rarely, if at all. For they were ignorant of the use of our knives. One of the natives put a knife under his belt in such a way as to cut open his stomach; and another, seeing how we closed our knives, wanted to do the same thing but would have cut his fingers, had we not forestalled it.

All these natives had copper-coloured skin and black hair. The custom that they have of painting their hair makes it blond, verging on yellow, but the original tone may be seen by the roots. They were naked, wearing only a belt below the belly to conceal what decency forbids us to show. And they had tattooed only the upper chest and, in a few cases, the face. The chief alone had tattooing right across his stomach in a green band. It seems that these people, inhabiting a solitary island, lack motives strong enough to cause them to lose time in embellishing the body. It is only in a large population, after all, that vanity grows and puts down deep roots, diversity of tastes and opinions deciding what is in fashion and producing those ornaments which are—frequently—so ridiculous. Not one of these natives wore any ornament that served to disfigure any part of the face. A few men only wore little tortoiseshell rings in their ears.[20]

One would not be too mistaken, I think, to believe that these people had come from the Friendly Islands. It is now known, beyond any doubt, that those intrepid islanders do make long voyages in their canoes. And, the Friendly Islands being to the east of Anouta, it would have been easy for the people of the former to come and settle there, merely by following the direction of the prevailing wind.[21]

According to Captain Edwards' observations, Mitre Island lies in latitude 11°49'S, longitude 170°42'E from Greenwich, and Cherry Island lies in latitude 11°57'30"S, longitude 169°55'30"E.[22] Astronomical observations made aboard our own ship, however, fixed Mitre's position as latitude 11°55'S, longitude 170°20'E, and Cherry or Anuta Isle's position as 11°5'S, 170°0'45"E. They lie on a NW-SE axis over a total distance of twenty-seven and a half nautical miles. The rock located 40°SE from Cherry or Anuta Isle at a distance of a nautical mile is connected to it by a reef, against which rollers break with force. Our marine watches had been checked, the previous night, by lunar observations. The day spent determining these islands' positions was a clear enough one. The natives having withdrawn, we continued on our way. . . .[23]

OBSERVATIONS ON ANUTA ISLAND

The European discovery of Anuta and Fataka, in 1791, was connected with the *Bounty* affair, for Edward Edwards, captain of HMS *Pandora* sent to arrest the mutineers, first sighted what he named Cherry's Island on his passage back to England.[24] No landing was attempted because of the raging surf, but a tolerably accurate description of Anuta was compiled from the notes of *Pandora*'s officers.[25] The island was about one mile long, seemingly very fertile, and populated. Groups of huts were observed on coastal flats along the island's southern shore (at modern Rotoapi village). Hilltops had a cultivated look. *Apollon* was certainly among the first few ships to follow HMS *Pandora* to Anuta; and Shabel'skii casts an interesting sidelight on the question of Anutans' ethnic origins and "homeland."

Two major hypotheses have been advanced in explanation of the presence of such Polynesian enclaves as Anuta in the Melanesian area. One is that such enclaves are remnant populations, left behind as Polynesian parties travelled eastward. Much linguistic evidence has been adduced to back that contention, now considered shaky.[26] The other is that outposts like Anuta were results of later west-to-east migration and/or drift by Polynesians from such areas as Samoa and Tonga.[27] Recent archaeology has shown that there were settlements on the Anutan coast 3,000 years ago; that human occupation ended, 1,500 years or so ago; and that another migrant wave or waves arrived perhaps 400 years ago.[28] As for the provenance of those more recent waves, from which the modern population is descended, it would seem to have been Tonga, as Shabel'skii intimates. There is, however, continuing debate on just this point.[29] The genealogies of both Anutan chiefly lines confirm linguistic, artefactual, and other evidence that that resettlement occurred about the early sixteenth century AD. Although genetic links between Anuta and the Tongan Archipelago have not been adequately studied, it is clear that the kinship terminology of the Anutans is allied more closely to the Tongan than to Samoan terminology.[30] The evidence is, all in all, for Tonga, though of course Samoan settlers may also have arrived and intermarried in historic times. It is of interest, in any case, that the Anutans should so gratifyingly and promptly have responded to the Russians' use of Admiral D'Entrecasteaux's short Tongan word list.[31]

Coming up to Tonga from New Zealand in mid-March 1793, on his protracted search for traces of the fate of La Pérouse, D'Entrecasteaux had brought the *Recherche* and *Espérance* to anchor on the north coast of Tongatapu. The French were soon surrounded by a multitude of noisy islanders who wished to trade with them at once. But there were language problems, notwithstanding Cook's and his companions' word lists. E.P.E. Rossel, of *L'Espérance*, made these remarks:

> The vocabulary found in Cook's last *Voyage* was of slight assistance, either because of the difference between the pronunciation of the English and ours, or because most of the words that Cook thought belonged to the language of the Friendly Islands were merely words badly pronounced by the English, which the natives had repeated as a sign of approval, which may have led each side to believe that they were in agreement. At the beginning, we were often misled by this. . . .[32]

The problem was that Tongan words had been "misspelt" by Cook's companions, from the standpoint of contemporary Frenchmen who were guided by different transliteration usages. Cook's people had produced quite serviceable word lists for that period and were a good deal more competent linguistically than was allowed for by Rossel. What is significant within the context of *Apollon*'s Anuta call, however, is that Shabel'skii, who spoke French as well as Russian, used a relatively new Tongatapu word list, which had been drawn up with a view to accurate Gallic transcription and correct pronunciation. The Anutans understood him instantly.

RUSSIAN EVIDENCE OF 1822

*Apollon* passed by the windward (eastern) shoreline of Fataka at a distance of perhaps a thousand metres, close enough to see the "two conical rocks" which, on 12 August 1791, had seemed to Edwards and his men like "two high hummocks."[33] It was clear to the Russians that the island was not permanently settled, though its west side seemed quite fertile. Khrushchev then swung NW, in HMS *Pandora*'s track, until Anuta came in view.

Through telescopes, the Russians saw the reef around its southeast rim (Te Aropi Penua) and up its eastern side to Te Tu Tereva. Behind this reef they saw "a hedge (*une haie*) and a man with fresh-cut coconuts." The "hedge," perhaps a field wall obscured by vegetation such as taro,[34] ran behind the Rotoapi coastal settlement. *Cocos nucifera*, the crucial staple food of the Anutans to this day, grew plentifully on the island's strand belt.[35]

Rotoapi was a centre of Anutan fishing. Large reef fish were driven into stone wall traps in front of it; and outrigger canoes were kept there for use in deep sea expeditions.[36] The canoes that ventured out to *Apollon* were of a size still used by fishermen today.[37] "Material made of reeds" was plainly *tapa* (bark-cloth) pieces of traditional variety.

Among the fourteen men who came aboard, it seems, was an Anutan chief or leader. This *ariki*, who was much deferred to, was perhaps with his descent group on the sloop.[38] He was tattooed "across his stomach" in a green-blue band. Such bands were to be seen on island chiefs, Pu Koroatu for example, in the 1970s.[39] Nor has tattooing on the "upper chest" died out. Anutans show conservatism where their body ornament and decoration are concerned. Today, indeed, they do not dye their hair with coral lime; but small shell ornaments are still in use. The "tortoise shell" observed by Shabel'skii in some Anutans' ears was, most likely, Trochus shell.[40]

The Russians were correct in thinking that the islanders had seldom dealt with Europeans, and the Russian evidence of local ignorance of clasp knives, thirty years having elapsed since Edwards' visit, underlines that point. They were correct, too, in suspecting that Anuta had been peopled from the east. Shabel'skii himself had never seen Tongans but was certainly familiar with Cook's or other British printed sources on the 1777 Tongan visit. And, as seen, he was acquainted with Rossel's *Voyage de D'Entrecasteaux* (1808), with its description of the French-Tongan encounter of March-April 1793.[41] That such a visitor should, independently and on the basis of his reading, link Anuta with Tongatapu is noteworthy.

Edwards' observations were available to Arrowsmith and other eminent cartographers and seemed reliable. Nevertheless, the charts used in 1810–40 marked both "Cherry" and "Mitre" as uncertain.[42] Arrowsmith's and Kruzenshtern's uncertainty was justified by *Apollon*'s surveying. Edwards had in fact placed "Mitre" six minutes too far north, and no less than thirty minutes east of its correct location.[43] As for "Cherry," or Anuta, he had placed it twenty-five minutes too far north, and approximately five minutes east of its actual position.[44] Russian reckonings of latitude were accurate within one minute—a conspicuously competent performance.

# APPENDIX

# FIJIAN ARTEFACTS IN LENINGRAD (MAE COLLECTIONS 736-37)

The inventory (*opis'*) to Collection No. 736 of the Peter-the-Great Museum of Anthropology and Ethnography (MAE), 3 University Quay, Leningrad, is stored and maintained by the relevant section (*otdel*) of that large institution (which has always been a branch of the Academy of Sciences).[1] The section in question is *Otdel Avstralii i Okeanii* (Australia and Oceania), and was headed until 1985 by the ethnologist Nikolai A. Butinov. The inventory is kept in a large buff folder, containing two lists. One, drawn up in 1903 by the pre-Revolutionary anthropologist E.L. Petri, has been superseded by another, prepared in 1957 by Miss L.G. Rozina-Bernstam. As source material, the 1903 list has been carefully preserved. The 1957 list of artefacts is the fifth largest at MAE, with 326 entries.[2] Rozina's *opis'* begins with these remarks:

> Inventory of Collection No. 736. Time of accession, 1826; Collector— from round-the-world voyages of the beginning of the 19th century; Method of acquisition—by transfer; Documents to the Collection— labels taken from objects; Number of articles 326; Time of Registration—Sept. 1957; Inventory on 99 sheets; Remarks—the first listing was undertaken in the year 1903 by E.L. Petri. The earliest Russian mariners did not call at New Guinea or the Admiralty Islands, and yet there are specimens from those islands in the collection.

The 326 objects in Collection No. 736 are from Australia and New Guinea, Fiji, Kiribati, New Zealand, Samoa, Tahiti, the Marquesas and Tonga Islands, Hervey Island, Easter Island, Hawaii, Mangareva, Vanuatu, and the Admiralty, Solomon, and Marshall Islands. The 1826 transfer was to the

*Kunstkamera*, or Curiosities Cabinet, of the Academy of Sciences from the Admiralty Department Museum; the transfer in fact continued until 1830. Regrettably, documentation for the actual transferral has been lost.[3] Rozina lists 21 artefacts as definitely Fijian and these are listed here. In addition, however, Collection No. 736 contains at least four dozen other articles which are described merely as Melanesian, some of which are almost certainly Fijian. These include 36 spears (736-40-75), 15 fish spears (736-83-97), and 13 bracelets of assorted types 736-98-110). Fijian objects are also held in several other collections, (e.g., 168, 737, 1198, 1352, 2009), and some lie hitherto unidentified in Collection No. 736 itself. Since *no* information on the Leningrad Fijian holdings is available in English, however, it seems useful to provide at least these limited data from Collection MAE 736:

1 (736-11) Club, straight and massive, with striking end curved like an arc; reminiscent in shape of an old gun's butt. The striking end is flattened out and covered with a mesh of carved ornamentation. Made of light brown, heavy wood. Overall length 114 cm; width of lower end 22 cm; maximum diameter 4.5 cm.

2 (736-12) Club, like 736-11. The haft is wrapped around with light brown lacing and with several lashings of palm leaf. The upper end has a flat, smooth knob; the curved and flattened lower end is embellished with a carved net-like pattern. Polished, light brown, and well preserved. Overall length 113 cm; haft diameter 5.4 cm; width of the striking end 2.8 cm; width without knob 16.5 cm.

3 (736-13) Club, like the preceding pair; the carved reticular patterning on the striking end is divided into triangular sections. In the rib passing along the lower end of the club, two transversal holes have been bored. The side knob is broken. Polished, brown. Overall length 108 cm; diameter 4.3 cm; width of striking end with knob 23 cm.[4]

4 (736-14) Club, spade-shaped, with a long and broad blade. There are triangular projections on the sides of the blade's upper part. The handle is rounded rectangular in cross-section. The whole surface of the blade, on both faces, is covered with a carved reticular ornament, against which background there stand out elongated vertical and horizontal cylinders which intersect to form a cross, two half-moons, two little stars, and two bows. The outer face of the blade is embellished by a border of little triangles; the carved netting has been rubbed with lime. The handle extremity has a rectangular knob. The ends of both lateral projections have been damaged. The whole is coloured

brown. Overall length 124.5 cm; length of blade 72 cm; thickness of blade 5 cm; width of blade including side projections 47 cm; without them, 17 cm.

5 (736–15) Club, similar to 736–14. Against the carved reticular background of the blade, which has been embellished with lime also, stand out in relief: four rounded rosettes and intersecting and prominent ribs. The haft, oval in cross-section, ends with a small knob and is wrapped round by a fine woven lace or ribbon, light and dark brown. This is now damaged. Lateral projections have broken ends. Overall length 128 cm; length of blade 76 cm.; width of blade 14.5 cm; width of haft 4.4 cm.

6 (736–16) Club, similar to 736–14–15. Both faces of the blade are covered with the carved reticular pattern, against which one sees carved, in relief, smooth intersecting ribs of a cross and 4 stripes, each forming a right angle. Lime embellishment on one face only; ribs and stripes are all black. Haft is oval in cross-section with a rhomboid knob. Overall length 120 cm; blade length 69.5 cm; blade width beneath 11 cm; haft diameter 5 cm.

7 (736–17) Club, similar to 736–14–16; blade with obliquely slanted carved reticular design, decorated with lime; against it, one sees carved intersecting ribs and 4 bows. One side projection broken. Bows and ribs coloured black, all the rest is brown. Length 114 cm; blade width 14 & 34 cm; blade length 64 cm; haft diameter 4 cm.

8 (736–18) Club, like 736–14–17, but lacking the carved reticulation and with two ribs only. One broken projection. The haft is rectangular with a conical knob; polished red timber. Overall length 114 cm; blade length 50 cm; blade width 17 and 33 cm; haft breadth 4.4 cm.

9 (736–19) Club, similar to 736–14–18. The outside edges of both blade faces are decorated, below the transversal rib, with teeth as of a saw. Rounded rectangular haft, with rhomboid knob; made of red wood. Overall length 130 cm; blade length 51; blade width 14 & 29 cm; haft width 4 cm.[5]

10 (736–20) Club with a straight handle, round in cross-section, and a striking end curved round to ninety degrees. This end has been conically sharpened and a spherical widening is carved thereon, the whole surface of which shows carved and sharp points. The haft's upper end also has a small knob. Made of red wood. Overall length along the arc 112 cm; length of striking end 23 cm; haft diameter 4.7 cm; diameter of spherical widening 10.7 cm.

11 (736–21)  Club, similar to 736–20. The little spikes have been damaged in places. Overall length 112 cm; length of the curving end 21 cm; haft diameter 4.2 cm; diameter of the widening 10.4 cm. This weapon was kept at the Hermitage Museum (Winter Palace, Leningrad) until 1965.

12 (736–22)  Club, straight, with curved striking end, suggestive of an old musket's butt end. Round in cross-section, with a round, smooth knob; similar to 736–11. Half the curved part is rough (unworked?). The rest is polished. The club's upper end is ornamented with a wide band of carved patterning: broken elongated lines. Heavy dark wood. Overall length 107 cm; haft diameter 4.2 cm; width of lower end 15 cm; width of ornamental band 28 cm.

13 (736–23)  Club, similar to 736–22. Overall length 110 cm; width of striking end 17.5 cm; width of ornamental band 24 cm.

14 (736–24)  Club, similar to 736–22–23. Decorated on the upper part with broken lines running diagonally. Overall length 103 cm; haft diameter 4 cm; width of ornamental band 25.5 cm.

15 (736–25)  Club, similar to 736–11–12. The flattened-out striking end is very smooth; on the concave side has deeply carved rectangular patterning. The club's upper end is embellished with a carved band of broken lines, which run diagonally. Smooth round knob at the extremity; and signs of insect damage. Length 103 cm; length of striking end 14.5 cm; half diameter 4 cm; width of ornamental band 26.5 cm.

16 (736–26)  Club, similar to 736–25. Decoration on the upper end is elongated carved lines, which are interrupted. The end has a mushroom-shaped knob. Overall length 97.5 cm; breadth of lower end minus projection 7 cm; haft diameter 3.8 cm; width of ornamental band 19.5 cm.

17 (736–27)  Club, similar to 736–11. The upper end is decorated with geometrical patterns—triangles of parallel lines; the lower end has a dotted embellishment. Overall length 107 cm; width of lower end 11.5 cm; diameter of upper part 3.5 cm.

18 (736–28)  Club, similar to 736–11; unornamented, with damaged knob. Length 110 cm; width of lower end 14.5 cm; haft diameter 4 cm. Also light brown in colour.

19 (736–29)  Club, similar to 736–11. A rough half of the striking end is fringed with an ornament of triangles. Polished brown. Overall length 102.5 cm; width of striking end 12.5 cm; diameter 3.5 cm.

20 (736–30)  Club, similar to 736–11. Half the striking end is rough, the rest

is polished. Overall length 102.5 cm; width of striking end 13 cm; diameter 4 cm.

21 (736–32) Club, a massive straight stick with a pear-shaped striking knob consisting of three long, rounded projections. In addition, there is a short cylindrical projection below. Three very short branches remain to one side of the stick. Upper end ornamented with long carved stripes. Polished heavy wood. Overall length 109 cm; length of striking end 14 cm; width thereof 11 cm; diameter of club 4.3 cm.

Other Fijian artefacts, of yet older provenance, are in Collection No. 737. That collection also was examined and described by L.G. Rozina. The *opis'* offers these preliminary remarks:

> Inventory of Collection No. 737. Provenance—from the Admiralty Museum; Time of Accession—1809(?); Collector unknown; Items from the Fiji, Samoa, Hawaii, and Tahitian Islands; Number of objects—44; First Inventory—by A. Piotrovskii.
>
> In the old Inventory Book of the Collections Division (*Otdela Fondov*), in Inventory K–IV (N. 7, page 38), Collection No. 737 is indicated as having arrived in the year 1782 and been a collection of Captain Cook.

Of the forty-four objects in the present Collection No. 737, five are Tahitian, three are Fijian, and at least twenty-six are Hawaiian. Several items have been broken or mislaid since the time of accession. All the Fijian pieces are *tapa* specimens (*masi-sula*), in good repair. Rozina added these comments to her *opis'* preface (1961): "In his inventory, Piotrovskii lists 28 items . . . and observes: 'in most cases, provenance is unexplained. The collection contained approximately 30 items, most no doubt coming from the Admiralty Museum collection or from Cook. In 1777, J.R. Forster, who accompanied Cook on his Second Voyage, presented the *Kunstkamera* with three specimens of tapa from Tahiti. The tapa specimens were accessed only in 1809, however'."

Whether or not the three Fijian specimens were also presented (or sold) to the St. Petersburg Academy of Sciences by Johann Reinhold Forster is unknown. It *is* known that Forster sold numerous objects of natural history and many artefacts to Continental museums during the 1780s;[6] and he had professional connections with St. Petersburg and with a number of Russo-German savants.[7] At all events, it is apparent that the three Fijian specimens now in Collection No. 737 are of some antiquity and likely were collected during the later eighteenth century. Rozina described them, on the basis of her own listing of 1961, in a paper entitled, "Tapa of Oceania," published in

*SMAE* (Vol. 30, 1974:95–96). Because the 1974 descriptions are rather fuller than the inventory entries of 1961, they are offered here instead:

1 (737–11)   *Masi-sula.* Single-layered, white, and strong, with a light brown and black ornamentation. The design is broken into large rectangles, the motifs repeating each other. The ends of the length of material are ornamented with large concentric diamonds—black stripes on a background of fine, parallel black lines. At one end there are two diamonds, at the other— one only. The latter has a fringe or edging of smooth terracotta and white triangular festoons. The rest of the material's surface has a decorative background consisting of thick light brown lines made by *vesi*. On these are rectangles filled with black triangles in a checkered manner. At the centre of these black triangles are figures, L-shaped angles, toothed and reddish in colour. These were stamped onto the *masi*. Overall length 15 metres 50 cm; width 64–70 cm.

2 (737–12)   *Masi-sula.* Double-layered, solid white stuff. The ornament consists of four elongated rows of patterning, broken into rectangles. Of these, some are filled with fine stamped ornamentation, a black-and-white stenciling, while others show sets of transversal lines on a background of pale brown parallels. There are broad red bands down the middle and on the sides of the material. The side edges also have white, unornamented, triangular festoons. Overall length 10 metres 9 cm; width 50–52 cm; length of festoons 3–4 cm.

3 (737–34)   *Masi-sula.* A single-layered, fine, strong piece of stuff, ornamented all over with a dark brown or black lacquer-like substance, on one face only. This face gleams dark brown. The whole surface has been stamped with a small reticular pattern, running diagonally, and with straight transversal lines 3–6 cm apart. There is a fringe at one end, consisting of a smooth stripe of light brown material and then white triangular festoons. The obverse face of the material is also white. Overall length 17 metres 28 cm; width 42–53 cm.

Rozina's 1961 inventory at MAE adds a few details that are missing from her 1974 paper, such as that No. 737–11 consists of four joined pieces of *masi* and that No. 737–12 shows seven different geometrical patterns.

# Notes

ABBREVIATIONS

ACLS        American Council of Learned Societies
AGO         Arkhiv Vsesoiuznogo Geograficheskogo Obshchestva
            SSSR
AKV         *Arkhiv kniazia Vorontsova*. 40 vols. Moscow 1870–95
AHR         *American Historical Review*
AVPR        Arkhiv Vneshnei Politiki Rossii
BCHQ        *British Columbia Historical Quarterly*
CHSQ        *California Historical Society Quarterly*
DNB         *Dictionary of National Biography*. London 1885–1900
ES          *Entsiklopedicheskii slovar'*. St. P. 1890–1904
GSE         *Great Soviet Encyclopaedia*
HAHR        *Hispanic American Historical Review*
IVGO        *Izvestiia Vsesoiuznogo Geograficheskogo Obshchestva*
JPH         *Journal of Pacific History*
JPS         *Journal of the Polynesian Society*
JRAHS       *Journal of the Royal Australian Historical Society*
L           Leningrad
M           Moscow
MM          *Mariner's Mirror*
OMS         *Obshchii morskoi Spisok*. St. P., 1885–1907
Op.         *Opis'*, Inventory
PHR         *Pacific Historical Review*
PNQ         *Pacific Northwest Quarterly*
Razr.       *Razriad*, Category

| SEER | *Slavonic and East European Review* |
|---|---|
| SIRIO | *Sbornik Imperatorskago Russkago Istoricheskago Obsh-chestva* |
| SMAE | *Sbornik Muzeia Antropologii i Etnografii* |
| St. P. | St. Petersburg |
| TIIET | *Trudy Instituta Istorii Estestvoznaniia i Tekhniki* |
| TsGADA | Central State Archive of Ancient Acts (Moscow) |
| TsGIAL | Central State Historical Archive in Leningrad |
| TsGAVMF | Central State Archive of the Navy of the USSR |
| ZADMM | *Zapiski Admiralteiskago Departamenta Morskago Minis-terstva* |
| ZGDMM | *Zapiski Gidrograficheskago Departamenta Morsk. Minis-terstva* |
| ZMNP | *Zapiski Ministerstva Narodnogo Prosveshcheniia* |
| ZUKMS | *Zapiski Uchonogo Komiteta Morskago Shtaba* |

CHAPTER ONE: ANGLO-RUSSIAN MARITIME ENTENTE

1 Barratt 1979 (1):218.
2 Grekov 1960:342–44; Sokolov 1851; Veselago 1939:57–78; Barratt 1981:23–25; Beskrovnyi 1957:306ff.; Divin 1971:164–66.
3 Barratt 1981:32–41; Sokolov 1851:206–8; Golder 1914:158ff.; Pokrovskii 1941:274–79; Waxell 1940:70–106; Müller 1758, 3:392–95.
4 Vize 1948:109–10; Lantzeff and Pierce 1973:179–80.
5 Deane 1899:87–90; Berkh 1831, 2:368–70.
6 Barratt 1981:25–26.
7 Divin 1961, passim; Divin 1971:95–96.
8 TsGADA, *fond* Senata, *delo* 666:104.
9 Divin 1971:94.
10 TsGADA, *fond* Gosarkhiva, *razr.* 31, *delo* 9:11–12.
11 Divin 1971:97.
12 Pokrovskii 1941:94–98.
13 Barratt 1979(1):218–19.
14 Chichagov 1886:35–53; Morozov 1952:765–78.
15 TsGAVMF, *fond* 315, *delo* 381; Belov 1956:2; Berg 1949:39–43.
16 Veselago 1939:85; Anderson 1956:132–36.
17 Veselago 1939:86–87; Anderson 1947:17–27; Barratt 1981:50. *SIRIO*, 10 (1876):28–29; *Materialy*, XI (1886):40–43.
18 *Materialy*, XI:48–52; Laird Clowes 1899, 3:326–27; Cross 1974:251–54; Cross 1980:156–59.
19 On personalia, Winter 1965, 3 and Soler 1970.
20 Cook 1973: 46–47; Tompkins and Moorehead 1949:231ff.
21 Barratt 1981:51–53.
22 See Bibliography.
23 Tompkins and Moorehead 1949:235–44; Chapman 1916:60–61, 87–90; Wagner 1944:219–25; Cook 1973:53ff.
24 Chapman 1916:221.
25 Ibid.:226–27.

26  Barratt 1981:59–66 (Krenitsyn-Levashev expedition).
27  Blue 1939:453–54; Humphrey 1938:95–101.
28  Archivo General de Indias, Catalogue 2901 (Bancroft Library copy):2–3.
29  Farrelly 1944:33–38.
30  *ES*, 79:199–202.
31  Smirnov 1967; Golder 1914:170–77, 193–96, etc.
32  Anderson 1956:136ff.; *Materialy*, XI:607–8; Anderson 1952:148–64; Tarle 1945:passim.
33  Cross 1980:159.
34  Anderson 1952:163–64; Cross 1980:160ff.
35  Berkh 1823:52–58; Divin 1971:212–25; Bancroft 1886:140–49.
36  Archivo General de Indias, Catalogue 2901 (Lacy to Grimaldi, 1 May 1775, etc.)
37  Tompkins and Moorehead 1949:251–55.
38  Divin 1971:196ff.; Makarova 1968: passim; Berkh 1823:52–56.
39  Barratt 1981:49–50; Divin 1971:212–14; Sokolov 1852:42–58.
40  TsGAVMF, *fond* 216, *delo* 77:1–2; *fond* 315, *delo* 381: Barratt 1981:58–60.
41  Beaglehole 1967, 3:649–66, 1242, 1338–39.
42  Ibid., Appendix, Ia. M. Svet, trans. P. Putz, "Cook and the Russians," pp. 6–8.
43  Ibid. 3:714 & 1550; TsGADA, *fond* A.R. Vorontsova, *delo* 754.
44  Beaglehole 1967, 3:1550; Williams 1962:210–11.
45  Sauer 1802:41–43, 275–78; Langsdorff 1814, 2:12; Kruzenshtern 1814, 2:108–12; Savin 1851:148–61.
46  Grenader 1957:22–30; Sokolov 1848:148ff.; Divin 1971:289–91.
47  Beaglehole 1967, 3:650–52 and (on Behm) clxiii–iv; Sgibnev 1869, no. 7:23–25; Lenz 1970:37.
48  Beaglehole 1967, 3:Appendix, "Cook and the Russians," pp. 6–7.
49  Ibid. 2:1553.
50  Watrous 1966:10–24; *DNB*, 11:782–83; *GDU*, 10:312.
51  Grenader 1957:22–25; Cook 1973:115; Barratt 1981:76–77.
52  Berkh, "Izvestie," pp. 97–99; Howay 1973:3–5, 9; Bancroft 1886:242–44.
53  La Pérouse 1798, 2:86–107.
54  Sauer 1802.
55  Penrose 1959:90–96; *OMS*, IV:406–8; Cranmer-Byng 1968:364.
56  Penrose 1959:28; Beaglehole 1967, 3:714.
57  Barratt 1979(1):223–24; Penrose 1959:89; Cross 1980:23–25; Shteinberg 1943:34ff.; Berkh, "Izvestie," pp. 97–98.
58  Penrose 1959:95–96; *AKV*, XVII:118 & XVIII:302.
59  Barratt 1979(1):224–25
60  TsGADA, *fond* Gosarkhiva, *razr.* 24, *delo* 61:3; *DNB*, 2:795–96.
61  Barratt 1981:89.
62  Penrose 1959:91, 94; Nevskii 1951:21–38; Barratt 1981:138–40.
63  TsGAVMF, *fond* 172, *delo* 367:1–13; Sokolov 1848:143–48.
64  *OMS*, IV:406–8; Cross 1980:159–60.
65  Clendenning 1974:passim; *Materialy*, XI—720–22.
66  Divin 1971:289–90; Sokolov 1848:148–50.
67  *PSZRI*, XXII, no. 16, 530; Sokolov 1848:174–76.
68  TsGAVMF, *fond* I.G. Chernysheva, *delo* 376:322–23; Frolov 1855:529–41; Wagner 1938:297–326.
69  Pavlov 1957:19–21; Lensen 1959:126–27; Barratt 1981:114–15, 121–22, 129–30.
70  TsGADA, *fond* Gosarkhiva, *razr.* 10, op. 3, *delo* 16:133.
71  TsGAVMF, *fond* 172, *delo* 376:262 (orders for V.P. Fondezin).
72  Okun' 1951:17.
73  Ibid. 17–18; Barratt 1981:96; Shemelin 1823:no.23; *ZUKMS*, XV (1840):361ff.
74  Veselago 1869:3; Nevskii 1951:23–25.
75  TsGAVMF, *fond* 7, op. 1, *delo* 2; Golovnin 1961:iii.
76  Aslanbegov 1873:3–5.
77  Golovnin 1961:ii–iii; Veselago 1869:3–4 (Cadet Corps).

78  TsGAVMF, *fond* 7, op. 1, *delo* 2 ("Zapisnaia knizhka"); *AKV*, IX:178, 198; Nozikov 1945:75.
79  TsGAVMF, *fond* 315, *delo* 381; Chichagov 1886:35ff.; Nevskii 1951:24; Krusenstern 1813:xxiv–xxv; Barratt 1981:108–12.
80  Anderson 1958:9, 71–72.
81  Anderson 1947:17–27; *AKV*, X:325; Divin 1959:44ff.; Rea 1955:245–49; *DNB*, 2:667; Cross 1980:156–57.
82  TsGAVMF, *fond* I.G. Chernysheva, *delo* 44 & Billings 1849:502 (round-the-world projects of 1781, 1786 linked with those two officers); *ZUKMS*, X (1833): "O medaliakh v Pamiat'. . ." (plan discussed in 1764 re Krenitsyn-Levashev expedition); Barratt 1981:66–69 and Tompkins and Moorehead 1949:231–55 (Spanish threat); Grenader 1957 (French arrival).
83  *AGM*, III:338; see also *AKV*, XXVIII (1883):146–47 and *Materialy*, XIV:439–40.
84  PRO Adm/1/498, cap.370; TsVMM, No.41821/1 (9170), Lisianskii, Iu. F., "Zhurnal . . . s 1793 po 1800 god," pp. 3–5; Lisiansky 1814:xv–xvii.
85  PRO Adm/1/498, cap. 370 (Murray to Stephen, 16 Aug. 1794); Krusenstern 1813, I:x xiv; Lisiansky 1814:xvi.
86  Krusenstern 1813, I:32–33; Marshall 1824, 2:61; Ralfe 1828, III:212, IV:98–99; James 1822, I:495; Lisiansky 1814:xvi.
87  Krusenstern 1813:xxiv–xxv; *ZAD*, III (1815), Kruzenshtern, I.F., "Puteshestvie . . .k Madrasu v 1797 godu"; TsVMM, No. 41821/1, Iu. F. Lisianskii, "Zhurnal," pp. 30ff.
88  PRO Adm/1/1516, cap. 404 (Boyles to Evan Nepean, 16 Mar. 1797); Nevskii 1951:34; Cross 1980:171; also Turner 1963 and Laird Clowes 1899, 4:279, 283, 296–97, 408–12 (Baskakov and others in Duncan's North Sea Fleet).
89  TsVMM, No. 41821/1:14ff.; Nevskii 1951:33–34.
90  Krusenstern 1813, I:xxv–xxvi & 2:289; Howay 1973:33, 35; Nevskii 1951:26–29.
91  Kruzenshtern 1809, I:20.
92  TsVMM, No. 41821/1, pp. 57–60; Hook 1832, I:168–70 (General David Baird in HMS *Sceptre*, etc.); Wellesley 1836, I:421 (Mornington's anxieties re Tipoo Sahib and de Suffren, 1797).
93  TsVMM, No. 41821/1, pp. 58–59; Pertsmakher 1972:252; *NC*, 3 (1800):147; *Fort William Correspondence*, XIII (1959).
94  Pertsmakher 1972:252.
95  TsVMM, 41820/2 ("Vakhtennyi zhurnal"); *DNB*, 8:295–96.
96  TsVMM, 41821/1, p. 60.
97  Ibid.:62; TsGAVMF, *fond* 406, op. 7, *delo* 62 & *fond* 198, op. 1, *delo* 36; Cross 1980:165–67 (1800 Armed Neutrality, etc.).
98  Sokolov 1883:137; Belinskii 1948, 3:112; *OMS*, IV:12ff.; Nevskii 1951:193–94.
99  Krusenstern 1813, I:xxx; Turgenev 1915:90–92 (Mordvinov's position); Barratt 1981:111.
100  *Russkaia starina*, 84 (1895), bk. 7:125–26; Novakovskii 1918: 77–78; Shemelin 1823:No. 23; Kruzenshtern 1809, I:3; Tikhmenev 1939, I:122–123.
101  Krusenstern 1813, I:14; Langsdorf 1813:x; Barratt 1981:115–17.
102  Barratt 1987:Chap. 1.
103  Armstrong 1979:121–25.
104  Hotimsky 1971; Barratt 1979 (1):228–29.
105  TsGADA, *fond* A.R. Vorontsova, *delo* 754:passim; Beaglehole 1967, 3:1553 & Appendix:6–7.
106  Beaglehole 1955:cclxxxiii.
107  Rozina 1966; Kaeppler 1978; Craig 1978:94–97.
108  Ryden 1963:68–69.
109  Barratt 1981:140–41; Friis 1967:186–97.
110  Fainberg 1960:52–66;l Krusenstern 1813, T:286; Lensen 1959:142ff.; Nevskii 1951:204–9; Voenskii 1919:60–64.
111  Kruzenshtern 1809, I:142–67; Shemelin 1816, I:106–35; Rezanov 1825:73–94; Vancouver 1798, 2:93.
112  TsGIAL, *fond* 853 (M.M. Buldakova), *delo* 1:No. 74 ("Zhurnal prikazov"); also, on the orders, Gvozdetskii 1947:85–88.

113 Tilesius 1806; Langsdorf 1810:99–118; Rozina 1963:110–19; Nevskii 1951:57–58, 270–71.
114 Rozina 1963:110–11; Rezanov 1825:93; Shemelin 1816, I:111–13; Korobitsyn 1952: 158–60.
115 Krusenstern 1813, I:11; Lenz 1970:40–41, 410, 468; Nevskii 1951:59–60.
116 Voenskii 1895:125ff.; Tikhmenev 1939, I:121–23; Lavrischeff 1938, 3:270; Krusenstern 1813, I:xxx; Dumitrashko 1947:15–17.
117 *Protokol Konferentsii Akademii Nauk*, 13 Apr. 1803.
118 Barratt 1981:113–15; Ivashintsev 1980:1–2; Mal'tebriun 1822.
119 Cited by Nevskii 1951:37.
120 Kruzenshtern 1809, I:2.
121 Golovnin 1816; Golovnin 1819: Chap. 3; Nozikov 1945:81–85.
122 TsGAVMF, *fond* 213, *delo* 97:1–2 ("Raport kapitan-leitenanta M.N. Vasil'eva"); *delo* 100:1–2 ("Raport komandira shliupa . . . G.S. Shishmareva . . .25 Aprelia 1820 goda"); Lazarev 1950: 162–66; Ivashintsev 1980:50–51.
123 Horsburgh 1827, II:595; Sharp 1960:195.
124 *Nantucket Inquirer*, 22 Oct. 1822.
125 Sementovskii 1951:141–60; Sharp 1960:198–99.
126 Rogers 1983:75–77; Maude 1964.
127 Barratt 1981:(1):13–14, 77; Suris 1962.
128 Kabo & Bondarev 1974:101–11; Vorob'ev 1949:497–504.
129 Barratt 1981:14, 20.
130 Gibson 1976:viii.
131 Hotimsky 1971:6–12. Results of the third voyage (1776–80) had been available to the Admiralty, through reports of Clerke, King, and Gore, even in 1780.
132 Armstrong 1979:121–25; Krusenstern 1813, I:190, 216, II:203, 222; Kotzebue 1821, I:6; Belov 1962:107–8.
133 Penrose 1959:94.
134 *Materialy dlia istorii*, III:passim; Barratt 1981:194–98.
135 Krusenstern 1813, I:11; Lisiansky 1814:318–19; Kohl 1843, 2:200–2; Lenz 1970:40–41, 468; Friis 1967:185ff.
136 Berg 1926:23; Zubov 1954:146–47; Friis 1967:185–97.
137 Barratt 1981(1):159–75.
138 Perm' District State Archive, Perm': *fond* 445 (K.T. Khlebnikova), op. 1, *delo* 58 ("Doneseniia Leitenanta L.A. Gagemeistera"):1–2; Ivashintsev 1980:14.
139 Ivashintsev1980:18–19, 66–67, 80, 101, 104, 110; Berens 1903:No. 3:19–20; Shabelsky 1826:37–42.
140 Gough 1973:4.
141 Veselago 1869:2–3; Golovnin 1961:ii–iv.
142 TsGAVMF, *fond* 7, op. 1, *delo* 1; Hotimsky 1971:6–12; Dunmore 1965:90–94 (Bougain-ville in the New Hebrides).
143 Golovnin 1961:iiff.
144 TsGAVMF, *fond* 7, op.1, *delo* 2 ("Zapisnaia knizhka"):240–43; *AKV*, XVIII:87–88; Turner 1963:215ff.
145 *AKV*, XXVIII:146–47; *AGM*, III:338–40; *Materialy*, XIV:439ff.; Lisiansky 1814:xvi–xviii.
146 Nelson 1844, V:448; Unkovskii, "Zapiski," pp. 11–12; Golovnin 1949:5–7; Anderson 1956:144–46.
147 TsGAVMF, *fond* 7, op.1, *delo* 2:246–52 (convoy duty, action in Bay of Servera, Feb. 1805, etc.); Nozikov 1945:76.
148 Ivashintsev 1980:15.
149 TsGAVMF, *fond* 7, op. 1, *delo* 2:256–57.
150 Ibid.:257–58.
151 Ivashintsev 1980:15; Noxikov 1945:76.
152 Golovnin 1816:177–200; Beaglehole 1974:402–7; Forster 1777, 2:261–62; Forster 1982, IV:583–85.
153 Mel'nitskii 1856; Rikord 1875: Chaps. 2–3.
154 Golovnin 1961:v; Laird Clowes 1899, 4:408–12.

155  Ivashintsev 1980:137.
156  Ivashintsev 1980:139 and Barratt 1984:6–7 (*Kamchatka*'s company).
157  Krusenstern 1813, 2:194–96, 217–19; Andreev 1948:365–67; Dobell 1830, I:297–98; 2:24–25; *AGM*, III:574–76.
158  Golovnin 1961:55–60.
159  Ibid.:72–73 (instruments by Arnold and Barraud, etc.); Shemelin 1816, I:22–23; Krusenstern 1813, I:8–9, 33.
160  Krusenstern 1813, I:68–79; Shemelin 1816, I:60–62; Nevskii 1951:86–96; Golovnin 1961:103–8.
161  Golovnin 1961:125–26; Nozikov 1945:78.
162  Golovnin 1961:134–48; Walker 1957:124–31 (political position at Cape Town); *DNB*, II:402–3 (Admiral Albermarle Bertie).
163  Golovnin 1961:149.
164  Ibid.:208–9; Ivashintsev 1980:18.
165  Nevskii 1951:57–58; Krusenstern 1813, I:10; Barratt 1981:116.
166  Golovnin 1961:47–48 (Pacific charts, atlases, etc.).
167  Kahn 1968:700–8; Hoare 1976:168–70; Beaglehole 1961, 2:cxliii–cxlviii.
168  Beaglehole 1961, 2:488ff.; Hoare 1976:117–20; Forster 1982, IV:484–536.
169  Beddie 1970:No. 1223; Larousse 1982, XIV:1664.
170  Details in Sopikov 1962: No. 5025; Hotimsky 1971:7.
171  Dunmore 1965:91–94; Sharp 1960:117–18.
172  Dunmore 1965:92.
173  Bougainville 1771:242ff.
174  Golovnin was apparently unacquainted with James Burney's *Chronological History*, Vol. II of which (London 1806) contained a chapter (XVII) on the Quiros voyage. He may well have known the relevant passage in Alexander Dalrymple's *Historical Collection* (London 1770:vol. 1); that, however, would have told him nothing about the Southern New Hebrides.
175  Survey in Beaglehole 1974:394–407 (Northern New Hebrides & Tana).
176  Sharp 1960:132–34.
177  Beaglehole 1974:394–401; Beaglehole 1961, 2:fig. 66, p. 456 (map of *Resolution*'s track); Hoare 1976:116–17.
178  Sharp 1960:136; Beaglehole 1961:518–19.
179  Beaglehole 1961, 2:460–61; Forster 1777, II:205–6.
180  Beaglehole 1961:470–83; Forster 1982, IV:572–83; Hoare 1976:116.
181  Forster 1777, II:261; also Beaglehole 1961:482, 524.
182  Forster 1982, IV:606–7; Wales 1778:97–98; Beaglehole 1961:495.
183  Beaglehole 1961:498–500; Wales 1778:83–88; Forster 1982, IV: 661.
184  Beaglehole 1961:493, 501; Forster 1982, IV:627–28; Golovnin 1961:227.
185  Forster 1777, II:226; Beaglehole 1961:483, n2.
186  Golovnin 1961:48 (*Diana*'s trade goods for Oceania).
187  TsGAVMF, *fond* 7, op. 1, *delo* 2; Golovnin 1961:29.
188  Golovnin 1961:231–50; Nozikov 1945:82–84.
189  Golovnin 1961:219; also Map 2 here.
190  The inlet was ESE of Anetchitchao Pt.; Beaglehole 1961:495, 524; Inglis 1887:Chap. 1.
191  Golovnin 1961:220; compare Forster 1777, II:261; Forster 1982, IV:584; Beaglehole 1961:482.
192  Golovnin 1961:220; Beaglehole 1961:482, n3, 486, n2 (ownership and exchanges of coconuts, etc.).
193  Forster 1778:254. The language was actually Kwamera.
194  Golovnin 1961:222; Beaglehole 1961:488 (Kwamera *buga*, a Polynesian term; cf. Tongan & Rarotongan *puaka*, pig).
195  Golovnin 1961:224, nl.
196  *Syn otechestva* (St. P. 1816), Pt. 31, no. 31:177–200, no. 32:217–33; Pt. 32, no. 33:3–23, no. 34:41–57; no. 35:84–101.
197  Golovnin 1961:225–26; Beaglehole 1961:485; Sparrman 1944:154; Forster 1777, II:272–73.

198  Golovnin 1961:227–28; Forster 1777, II:277; Turner 1861:77; Beaglehole 1961:505; Forster 1982, IV:622–23.
199  Golovnin 1961:228; Forster 1982, IV:591, n6.
200  Golovnin 1961:229; Forster 1982, IV:619–20.
201  Golovnin 1961:230. Gunama had not supposed that the Russians were returning ancestors (cf. Beaglehole 1961: 484, n4, etc.); nor can the modest volume of foodstuffs provided by his people for Golovnin be explained in those terms (Ibid.:489, nl).
202  Golovnin 1961:243, 250.
203  Barratt 1981:164–69.
204  Golovnin 1851:II:135–47; Lensen 1959:240–41.
205  Golovnin 1961:250; Beaglehole 1961:481, 489, n4. Cook in fact refers to Immer, not Emir, Island.
206  Golovnin 1961:251; Ivashintsev 1980:19; Sharp 1960:63.
207  Sharp 1960:164–65; Golovnin 1961:251–52.
208  Khrushchev 1826:244ff.; Shabelsky 1826:37–42.
209  Ivashintsev 1980:114.
210  Ibid.:101, 104; Berens 1903:12–13 (*Krotkii* and Rotuma).
211  Both *Krotkii* and *Elena* touched at the Ellis Islands (Tuvalu) in 1829: Ivashintsev 1980:102, 104; Lazarev 1950:163–69, 373–75; Khromchenko 1832:306–8. *Elena* evidently sighted both Nui (Koerzen's Nederlandsch Eyland; see Sharp 1960:208) and Nanumanga (Maurelle's Cocal: Ibid:150–51.) *Krotkii* passed two days, 7–8 May 1829, examining "D'Urville's Candaboque" in lat. 19°07'S, long. 177°58'E. *Otkrytie* and *Blagonamerennyi* passed through the same area in April 1820, also heading north; and Nukufetau was sighted and surveyed from the west by Captain-Lt. Gleb Shishmarev of *Blagonamerennyi*, with whom natives in four canoes traded lethargically on the 17th of that month: Lazarev 1950:166–68.
212  Golovnin 1961:252–54; Duperrey 1827: 45–53; Sharp 1960:191.
213  Golovnin 1961:262.

## CHAPTER TWO: GOLOVNIN'S ACCOUNT OF THE VISIT TO ANEITYUM AND TANA

1  Also Forster 1777, II:260–61 and Beaglehole 1961, 2:481–82.
2  Golovnin follows Cook's nomenclature for the Southern New Hebrides: see Forster 1982, IV:594; Sharp 1960:133–34.
3  The plural form is correct.
4  From the vicinity of Anelgowhat village, situated behind a wide sandy beach.
5  East of Anetchitchao point.
6  I.e., due west of that same point, in lat. 20°15'S.
7  Conventional usage: the Aneityumese wore the very narrow loin-strip or the penis wrapper; women wore the grass skirt that was usual in the New Hebrides: Forster 1777, II:266; Turner 1861:79–80.
8  Turner 1861:80–82; Beaglehole 1961, 2:483.
9  See discussion in Haddon & Hornell 1975, II:15–18.
10  Or, narrow strips.
11  George Forster's "Mother of Pearl Shell": Forster 1982, IV:608.
12  Ibid.:IV:594; Sharp 1960:133–34.
13  Beaglehole 1961, 2:482ff.
14  *Diana* now stood two or three miles north of Samoa Pt. and SW of Aniwa.
15  Golovnin had been reading Cook and Forster overnight.
16  The "boar-spears" were javelins thrown with the aid of a cord loop on the Tannese clubs. See Forster 1777, II:279–80, 326 and Beaglehole 1961, 2:506–7.
17  All this exactly echoed events of 5 Aug. 1774, when *Resolution* had arrived in the same spot: Forster 1982, IV:584.
18  Forster 1777, II:260–61.
19  Golovnin 1961:110ff.
20  Forster 1982, IV:591–92, 602, 635 (foodstuffs obtained in 1774).
21  Sharp 1960:174. Golovnin had a copy of J.J. de Labillardière's *Relation du voyage à la*

*recherche de La Pérouse* (Paris 1800), so could trace the tracks of *Recherche* and *Espér-ance* past the New Hebrides of Apr. 1793.

22 Golovnin was acquainted with Dalrymple's *Historical Collection* (London 1770–71), Vol. I:166ff. of which dealt with Malekula and Espiritu Santo in the Northern New Hebrides.

23 Thus fulfilling the function of Cook's Paowang and the Forsters' Pawyangom in 1774: Forster 1777, II:270–71.

24 Forster 1777, II:359–60; Forster 1982, IV:629. The Russians apparently consulted J.R. Forster's *Observations* (London 1778) for its "Comparative Table of Various Languages" (p. 254), though Golovnin does not specify that Forster senior is meant.

25 Forster 1777, II:266 ("a Pool . . . not above Twinty yards from the shore"); Beaglehole 1961, 2:483, n2.

26 Forster 1982, IV:594.

27 I.e., 1816. On the effects of the earliest European contacts with the Tannese, see Guiart 1956:Chaps. 1–3.

28 Tannese *pukas*, deriving from the Polynesian word *puaka*: further on hogs and dogs, Forster 1777, II:289; Beaglehole 1961, 2:488; Turner 1861:87. Gunama recognized the immense superiority of *Diana*'s cutter over the local dugout (*negau* or *niko*), which was much inferior even to Futunese or Aniwan craft: Forster 1982, IV:630, n4 & 634, n4.

29 Forster 1982, IV:594 (*booga*, etc.); Beaglehole 1961, 2:483 and Sparrman 1944:154 (*Resolution*'s volley of 6 Aug. 1774.) See below for discussion of the true reasons for *Diana*'s kindly reception by the people (?Karumene) on the east side of Port Resolution.

30 Despite the natives' relative indifference to iron axes and other British implements: Forster 1777, II:336.

31 The landing was not on Cape Cook, half a mile south of Samoa Pt., but on the bay's west shore. See Plate 1 for Tannese weaponry.

32 The condition of the watering pond varied week by week. Like Port Resolution itself, it was dried out by earthquakes in 1878 and 1888: see Gunn 1914:178, etc. and Forster 1982, IV:608, on the swampiness and mosquitos of the area.

33 *Diana* was now anchored, slightly south of *Resolution*'s anchorage: Forster 1777, II:268 and Beaglehole 1961, 2:483.

34 Local yams often weighed over 200 lbs.: Forster 1982, IV:627, nl.

35 Like Kruzenshtern's "Marquesan Orders" of May 1804 (see Barratt 1981:6–7), which they strongly resemble, these instuctions were based on Cook's of forty years before.

36 Lensen 1959:205–78. See also Forster 1982, IV:624–25 (weapons), 588 (the people of the Enekahi side of the bay, towards Mount Yasur).

37 Probably the local *nipn*, i.e., *Musa sp.*, the Forsters' "Horse plantains" (Forster 1982, IV:592), *Saccharum officinalum L.*, and varieties of *Dioscorea alata L.* (Ibid., IV:627, nl). The Russians had arrived at Tana only two weeks earlier in the year than had Cook in 1774, so the foodstuffs available for barter were virtually the same for both.

38 Half-way up Cape Cook towards Samoa Pt.

39 Forster 1777, II:337 (Cook's inability to purchase hogs).

40 Ibid., II:299–301; Beaglehole 1961, 2:488–90. The Russians were heading towards the sacred place at Ile Pou, at the end of Samoa Pt. Forster 1777, II:337 on the Yatta met in 1774.

41 For game to feed the ship's company.

42 Evidently on the Enekahi side of the bay, towards the volcano, and so among the natives who frequently fought the Karumene, Gunama's people.

43 For brief comments on Russian linguistic evidence, see below.

44 *Yerumanu*, "chief" in the Kwamera dialect.

45 Forster 1777, II:292 (confluence of men from other districts to meet Europeans); Beagle-hole 1961, 2:507–8 and Guiart 1956:9–12 (Tannese chiefly systems); Beaglehole 1961, 2:504–5, Forster 1777, II:324; Forster 1982, IV:622 (female drudgery).

46 Turner 1861:76ff. and Forster 1982, IV:622–23 (body painting); Forster 1777, II:277 (painted patterns); Ibid., II:288 (the indifference shown towards alcohol by Fannokko in 1774).

47 Golovnin was essentially correct about this complex ritual question, on which see Beagle-

hole 1961, 2:487, n4 and Forster 1982, IV:591, n6 & 627, n4. Iata feared that he might contract elephantiasis or lay himself open to later sorcery, should a sacred man burn the left-over fish (as *nahak*, "rubbish"), in due course. Nor, we may think, was he sure that the fish was untouched by women.

48 Like Cook's men, the Russians relished Tana's numerous kinds of fig–locally, *nihm*, *Ficus spp.*: see Seeman 1865:247–48 and Forster 1982, IV:591–92, 602, 620. They acquired some 1,090 coconuts (*Cocos nucifera*) and 232 lbs. of yam (*Dioscorea alata L.*) but practically no breadfruit.

49 These were Enekahi men hoping for good payment and, as Golovnin says, full of respect for *Diana*'s guns.

50 Forster 1777, II:311; Beaglehole 1961, 2:469, n5 Forster 1982, IV:569, n7 & 602, n2; Sparrman 1944:154.

51 Forster 1982, IV:625; Forster 1777, II:278–80.

52 Golovnin followed the Forsters, the astronomer William Wales, and Cook himself in pondering the effects of winds and rains on Tanna's volcanoes: see Beaglehole 1961, 2:497–98 and Forster 1982, IV:618, etc.

53 Forster 1777, II:300 (cannibalism); aslo Turner 1861:83 and Guiart 1956:401. Golovnin's fears were probably unjustified.

54 Golovnin translates from Chapter 2 of Vol. II of George's *Voyage Round the World* (London 1777), "Account of Our Stay at Tanna, and departure from the New Hebrides" (pp. 262–364), and incorporates the translated passages into a continuous Russian text. I here restore Forster's original remarks, indicating (as Golovnin does not) the page references to the 1777 edition. *Diana*'s also carried copies of Cook's own *Voyage* (1777), as well as of the older Forster's *Observations* (1778), but George Forster was always Golovnin's main yardstick in the New Hebrides.

55 *Piper methysticum Forst.*, one of Tana's most valued domestic plants, associated with numerous rituals and ceremonies.

56 The Russians saw only *niko* in Uea Bay, dugouts made from the trunks of breadfruit trees, described by Wales (Beaglehole 1961, 2:503, 863). No better-made Futunese canoes were present, as they had evidently been in 1774.

57 Forster 1982, IV:592, n5, 623.

58 On the Enekahi (west) side of the bay. Banana leaves, and not ginger, were actually used for covering, as a rule: Forster 1982, IV:623. The Russians were offered ochre-based red colouring substance: Turner 1861:77. Like the local blacklead, it was often imported, from Erromanga. The nephrite, too, was brought from afar, from New Caledonia: de La Rue 1956:69.

59 Forster 1982, IV:622, n1, 626 (abuse of woman); Ibid., IV:625 (esteemed hardwood clubs based on Fijiian exemplars.) Golovnin's "most esteemed weapon" was imported from Erromanga or, at least, fashioned from Erromangan timber.

60 See note 47 (contamination by foodstuffs); Forster 1777, II:318–23 (conches, reed pipes, and Tannese music); Forster 1982, IV:623 (tortoise shell earrings, etc.). The Russians retraced the steps along the Samoa Pt. side of the bay that the British had taken often in 1774, not realizing that the local (?Karumene) tribe considered themselves "allied" to Europeans. Gunama was living at Samoa village.

61 As George Forster regretted the absence of James Burney at Tana when music was to be recorded and discussed (Forster 1982, IV:602, n8), so Golovnin, a thorough but unmusical man, could have used the services of Kruzenshtern's borrowed savant, Tilesius von Tilenau, whose commentaries on Marquesan and Kamchadale music remain of value: Kruzenshtern 1809–12:3. Forster 1982, IV:629, on George's contribution to Melanesian linguistics.

62 Perhaps a printer's or copyist's error: Mount Yasur stands four miles west of Port Resolution, not north of it.

63 Forster 1982, IV:619–20 (food plants cultivated); palings round plantations were usually of sugarcane reeds, not timber.

64 I.e., the only quadrupeds.

65 Beaglehole 1961, 2:488; Forster 1777, II:289; Turner 1861:87.

66 Details in Forster 1982, IV:621. Here again, Golovnin vaguely refers to "Forster," not to

Johann Reinhold as the context plainly requires.

67 The "flycatchers" included the yellow white-eye and the collared flycatcher; the green palm lorikeet and coconut lory, sighted in 1774, were probably present in 1809 also. *Diana's* officers were not ornithologists, and had little time to spare for non-edible birds.

68 Sparrman 1944:154; Forster 1982, IV:593, 595, 602.

69 *Esox argenteus*, a *Mullus* species.

70 Forster 1777, II:334-35, 340 (noxious swamps); Belkin 1962, I:457-61 (the mosquito *Aedes hebrideus*); Turner 1861:70-72 (heat caused by the Yenkahe volcanic system of Tana). Port Resolution is actually malaria-free–a happy result of superior drainage of all surface water through volcanic ash, which also favours root vegetables like yams.

71 Particularly *Ptosis palpebrae* and progressive external opthalmonplegia resulting in excessively relaxed muscles in the eyelid and retina pigmentation: Sparrman 1944:156-57; Walton 1974:583-85.

72 Forster 1777, II:321; Forster 1982, IV:627.

73 Large numbers of swine were raised for use in ritual exchanges at the competitive Tannese feast called *nekowiar*. See Forster 1982, IV:622, n5. Their meat was not reserved for the use of particular classes.

74 Forster 1982, IV:621 (birds as food); Sparrman 1944:158 (rats).

75 Beaglehole 1961, 2:503, 863.

76 Forster 1982, IV:634.

77 Forster 1777, II:321; Forster 1982, IV:602, n8.

78 For example, for carrying infants on the back.

79 Discussion in Guiart 1956:11-14. Estimates of 1774 in Sparrman 1944:153; Forster 1777, II:271; Beaglehole 1961, 2:483.

80 Stones and shells for hatchets were brought to Tana from both Aniwa and Aneityum: Forster 1982, IV:630); the "business" may well therefore have been trade in raw materials. In addition, there was a close connection between the Karumene and Neraymene people of Port Resolution and those of Anelgowhat, SW of Aneityum, where *Diana* had paused five days earlier.

81 Lensen 1959:205-78; Ivanshintsev 1980:137 (Moore's suicide).

## CHAPTER THREE: THE ETHNOGRAPHIC RECORD

1 Descriptions in Forster 1777, II:508; Beaglehole 1967, 2:855.

2 Forster 1777, II:321.

3 It must, of course, be collated with the 1774 word list in Forster 1778, II:254; see also Ray 1926 in this connection.

4 Robertson 1902:376-77.

5 Modern *nekowiar*.

6 *Diana's* Tannese collection reached Petropavlovsk-in-Kamchatka on 25 Sept. 1809, but apparently never reached St. Petersburg intact.

7 Robertson 1902:380ff.

8 Forster 1982, IV:627, nl.

9 Forster 1777, II:280..

10 Turner 1861:79-80.

11 Ibid., 77; Forster 1982, IV:586, n5, 622.

12 Forster 1777, II:275-76.

13 Forster 1982, IV:621.

14 Forster 1777, II:357.

15 De la Rue 1956:69.

16 Forster 1777, II:270-71; Sparrman 1944:151.

17 Guiart 1956:11ff.; Forster 1982, IV:588.

18 Forster 1777, II:292; Beaglehole 1961, 2: 507-8; Guiart 1956:9-12, 107 (multiplicity of chiefs, etc.).

19 Forster 1777, II:300-1; Beaglehole 1961, 2:488; Forster 1982, IV:594-95 (Ile Pou in Neraymene territory), 628.

20 Guiart 1956:Chap. 2.
21 Forster 1777, II:278–80; Turner 1861:81; Forster 1982, IV:624.
22 Forster 1777, II:280: Robertson 1902:371.
23 Beaglehole 1961, 2:503, 863; Forster 1982, IV:634, n4.
24 Tryon 1972:68–69.
25 Ibid., 67.
26 See Green 1977.
27 Whiteman 1983:50–51.
28 Dougherty 1983.

## CHAPTER FOUR: PREPARATIONS FOR THE BELLINGSHAUSEN VISIT, 1820

1 "Prodolzhenie ob otkrytiiakh Tasmana," pp. 120–33; on Tasman's route in 1643, see Sharp 1960:80–85; on *Nadezhda*'s library, Krusenstern 1813, I:9. The journal was *Tekhnologicheskii zhurnal*, 1806 (No. III, Pt. IV); the article was "Concerning Tasman's Discoveries: Continuation.".
2 PRO Adm/1/498, cap. 370; TsVMM, No. 41821:3–5; Nevskii 1951:25; Pertsmakher 1972:248–50.
3 *Gentleman's Magazine*, 1838, ii:100; *DNB*, 19:902.
4 Bligh 1792; Henderson 1933; Sharp 1960:157–60.
5 *DNB*, 1:595–96; Nevskii 1951:250–51.
6 Sharp 1960: 179; Kruzenshtern 1806:126.
7 Ward 1967, 2:359–60.
8 TsGAVMF *fond* 198, op. 1, *delo* 36; Kruzenshtern 1809, I:19–21.
9 Kruzenshtern 1815, passim; Pertsmakher 1972:249–50; Barratt 1981:110–11, 125.
10 Howay 1973:30; Dermigny 1964, 3:1240ff.
11 *Albany Sentinel* (NY), 29 Aug. 1797 ("Discoveries"); Stackpole 1953:375 (*Arthur's* voyage).
12 Kruzenshtern, "Prodolzhenie ob otkrytiiakh Tasmana," pp. 126–28.
13 Krusenstern 1813, I:9; Sharp 1960:82–83.
14 Dunmore 1965:90–93.
15 Nevskii 1951:250–54; Veselago 1869:11–12.
16 Rossiiskii 1820; Ivanshintsev 1980:20–23.
17 Kotzebue 1821, I:Introduction.
18 Gough 1973:4.
19 Williams 1962:271–72.
20 Kotzebue 1821, 1:2ff.
21 Kirwan 1960:77. Barrows' statements mirrored ignorance of his day, where Russian exploration of the Artic was concerned. In fact, Russians had been pushing east along the polar shorelines of Siberia by 1609.
22 Day 1967:27–29.
23 Barratt 1981:178–80; Veselago 1939:290–91.
24 Bellinsgauzen 1960:8–10.
25 Beaglehole 1955:cclxxiii; Barratt 1981:1:5–6.
26 Surveys in Henderson 1933; Ivanshintsev 1980:46; Sharp 1960:198.
27 Bellinsgauzen 1960:10.
28 Barratt 1979:9–11.
29 TsGAVMF, *fond* 25, op. 1, *delo* 114:21.
30 Lenz 1970:40–41.
31 Kohl 1843, 2:200ff.; Haxthausen 1856:344–46; Barratt 1981:140.
32 Kohl 1843, 2:201; Lenz 1970:40, 52, 410, 284, etc.
33 Krusenstern 1813, I:113–14; Shemelin 1816, I:104–6; Rezanov 1825:73–74.
34 TsGIAL, *fond* 853 (M.M. Buldakova), *delo* 1:No. 74 ("Zhurnal prikazov kapitana Kruzenshterna komande sudov"); Gvozdetskii 1947:85–88; Barratt 1981:119–21.
35 Lisiansky 1814:88–89; Shemelin 1816, I:106–8.
36 Rozina 1963:110–19.

37  Bellinsgauzen 1960:281ff.
38  Samarov 1952, I:3–5.
39  Ivanshintsev 1980: 20–23; Barratt 1981:174–75.
40  Bellinsgauzen 1960:20–21.
41  Ibid.:21.
42  Hunter Christie 1951:109.
43  Full details in Bellinsgauzen 1960:66; also Ryden 1963:67 and Barratt 1979:101–3.
44  Ryden 1963:68.
45  Bellinsgauzen 1960:26.
46  *Allgemeine Deutsche Biographie*, 21:470; 17:401–2; Barratt 1979:10.
47  Aleksandrov 1950:passim; Barratt 1979:14–15, 169; Vorob'ev 1949:497–504.
48  Pasetskii 1977:34–52 (Torson in Oceania); Ivanshintsev 1980:145. A number of other naval officers who had served in round-the-world expeditions of 1820–24 (including M.K. Kiukhel' beker, D.I. Zavalishin, F.P. Vishnevskii) were also involved in the anti-autocratic revolt that was staged in St. Petersburg on 14 December 1825–and so was known as the Decembrist Revolution. The revolt was quashed by the new tsar, Nicholas I, and the rebels, almost all of whom were of noble origins, were hanged or banished to Siberia in 1826–27.
49  Barratt 1981:1:13–14, 77; Fedorov-Davydov 1953:220, 324; Petrov 1864, I:327, 467, 485–86. Mikhailov returned to Oceania in 1827–28, with the *Moller* (Capt. M.N. Staniukovich), and again did excellent work as an artist.
50  Bellinsgauzen 1960:83.
51  Novosil'skii 1853:17–18.
52  Bellinsgauzen 1960:192–93; Sementovskii 1951:168–69; Barratt 1981:203–04; Fitzhardinge 1965:140–42.
53  Full details in Barratt 1979 & 1987.
54  Bellinsgauzen 1960:308.
55  Survey in Sharp 1960: 198 & Ivanshintsev 1980:45–46.
56  Bellinsgauzen 1960:317.
57  Rogers 1983:73–74.
58  Maude 1964:217–35; Rogers 1983:75–76.

## CHAPTER FIVE: THE RUSSIAN RECORDS OF THE LAUAN VISIT, 1820

1  See above for discussion of the *Bounty* mutineers' visit to Ono of 28 June 1791. Text here based on Sementovskii 1951:41–42.
2  Ibid.:144–59 for survey of dealings with the peoples of Tuamotu Archipelago, Tahiti, in July 1820.
3  These were *wangga vothe* (paddling craft) and sailing canoes with outrigger (*thamakathu*).
4  Strips of pandanus matting sewn with sennit.
5  This is confusing. Simonov apparently refers here to natives other than the Lauans he has been discussing.
6  Mangrove.
7  *Vetau* (*Mammea odorata*). the juice of pulped bark, as well as the leaves, produced a copper red dye: see Clunie 1982:6.
8  Vuata Ono: Bellinsgauzen 1960:318, 324.
9  *Ndrua*.
10  Simonov is correct in this surmise regarding the Tongans at Ono. Despite a liquid final "l," the Cyrillic rendering suggests an effort to convey the sound actually heard, i.e., not as Pavel.
11  Fio's *alofi*: Simonov had evidently heard of Fijian word *turaga* spoken. Disappointingly, he offers no clue as to how Paul had come by such a name.
12  See below, pp. 118–20, on the "Ceremony of Introduction" on this modified ceremony of "anchor-raising" (*thavu i kelekele*) and symbolic acceptance of welcome.
13  Probably, *a--u, a--u!*: see Thompson 1940:67.
14  *Kinikini*: see "Weaponry and Social Order," pp. 130–33.
15  *Masi* barkcloth pieces.

16 Bellinsgauzen 1960:329–31 (naval work at Sydney, etc.).

17 *Tobe* ringlets: see Clunie 1982:3.

18 Ibid., Plate 1, centre row. Mikhailov's study of this Lauan (Plate 11 here), whose "downy flower" is bright red, has lightly pencilled beneath it the name Dovli or Dovili.

19 See Clunie, 1982:4 (*i seru balabala* and *sasa* combs).

20 Details in Clunie and Ligairi, 1983, Mikhailov shows the use of carved sperm-whale tooth earrings (*sau-ni-daliga*, "ornamental plugs") in slit and distended earlobes.

21 Tuvana-i-Ra and Tuvana-i-Tholo or -Colo. The "powder" employed by these "marquises" was probably fragrant yellow grated sandalwood. The coral reef mentioned was, of course, Vuata Ono.

22 *Vostok* stood east of the Mana Islets.

23 I.e., the reef by Yanuya Islets..

24 Literally, "as if among their own people" (*kak mezhdu svoimi*).

25 Fio later confirmed this. Bellinsgauzen, 1960:66 (trade articles).

26 On Polynesian (principally Tongan) influence in the Lau Group, see Henderson 1937, Thompson 1940.

27 Captain-Lieutenant Ivan A. Zavadovskii.

28 Or, to chant (Russian: *pet'*).

29 *Kiakavo* or *gata* clubs: discussion above, "The '1820 Ono' Artefacts in Leningrad," pp. 130–33.

30 A *kinikini* club, apparently painted with burnt coral lime. MAE has no fewer than six such clubs (Nos. 736–14–19), several of which retain the white lime ilustrated by Mikhailov in his portrait of Fio.

31 A yellow paint produced, in Russia, by the boiling of birchleaf.

32 The hill was Nawamaji on Onolevu. The modern villages of Nukuni and Lovoni stand near the "Russians' village." See also Derrick 1951:325.

33 Udui, Doi, and Davura are indeed fertile, to varying extents.

34 Discussion in Clunie 1983:3–4.

35 *Tobe* ringlets are illustrated by Mikhailov: see Plate 12.

36 Ornamental *i seru sasa* or *i seru balabala* combs, of coconut leaf midribs or slivers of ebony-like tree-fern wood.

37 These "pins" were *i milamila*, head-scratching skewers.

38 Erroneous. See Clunie 1983:4–5.

39 Illustrated by Clunie 1983, Plate 1, upper row, but not by Mikhailov.

40 All this reflects a misreading of the 1784 edition of Cook's and King's *Voyage* by the paraphrast whom Bellinshausen follows, the original having "Fidjee." The downstroke of the "j" was perhaps taken as "f," that is, modern "s." See also Beaglehole 1967, Pt. 2:958–59 (Anderson) and 1311–12 (Clerke).

41 Ibid., Pt. 2:163. Cook's encounter with these Fijians was in June 1777, 54 years before the appearance of Bellingshausen's text..

42 Typographical error in 1831 edition of Bellingshausen's narrative: Pulago should have read Poulago. But Fatafehi Paulaho, Tu'i Tonga in 1777, was long dead by 1831.

43 See Sementovskii 1951:164.

44 Lakemba, in fact lying NNE from Ono-i-Lau in long. 178°52′W. For possible interpretations of "Pau," see "The Canoe," pp. 127–29.

45 Discussion by Paul Geraghty above; see pp. 139–46.

46 *Davui.*

47 These were *i sala*, chiefs' gauzy white headdresses or "turbans." They both protected the elaborate coiffures and indicated rank.

48 That is, longer than five weeks, as earlier in 1820.

49 Immediately west of Yanuya Islets.

50 See n21.

51 Vuata Ono, fixed by the Russians in lat. 20°45′S, long. 178°49′49″W. Further details in Bellinsgauzen 1960:324.

52 Text taken from Sementovskii 1951:258. The "long pins" were not combs but *i milamila* skewers, and Mikhailov drew the "pearl-shell necklaces" (see Plate 11).

53  Text taken from Sementovskii 1951:185. Ono seemed "very big" compared to the atolls lately seen in the Tuamotu archipelago. "Tarunarr" was possibly a mangled form of Tuvana but more likely a corruption of *turaga* (Simonov's *turan*), which Kiselev heard on Fio's approach towards *Vostok*. Paul' would have uttered the word, indicating the king and shore beyond.

54  The other texts do not support this claim that the Lauans meant, from the outset, to trade in or to present pearls.

55  Bellinsgauzen 1960:65 (bronze medallions with the bust of Tsar Alexander I on one face and, on the other, the inscription "The Sloops *Vostok* and *Mirnyi*, 1819").

## CHAPTER SIX: OBSERVATIONS ON THE RUSSIANS NARRATIVES AND DRAWINGS

 1  Barsukov 1896, 10:389; Barratt 1979:21–22.
 2  See Lurie 1961:87.
 3  Bellinsgauzen 1960:212–13.
 4  Ibid., 317; Sementovskii 1951:162–63, 258; Rogers 1983:76.
 5  Sementovskii 1951:163; Bellinsgauzen 1960:318.
 6  Derrick 1951:325.
 7  For attacks on *vavalagi* shipping at Tongatabu in 1802–4, etc., see Angas 1866:251–52 and Ward 1967, 7:306–9.
 8  Beaglehole 1961, 2:452–53; Forster 1982, 3:550.
 9  Bellinsgauzen 1960:65, 320.
10  Maude 1964:217ff.; Rogers 1983:75–76.
11  Sementovskii 1951:163.
12  Barratt 1979:30, 74.
13  For more on this, see Deane 1921:47–49, 90; Roth 1953:69–70.
14  Bellinsgauzen 1960:318–19; Sementovskii 1951:163; Henderson 1931:intro.
15  Roth 1953:101; see also Thomson 1908:25–31 (violent European-Fijian contacts, 1794–1814).
16  Plate 5 and Clunie 1977 (classical *totokia*, etc.).
17  The Soviet collections of early contact period Fijian artefacts have yet to be described, but see Appendix A below, pp. 197–202.
18  Ryden 1963:67–68.
19  No landing was made, however, to confirm that evidence.
20  Gabel 1958:passim; France 1969:7–8; Thomson 1908:14–15, 52.
21  See Derrick 1951:122.
22  Ibid.:123.
23  Thomson 1908:52, 295.
24  Deane 1921:4; Thomson 1908:172–81.
25  Thompson 1940:147.
26  Thomson 1908:255–76.
27  Ibid.:217–19.
28  Discussion in Clunie and Ligairi 1983:22ff.; on *mundulinga* ("the lopped finger") see Thomson 1908::375–76.
29  Clunie and Ligairi 1983:31, 33.
30  Ibid.:25; Thomson 1908:17–19.
31  Clunie and Ligairi 1983:33, 37.
32  Sementovskii 1951:165; Bellinsgauzen 1960:320.
33  Clunie 1982:3.
34  State Russian Museum (*Gosudar. Russkii Muzei*), *Otdel risunka*: P.N. Mikhailov Portfolio, R-29072/54–55.
35  Sementovskii 1951:42, 166; Clunie 1982:5–6.
36  Clunie 1982:4.
37  Bellinsgauzen 1960:320; Clunie 1982:7.
38  MAE, *Opis' Kollektsii* No. 736 (compiler L.G. Rozina, 1957). Those inventories (*opisi*) listing Fijian holdings at the Peter-the-Great Museum of Ethnography now at MAE are

held by the "Australia and Oceania Division" (*Otdel Avstralii i Okeanii*), and are now (1988) in the care of the records-keeper for that Division, Tamara K. Shafranóvskaia.
39 MAE, *Opis' Kollektsii* No. 737 (compiled originally by Piotrovskii; revised and enlarged inventory by L.G. Rozina, 1961), p. 1.
40 Further details in Appendix A, pp. 197–202.
41 Thomson 1908:321; Hocart 1929:117.
42 Hocart 1929:116ff.
43 Haddon and Hornell 1936–38 remain the essential source on Fijian craft, canoe-building, and even navigation, but see also Thomson 1908:290–96 and Williams 1884:71–76.
44 Sementovskii 1951:166; Bellinsgauzen 1960:323; Thomson 1908:292.
45 Thompson 1940:177.
46 Deane 1921:29; Hocart 1929:110; see also Bougainville 1772:278, Forster 1778:509, and Golson 1972:119, on the use of Orion's Belt by native navigators in Oceania.
47 Thomson 1908:23–33.
48 Ibid.:52, 295.
49 Butinov and Rozina 1963:85 and Barratt 1979:106, 130–31 (Coll. No. 736 and others at *MAE* containing "pre-1828" articles).
50 Technical details in Clunie 1977.
51 Plate 6 and Wilkes 1845:343.
52 Clunie 1977:vii.
53 Ibid.:2.
54 Beaglehole 1961:450.
55 Cary 1972:40.
56 See Clunie 1977.
57 Ibid.:Plate 11; Endicott 1923:60.
58 See Appendix A, pp. 197–202.
59 Thomson 1908:322.
60 No. 736-19 closely resembles the instrument in Fio's hands as drawm by Mikhailov.
61 Tippett 1968:42.
62 Ibid.:48–49.
63 See Deane 1921:29, 152.
64 Thompson 1940:67.
65 Waterhouse 1866:305.
66 Tippett 1968:66.
67 Ibid.:71–772; Larsson 1960:88.
68 Deane 1921:90.
69 Hocart 1929:49.
70 Deane 1921:196; also Thomson 1908:62.
71 See Barratt 1981:140–41 (Baltic-German scientific influences).
72 Fedorov-Davydov 1953:324; Suris 1962:66–67.
73 Arkhiv Akademii Khudozhestv (1819), op. 20, *delo* 28; Petrov 1864:327, 460, 467, 485–6.
74 Barratt 1981:1:Plates 2, 4.
75 Bellinsgauzen 1960:77–78.
76 Fedorov-Davydov 1953:219–20, 323.
77 Suris 1962, passim.
78 For more about Mikhailov, see Isakov 1915 and Shur and Pierce 1978.
79 Bellinsgauzen 1960:5.
80 Bellinsgauzen 1949:169 n8.
81 Pasetskii 1979:Chap. 3; Gibson 1976:84.
82 Barratt 1981:213–32; Barratt 1981:1:94–95; Okun':107; O'Meara 1984:142–45. Among the other revolutionaries who had participated lately in Pacific voyages or had connections with Russian-American Company outposts in the North Pacific basin were suce would-be authors as Dmitri I. Zavalishin (or *Kreiser*), Mikhail K. Kiukhel'beker (of *Apollon*), and the poet-publicist Kondrati Ryleev.
83 Bellinsgauzen 1960:5–6.
84 Bellinsgauzen 1831:I:into., vii.

85  Nos. R29188–28196, 29131-29134, 29272 in the Mikhailov portfolio, held at the State Russian Museum, Leningrad, Drawings Division.
86  Shur and Pierce 1978:360–63. I thank A.M. Cheremisin, Academic Secretary of the State Historical Museum (½ Red Square, Moscow 103012), for much information on the P.N. Mikhailov album held there.
87  Fedorov-Davydov 1953:324; Barratt 1981:1:77.
88  Linguistic fieldwork was undertaken on Ono in 1979, and assistance was rendered by Meli Suka, the Tui Matokana, and the people of Matokana in Ono.
89  By Glynn Barratt.
90  Further on this, see A.J. Schütz and P. Geraghty, *Fijian Language Studies, II: David Cargill's Fijian Grammar* (Suva, Bulletin of the Fiji Museum No. 6, 1980):3–5. Cargill's description of the phonetics of Lakeba Lauan of circa 1836 fits the contemporary language very well. Lauan pronunciation differs from that of Bau-based standard Fijian mainly in the palatalization of /t/ and /d/ before a high frontal vowel.
91  *Pandora*'s tender may have brought small knives to Ono in 1791. The word list demands brief comments, such as that Nos. 9 and 32 illustrate overspecification, that the Russians were inconsistent in recording words with or without nominal article *a*, and that the f in No. 14 suggests influence by the Tongan cognate *fonua*. In Ono, the three stars of Orion's belt, plus the sword and shoulders, comprise the *iribuli* constellation.

## CHAPTER SEVEN: THE ARTEFACTS FROM ONO IN KAZAN' AND LENINGRAD

1  Vorob'ev 1949:497–504; Kabo & Bondarev 1974:101–10.
2  MAE, *Otdel Avstralii i Okeanii: Opis'* Koll. No. 737:1.;also Shafranovskaia 1984:16.
3  LOAAN: *Arkhiv Otdela fondov*, K-IV, *opis'* No. 7:0038; on Forster's artefact collection and donations and sales thereof in 1775–85, Fiedler 1970:61–92; Kaeppler 1971:204–20; Hoare 1976:146–47, 177.
4  Gennadi 1914:I:133; Sopikov 1816, Pt. 4:Nos. 9206–8; Barratt 1979 (1):228–29.
5  Bellinsgauzen 1960:65.
6  Beaglehole 1955:520–21.
7  Ryden 1963:66.
8  Bellinsgauzen 1960:66–67. An *arshin* of material was a 28-inch strip.
9  One likely collector at Ono-i-Lau was *Mirnyi*'s surgeon, Nikolai Galkin, who had been collecting in New Zealand three months earlier: see *Syn otechestva* (St. P. 1822), No. 49:103n; Kabo & Bondarev 1974: 103, n7; Barratt 1979:15, 23. Imperial orders of 1819 encouraged other offficers to collect—Bellinsgauzen 1960:77–78.
10  Bellinsgauzen 1960:77–78 (Third Set of Instructions, para. 15); for comparison with Dumont D'Urville's people's dispostion of Pacific artefacts acquired in situ, see Wright 1950:73 and Barratt 1979:103–6.
11  Lisiansky 1814:102.
12  Aleksandrov 1964:75–87; Kabo & Bondarev 1974:101–2.
13  Karimullin & Laptev 1979:111–12 (N.I. Lobachevskii's report to Kazan' University, dated 4 May 1822).
14  RBS, 19:302–14.
15  Kabo & Bondarev 1974:103.
16  Kabo & Bondarev 1974:104. Lauan items are mentioned in the 1957 guide to Kazan' University's ethnographic collection, *Kratkie putevoditeli po universitetu: etnograficheskii muzei* (Kazan').
17  Ibid.:102; Vorob'ev 1949:497–98; Barratt 1979:18–22.
18  See Andreev 1949, passim.
19  Sementovskii 1951:4–5; connected material in *Izvestiia* (Moscow) for 10 June 1950.
20  *IVGO* (1949), no. 5:497–504.
21  Plate 1 (p. 498); see also Staniukovich 1978:76.
22  *Slovo ob uspekhakh plavaniia . . .* appeared as a pamphlet (Kazan' 1822); a slightly variant piece appeared in *Kazanskii vestnik*, No. 3, that same year.
23  On Magnitskii, Feokistov 1865; on Kazan' University's struggles in this period, Vucinich

1970, Vol. 1. For more information on his career at Kazan', see *ES*, 58:934.
24 Vorob'ev 1949:503; also *Kazanskii vestnik*, 1821, No. 3:166–68.
25 "Znak s Ostrova Ono," *Izvestiia Obshchestva Arkheologii, Istorii i Etnografii*, Vol. 29 (Kazan' 1916):253–59.
26 Printed as No. 9 of the *Uchennye Zapiski Kazanskogo Pedagogich: Instituta* (Kazan') for that year.
27 *SMAE*, 30 (1974):101–11.
28 Ibid.:109–11.
29 MAE: *Otdel Avstralii i Okeanii, Opis'* No. 736:7ff. (attribution by L.G. Rozina, in 1956–57).
30 Butinov 1963:85.
31 On Miklukho-Maklai as a collector of Melanesian objects, see his collected works, *Sobranie sochinenii*, 5 vols. (Moscow 1950–54), and Putilov 1981; on Sviatlovskii, see Rozina 1974:127–39.
32 Shafranovskaia 1984:15.
33 LOAAN: *fond* 142, op. 1, *delo* 55.
34 Arkhiv Instituta Etnografii, K-V, op. 1, No. 604.
35 Cited in Rozina 1974:138.
36 Ibid.:132 & Plate 8 (MAE Coll. 2798–3)..
37 Rozina in *SMAE*, 30 (1974): 96.
38 Shafranovskaia 1984:17–18. Fijian items in Collection No. 2798 were retained by the collector until 1921, but some had also been acquired in 1908.
39 See, for instance, B.N. Putilov's descriptions of Fijian musical instruments in *SMAE*, 30 (1974):42–45, and P.M. Kozhin's and L.A. Ivanov's treatment, in the same issue (pp. 122ff.), of Fijian ceramics

CHAPTER EIGHT: ENVOI

1 Ivanshintsev 1980: 50, 80, 101, 104, 110, 114; Gibson 1976: Table 7 76–89; McCartan 1963:30–37; Friis 1967:185–99.
2 TsGAVMF, *fond* 203, op. i, *delo* 730:228–42; *fond* 166, *delo* 660, pt. 2:240ff. (materials on *Otkrytie*'s and *Blagonamerennyi*'s voyages to Sydney); Lazarev 1950; Kuznetsova 1968:237–45; Gillesem 1849:Nos. 9–10; Fitzhardinge 1965:113–47.
3 *Sydney Gazette*, 14 Apr., 28 Apr., 26 May 1825 and *The Australian* 27 Mar. 1829 (the 400-ton *Elena* at Sydney, her officers, crew); Zubov 1954:205; Fitzhardinge 1965:140–41; Liapunova & Fedorova 1979:221–24, 276 and Kotzebue 1821, I:256, 328 (Khromchenko).
4 Ivanshintsev 1980:101, 104, 110, 114; Kuznetsova 1968:237–38 on *Blagonamerennyi*'s voyage); *ZUKMS*, 12 (1835):338–40 (Shishmarev as see officer); Lazarev 1950:27–30 (Vasil'ev and Shishmarev, etc.); *RBS*, 22:516–18 (von Schantz in *Amerika*); Berezhnoi 1984:56–57.
5 TsGAVMF, *fond* 402, op. 1, *delo* 88, for instance, holds Hagemeister's report on *Krotkii*'s passage to Kamchatka and related papers; and, in that same archive, *fond* 203, op. 1, *delo* 730, are the original journal and notes of Midshipman Nikolai D. Shishmarev of *Blagonamerennyi*. For hydrographic records and chart collecting, Churkin 1975:1–20, Shibanov 1975:Chap. 6.
6 Ivanshintsev 1980:110; on *Amerika*, see Anon 1832 and Zavoiko 1840:Pt. 1:4–5.
7 Kuznetsova 1968:237–39; Lazarev 1950:23–27, 37–40; Ivanshintsev 1980:140–41; Gillesem 1849: No. 9. M.N. Vasil'ev's unpublished account of his Pacific crossing of 1820 remains at TsGAVMF, *fond* 213, op. 1, *delo* 118; *delo* 52 of the same file offers correspondence regarding diaries and journals by others who crossed Melanesia with him in 1820. For materials concerning Emel'ian E. Korneev, *Otkrytie*'s artist in 1819–21, see Goncharova 1973.
8 TsGIAL, *fond* 789, op. 20, *dela* 28–30, etc. (possible illustration of Gillesem's narrative by Korneev, 1828–30); Kuznetsova 1968:237.
9 TsGAVMF, *fond* 213, op. 1, *dela* 52, 101 (Vasil'ev's brief notes); but see *ZADMM*, 5 (1823), for a finished paper by on New South Wales; also Lazarev 1950:27–29.

10  *Morskoi sbornik* (St. P.), No. 3, "Neofitsial'nyi otdel":11ff.
11  M.D. Ol'khin, *Ukazatel' Vnov' Vykhodiashchikh knig* (St. P. 1841); A.F. Smirdin, *Rospis'* (St. P. 1840); Zdobnov 1951:135–36, 158–60; *GSE*, 9:599 (Zavoiko's career).
12  Lazarev 1832; Ivanshintsev 1980:70–71.
13  Rossiiskii 1820; Samarov 1952, Vol. I: Sokolov 1951; Sementovskii 1951:19–28, etc. (*Mirnyi*'s voyage); Zavalishin 1877 (*Kreiser*'s voyage).
14  Lazarev 1950:33.
15  Pasetskii 1977:34–52, 70–81.
16  Holograph now in TsGAVMF, *fond* 1152, *delo* 1; see Lazarev 1950:6–8 and Kuznetsova 1968:237, on variant ms journal now held by GPB (Leningrad), F.17.106, etc.
17  A.P. Lazarev 1950:158–59; TsGAVMF, *fond* 213, op. 1, *delo* 118.
18  TsGAVMF, *fond* 203, op. 1, *delo* 730:Pt.VI (N.D. Shishmarev's 1820 journal); Lazarev 1950:160.
19  Lazarev 1950:161.
20  Ibid., 265–67; Starbuck 1878; Stackpole 1953.
21  Seemann 1862:137–38 and Starbuck 1878 (early New England whaling off Fiji); on other early traders, see Derrick 1946; Henderson 1937; Ward 1967, 2:366–78. Vasil'ev and Shishmarev knew of the loss the brig *Eliza* (Captain Rogers) at the Fijis in 1808 (details in *Columbian Centinel*, Boston, 27 May 1809), and evidently knew something of the subsequent trading visits there of *Hunter* and *Brutus* (*Salem Gazette*, 24 Mar. 1812:26). Shipping reports were much reprinted in that period.
22  Ivanshintsev 1980:80, 101; on Chistiakov, see Pierce 1971:38–40 and *Sydney Gazette*, 14, 28 Apr. 1825; on Khromchenko, n3 above.
23  Captain Edward Edwards' visit of 1791 (see Sharp 1960:164) had been followed by that of James Wilson in the missionary ship *Duff* (1797); Kruzenshtern had exploited all hydrographic data in Wilson's *Missionary Voyage* (London 1799) for his 1823 *Atlas*.
24  Ward 1967, 6:318.
25  See Ch.1, nn. 66–69.
26  Howard 1970:10.
27  Veselago 1869:12ff.; Nevskii 1951:250–52.
28  Hamilton 1793:88; Sharp 1960:164; Ivanshintsev 1980:101.
29  *ZUKMS*, 9 (1832):304.
30  Ivanshintsev 1980:25–26 (*Riurik*'s path NW from the northern Cooks); Golovnin 1819 and Klochkov 1826, among other printed sources, gave data on Russian routes from Sydney or the Tasman Sea.
31  *ZUKMS*, 9 (1832), "Plavanie sudna Eleny," 304–5.
32  Sharp 1960:152–53.
33  *ZUKMS*, 9 (1832):305; Ivanshintsev 1980:101.
34  Kashevarov was a creole from Novo-Arkhangel'sk. Sent to St. Petersburg by the Russian-American Company, and trained there at its expense, he returned to the Northwest Coast with *Elena* and served as manager on Kodiak (1831–38?).
35  In addition, one may consult Gibson 1973:13; Tikhmenev 1939, 1:407–11; and *The Australian* (Sydney), 27 Mar. & 8 Apr. 1829).
36  Ivanshintsev 1980:104; on Hagemeister's naval career, *ZUKMS*, 11 (1834):355–57; *Dorpater Jahrbücher*, 1835, Bd. IV, no. 2; *RBS*, 4:97–98; Berezhnoi 1984. A biographical sketch by Kirill T. Khlebnikov is unpublished: MS in Perm' District State Archive, *fond* 445, op. 1, *delo* 43. On *Krotkii* herself, Wrangel 1828:48ff. and Komissarov 1977:150.
37  Fitzhardinge 1965:141–43; *ZUKMS*, 9 (1832):304; TsGAVMF, *fond* 402, op. 1, *delo* 88:45.
38  Ivanshintsev 1980:104. Dumont D'Urville's *Voyage de la corvette "L'Astrolabe"* (Paris 1830–33) belatedly presented details of the 1827 Fijian probe (vol. 4:424–30.).
39  This was Niuafou, or Onaseuse, sighted by Captain Hunter of *Donna Carmelita* in July 1823 (but long before him by Jacob Le Maire in 1616). Hunter reported its latitude correctly enough, at 15°31'S, but its longitude was reported (by Hunter or by a printer) at 176°11'E, instead of W. It is actually a northern outlier of the Tonga Group, not the Fijis (not to be confused with modern Hunter Island, SE of the Loyalty Islands: see Sharp 1960:75, 181). Hagemeister had the false data from Kruzenshtern. Findlay 1884: 787; *New*

*Bedford Mercury*, 9 June 1826:19; Ward 1967, 3:475–77.
40  Ivanshintsev 1980:104.
41  Sharp 1960:171; Henderson 1937.
42  *Columbian Centinel*, Boston, 9 Aug. 1800: 33; Ward 1967, 2:366ff.
43  TsGAVMF, *fond* 402, op. 1, *delo* 88:46.
44  Dumont D'Urville 1834, 4:426–29; Dunmore 1969:205–6.
45  Berens 1903:11–12.
46  Nevskii 1951:250–52; Wilson 1799; Sharp 1960:159–60, 171; Ward 1967, 2:366–78.
47  *Salem Gazette* 24 Mar. 1812:26; *H.O. Publ.*, Chart 2858, No. 166 (Vol. 2, 1933):288
    (Kandavu Island); Derrick 1946:Chaps. 3–4.
48  See Map 6 (*Krotkii*'s approach from the south).
49  Berens 1903:12.
50  Sharp 1960:160.
51  Kruzenshtern had data on Ebon, a detached atoll in the SW Marshalls, from Louis Isidor
    Duperrey. The two had corresponded (1824–27) before the French material was printed in
    Duperrey 1827:54. The French had had their information from the New England whaler
    *Boston*, which had sighted Ebon in May 1824—Findlay 1886:966; Ward 1967, 2:242;
    Sharp 1960:207–8. Kotzebue's many discoveries in the Marshalls in 1816–17 (Ivanshintsev
    1980:26–28) combined with the Russians' natural routes to Kamchatka to provoke much
    practical interest, on Gagemeister's part, in the geography of that part of Micronesia.
52  On Vasilii Stepanovich Khromchenko (1792–1849), see n3 above; on the 130-foot armed
    transport *Amerika*, see Zavoiko 1840:5–6 and Anon. 1832:4 July section.
53  *OMS*, 8:464–68; *RBS*, 22:516–18. Despite his early service in merchant shipping, von
    Schantz became a full admiral in 1866 during the age of ironclad steamers.
54  On Vasilii S. Zavoiko (1810–98), Military Governor of Kamchatka (1849–55) and hero of
    the Crimean War on the Pacific, see *GSE*, 9:599.
55  Ivanshintsev 1980:110.
56  Purdy 1816:697–98; Horsburgh 1827, 2:593–94; see also n39 above.
57  Ivanshintsev 1980:102, 110; Sharp 1960:150–51 (*Elena* and *Amerika* at Nukufetau, Nano-
    mana, and Nanumea in the Ellice Islands, 1829 and 1832).
58  Zavoiko 1840, Pt. 1:61.

CHAPTER NINE: "DISCOVERING" DISCOVERED ATOLLS

1  Cited in Hoare 1976:265.
2  Burrows 1936:passim; Yen 1978:Chs.1–2; Hedley 1897:229ff.
3  Butinov 1978, 1982:12–13; Svet 1966; Maude 1961:93–95.
4  Ivanshintsev 1980:80, 101.
5  A.P. Lazarev 1950:162.
6  Ivanshintsev 1980:104; Horsburgh 1827:594–95.
7  TsGAVMF, *fond* 213, op. 1, *delo* 97: 1 (M.N. Vasil'ev on Russian use of charts of Oceania
   by Aaron Arrowsmith [1750–1833] and his son); also Chambers & Munro 1980:passim;
   Butinov 1982:9–16.
8  A.P. Lazarev 1950:167; Maude 1961:93ff. The basic hydrographic and investigative
   research was undertaken for the Russians, almost inevitably, by I.F. Kruzenshtern: see his
   *Sobranie soch.* (1826) and *Dopolnenie* (1836). With regard to early European records of
   sightings of atolls in Tuvalu, Kruzenshtern consulted James Burney's *Discoveries in the
   South Sea* (1803–17: Vol. I for Alvaro de Mendaña's voyage of 1567–68), La Pérouse's
   *Voyage* in the 1798 (London) edition of M.L. Milet-Mureau (for Maurelle's visit to Tuvalu
   of May 1781), older Spanish sources suggested by Mr. Burney and/or Alexander Dalrymple (*Historical Collection* 1770), and such New England publications as the *Boston Commercial Gazette*, the *Independent Chronicle*, and *Nantucket Inquirer*. (For a Soviet
   account of Mendaña's discoveries, see Svet 1966:78–90.).
9  Discussions in Koch 1961 and Roberts 1958.
10 See Buck 1930:7 (independent names for all islets); for detailed maps, *H.O. Publ.* No. 166,
   Vol. II (1933, 4th ed.):438–45.

11 See Chambers 1984 and Butinov 1982, on recent economic and social developments in the Government of Tuvalu; on nineteenth-century changes, Hedley 1896 and Kennedy 1931 (emphases on Funafuti and Vaitupu).
12 Smith 1897:passim; Butinov 1982:98 (citing R.G. Roberts on the Tongan discoverer of Nukufetau, Chief Laupepa of Fale, etc.); Chambers 1984:78–82.
13 Sharp 1960:43–44, 53.
14 Maude 1961:299–304; *Pacific Islands Pilot*, 2:425;Butinov 1982:9–10.
15 La Pérouse 1798, I:cxv-clxiii; *Pacific Islands Pilot*, 2:433–34; Maude 1961:73–74; Maude 1968:93.
16 Sharp 1960:150–51; Butinov 1982:10.
17 La Pérouse 1798, I:cxv. Maurelle's account had also appeared in Peter Simon Pallas's *Neue Nordliche Beyträge*(St. P. 1796).
18 Further details in Ward 1967, 2:564–65.
19 *H.O. Publ.* No. 166, Vol. II (1933):445; *Independent Chronicle* (Boston), 9 Feb. 1820:52.
20 TsGAVMF,*fond* 213, op. 1, *delo* 97:1.
21 Misprinted, Lazarev 1950:374, as "January 1820."
22 Ivanshintsev 1980:56.
23 See Ward 1967, 2:564; Horsburgh 1827, 2:595.
24 Stackpole 1953:279–82; Sharp 1960:195.
25 *Nantucket Inquirer*, 25 Nov. 1826: 6; Ward 1967, 2:269–70; see also Horsburgh 1827, 2:596 and Sharp 1960:208 (Eeg's sighting of Nui in 1825).
26 *Independent Chronical and Boston Patriot*, 9 Feb. 1820:52.
27 *H.O. Publ.* No. 166, Vol. II (1933):445.
28 A.P. Lazarev 1950:162.
29 Ibid.:163–68. Both Russian sloops carried copies of J. Purdy's *Tables of Positions* (London 1816), which gave data on Captain Patterson's track of 1809 in the *Elizabeth*, as well as Maurelle's of 1781 in *La Princessa*. On Aaron Arrowsmith's work, see *DNB*, 1:595–96 and Nevskii 1951:250. The Russians carried revised editions of his celebrated world map on Mercator's projection (1794), valuing the accompanying hydrographic commentaries.
30 Career data in *ZUKMS*, 12 (1835): 338–40 and Lazarev 1950: 29–30.
31 TsGAVMF,*fond* 213, op. 1, *delo* 100:1–2 ("Raport komandira . . . nachal'niku ekspedit-sii").
32 Lazarev 1950:374–75; on Rikord's visit to Vanuatu in 1809, see above, Part One, Ch. 2.
33 Lazarev 1950:374 ("Raport kapitan-leitenanta M.N. Vasil'eva morskomu ministru").
34 Ibid.34–35; Ivashintsev 1980:140–41 (ships' personnel).
35 Kotzebue 1821, 1:16; Bellinsgauzen 1960:88; Novosil'skii 1853:5–6 (acquisitions of instruments in London by the makers Edward Troughton, Dolland, Tully, and Arnold, etc.).
36 Chambers 1984:78–81; Roberts 1958:394ff.; Butinov 1982:106–7.
37 Kennedy 1931: passim; Butinov 1982:72–77.
38 Butinov 1982:98.
39 Burrows 1938:88–90, etc.
40 Butinov 1982:23–25.
41 Burrows 1938:88, 192; Vaida 1959:832ff.
42 TsGAVMF,*fond* 213, op. 1, *delo* 97:2.
43 See Beaglehole 1974:532–35 (the Tongan stay of 1777).
44 Butinov 1982:98; Lazarev 1950:163.
45 Haddon & Hornell 1975, I:292–99 (the "southern type," which predominated at Nukufetau in the nineteenth century).
46 Chambers 1984:285–86.
47 Koch 1961:194.
48 Ibid.:143 (use of *asu* bailers, etc.).
49 Chambers 1984: passim.
50 Ibid.:285ff.
51 Hale, H.H. in Wilkes 1845, v. 6 (1846):309ff.; Koch 1961:91.
52 Hale in Wilkes 1845,6:164, 167.
53 Kennedy 1931:311; Koch 1961:90.

54 Wilkes 1845, 5:41; Kennedy 1931:301; Hedley 1897:238-40.
55 Koch 1961:132-33. The Russians may also have seen *manaui*, craft of similar construction but smaller size, used in fishing.
56 Lazarev 1950:168.
57 Ibid. The Soviet editor A.I. Solov'ev's identification of "Shevsons Island" with Rotuma (n. 118) is as ridiculous as his assertion that Rotuma is in the "Gilbert Archipelago." The very typesetting of this part of Lazarev's *Zapiski*, however, is full of slips: Arrowsmith is disguised in the cited remark as "Arrovelist" despite the fairly correct transliteration of that proper name in Lazarev's holograph (TsGAVMF, *fond* 1153, op. 1, *delo* 1).
58 *Naval Chronicle*, 24 (1810):313; Purdy 1816:153.
59 La Pérouse 1798, I:235; Brand 1967:132; Chambers 1980:173-75
60 Sharp 1960:43-44; Maude 1968:53-64; Broeze 1975:35-36.
61 *Nantucket Inquirer*, 25 Nov. 1826; Sharp 1960:205; Ward 1967, 2:270; Maude 1968:126.
62 *DNB*, 1:595-96
63 Chambers 1980:171, 180-81.
64 Ibid.:194, n10.
65 Sharp 1960:150.
66 See Maude 1968:93-94; Chambers 1980:171ff.
67 Lazarev 1950:168; Purdy 1816:153-54; Duperrey 1827 (*Mémoire*), 47-52.
68 Kruzenshtern 1824, 1:23; *Bombay Courier*, 12 Aug. 1809; Purdy 1816:153; Maude 1968:107; also Findlay 1877:755.
69 Duperrey, *Voyage*:15; Duperrey 1827:45; Dunmore 1969:145.
70 Lesson 1839:445-46; Duperrey 1827:46-47.
71 See Dunmore 1969, for discussion of these materials.
72 Chambers 1980:184-85.
73 Khromchenko 1832:306ff.; Ivashintsev 1980:110.
74 Kotzebue 1821, 1:256, 328; Liapunova & Fedorova 1979:221-24.
75 *Sydney Gazette*, 14, 28 Apr. 1825; *The Australian*, 27 Mar. 1829 (*Elena*); Ivashintsev 1980:101-3, 146; *ZUKMS*, 9 (1832):305ff.
76 Anon. 1832; Ivashintsev 1980:109; Fitzhardinge 1965:143-44.
77 See Gibson 1976:74 (Table 7).
78 Ivashintsev 1980:102, 111; *The Australian*, 31 Mar. 1829; *Sydney Gazette*, 24 May 1832.
79 Fitzhardinge 1965:141; Zubov 1954:205.
80 Ivashintsev 1980:104; Dumont D'Urville 1833, 4:424-30 (Fiji).
81 Maude 1968:53ff.; Chambers 1980:170-71.
82 H.O. Chart No. 198, *Pacific Islands*, Vol. II (1933), 446; Horsburgh 1827, 2:596; Findlay 1871:667; Ward 1967, 5:205-9.
83 Wilkes 1845, 5, frontispiece (1841 chart of "Ellice's Group"); Chambers 1980:172.
84 *New England Palladium* (Boston), 14 Apr. 1826, 62.
85 Khromchenko 1832:306ff.; Ivashintsev 1980:102.
86 Kruzenshtern 1836:19.
87 Ward 1967, 5:205; further on European rediscovery of Nui, see Broeze 1975:30-47.
88 Ivashintsev 1980:102.
89 Further details in Kromchenko 1832.
90 Ivashintsev 1980:110.
91 Ibid., 51; *Boston Commercial Gazette*, 10 Feb. 1820; Ward 1967, 3:565; Paulin 1947:32-45.
92 Likhtenberg 1960:168-69; Rozina 1963; Friis 1967:185-97.
93 Ivashintsev 1980:110.
94 TsGAVMF, *fond* 213, op. 1, *delo* 97:2; H.O. *Publ.* No. 166, Vol. II (1933), 445.
95 Chambers 1980:186, for discussion.
96 Ibid.:175-77.

## CHAPTER TEN: ANUTA ISLAND

1 Barratt 1981:207-9; Gibson 1976: Chap. 3-4.
2 Lazarev 1832; Klochkov 1826; Khrushchev 1826; Ivashintsev 1980:60-74.

3  Ivashintsev 1980:62–64.
4  AVPR, *fond* Kantseliarii Ministerstva Vneshnikh Del, 1822; *delo* 3645:31ff.; Khrushchev 1826:200–2; Barratt 1981:216–20.
5  Ivashintsev 1980:65.
6  Ibid.:139, 142.
7  Shabel'skii 1826, Chaps. 1–2.
8  Khrushchev 1826:209–13; *Sydney Gazette*, 28 June & 2 Aug. 1822; Fitzhardinge 1965:134–35.
9  Ivashintsev 1980:66.
10  Ibid.:19.
11  Khrushchev 1826:215ff.
12  Biographical data in Grot 1899:238, Cheriskii 1975:466.
13  *Severnaia pchela*, 1827, No. 58 (Shabel'skii to A.B. Kurakin); Hotimsky 1967:86; Bolkhovitinov 1975:Chaps.5–7.
14  *Pushkin i ego sovremenniki*, Nos. 9–10:330–31.
15  E.g., in *Severnyi arkhiv*, 1826, Pt. 23, Nos. 17–18:43–61 (New South Wales).
16  A correct assumption: see Sharp 1960:164.
17  In fact, HMS *Pandora's* surgeon, George Hamilton, had published his *Voyage Round the World* as early as 1793, in Berwick, Scotland, and subsequent reprints had appeared in London. One of these, of 1799, had then been translated into German by Johann Reinhold Forster, and published in Berlin (?) in 1804. All contained a few lines on "Cherry's Island" and its populace.
18  Presumably, the Kwamera-English word list printed in Forster 1778; on which, see above, Part One, Ch. 3.
19  La Billardière 1800, 2:92ff.; Dunmore 1969:314–15.
20  Further on Anutan ornaments, see Yen & Gordon 1973:86–88.
21  Literally, the "trade wind" (*vent alisé*).
22  Details in Thomson 1915 and Ward 1967, 1:152.
23  Shabel'skii 1826:42. The equator was crossed in long. 168 E, on 23 July 1822. Like the *Krotkii* in May 1829, *Apollón* passed near Ocean Island (Ivashintsev 1980:67, 104).
24  Thomson 1915:67; Findlay 1871:629; Sharp 1960:164.
25  See also n17 here, on Surgeon Hamilton's account.
26  Capell 1962:380 and Yen & Gordon 1973:25, for surveys.
27  See Pawley 1967:261–63.
28  Yen & Gordon 1973:100.
29  Ibid.:101; Green 1971, passim.
30  Firth 1954:121–22; Kaeppler in Yen & Gordon 1973:23–24.
31  Shabel'skii 1826:40.
32  Rossel 1808 1:300.
33  See Sharp 1960:164. For details of *Apollón's* movements, see Khrushchev 1826.
34  Yen & Gordon 1973:119, 122 (walls, terraces, etc.).
35  Ibid.:114.
36  Ibid.:132, fig. 8.
37  He controlled distribution of island resources.
38  Ibid.:2, 27.
39  Ibid.:15, fig. 1.
40  Ibid.:86.
41  Rossel 1808, 1:276ff.
42  Ward 1967, 1:150 ("shown on the chart as doubtful").
43  H.O. *Publ.*. No. 165, Vol. 1 (1938):273.
44  Ibid.:272; also Markham 1873:129–37; Thomson 1915:67; and British Admiralty, *Pacific Islands Pilot: Western Groups* (1920):317.

APPENDIX

1  Russov 1900: Butinov 1983.

2 Shafranovskaia 1984:15–20.
3 Butinov 1963:85; Likhtenberg 1960:168–69; Barratt 1979:131.
4 These three clubs are *sali*, spurred or "gunstock" cutting clubs: see Derrick 1957:392.
5 *Thulathula* clubs—Derrick's Type 3b. Of other clubs in this MAE collection, suffice to note that 736–22 and 26 are *kiakavo* dance clubs; 736–30 is a *nggata*; 736–31 is a *totokia*; and 736–32 is a mace-headed *waka* (Derrick's Type 2b).
6 Kaeppler 1971:204ff.; Hoare 1976:177. Even in 1784, the elder Forster was seeking a post at the St. Petersburg Academy of Sciences (see Hettner 1877:651–53), of which he was a foreign correspondent and to which he had sold numerous Pacific artefacts. Moreover, he had sold Melanesian and Polynesian artefacts to other Russian institutions, notably the Mittau Museum in Courland. See *Sitzungsbericht der kurländischen Gesellschaft für Literatur und Kunst aus den Jahren 1864 bis 1867* (Mitau 1867):208–9.
7 Hoare 1976:207–8, 249–50.

# BIBLIOGRAPHY

BIOGRAPHICAL AND BIBLIOGRAPHICAL AIDS: A SELECT LIST

Beddie, M.K. *A Bibliography of Captain James Cook*. Sydney 1970
Bilbasov, V., ed. *Arkhiv grafov Mordvinovykh*. 10 Vols. St. P. 1901-3
Chentsov, N.M. *Vosstanie dekabristov: bibliografiia*. M. 1929
*Dictionary of National Biography*, ed. L. Stephen. London 1885-1900
*Entsiklopedicheskii slovar'*, ed. I, Andreevskii & K. Arsen'ev. St. P. 1890-1904
*Entsiklopediia voennykh i morskikh nauk*. St. P. 1893
Hotimsky, C.M. "A Bibliography of Captain James Cook in Russian—1772-1810," *Biblionews and Australian Notes and Queries*, 5 (1971): no. 2:3-12
Gennadi, G. *Slovar' russkikh pisatelei i uchenykh*. 2 vols. Berlin 1876-80
Granat, *Entsiklopedicheskii slovar'*. 53 Vols. M. 1937, 7th ed.
Larousse *Grand dictionnaire universel du XIXe siècle*. Geneva, Paris: Slatkine & Cie reprint 1982
Lenz, W., ed. *Deutsch-Baltisches Biographisches Lexikon, 1710-1960*. Köln, Wien 1970
*Materialy dlia istorii russkogo flota*, ed. S.I. Elagin, F. Veselago, and S.F. Ogorodnikov. 17 Vols. (St. P. 1865-1904)
*Obshchii morskoi spisok*, ed. F.F. Veselago et al. St. P. 1885-1907
Pypin, A.N. *Istoriia russkoi etnografii*. 4 Vols. St. P. 1890-92
Ralfe, J. *Naval Biography*. 5 Vols. London 1828
Rudovits, L.F. "Pervoe russkoe krugosvetnoe plavanie, 1803-06: obzor nauchnykh rabot," in *Trudy Gosudarstvennogo Okeanograficheskogo Instituta*, 27 (L. 1954):3-12

*Russkii biograficheskii slovar'*, ed. A.A. Polovtsov and B. Modzalevskii. 25 Vols. St. P. 1896-1916

Marshall, J. *Royal Navy Biography* London 1824

*Sbornik Imperatorskago Russkago Istoricheskago Obshchestva.* 148 Vols. St. P. & Petrograd 1867-1916

Smirdin, A. *Rospis' rossiiskim knigam dlia chteniia.* St. P. 1828

Sopikov, V. *Opyt rossiiskoi bibliografii, ili polnyi slovar' sochinenii i perevodov.* St. P. 1813-21, 5 pts. Facsimile reprint by Holland House, London 1962

*Svodnyi katalog russkoi knigi grazhdanskoi pechati XVIII veka: 1725-1800.* 5 Vols. M. 1963-67

Vengerov, S.A. *Istochniki slovaria russkikh pisatelei.* 2 Vols. St. P. 1900-17

Winter, O.F. *Repertorium der diplomatischen Vertreter aller Länder, 1764-1815.* Graz 1965

Zubov, V.P. *Istoriografiia estestvennykh nauk v Rossii: XVIII-pervaia polovina XIX veka.* M. 1956

PACIFIC NAVAL HISTORY AND EXPLORATION: BASIC REFERENCES

Akademiia Nauk SSSR. *Tikhii okean: russkie nauchnye issledovaniia*, ed. A. Fersman. L. 1926

Andreev, A.I. *Russkie otkrytiia v Tikhom okeane i Severnoi Amerike v XVIII-XIX vekakh: sbornik dokumentov.* M. 1944

Berg, L.S. *Ocherki po istorii russkikh geograficheskikh otkrytii.* M.-L. 1949, 2d ed.

Burney, J. *Chronological History of North-Eastern Voyages of Discovery.* London 1819

Burney, J. *Discoveries in the South Sea.* 5 Vols. London 1803-17

Brosses, C. de *Histoire des navigations aux terres australes* 2 Vols. Paris 1756

Buck, P.H. (Te Rangi Hiroa) *Explorers of the Pacific.* Honolulu 1953

Charnock, J. *Biographia Navalis, or, Impartial Memoirs of the Lives and Characters of Officers of the Navy of Great Britain.* 6 Vols. London 1794-98

Dumont D'Urville, J.S.C. *Voyage pittoresque autour du monde.* Paris 1835

Duperrey, L.I. *Mémoire sur les opérations géographiques . . . de la "Coquille".* Paris 1827

Davydov, Iu.V *V moriakh i stranstviiakh.* M. 1956

Dunmore, J. *French Explorers in the Pacific*, Vol. II: *The Nineteenth Century*, Oxford 1969

Esakov, V.A. *Russkie okeanicheskie i morskie issledovaniia v XIX-nachale XX veka.* M. 1964

Faivre, J.P. *L'Expansion française dans le Pacifique, 1800-42*. Paris 1960

Findlay, A.G. *Directory for the Navigation of the Pacific Ocean*. 3d ed., London 1871; 4th ed., 1877; 5th ed., 1884

Friis, H.R., ed. *The Pacific Basin: A History of Its Georgraphical Exploration*. NY 1967

Hawkesworth, J. *Voyages*. 3 Vols. London 1773

Horsburgh, J. *India Directory*. 3rd ed., London 1827

Ivanshintsev, N.A. *Russkie krugosvetnye puteshestviia s 1803 po 1849 god*. St. P. 1872. English translation by Glynn Barratt, *Russian Round-the-World Voyages, from 1803 to 1849*. Kingston, Ont.: Limestone Press 1980

Hydrographic Department, Admiralty. *Pacific Islands Pilot*. 3 Vols. & supplements. 1931-57

James, W. *Naval History of Great Britain from the Declaration of War by France*. London 1822-26

Kruzenshtern, I.F. (Krusenstern, Adam Johann von). *Receuil de mémoires hydrographiques, pour servir d'analyse et d'explication à l'Atlas de l'Océan Pacifique*. 4 Vols. St. P. 1824-35

Laird-Clowes, W. *History of the Royal Navy*. 7 Vols. London 1899-1904

Magidovich, I.P. *Ocherki po istorii geograficheskikh otkrytii*. M. 1957

Maude, H.E. *Of Islands and Men: Studies in Pacific History*. Melbourne 1968

Moerenhout, J.A. *Voyages aux iles du Grand Océan*. 2 Vols. Paris 1837

Morison, S.E. *The Maritime History of Massachusetts, 1783-1860*. Boston 1941

Navarrete, M.F., ed. *Coleccion de Documentos*, Vols. 4-5. Madrid 1837

Marshall, J. *Royal Navy Biography*. London 1824

*Otechestvennye fiziko-geografy i puteshestvenniki*, ed. N. Baranskii. M. 1959

Purdy, J. *The Oriental Navigator*, ed. J. Stevens. London: Whittle & Laurie 1816

Spate, O.H.K. *The Pacific since Magellan*, Vol. 1, *The Spanish Lake*. Canberra 1979

Stackpole, E.A. *The Sea-Hunters: The New England Whalemen during Two Centuries, 1635-1835*. Philadelphia 1953

Starbuck, A. *History of the American Whale-Fishery*. Washington, D.C. 1878

Shokal'skii, Iu.M. *Okeanografiia*. L. 1959

Svet, Ia. M. *Istoriia otkrytii i issledovaniia Avstralii i Okeanii*. M. 1966

Ward, R.G., ed. *American Activities in the Central Pacific, 1790-1870*. 8 Vols. Ridgewood, NJ: Gregg 1967

ARCHIVAL MATERIALS

Central State Archives of the USSR

(a) Tsentral'nyi Gosudarstvennyi Arkhiv Voenno-Morskogo Flota SSSR

*fond* 7, op. 1, *delo*2 (Vasilii M. Golovnin's notebook, 1802-5; service as a
   Volunteer, early actions); *delo* 16 (holograph of Golovnin's "Puteshestvie na Voennom Shliupe *Kamchatka*")
*fond* 25, op. 1, *delo* 114:7-21 (I.F. Kruzenshtern, Memoir of 31 March 1819,
   "Investigation of Lands Situated around the South Pole"; recom-
   mendation of Bellingshausen as commander of the two-ship squadron bound for the South, etc.)
*fond* 162, op. 1, *delo* 44 (materials on the publication plans for M.N. Vasil'-
   ev's, A.P. Lazarev's, and K. Gillesem's accounts of the *Otkrytie-
   Blagonamerennyi* expedition, 1819-22; A.S. Menshikov-Kutuzov
   corresp., 1823-30
*fond* 166, *delo* 600, pt. 2 (M.N. Vasil'ev to Naval Staff re hydrography); *delo*
   691 (documents re participation of Pavel Mikhailov in the *Vostok-
   Mirnyi* venture, his terms of service and duties); *delo* 666:314-16
   (Orders for Captain Irinarkh Tulub'ev of *Kreiser*, 1822
*fond* 172, op. 1, *delo* 376 (administrative preparations for Mulovskii's
   Pacific expedition, chart collecting); *delo* 589 (would-be participants
   in that expedition, 1786-87)
*fond* 198, op. 1, *delo* 36 (Iu. F. Lisianskii's return to Kronstadt from London and Madras by May 1800; activities in England, routes, plans,
   and logistics)
*fond* 203, op. 1, *delo* 730b (Nikolai D. Shishmarev's journal, 1819-21; *Blagonamerennyi*'s contact with Nukufetauans, ships' tracks west of the
   Southern Tuvalus, hydrography)
*fond* 205, op. 1, *delo* 644 (Discussion of publication of Vasil'ev's MS; list of
   available primary materials, expenses, etc.)
*fond* 213, op. 1, *delo* 52 (correspondence re journals of former members of
   the Vasil'ev-Shishmarev expedition; drawings and aquarelles submitted by E.M. Korneev, artist in the *Otkrytie*; their return to him for
   completion, 1822); *delo* 97 ("Raport kapitan-leitenanta M.N. Vasil-
   'eva Morskom Ministeru o plavanii Shliupov . . . ot porta Rio-Zha-
   neiro," June 1820: the discovery of the so-called "Blagonamerennyi
   Group"); *delo* 100:1-2 ("Raport Komandira shliupa *Blagonamerennyi*' . . . s opisaniem Zhitelei Ostrova Gruppy 'Blagonamerennogo',"
   25 Apr. 1820: details of the Russian encounter with the natives of

Nukufetau, Tuvalu, provided by Gleb S. Shishmarev); *delo* 118 (remarks on the expedition by Vasil'ev)

*fond* 215, op. 1, *delo* 1203 (list of ethnographica and objects of natural history brought from Oceania to St. Petersburg aboard *Otkrytie* and *Blagonamerennyi*; their deposition, etc.)

*fond* 315, op. 1, *delo* 381:4-8 (V. Ia. Chichagov to attempt to find a seaway from Bellsund into the North Pacific, 1764)

*fond* 402, op. 1, *delo* 88 (L.A. Hagemeister: despatches re *Krotkii*'s voyage past the Fiji Islands, May 1829, conditions)

*fond* 406, op. 7, *delo* 62 (Lisianskii's passage to London in the East Indiaman *Royalist*, May-Dec. 1799; reflections on the Russians' prospects in the East and Oceania, etc.)

*fond* 1153, op. 1, *delo* 1 (Aleksei P. Lazarev's "Zapiski o plavanii Voennogo Shliupa *Blagonamerennogo* v Beringov proliv": 325-page holograph. Russians at Nukufetau, 1820)

*fond* I.G. Chernysheva, *delo* 376 (collapse of the Mulovskii expedition)

(b) Tsentral'nyi Gosudarstvennyi Arkhiv Drevnikh Aktov (Moscow)

*fond* 30, *delo* 67 (Russian Volunteers with foreign navies, 1802-11, incl. V.M. Golovnin, L.A. Hagemeister, and M.P. Lazarev)

*fond* Senata, *delo* 666 (memorandum of 12 Sept. 1732 re despatching warships from the Baltic Sea to Kamchatka; Saunders)

*fond* Gosarkhiva, *razr.* 10, op. 3, *delo* 16 (qualifications for the 1787 Pacific-bound squadron, procedures to be followed); *razr.* 24, *delo* 61 (Willem Bolts to I.A. Ostermann, 17 Dec. 1782, re Russia's annexation of Pacific Islands, sugar plantations in Oceania, etc.); *razr.* 31, *delo* 9 (N.F. Golovin on the advantages of stationing Russian warships at Kamchatkan harbours, 1732)

(c) Tsentral'nyi Gosudarstvennyi Istoricheskii Arkhiv SSSR (Leningrad)

*fond* 13, op. 1, *delo* 287 (Count N.P. Rumiantsev to Alexander I re Russian-American Company affairs, Hagemeister's voyage out in *Neva*; A.A. Baranov on Hagemeister; orders to Golovnin to take *Diana* to the Northwest Coast, assist *Neva*, etc.)

*fond* 789 (Akademii Khudozhestv), op. 1, *dela* 1854, 1948, 2460 (material on the release of the artists P.N. Mikhailov and E.M. Korneev on secondment to the Navy, 1819); op. 20, *dela* 7-9, 17 (Korneev's duties in *Otkrytie*); *delo* 28 (A.N. Olenin praises Korneev's work); *delo* 30 (Korneev's portfolios, their entrusting to Vasil'ev in 1822)

*fond* 853, *delo* 1, item 74 (I.F. Kruzenshtern's orders to the companies of

*Nadezhda* and *Neva*, Apr. 1804, etc., re collection of artefacts, barter with Pacific Islanders, etc.)

(d) Arkhiv Vneshnei Politiki Rossii.

*fond* Sankt-Peterburgskogo Glavnogo Arkhiva (Glavarkhiva), II-3, op. 34 (Company orders re vessels bound for the Pacific, with associated memoranda and reports)
*fond* Kantseliarii Ministerstva Vneshnikh Del: 1822, *delo* 3645 (the *Apollón* to patrol the Northwest Coast until relieved; political stresses on the North Pacific front, 1822)

(e) Arkhiv Vsesoiuznogo Geograficheskogo Obshchestva SSSR (AGO)

*razr.* 99 (Rossiisko-Amerikanskoi Kompanii), op. 1, *delo* 65 (crew list of the Company ship *Elena*, 1828-30); *delo* 139 (Efim Klochkov's reports to Company Main Office, *Riurik*'s passage from Sydney across the Pacific, 1822, etc.)

(f) Gosudarstvennaia Publichnaia Biblioteka imeni Saltykova-Shchedrina: Otdel Rukopisei (ORGPB)

F.XVII.106.11, pp. 213-57 (scribe's copy of Aleksei P. Lazarev's diary, kept aboard *Blagonamerennyi* in 1820; editorial notes)
*fond* Ivana T. Pomialovskogo, No. 72, pp. 1-140 (variant of Aleksei P. Laza-rev's *Zapiski*, based on above, with numerous correction)
*fond* 1000, op. 2, *delo* 1146 (Makar' I. Ratmanov's journal from *Nadezhda*, 1803-6; Kruzenshtern as commander; routines in South Pacific waters)

(g) Arkhiv Adademii Khudozhestv SSSR (Leningrad)

*fond* 1819 goda, op. 20, *delo* 28 (Pavel N. Mikhailov's election to the Academy for a portrait of F.P. Tolstoi; his career)

(h) Leningradskoe Otdelenie Arkhiva Akademii Nauk SSSR (LOAAN)

*Arkhiv otdela fondov*, K-IV, op. 7, item 0038 (Johann Reinhold Forster as supposed source of Pacific artefacts acquired in 1782 and stored in the *Kunstkamera*;) *fond* 142, op. 1, *delo* 55 (V.V. Sviatlovskii's acquisition of Fijian and other Pacific artefacts in 1907-8, for MAE)

(i) Tsentral'nyi Voenno-Morskoi Muzei (Leningrad)

MS 41821/1 ("Zhurnal leitenanta Iuriia Lisianskago s 1793 po 1800 god")
MS 41820/2 ("Iu. F. Lisianskii: Vakhtennyi zhurnal," 1797-1800)

PRIMARY PRINTED MATERIAL

Alaska History Research Project. *Documents Relative to the History of Alaska*, ed. T. Lavrischeff. College, Alaska 1936-38
Angas, G.F. *Polynesia: A Popular Description of the Islands of the Pacific*. Oxford 1866)
Anon "Pis'ma russkogo puteshestvennika iz Brazilii," in *Severnaia pchela* (4-5 July 1832):4-6
Arrowsmith, A. *A Chart of the Pacific Ocean, Drawn from a Great Number of Printed and MS Journals*. London 1798. 9 sheets; rev. eds. in 1808, 1810, 1832
*Arkhiv admirala P.V. Chichagova*. St. P. 1885
Bartenev, P., ed. *Arkhiv kniazia Vorontsova*. 4 vols. M. 1870-95
Beaglehole, J.C., ed. *The Journals of Captain James Cook*, Vol. 1, *The Voyage of the Endeavour, 1768-1771*. Cambridge: Hakluyt Soc. Extra Series, no. 34, 1955; Vol. 2, *The Voyage of the Resolution and Adventure, 1772-1775*. Cambridge 1961; Vol.3, *The Voyage of the Resolution and Discovery, 1776-1780*. Cambridge 1967; 2 pts. *The Life of Captain James Cook* (Stanford 1974—companion volume to the journals)
Belinskii, V.G. *Sobranie sochinenii*. M. 1948
Bellinsgauzen (Bellingshausen), F.F. *Dvukratnye izyskaniia v iuzhnom ledovitom okeane i plavanie vokrug sveta, svershennye na shliupakh Vostoke i Mirnom v 1819, 1820, i 1821 godakh*. St. P. 1831; 2d ed., intro. and ed. A.I. Andreev. M. 1949; 3d ed., intro. and ed. E.E. Shvede. M. 1960
Berens, E.A. "Zapiski, vedennye v krugosvetnom plavanii na shliupe 'Krotkii' v 1828-1830 godakh," *Morskoi sbornik*. St. P. 1903: no. 2:45-66
Berkh, V.N. "Izvestie o mekhovoi torgovle, proizvodimoi . . . pri ostrovakh Kuril'skikh," *Syn otechestva*, 88 (1823):243-64; 89: 97-106
Bligh, W. *A Voyage to the South Sea*. London 1792
Bougainville, L.A. de *Voyage autour du monde*. Paris 1771
Chichagov, P.V. "Zapiski," in *Russkaia starina*. (Oct. 1886):35-53
Cook, J. *A Voyage towards the South Pole*. 2 Vols. London 1777
____& King, J. *A Voyage to the Pacific Ocean . . . for Making Discoveries in the Northern Hemisphere*. 3 Vols. London 1784. Translated by L.I. Golenishchev-Kutuzov as *Puteshestvie v Severnyi Tikhii Okean*. St.

P. 1805-10. The same translator produced a Russian version of Cook's 1777 *Voyage*, using the text of J.B. Suard's *Voyage dans l'hémisphere australe* (Paris 1778), under the title: *Puteshestvie v iuzhnoi polovine zemnago shara.* 2 Vols. St. P. 1796-1800

Dalrymple, A. *Historical Collection of the Several Voyages.* London 1770-71

Deane, J. *The Russian Fleet under Peter the Great, by a Contemporary Englishman*, ed. C.A. Bridge. London 1899

Dobell, P. *Travels in Kamtschatka and Siberia.* London 1830

Dumont D'Urville, J.S.C. *Voyage de la corvette "l'Astrolabe".* 5 Vols. & atlas. Paris 1830-33

—— *Voyage pittoresque autour du monde.* 2 Vols. Paris 1834-35

Duperrey, L.I. *Voyage autour du monde . . . sur la corvette de Sa Majesté la "Coquille," pendant les années 1822, 1823, 1824 et 1825.* Paris: Bertrand 1827

—— *Mémoire sur les opérations géographiques faites dans la campagne de la corvette la "Coquille".* Paris, n.d., but evidently 1827

Edwards, E. *The Voyage of HMS Pandora*, ed. B. Thomson. London 1915

Forster, J. George A. *Voyage Round the World, in His Britannic Majesty's Sloop, "Resolution".* London: White, Robson, Elmsly 1777

—— *Reply to Mr. Wales' Remarks.* London 1778

—— *Werke: Samtliche Schriften, Tagebucher, Briefe*, ed. R.L. Kahn, G. Steiner et al. Berlin: Akademie der Wissenschaften 1958-74

Forster, J.R. *Observations Made during a Voyage Round the World, on Physical Geography, Natural History, and Ethnic Philosophy.* London: Robinson 1778

——, ed. M.E. Hoare. *The Resolution Journal of Johann Reinhold Forster, 1772-1775.* 4 Vols. London: Hakluyt Soc. 1982

Galkin, N. "Pis'ma g. Galkina o plavanii shliupov Vostoka i Mirnago v Tikhom okeane," *Syn otechestva* (1822):pt. 49:97-121

Gillesem, K. "Puteshestvie na shliupe Blagonamerennom dlia issledovaniia beregov azii i Ameriki," *Otechestven. Zapiski*, 66 (1849): pt. 8-10; 67 (1849): pt. 11

Golovnin, V.M. "Ostrov Tana: iz zapisok," *Syn otechestva*, (1816): pt. 31, no. 31:177-200; no. 32:217-33; pt. 32, no. 33:3-23; no. 34:41-57

—— *Puteshestvie russkogo imperatorskago voennogo shliupa 'Diana' iz Kronshtadta v Kamchatku, v 1807, 1808, i 1809 godakh.* St. P. 1819

—— *Puteshestvie vokrug sveta . . . na voennom shliupe "Kamchatku" v 1817, 1818 i 1819 godakh.* 2 Vols. St. P. 1822. Soviet edition (M. 1965) by V.A. Divin, S.D. Osokin, and K.F. Fokeev, with very useful annotations and appendices

—— *Sochineniia i perevody.* 5 vols. St. P. 1864

____ed. I.P. Magidovich, *Sochineniia*, M. 1949

Hamilton, George *A Voyage Round the World, in His Majesty's Frigate "Pandora"*. Berwick 1793; London ed., slightly varient 1799

Hawkesworth, J. *Voyages*. 3 Vols. London 1773

Hotimsky, C.M., ed. "A Russian Account of New South Wales in 1822," *Melbourne Slavonic Studies*, 1 (1967):82-95 (account by Akhilles P. Shabel'skii of the sloop *Apollon*)

Khlebnikov, K.T. "Vzgliad na polveka moei zhizni," *Syn otechestva* (1836):299-324, 345-73, 413-28

____ed. R.G. Liapunova and S.G. Fedorova. *Russkaia Amerika v neopublikovannykh zapiskakh K.T. Khlebnikova*. L. 1979

____ed. J.R. Gibson. "Russian America in 1833: The Survey of Kirill Khlebnikov," *PNQ*, (1972): no. 1:1-13

Khromchenko, V.S. "Puteshestvie . . . sudna *Eleny*," *ZUKMS* (1832): pt. 9:304-12

Khrushchev, S.P. "Plavanie shliupa *Apollona* v 1821-1824 godakh," *ZADMM*, 10 (1826):200-72

Kiselev, E. "Pamiatnik prinadlezhit matrozu pervoi stati Egoriu Kiselevu," ed. Ia. Tarnapol'skii, in *Vokrug sveta* (1941):no. 4:40-43

Klochkov, E.A. "Puteshestvie vokrug sveta v kolonii Rossiisko-Amerikanskoi Kompanii," *Severnyi arkhiv*, 24 (1826):202-29

Korobitsyn, N.I. "Zhurnal," in A.I. Andreev, ed., *Russkie otkrytiia v Tikhom okeane* (1944); see English version of a text by Andreev by Carl Ginsburg, *Russian Discoveries in the Pacific and in North America in the 18th and 19th Centuries*. Ann Arbor: ACLS 1952

Kotzebue, O.E. *Puteshestvie v iuzhnyi okean i v Beringov proliv v 1815, 1816, 1817 i 1818 godakh*. St. P. 1821. Cf. English translation by H.E. Lloyd, *Voyage of Discovery into the South Sea and Beering's Straits* (London 1821), used here

Kruzenshtern, I.F. "Otkrytiia Tasmana, s prilozheniem sochineniia o polozhenii Ontong-Iavy," *Tekhnologicheskii zhurnal*, 3 (St. P. 1806):134-85

Kruzenshtern, I.F. "Puteshestvie ot Mysa Dobroi Nadezhdy k Madrasu v 1797 godu," *ZADMM*, 3 (1815)

____ *Puteshestvie vokrug sveta v 1803, 1804, 5 i 1806 godakh na korabliakh 'Nadezhda' i "Neva"*. 3 pts. St. P. 1809-12. English version by R.B. Hoppner, *A Voyage Round the World*. 2 Vols. London 1814

____ *Atlas Iuzhnago Moria*. 2 Vols. St. P. 1824-27

____ *Sobranie sochinenii, sluzhashchikh razborom i iz'iasneniem Atlasa Iuzhnago Moria*. 2 Vols. St. P. 1823-26. French text printed in St. P. as *Receuil de mémoires hydrographiques, pour servir d'analyse et d'expliction* . . .

——*Dopolnenie k izdannym v 1826 i 1827 godakh ob'iasneniiam osnovanii.* St. P. 1836

La Billardière, J.J. de *Relation du Voyage à la recherche de La Pérouse.* 2 Vols. & atlas. Paris 1800

Langsdorf, G.H. "Opisanie uzorov, navodimykh zhiteliami ostrova Vashingtona na ikh tele," *Tekhnologicheskii zhurnal*, 7 (St. P. 1810):pt. 2

—— *Voyages and Travels in Various Parts of the World, during the Years 1803-1807.* London 1813; based on the 1812 (Frankfurt) text *Bemerkungen auf einer Reise um die Welt*

La Pérouse, J.F.G. de *Voyage autour du monde.* 4 Vols. Paris 1797. English version, *Voyage Round the World.* London 1798-99, and Russian version, by L. Golenishchev-Kutuzov, *Puteshestvie La Peruza v iuzhnom i severnom Tikhom okeane.* St. P. 1800

Lazarev, Aleksei P. *Zapiski o plavanii voennogo shliupa Blagonamerennogo v Beringov proliv i vokrug sveta v 1819, 1820, 1821 godakh*, ed. A.I. Solov'ev. M. 1950

Lazarev Andrei P. *Plavanie vokrug sveta na shliupe "Ladoga" v 1822, 1823, i 1824 godakh.* St. P. 1832

Lazarev, Mikhail P. "Pis' mo A.A. Shestakovu," *Morskoi sbornik* (1918): no. 1:53-63

—— ed. A.A. Samarov. *Russkie flotovodtsy: M.P. Lazarev: sbornik dokumentov.* 2 Vols. M. 1952. Many original papers

Lavrischeff, T. See Alaska History Research Project.

Liapunova, R.G. & Fedorova, S.G., eds. *Russkaia Amerika v neopublikovannykh zapiskakh K.T. Khlebnikova.* L. 1979

Lisianskii, Iu. F. *A Voyage Round the World in the Years 1803, 4, 5 & 6 . . . , in the Ship "Neva".* London 1814; translated by the author from his *Puteshestvie vokrug sveta.* St. P. 1812

Lesson, P. *Voyage autour du monde, entrepris . . . dans la corvette "La Coquille".* Paris: Pourrat 1839

Lockerby, W. "A William Lockerby Manuscript in the Peabody Museum of Salem," ed. E.S. Dodge, *JPH*, 7 (1972)

Mal'tbriun, V. "O plavanii vokrug sveta korablei 'Nadezhda' i 'Neva' v 1803-1806 godakh," *Vestnik Evropy*, 121 (1822):no. 1

*Materialy dlia istorii russkikh zaselenii po beregam Vostochnago Okeana.* St. P. 1861, supplement to *Morskoi sbornik*, 1st issue for that year

Markham, A.H. *The Cruise of the "Rosario" among the New Hebrides and Santa Cruz Islands.* London: Dawson 1873

*Materialy dlia istorii Imperatorskoi Akademii Nauk.* St. P. 1885-1900

Martin, J. *An Account of the Natives of the Tongan Islands in the South Pacific Ocean.* L. 1827

Müller, G.F. *Sammlung Russischer Geschichte*. 9 Vols. St. P. 1732-64. Vol. 3 printed in 1758, with crucial maps

Mourelle, F.A. "Narrative of an Interesting Voyage in the Frigate 'La Princesa' . . . in 1780 and 1781," in La Pérouse, *Voyage Round the World*, ed. L. Milet-Mureau. L. 1799

Nelson, H. *The Despatches and Letters of Vice-Admiral Lord Viscount Nelson*, ed. N.H. Nicolas. L. 1844

Novosil'skii, P.M. *Iuzhnyi polius: iz zapisok byvshego morskago ofitsera*. St. P. 1853

Pavlov, P.N., ed. *K istorii Rossiisko-Amerikanskoi Kompanii: sbornik dokumental'nykh materialov*. Krasnoiarsk 1957

Penrose, C.V. *A Memoir of James Trevenen, 1760-1790*, ed. R.C. Anderson and C. Lloyd. London: Navy Record Soc. 1959

Petrov, P.N., ed. *Sbornik materialov dlia istorii Imperatorskoi St. Peterburgskoi Akademii Khudozhestv za sto let eio sushchestvovaniia*. St. P. 1864-66

Pokrovskii, A. *Ekspeditsii Beringa: sbornik dokumentov*. M. 1941

Purdy, J. *The Oriental Navigator*, ed. J. Stevens. London 1816. Contains the (1814) "Tables of Observed Positions" used by the Russian Navy for 25 years

Rezanov, N.P. "Pervoe puteshestvie Rossiian vokrug sveta, opisannoe N. Riazanovym," *Otechestvennye zapiski*, 23 (1825):173-88; 24 (1825):73-96

Reynolds, J.N. "Report of 1828 . . . ," in U.S. House of Representatives, Navy Department, *23rd Congress, 2nd Session*. Washington, D.C. 1835, Doc. 105

Rossel, E.P. de *Voyage de Dentrecasteaux, envoyé à la recherche de La Pérouse*. 2 Vols. Paris 1808

Rossiiskii, A. "Vypiska iz zhurnala shturmana Alekseia Rossiiskago," *Sorevnovatel' prosveshcheniia i blagodeianiia* (St. P. 1820): no. 11:125-46; no. 12:246-56

Samarov, A., ed. See Lazarev, Mikhail P.

Sauer, M. *An Account of a Geographical and Astronomical Expedition to the Northern Parts of Russia*. L. 1802

Sementovskii, V.N., ed. *Russkie otkrytiia v Antarktike v 1819-1821 godakh* M. 1951

Shabel'skii, A.P. *Voyage aux colonies russes de l'Amérique, fait à bord du sloop de guerre "l'Apollon" pendant les années 1821, 1822, et 1823*. St. P. 1826

Shemelin, F.I. "Istoricheskoe izvestie o pervom puteshestvii Rossiian vokrug sveta," *Russkii invalid*, 146 (St. P. 1823):nos. 23-28, 31-36

Smirnov, V., ed. *Leonard Eiler: perepiska: annotirovannyi ukazatel'*. L. 1967

Simonov, I.M. "Précis du voyage de découvertes, fait . . . par le capitain Bellingshausen," *Journal des voyages*, 23 (Paris 1824):69 cahier:10ff.

——"Slovo o uspekhakh plavaniia shliupov 'Vostok' i 'Mirnyi' okolo sveta," in V.N. Sementovskii, ed., *Russkie otkrytiia v Antarktike v 1819-1821 godakh* (M. 1951):29-47

—— "Opredelenie geograficheskogo polozheniia mest iakornogo stoianiia shliupov 'Vostok' i 'Mirnyi'," *ZMNP*, 22 (St. P. 1828):44-68

——"Kratkii istoricheskii vzgliad na puteshestviia znameniteishikh moreplavatelei do nachala XIX veka," ibid., 42 (1844):92-115

Skelton, R.A., ed. *The Voyages of Captain Cook: Charts and Views Drawn by Cook and His Officers*. Cambridge. Hakluyt 1955

Sparrman, A. *A Voyage Round the World with Captain James Cook in HMS Resolution*. London: Golden Cockerel 1944; 1st English translation of Sparrman's Swedish text of 1802-18

Tikhmenev, P.A., comp. *Istoricheskoe obozrenie obrazovaniia Rossiisko-Amerikanskoi Kompanii i deistvii eio*. 2 Vols. St. P. 1861-63. Translated by D. Krenov as *The Historical Review of the Formation of the Russian-American Company*. Seattle 1938. Poor translation, but contains many valuable documents, 1795-1825 esp.

Tilesius von Tilenau, W.G. "Izvestie o estestvennom i politicheskom sostoianii zhitelei ostrova Nukagivy," *Tekhnologicheskii zhurnal*, 3 (1806):pt. 4

Tompkins, S.R. & Moorehead, M.L., eds. "Russia's Approach to America: From Spanish Sources, 1761-1775," *BCHQ*, 13 (1949):231-55

Turgenev, N.I. *Rossiia i Russkie*. M. 1915. From *La Russie et les Russes*. Paris 1848

Turner, G. *Nineteen Years in Polynesia*. L. 1861

Unkovskii, S. Ia. "Istinnye zapiski moei zhizni," in Samarov, ed., *Russkie flotovodtsy: M.P. Lazarev* (M. 1952):1:11-26

Vancouver, G. *A Voyage of Discovery*. 3 Vols. L. 1798

Wales, W. *Remarks on Mr. Forster's Account of Cpatain Cook's Last Voyage Round the World, in the Years 1772, 1773, 1774, and 1775*. L. 1778

Waxell, S. *Vtoraia Kamchatskaia ekspeditsiia Vitusa Beringa*. M.-L. 1940

Wellesley, Lord *The Despatches, Minutes, and Correspondence of the Marquess of Wellesley . . . during his Administration in India*, ed. Montgomery Martin. 10 Vols. L. 1836

Wilkes, C. *Narrative of the United States Exploring Expedition during the Years 1838-1842*. 5 Vols. Philadelphia 1845

Williams, T., Rev. *Fiji and the Fijians*, Vol. 1, *The Islands and Their Inhabit-*

*ants*. L.: Heylin 1858; reprinted with Vol. 2, in James Calvert, *Mission History*. L. 1884

Wilson, W. et al. *A Missionary Voyage to the Southern Pacific Ocean*. L. 1799

Wrangel, F.P. "Otryvok iz rukopisi, pod zaglaviem: Dnevnye zapiski o plavanii voennogo transporta Krotkago v 1825-1827 godakh," *Severnyi arkhiv* (1828): no. 36:49-106

Wright, O., trans. & ed. *New Zealand, 1826-27: From the French of Dumont D'Urville*. Wellington 1950

Zavalishin, D.I. "Krugosvetnoe plavanie fregata 'Kreiser' v 1822-25 godakh, pod komandoiu Mikhaila Petrovicha Lazareva," *Drevniaia i novaia Rossiia* (1877): nos. 6-7, 10-11

___ *Zapiski dekabrista*. Munich 1904

Zavoiko, V.S. *Vpechatleniia moriaka vo vremia dvukh puteshestvii krugom sveta: sochinenie leitenanta V. Zavoiko*. St. P. 1840, Pt. 1, "Puteshestvie v 1834, 1835, i 1836 godakh"

SELECTED SECONDARY SOURCES

Adler, B.F. "Znak s ostrova Ono," *Izvestiia Obshchestva Arkheologii, Istorii, i Etnografii*, 29 (Kazan' 1916):253-59

Aleksandrov, I.N. "Professor I.M. Simonov—uchastnik antarkticheskoi ekspeditsii F. Bellinsauzena i Lazareva," *Uchenye Zapiski Kazanskogo Pedinstituta*, bk. 9. Kazan' 1950

___ *Problemy geografii v Kazanskom universitete*. Kazan' 1950

Anderson, M.S. "Great Britain and the Growth of the Russian Navy in the Eighteenth Century," *MM*, 42 (1956):132-46

Anderson, R.C. "British and American Officers in the Russian Navy," *MM*, 32 (1947):17-27. Incomplete, flawed list

Andreev, A.I. *Russkie otkrytiia v Tikhom okeane i severnoi Amerike v XVIII-XIX vekakh*. M. 1944; modified ed. 1948. Trans. by Carl Ginsburg as *Russian Discoveries in the Pacific and in North America in the Eighteenth and Nineteenth Centuries*. Ann Arbor: ACLS 1952

Armstrong, T. "Cook's Reputation in Russia," in *Captain James Cook and his Times*, ed. R. Fisher and H. Johnston. Vancouver 1979

Aslanbegov, A.B. *Zhizneopisanie admirala Alekseia Samuilovicha Greiga*. St. P. 1873

Bancroft, H.H. *A History of Alaska, 1730-1885*. San Francisco 1886

Barratt, G.R. *Bellingshausen: A visit to New Zealand, 1820*. Palmerston North, NZ: Dunmore 1979

___ "The Russian Navy and New Holland," *JRAHS*, 64 (1979:no. 1):217-34

—— *Russia in Pacific Waters, 1715-1825: A Survey of the Origins of Russia's Naval Presence in the North and South Pacific*. Vancouver 1981

—— *The Russians at Port Jackson, 1814-1822*. Canberra: AIAS, 1981:1

—— *Russian Exploration in the Mariana Islands, 1816-1828*. Saipan: Micronesian Archaeological Report No. 17, 1984

—— *The Russian Discovery of Hawaii, 1804: The Journals of Eight Russian Explorers*. Honolulu: Editions Limited 1988

Barsukov, N.P. *Zhizn' i trudy M.P. Pogodina*. M. 1896

Belkin, J.N. *The Mosquitoes of the South Pacific (Diptera and Culicidae)*. Berkeley 1962

Belov, M.I. *Istoriia otkrytiia i osvoeniia Severnogo morskogo puti*, 3 vols. M.-L. 1956-59

Berezhnoi, A.S. "Krugosvetnyi moreplavatel' L.A. Gagemeister," *Izv. Akademii Nauk Latviiskoi SSR*. (1984):no. 8:48-59

Berg, L.S. "Otkrytiia russkikh v Tikhom okeane," in *Tikhii okean: russkie nauchnye issledovaniia*, ed. Fersman. L. 1926

—— *Ocherki po istorii russkikh geograficheskikh otkrytii*. 2d ed. M.-L. 1949

Belov, M.I. "Shestaia chast' sveta, otkryta russkimi moriakami," *IVGO*, 90. L. 1962

Berkh, V.N. *Khronologicheskaia istoriia otkrytiia Aleutskikh ostrovov, ili podvigi rossiiskago kupechestva* St. P. 1823

—— *Zhizneopisaniia pervykh rossiiskikh admiralov, ili opyt istorii Rossiis-kago Flota*. St. P. 1831

Beskrovnyi, L.G. "Armiia i flot," in *Ocherki istorii SSSR*. M. (1957):127-59

Blue, G.V. "A Rumor of an Anglo-Russian Raid on Japan, 1776," *PHR*, 8 (1939):453-4

Bolkhovitinov, N. *Stanovlenie russko-amerikanskikh otnoshenii, 1785-1815*. M. 1966

—— *Russko-amerikanskie otnosheniia, 1815-1832*. M. 1975

Broeze, F. "A Second-Hand Discovery: The Netherlands and the Pacific in the First Half of the Nineteenth Century," *JPH*, 10 (1975):30-47

Burrows, E.G. *Ethnology of Futuna*. Honolulu: Bishop Mus. Bull. 138, 1936

Burrows, E.G. "Western Polynesia: A Study in Culturnal Differentiation," *Ethnologiska Studier*, 7 (1938):70-91

—— "Culture Areas in Polynesia," *JPS*, 49 (1940

Butinov, N.A. *Polineziitsy ostrovov Tuvalu* (M., 1982)

—— & Rozina, L.G. "Nekotorye cherty samobytnoi kul'tury Maori," *SMAE*, 21 (1963):78-109

Brand, D.D. "Geographical Exploration by the Spaniards," in H.R. Friis, ed., *The Pacific Basin: A History of Its Geographical Exploration*. NY 1967

Capell, A. "Oceanic Linguistics Today," *Current Anthropology*, 3 (1962):no. 4:371-428

Chambers, A. *Nanumea: Atoll Economy. Social Change in Kiribati and Tuvalu*. Canberra: ANU Development Studies Centre, No. 6, 1984

Cary, W.S. *Wrecked on the Feejees*. Fairfield, WA: Galleon Press 1972

Chambers, K. & Munro, D. "The 'Mystery' of Gran Cocal: European Discovery and Mis-Discovery in Tuvalu," *JPS*, 89 (1980):167-99

Chapman, C.E. *The Founding of Spanish California: Northwestward Expansion of New Spain, 1687-1773*. NY 1916

Chereiskii, L.A. *Pushkin i ego okruzhenie*. L. 1975

Churkin, V.G. "Atlas Cartography in Pre-Revolutionary Russia," trans. J.R. Gibson, *Canadian Cartographer*, 12 (1975):1-20

Clendenning, P. "Admiral Sir Charles Knowles and Russia, 1771-74," *MM*, 61 (1974):39-40

Clunie, F. "Traditional Fijian Hairdressing," *Fiji Heritage* (Feb. 1982):1-10

____& Ligairi, W. "Fijian Mutilatory Practices: Earlobe Slitting and Distension," *Domodomo*, 1 (Suva 1983):22-44

____ *Fijian Weapons and Warfare*. Suva: Fiji Mus. Bull. 2, 1977

Cook, W.L. *Flood Tide of Empire: Spain and the Pacific Northwest, 1543-1819*. New Haven & L. 1973

Craig, R.D. "The 1780 Russian Inventory of Cook Artifacts," *Pacific Studies*, 2 (1978):no. 1:94-97

Cranmer-Byng, J. "Russian and British Interests in the Far East," *Canadian Slavonic Papers*, 10 (1968):357-75

Cross, A.G. "Samuel Greig, Catherine the Great's Scottish Admiral," *MM*, 60 (1974):251-65

____ *"By the Banks of the Thames": Russians in Eighteenth Century Britain*. Newtonville, MA 1980

Day, A. *The Admiralty Hydrographic Service, 1795-1919*. London 1967

Dougherty, J.W. *West Futuna-Aniwa: An Introduction to a Polynesian Outlier Language*. Berkeley 1983

Deane, W. *Fijian Society*. L. 1921

De la Rue, A. "La géologie des Nouvelles-Hébrides," *Journal de la Société des Océanistes*, 12 (1956):177-91

Derrick, R.A. *History of Fiji: To 1874*. Suva 1946

____ *The Fiji Islands: A Geographical Handbook*. Suva 1951

____ "Notes on Fijian Clubs, with a System of Classification," *JPS*, 66 (1957):391-95

Divin, V.A. "O pervykh proektakh russkikh krugosvetnykh plavanii," *TIIET*, 32 (1961):330-42

____ *Russkie moreplavaniia na Tikhom okeane v XVIII veke*. M. 1971

Dumitrashko, N.V. "Iu. F. Lisianskii i russkie krugosvetnye puteshestviia," in the 1947 Moscow ed. of Lisianskii's *Puteshestvie vokrug sveta na korable Neva*. St. P. 1812

Dunmore, J. *French Exploration in the Pacific: The Eighteenth Century*. Oxford 1965

—— *French Exploration in the Pacific: The Nineteenth Century*. Oxford 1969

Endicott, W. *Wrecked among the Cannibals in the Fijis*. Salem. MA 1923

Fainberg, E. Ia. *Russko-iaponskie otnosheniia v 1697-1875 godakh*. M. 1960

Farrelly, T.S. "A Lost Colony of Novgorod in Alaska," *SEER* (American series), 3 (1944):33-38

Fedorov-Davydov, A. *Russkii peizazh XVIII-nachala XIX veka*. M. 1953

Feokistov, E.M. *M.L. Magnitskii*. St. P. 1865

Fiedler, H. et al. *Georg Forster: Naturforscher, Weltreisender, Humanist, und Revolutionär*. Worlitz 1970

Fitzhardinge, V. "Russian Ships in Australian Waters, 1807-1835," *JRAHS*, 51 (1965):113-47

Frolov, N. *Sobranie starykh i novykh puteshestvii*. M. 1855

France, P.L. *The Charter of the Land*. Melbourne 1969

Gabel, N.E. *A Racial Study of the Fijians*. Berkeley & Los Angeles, Anthrop. Records XX, No. 1, 1958

Gibson, J.R. *Imperial Russia in Frontier America: The Changing Geography of Supply of Russian America, 1784-1867*. NY 1976

Golder, F.A. *Russian Expansion on the Pacific: 1641-1850*. Cleveland 1914

Golson, J., ed. *Polynesian Navigation: A Symposium on Andrew Sharp's Theory of Accidental Voyages*. 3d ed. Wellington 1972

Goncharova, N.N. "Vidopisets E. Korneev," *Iskusstvo* (1972):no. 6:60-64

—— "Khudozhnik krugosvetnoi ekspeditsii 1819-1822 godov E. Korneev," *IVGO*, 105 (1973):67-72

Gough, B.M., ed. *To the Pacific and Arctic with Beechey*. Cambridge, Hakluyt Soc. 1973

Green, R.C. "Anuta's Position in the Subgrouping of Polynesia's Languages," *JPS*, 80 (1971):355-70

Grekov, V.I. *Ocherki iz istorii russkikh geograficheskikh issledovanii v 1725-65 godakh*. M. 1960

Grenader, M.B. "Istoricheskaia obuslovlennost' vozniknoveniia severovostochnoi ekspeditsii 1785-1795 godov," *Uchennye zapiski Petropavlovskogo Gos. Pedinstituta* (1957):bk. 2:55-72

Grot, Ia.K. *Pushkin, ego litseiskie tovarishchi i nastavniki*. St. P. 1899

Gunn, W. *The Gospel in Futuna*. L. 1914

Guiart, J. *Un siècle et demi de contacts culturels à Tanna, Nouvelles-Hébrides*. Paris 1956

Gvozdetskii, N. "Pervoe morskoe puteshestvie Rossiian vokrug sveta," *Priroda* (1947): no. 1:85-88

Haddon, A.C. & Hornell, J. *Canoes of Oceania*. Honolulu: Bishop Museum Spec. Pubs. 27-29, 1975, reprint in vol. of 1936-38 vols.

Haxthausen, A. von *The Russian Empire, Its Peoples, Institutions, and Resources*. L. 1856

Hedley, C. *The Ethnology of Funafuti*. Sydney: Australian Mus. Memoir 3, 1897

Henderson, G.C. *The Discoverers of the Fiji Islands*. London 1933; 2d ed. 1937

Hettner, T., ed. *Georg Forsters Briefwechsel mit S. Th. Sömmering*. Brunswick 1877

Hoare, M. *The Tactless Philosopher: Johann Reinhold Forster, 1792-98*. Melbourne 1976

Hocart, A.M. *The Lau Islands*. Honolulu: Bishop Museum Bull. 62, 1929

Howard, A. *Learning to Be Rotuman: Enculturation*. NY 1970

Howay, F.W. *A List of Trading Vessels in the Maritime Fur Trade, 1785-1825*. Ed. and intro. by R.A. Pierce. Kingston, Ont. 1973

Humphrey, R.A. "Richard Oswald's Plan for an English and Russian Attack on Spanish America," *HAHR*, 18 (1938):95-101

Hunter Christie, E.W. *The Antarctic Problem: An Historical and Political Study*. L. 1951

Isakov, I.A. *Imperatorskaia Akademiia Khudozhestv: Muzei: russkaia zhivopis', katalog*. Petrograd 1915

Kabo, V.R. & Bondarev, N. "Okeaniiskaia kollektsiia I.M. Simonova," *SMAE*, 30 (L. 1974):101-11

Kaeppler, A.L. "Eighteenth Century Tonga: New Interpretations," *Man*, 6 (1971):no. 2:204-20

___ *Cook Voyage Artifacts in Leningrad, Berne, and Florence Museums*. Honolulu: Bishop Museum 1978

Kahn, R.L., ed. *Georg Forsters Werke: Sämtliche Schriften*. Berlin 1968:1:700-8 ("Influence and Reception of the Work")

Karimullin, A.G. *Chto chital N.I. Lobachevskii: zapisi knig i zhurnalov, vydannykh iz biblioteki Kazanskogo Universiteta*. Kazan' 1979

Kennedy, D.G. "Field Notes on the Culture of Vaitupu, Ellice Islands," *Polynesian Society Memoirs*, 9 (1931).

Kirwan, L.P. *The White Road: A Survey of Polar Exploration*. L. 1960

Koch, G. *Die Matierelle Kultur der Ellice-Inseln*. Berlin: Museum für Volkerunde, Neue Folge 3, 1961

Kohl, J.G. *Russia and the Russians in 1842*. L. 1843

Komissarov, B.N. *Russkie istochniki po istorii Brazilii pervoi treti XIX veka*. London 1977

Kuznetsova, V.V. "Novye dokumenty o russkoi ekspeditsii k severnomu poliusu," *IVGO* (1968):no. 3:237-45

Lantzeff, G.V. & Pierce, R.A. *Eastward to Empire: Exploration and Conquest on the Russian Open Frontier to 1750.* Montreal 1973

Larsson, K.E. *Fijian Studies.* Göteborg, Ethnologiska Studier, No. 25, 1960

Lensen, G.A. *The Russian Push toward Japan: Russo-Japanese Relations, 1697-1875.* Princeton 1959

Likhtenberg, Iu. M "Gavaiskie kollektsii v sobraniiakh Muzeia Antropologii i Etnografii," *SMAE*, 19 (1960:168-205

Lipshits, V.A. "Etnograficheskie issledovaniia v russkikh krugosvetnykh ekspeditsiiakh," in *Ocherki istorii russkoi etnografii, fol'kloristiki, i antropologii*, Vol. 1 M. 1956

Lurie, N.O. "Ethnohistory: An Ethnological Point of View," *Ethnohistory*, 8 (1961):78-92

Makarova, R.V. *Russkie na Tikhom okeane vo vtoroi polovine XVIII veka.* M. 1968

Maude, H.E. "Bligh's Men at Ono-i-Lau in 1791," *MM*, 50 (1964):217-35

—— "Post-Spanish Discoveries in the Central Pacific: A Study in Identification," *JPS*, 70 (1961):67-111

—— *Of Islands and Men: Studies in Pacific History.* Melbourne 1968

McCartan, E.F. "The Long Voyages: Early Russian Circumnavigation," *Russian Review*, 1 (1963):30-37

Mel'nitskii, P. *Admiral Rikord i ego sovremenniki.* St. P. 1856

Morozov, A. *Mikhail Vasil'evich Lomonosov.* L. 1952

Nevskii, V.V. *Pervoe puteshestvie Rossiian vokrug sveta.* M. 1951

Novakovskii, S.I. *Iaponiia i Rossiia.* Tokyo 1918

Nozikov, N., trans. Lesser. *Russian Voyages Round the World.* L. 1945

Okun', S.B. *Rossiisko-Amerikanskaia Kompanii.* M. 1939, translated by Carl Ginsburg as *The Russian-American Company.* Cambridge, MA, ACLS 1951

O'Meara, P. *K.F. Ryleev: A Political Biography of the Decembrist Poet.* Princeton 1984

Ostrovskii, B.G. "O pozabytykh istochnikakh i uchastnikakh ekspeditsii Bellinsgauzena-Lazareva," *IVGO*, 81 (1949): pt. 2

Pasetskii, V.M. *Geograficheskiie issledovaniia dekabristov.* M. 1977

Paulin, A. "Oscar's Island," *Forum Navale Skrifter utg. av Sjohistoriska Samfundet* (Uppsala), 8 (1947):32-45

Pawley, A. "The Relationships of Polynesian Outlier Languages," *JPS*, 76 (1967):no. 3:259-96

Pertsmakher, V.V. "Iu. F. Lisianskii v Indii (1799)", *Strany i narody Vostoka*, ed. D.A. Olderogge, 12 (M. 1972):248-59

Pierce, R.A. "Alaska's Russian Governors," *Alaska Journal*, 1 (1971):no. 4:38-42

Putilov, B.N. *Nikolai Miklouho-Maclay: Traveller, Scientist, and Humanist*. M. 1982

Ray, S.H. *A Comparative Study of the Melanesian Languages*. Cambridge 1926

Rea, R. "John Blankett and the Russian Navy," *MM*, 41 (1955):245-49

Rikord, L.I. *Admiral P.I. Rikord: biograficheskii ocherk*. St. P. 1875

Roberts, R.G. "Te Atu Tuvalu: A Short History of the Ellice Islands," *JPS*, 67 (1958):394-423

Robertson, H.A. *Erromanga: The Martyr Isle*. L. 1902

Rogers, G. "The First Recorded Contact between Fijians and Europeans," *Domodomo*, 1 (1983):72-77

Roth, G.K. *The Fijian Way of Life*, Melbourne 1953

Rozina, L.G. "Kollektsiia Dzhemsa Kuka v sobraniiakh Muzeia Antropologii i Etnografii," *SMAE*, 23 (1966):234-57

_____ "V.V. Sviatlovskii—sobratel' kollektsii iz Okeanii," ibid., 30 (1974):127-39

_____ "Tapa Okeanii (po materialam MAE)," ibid., 30 (1974):51-100

Russov, F. "Beiträge zur Geschichte der etnographischen und antropologischen Sammlungen der Kaiserlichen Akademie der Wissenschaften zu St. Petersburg," *Sbornik Muzeia po Antropologii i Etnografii pri Imp. Akademii Nauk* (St. P. 1900): no. 1

Ryden, S. *The Banks Collection: An Episode in Eighteenth-Century Anglo-Swedish Relations* Stockholm, Ethnographical Museum of Sweden Monographs no. 8, 1963

Savin A.S. "Okhotsk," *ZGDMM*, 9 (1951):148-61

Seeman, B.C. *Flora Vitiensis*. L. 1865

_____ "Fiji and Its Inhabitants," in F. Galton, ed., *Vacation Tourists and Notes of Travel*. L. 1862

Sharp. A. *The Discovery of the Pacific Islands*. Oxford 1960

Stackpole, E.A. *The Sea-Hunters*. Philadelphia/NY 1953

Sgibnev, A.S. "Popytki russkikh k zavedeniiu torgovykh snoshenii s Iaponieiu," *Morskoi sbornik*, 100 (1869), no. 7

Shafranovskaia, T.K. "Katalog kollektsii otdela Avstralii i Okeanii MAE," *SMAE*, 39 (1984):5-25

Shibanov, F.A. "Studies in the History of Russian Cartography," trans. L. Morgan, in *Cartographica*. Toronto: Monograph Series no. 15, 1975

Shteinberg, E.L. *Zhizneopisanie russkogo moreplavatelia Iuriia Lisianskogo*. M. 1948

Shur, L.A. "Dnevniki i zapiski russkikh puteshestvennikov kak istochnik po istorii i etnografii stran Tikhogo okeana," in *Avstraliia i Okeaniia* (M. 1970):201-12

Shur, L.A. & Pierce, R.A. "Pavel Mikhailov: Artist in Russian America," *Alaska Journal*, 8 (1978):no. 4:360-63

Smith, S.P. "The First Inhabitants of the Ellice Islands," *JPS* 6 (1987):12-20

Sokolov, A.P. "Prigotovlenie krugosvetnoi ekspeditsii 1787 goda pod nachal'stvom Mulovskogo," *ZGDMM*, 6 (1848):142-91

―― *Proekt Lomonosova i ekspeditsiia Chichagova 1765 goda.* St. P. 1852

Soler, A.M. *Die Spanisch-Russischen Beziehungen im 18-em Jahrhundert.* Wiesbaden 1970

Staniukovich, T.V. *Etnograficheskaia nauka i muzei.* L. 1978

Starbuck, A. *History of the American Whale-Fishery.* Washington, D.C. Appendix to Report of the Commissioner for Fisheries for 1875-76, 1878

Suris, B. "P.N. Mikhailov—khudozhnik i puteshestvennik," *Iskusstvo* (1962):no. 7:66-70

Tarle, E.V. *Chesmenskii boi i pervaia russkaia ekspeditsiia v Arkhipelag.* M. 1945

Thompson, L.M. *Southern Lau, Fiji: an Ethnography.* Honolulu: Bishop Mus. Bull. no. 162, 1940

Thomson, B. *The Fijians: A Study in the Decay of Custom.* L. 1908

―― ed. *The Voyage of HMS "Pandora."* L. 1915

Tippett, A.R. *Fijian Material Culture: A Study of Cultural Context, Function, and Change.* Honolulu: Bishop Mus. Bull. no. 232, 1968

Tryon, D.T. et al. *Papers in the Linguistics of Melanesia, No. 3: The Languages of the New Hebrides: A Checklist.* Canberra: ANU Pacific Linguistics Series A, no. 36, 1972

Tumarkin, D.D. "Materialy ekspeditsii M.N. Vasil'eva—tsennyi istochnik po istorii i etnografii Gavaiskikh ostrovov," *Sovetskaia etnografiia* (1983): no. 6:48-61

Turner, E.H. "The Russian Squadron with Admiral Duncan's North Sea Fleet, 1795-1800," *MM*, 49 (1963):212ff.

Vayda, A.P. "Polynesian Cultural Distribution in New Perspective," *American Anthropologist*, 61 (1959):817-28

Veslago, F.F. *Admiral Ivan Fedorovich Kruzenshtern.* St. P. 1869

―― *Kratkaia istoriia russkogo flota.* M. 1939

Vize, V. Iu. *Uspekhi russkikh v issledovanii Arktiki.* M. 1948

Voenskii, K. "Russkoe posol'stvo v Iaponiiu v nachale XIX veka," *Russkaia starina*, 84 (1895):123-41, 201-35

Vorob'ev, N.I. et al. "Etnograficheskie nabliudeniia I.M. Simonova na ostrovakh Tikhogo okeana," *IVGO* (1949):no. 3:497-504

Vucinich, A. *Science in Russian Culture: A History to 1860*. Stanford 1963; Vol.2, 1970

Wagner, H.R. "The Memorial of Pedro Calderon y Henriquez . . . with a View to Preventing Russian Encroachment in California," *CHSQ*, 23 (1944):219-25

Walker, E.A. *A History of Southern Africa*, 2d ed. L. 1957

Waterhouse, J. *The King and People of Fiji: Containing a Life of Thakombau*. London 1866

Watrous, S.D., ed. *John Ledyard: Journey through Russia and Siberia in 1787-88*. Madison 1966

Whiteman, D. *Melanesians and Missionaries: An Ethnohistorical Study*. Pasadena 1983

Williams, G. *The British Search for the Northwest Passage in the Eighteenth Century*. L. 1962

Yen, D.E. & Gordon, J., eds. *Anuta: A Polynesian Outlier in the Solomon Islands*. Honolulu, Bishop Mus., Pacific Anthrop, Records no. 21, 1973

Zdobnov, V.N. *Istoriia russkoi bibliografii*. M. 1951

Zubov, N.N., ed. *Otechestvennye moreplavateli- issledovateli morei i okeanov*. M. 1954

# Name Index

# Place Index

# Ship Index